Warren, Gorham & Lamont Titles of Interest

Books and Services

Basic Legal Forms
  by Marvin Hyman
Basic Legal Transactions
  by Marvin Hyman
Computer Software Agreements
  by Clarence H. Ridley, Peter C. Quittmeyer, and John Matuszeski
Copyright Law in Business and Practice
  by John W. Hazard, Jr.
Corporate Acquisitions, Mergers, and Divestitures
  by Lewis D. Solomon
The Law of Computer Technology
  by Raymond T. Nimmer
The Law of Personal Property Leasing
  by William H. Lawrence and John H. Minan
The Law of Products Liability
  by Marshall S. Shapo
The Law of Product Warranties
  by Barkley Clark
The Law of Secured Transactions
  by Barkley Clark
Modern Law of Contracts
  by Howard O. Hunter
Quinn's Uniform Commercial Code Commentary and Law Digest
  by Thomas M. Quinn

Newsletters and Journals

Clark's Secured Transactions Monthly
  by Barkley Clark and Barbara Clark
Multimedia and Technology Licensing Law Report
  by Gregory J. Battersby and Charles W. Grimes
Uniform Commercial Code Law Letter
  by Thomas M. Quinn
Uniform Commercial Code Law Journal
  by Thomas M. Quinn

If you have any questions about these or any other WG&L publications, please call our Customer Service representatives at this toll-free number:
1-800-950-1216
Our representatives will be happy to help you.

Warren, Gorham & Lamont
31 St. James Avenue
Boston, MA 02116

COMPUTER AND INFORMATION LAW DIGEST

JAMES A. DOUGLAS

Member of the New York Bar
Lecturer, New York University

LAUREL BINDER-ARAIN

Member of the New York and Connecticut Bars

Editorial Consultant
RAYMOND T. NIMMER

Leonard Childs Professor of Law,
University of Houston Law Center

of Counsel
Weil, Gotshal & Manges

WARREN, GORHAM & LAMONT

Warren, Gorham & Lamont
31 St. James Avenue
Boston, Massachusetts 02116

ISBN 0-7913-2217-3

Library of Congress Catalog Card No. 94-062096   This publication is designed to provide accurate and authoritative information in regard to the subject matter covered. In publishing this book, neither the authors nor the publisher is engaged in rendering legal, accounting, or other professional service. If legal advice or other expert assistance is required, the services of a competent professional should be sought.

Printed in the United States of America

PREFACE

Publication of this *Computer and Information Law Digest* marks another step in the development of legal research and resources pertaining to an industry that has now become a dominant force in our modern economy.

Conservatively measured, by the early 1990s, the computer and electronic information industries accounted for over three percent of our gross national product; their market share was and is growing rapidly. In terms of their impact on society, however, the role of these industries is already hugely more significant than their large share of the gross national product. These industries and their products are actively creating a fundamental reshaping of the global community, including its legal, political, and business environments.

We are in the midst of a revolution that is at least equivalent in force to the industrial revolution that irrevocably transformed the fabric of our legal and social culture. Today's revolution is based on the burgeoning cultural dominance of information and information technologies. Information technologies are expanding at a truly incredible rate, often outracing even their own developers' expectations. Driven in part by this technological explosion, the role of information in society has also changed. Information is now a major commodity. It is at once a lifeblood for decision making and at the same time the most flexible modern focus of commercial trade and business transactions.

One consequence of this revolutionary transformation of society and of the technologies that underlie it is that traditional categories of thought and political-legal analysis are breaking down with a speed that is remarkable. How today do we define, for example, the line between telecommunications and computing? The answer is that the line may no longer make sense. How do we draw a line in terms of political and legal policy between book publishers and software distributors? The line blurs as technology evolves. Similar comments can be made about the distinction between delivering goods and performing services, of distinctions among the various facets of the entertainment industry, and of distinctions among trade in goods, services, and intangibles.

Of course, lawyers and the legal system are not isolated and held apart from this revolutionary change. The technologies have provoked massive changes in how law is practiced: new sections of the bar, new businesses focused on law office automation and similar themes, and new computers on the desks of most lawyers.

But, for many lawyers, the greater effect lies in the changing contours of the law as it relates to this industry and to its by-product effects on society. Here, both the challenges and the opportunities are awesome. The pace of legal change is staggering. In 1985, I wrote *The Law of Computer Technology*, which achieved some commercial success and received a national book award. We revised that book in 1992, in part because the supplement of recent cases and legislation had reached a size equivalent to the original book. Less than two years later, as the pace of legal change continues unabated, we have almost reached that same position with the second edition.

This is an area of opportunity for the practicing lawyer to affect the emerging shape of our culture. It is also a challenge for the lawyer to remain current and aware of the many changes and legal developments that seem to occur in this field on almost a daily basis. These changes affect the computer law specialist and the lawyer who works in or with the industry. But, the effect is broader. It extends to all lawyers involved in virtually any area of practice.

Consider just a few of the changes that the industry has caused in law:

- Intellectual property laws have been challenged and transformed in the face of a need to evolve systems of software protection.
- Commercial contract law in the UCC is undergoing transformative change as traditional categories between goods and intangibles are less and less tenable in commercial practice.
- The criminal laws of all fifty states have been revisited, defining criminal conduct in the age of information.
- Antitrust law has floated forward and back as policy perspectives shift on proper and improper use of control over information and intellectual property rights.
- Telecommunications law and practice have been irrevocably altered.
- Privacy rights are evolving in the face of increasingly cogent threats from massive computing capability and massive systems of data storage.
- A law of electronic transactions is evolving as modern commerce is often conducted entirely by computer.

It is to this activity and to the almost overwhelming velocity of legal change that this *Law Digest* is directed.

RAYMOND T. NIMMER

November 14, 1994

HOW TO USE

Computer and Information Law Digest is a handy, easy-to-use reference to selected cases dealing with computer and information law. Included in this *Digest* are all U.S. and state supreme court cases, all federal court of appeals cases, and selected state appellate and federal district court cases, chosen for their importance, timeliness, and relevance. The goal of the *Digest* is to provide in a single and structured source access to the major decisions and patterns that are emerging in the field of computer and electronic information law.

The *Digest* is organized by a topical outline that follows the structure of *The Law of Computer Technology*, a treatise on computer law written by Raymond T. Nimmer. Professor Nimmer, the Leonard Childs Professor of Law at the University of Houston Law Center and of Counsel to Weil, Gotshal & Manges, is a recognized authority on computer and information law and serves as Editorial Consultant to this *Digest*. Those relying on Professor Nimmer's treatise as a main reference can refer to *Computer and Information Law Digest* for synopses of cases cited in the treatise. Likewise, those who desire analysis of the law and the manner in which it has developed should refer to *The Law of Computer Technology*.

Additional research aids in the *Digest* include the table of contents, a table of abbreviations that explains acronyms used throughout the *Digest*, an alphabetical table of cases that enables the reader to locate any case by name, and a comprehensive topical index.

SUMMARY OF CONTENTS

TABLE OF CONTENTS

2 Patent Law: Software and Systems Protection

3 Trade Secrets and Confidentiality

TABLE OF CONTENTS

4 Research, Development, and Ownership

5 International Intellectual Property Issues [Reserved]

PART II Transactions and Third-Party Liability

6 Computer and Systems Sales Contracts

7 Technology Licensing and Computers

8 Computer and Software Leasing

9 Computer and Information Services Contracts

10 Fraud and Computer-Related Torts

PART A. FRAUD: GENERAL ISSUES AND ELEMENTS

11   International Technology Export and Import [Reserved]

PART III   Information Age Issues

12   Computer Crime

PART A. COMPUTER CRIME IN GENERAL

PART B. FINANCIAL CRIMES

PART C. INFORMATION AND SOFTWARE THEFT CRIMES

13 Computer Error and Use Liability

14 Electronic Transaction Environments

15 Information Products: Electronic Publishing

16 Privacy, Disclosure, and Access to Information

PART D. PRIVATE DATA

TABLE OF ABBREVIATIONS

APA   Administrative Procedure Act
ATM   automatic teller machine
CBCT   customer-bank communication terminal
CPU   central processing unit
DOD   Department of Defense
EDI   electronic data interchange
EFTA   Electronic Funds Transfer Act
EPA   Environmental Protection Agency
FBI   Federal Bureau of Investigation
FCC   Federal Communications Commission
FCRA   Fair Credit Reporting Act
FDIC   Federal Deposit Insurance Corporation
FEA   Federal Energy Administration
FIFRA   Federal Insecticide, Fungicide, and Rhodonticide Act
FOIA   Freedom of Information Act
FTCA   Federal Tort Claims Act
IRC   Internal Revenue Code
NAACP   National Association for the Advancement of Colored People
NASA   National Aerospace Science Administration
OEM   original equipment manufacturer
RAM   random access memory
RICO   Racketeer Influenced Corrupt Organizations
ROM   read only memory

PART I

INNOVATIONS AND INCENTIVES

CHAPTER 1

COPYRIGHT AND COMPUTER TECHNOLOGY

PART A.   OVERVIEW

¶ 1.01 FRAMING THE SOFTWARE COPYRIGHT ISSUES

Copyright infringement claim cannot be maintained when plaintiff fails to establish that original elements of selection, coordination, or arrangement had been copied.
Bellsouth Advertising & Publishing Corporation, the publisher of a classified business directory, brought an action against Donnelley Information Publishing and others for copyright and trademark infringement and unfair competition. The district court found, and Donnelley admitted, that Bellsouth owned a valid compilation copyright in its classified directory. Donnelley stipulated that, in preparing its data base and sales lead sheet, it obtained from each listing in the Bellsouth directory the telephone number, name, address, kind of business, and unit of advertising for the listed subscriber. From the process by which Donnelley prepared its competitive yellow pages directory, the district court identified three acts of copying. Based on these acts of copying, the court granted Bellsouth's motion for summary judgment on its copyright infringement claim. *Held:* By copying the name, address, telephone number, business type, and unit of advertisement purchased for each listing in the Bellsouth directory, Donnelley copied no original element of selection, coordination, or arrangement; accordingly, Donnelley was entitled to summary judgment on Bellsouth's claim of copyright infringement. The circuit court held that the district court erred in finding that certain acts of selection, such as Bellsouth's determination of the geographic scope of its directory and various marketing techniques, were sufficiently original to merit copyright protection. These acts of selectivity did not meet the level or originality required to extend the protection of copyright to Bellsouth's selection; the acts were not acts of authorship, but rather techniques for the discovery of facts. Moreover, the district court erred in finding that Bellsouth's acts of coordination and arrangement in the particular system of alphabetized lists under applicable headings used in the directory warranted copyright protection. Here, Bellsouth's arrangement and coordination was "entirely typical" for a business directory and lacked the

requisite originality required for copyright protection. The court further noted that because there is only one way to construct a useful business directory, the arrangement had "merged" with the idea of a business directory, and thus was uncopyrightable. Finally, the court noted that given that the copyright protection of a factual compilation is "thin," a competitor taking the bulk of a factual material from a preexisting compilation without infringement of the author's copyright is not surprising. Copyright assures authors of the right to their original expression, but encourages others to build freely on the ideas and information conveyed by a work.

[Bellsouth Advertising & Publishing Corp. v. Donnelley Info. Publishing, 999 F2d 1436 (11th Cir. 1993)]

¶ 1.02 COPYRIGHT LAW AND COMPUTER TECHNOLOGY

Copyright Act does not protect work in limited distribution, but suit may be brought for misappropriation of trade secrets. Technicon and Green Bay provided computer services to a hospital. To enable the hospital to properly use its services, Technicon gave the hospital a user's guide, which it improperly provided to Green Bay. Technicon alleged that Green Bay misappropriated trade secrets from the guide, but Green Bay countered that since Technicon included a copyright notice in the guide—thereby invoking the protection of the Copyright Act—it could not claim trade secrets were included in the guide. *Held:* A copyright notice does not preclude the creator of the material from claiming that trade secrets are located therein where the work is for limited publication. The court noted that the user's guide was not generally available. Where the distribution of a work is only a "limited publication," the distribution requirement of the Copyright Act is not met. Therefore, the work is not under the Copyright Act's protection. Since Technicon could not avail itself of the protection of the Act, it was not estopped from claiming trade secrets were contained in the user's guide.

[Technicon Medical Info. Sys. Corp. v. Green Bay Packaging, Inc., 687 F2d 1032 (7th Cir. 1982), cert. denied, 459 US 1106 (1983)]

Abstraction-filtration-comparison test must be used when determining which elements of computer program are entitled to copyright protection. Gates, the owner of a copyright for computer software designed to aid in the selection of replacement industrial belts, brought suit against its competitor, Bando, seeking permanent injunction against Bando's use of an allegedly infringing computer program. The district court found, among other things, that Bando had infringed Gates's copyright on its engineering computer program, and granted motion for permanent injunction in part. Bando claimed that the district court erred when it extended copyright protection to facts and ideas in Gates's computer program. *Held:* The district court erred in extending copyright protection to certain unprotectable elements of the computer program, and the district court failed to properly determine the protectability of many of the elements of Gates's program that it found to have been copied by Bando. The court of appeals remanded the copyright claim to the district court for a reconsideration of which elements of the program were protectable in light of the "abstraction-filtration-comparison" test. Under this test, the first step in the analysis involves dissecting the allegedly infringed program according to the abstractions test; i.e., parsing the program into at least six levels of generally declining abstraction: (1) main purpose, (2) program structure or architecture, (3) modules, (4) algorithms and data structures, (5) source code, and (6) object code. Once the court has succeeded in identifying the various levels of abstraction of a computer program, it must filter out those elements of the program that are not protected by copyright. After filtering, the court is left with a core of protected elements that can be compared to the alleged infringing program. Ultimately, the court must decide whether those protectable portions of the original work that have been copied constitute a substantial part of the original work; i.e., matter that is significant in the plaintiff's program.

[Gates Rubber Co. v. Bando Chem. Indus., Ltd., 9 F3d 823 (10th Cir. 1993)]

Originality requirement of Copyright Act does not place stringent requirements on party seeking copyright.   Apple Computer developed a user interface for its Macintosh computer using icons, pull-down menus, and overlapping screens. Microsoft developed for IBM computers the Windows program, which employed a similar user interface. To challenge the validity of Apple's copyright, Microsoft claimed that Apple's interface lacked originality, a requirement for copyright. Microsoft contended that Apple's idea had been taken from Xerox. *Held:* The copyright was valid. The court noted that the originality requirement was not a stringent requirement; its main purpose was to prevent exact copying from another source by the party claiming the copyright. Furthermore, even if the Xerox program was similar, there was no evidence that Apple copied protected elements of expression from Xerox programs.

[Apple Computer, Inc. v. Microsoft Corp., 759 F. Supp. 1444 (ND Cal. 1991)]

Programs on ROM chips are copyrightable even though in binary code and part of computer.   Midway developed the Pac-Man video game. Strohon developed new ROM chips to be placed in the Pac-Man circuit board to create a new game, CUTE-SEE. This game looked different from Pac-Man, but the new ROM chips used a substantially similar code to the old Pac-Man ROM chips. Midway sued for copyright infringement. *Held:* CUTE-SEE violated the copyright. The court noted that information on ROM chips is copyrightable as literary works. The fact that ROM chips contain binary code readable only by the computer or computer experts does not destroy the ability to copyright. The 1980 amendments to the Copyright Act made it clear that literary works readable only by machine are copyrightable. Furthermore, the court held that ROM chips, although a part of the computer, can still contain copyrightable material. The court would not draw a line making information on floppy disk copyrightable and material on ROM chips noncopyrightable.

[Midway Mfg. Co. v. Strohon, 564 F. Supp. 741 (ND Ill. 1983)]

User interface is not copyrightable. EDI developed an engineering program for use on a mainframe. SSI developed a similar program for use on a personal computer. EDI alleged that SSI infringed its copyright by copying its user interface (input and output reports). SSI countered that a user interface is not copyrightable. *Held:* The user interface was not copyrightable. The court felt bound to follow *Plains Cotton Coop. v. Good Pasture Computer Service*, 807 F.2d 1256 (5th Cir. 1987), which held that computer input formats were ideas rather than expression. Since ideas are not copyrightable, EDI could not hold a copyright on the user interface.

[Engineering Dynamics, Inc. v. Structural Software, Inc., 785 F. Supp. 576 (ED La. 1991)]

User interface is "most unique" portion of computer program and is subject to copyright. Lotus sued Paperback for copyright infringement, claiming that Paperback had copied Lotus's user interface. Lotus developed the 1-2-3 spreadsheet. Paperback used similar commands and menu structure in its spreadsheet. Lotus claimed that its copyright was infringed, and Paperback countered that only the literal elements (source and object codes) are protected by copyright; the nonliteral elements had no such protection. *Held:* The user interface is copyrightable. According to the court, the user interface is more than an idea—a spreadsheet—but rather an expression and the "most unique" portion of a spreadsheet program. In no way was the Lotus user interface obvious or the only way of establishing spreadsheet commands or presenting menus. The court looked at other spreadsheet programs to demonstrate the variety of user interfaces.

[Lotus Dev. Corp. v. Paperback Software Int'l, 740 F. Supp. 37 (D. Mass. 1990)]

PART B.   COPYRIGHT AND PROGRAM CODE OR STRUCTURE

¶ 1.03 FLOW CHARTS AND SOURCE CODE

Random notes are not fixed tangible expression protected by copyright. Wigginton and Ross set out to develop a spreadsheet program. Ross was to program the computational component and Wigginton the user interface. During the collaboration, Ross gave Wigginton some notes as to what he believed should be contained in the user interface. After a dispute, Wigginton left the project and took his user interface to Ashton-Tate, which used the interface in its own program. Ross sued for copyright infringement, claiming joint authorship of the interface. *Held:* There was no infringement. Noting a split in authority, the court determined that where one person supplies only ideas, which are not copyrightable, that person is not a joint author. A joint author needs to supply fixed tangible expression. Although Ross claimed his notes to Wigginton constituted such, the court disagreed, stating that a random list does not qualify for copyright protection.

[Ashton-Tate Corp. v. Ross, 916 F2d 516 (9th Cir. 1990)]

Where plaintiff cannot establish that defendant copied work substantially similar to its work, infringement action cannot be maintained.   Infodex, brought an action against Meredith-Webb Printing Company for infringement. Meredith-Webb filed a motion for partial summary judgment, arguing that Infodex's evidence failed to sufficiently establish the essential elements of copyright infringement. *Held:* Infodex failed to establish that Meredith-Webb copied the constituent elements of the work that were original. Infodex could not prove that the works were substantially similar. Because Meredith-Webb's work was essentially combinations of numbers, any similarity between the two works would be found through a comparison of the sequences of numbers used in the two works. Individual numbers and sets of numbers by themselves are not copyrightable. However, when numbers are combined in sequences to express ideas or information, any original expression that results from the use of the numerical sequences is copyrightable. After reviewing the various sequences of numbers in the two works, the court held that no degree of similarity between Meredith-Webb's work and the original expression in Infodex's work existed. The only two number combinations similar to both works were in different positions within their respective number sequences. As such, any similarity that existed between the two works was of noncopyrightable elements.

[Infodex, Inc. v. Meredith-Webb Printing Co., 830 F. Supp. 614 (ND Ga. 1993)]

¶ 1.04 MACHINE CODE FORMATS

Binary object codes are protected by copyright.   Franklin admitted copying various Apple programs. In Apple's suit for copyright infringement, Franklin alleged that computer object codes, which are a binary code, are not protected by copyright law, and that Apple had no basis for its suit. Franklin contended that object codes, which are readable only by machine, are not copyrightable because they are not easily decipherable by humans. *Held:* Under the 1976 copyright law, copyright protection is not based on whether or not a work can be read and understood by a lay reader. If a work can be read by machine, it can be protected (17 USC § 102(a)). When the codes, rather than method or processes, are copied, there is a violation of copyright. Furthermore, that the program is imbedded in a computer as its operating system does not defeat copyright protection.

[Apple Computer, Inc. v. Franklin Computer Corp., 714 F2d 1240 (3d Cir. 1983), cert. dismissed, 464 US 1033 (1984)]

Operating systems are protected expression. Formula developed a computer kit that had an internal processor with an operating program that made its computer compatible with Apple computers. Apple claimed that the program was copyrighted. Formula contended that operating programs are processes or ideas that are not protected by copyright. *Held:* Operating programs are protected by copyright. The court rejected Formula's suggestion that (1) an operating system is an idea because it only supplies information to the computer and (2) the expression is only that information the computer presents to the user. The court noted that an idea becomes expression when there are numerous ways to express the idea. Here, the operating system could have been written in several ways. Therefore, Apple's way of writing the program was protected; different programs creating the same operating system, however, would not violate the copyright.

[Apple Computer, Inc. v. Formula Int'l, 725 F2d 521 (9th Cir. 1984)]

Source code copyright also protects object code. GCA developed an integrated circuit, the chips of which contained a computer program. GCA alleged that Chance and others, all former employees, violated its copyright. Chance alleged that GCA did not have a valid copyright because it did not publish the copyrighted work. In particular, Chance contended that GCA held a copyright on the source code, but published only the object code. Chance contended that the Copyright Office was misled and, therefore, GCA lacked a valid copyright. *Held:* GCA held a valid copyright. According to the court, the source and object codes are treated as one; therefore, the copyright of one protects the other. The source code is protected as a work of authorship in a fixed medium: a computer chip. GCA had a valid copyright because it complied with all requests of the Copyright Office. According to the court, the office was not misled.

[GCA Corp. v. Chance, 217 USPQ 718 (ND Cal. 1982)]

Copyright Act does not allow copying of ROM chips. Tandy claimed that PMC had copied its program, which allowed source code to be translated into object code. This program was on a ROM chip. PMC claimed that copying a ROM chip was not covered by copyright law at the time of the alleged copying. *Held:* The Copyright Act does include copying of ROM chips. The Act allows the copyrighting of a work of authorship in a fixed medium. The program is the work and the chip is the fixed medium. The exception to the rule—allowing material to be downloaded into computer memory—was inapplicable. The exception applies to copying a program "in conjunction with" the use of the computer. This exception does not allow for the copying of material fixed on a chip. The court noted that to hold any copying of computer programs acceptable would be to render copyright protection of computer programs meaningless.

[Tandy Corp. v. Personal Micro Computers, Inc., 524 F. Supp. 171 (ND Cal. 1981)]

Five computer tapes that represent one program are not five works but one for copyright purposes. IBM developed a computer that functioned using a microcode it also developed. In case the microcode were damaged or destroyed, the purchasers of the computer received five computer tapes that included the microcode. Allen-Myland copied these tapes for its use in reconfiguring IBM computers. In defense to IBM's claim of copyright infringement, Allen claimed that the second of the five tapes lacked sufficiently original material to be copyrighted, making the whole not copyrightable because of the relationship of tape 2 to the whole. *Held:* The program was copyrightable. The court declined to view the parts of the program in isolation, because IBM's separation of the program onto five tapes did not indicate that there were five separate works. When the program tapes were loaded into the computer, the distinction among the tapes was not maintained. According to the court, tape 2 contained a substantial, necessary part of a single work.

[Allen-Myland, Inc. v. IBM, 746 F. Supp. 520 (ED Pa. 1990)]

¶ 1.05 INFRINGING COPIES OF CODE

Computer microcode has requisite creativity to be protected by copyright. Intel developed a microprocessor chip that contained a microcode—the instructions to the microprocessor. Intel alleged that NEC had violated its copyright when NEC developed a substantially similar chip. NEC contended that a microcode cannot be copyrighted because the code lacks originality and is an idea rather than expression. *Held:* A microcode can be copyrighted. Although a microcode does involve many obvious steps showing little creativity, the program as a whole shows the creativity necessary for copyright. The court noted that the Intel microcode may be an idea if it can be expressed in only one way, but this fact would not have been known when Intel applied for a copyright. Therefore, the copyright should be presumed valid unless the party challenging the copyright can show the program cannot be expressed in any other way.

[NEC Corp. v. Intel Corp., 10 USPQ2d 1177 (ND Cal. 1989)]

Subroutines of computer program are copyrightable. Competition Electronics developed a device with internal software for use in gun-shooting competitions. Pearl later introduced a similar device. Competition alleged that two of the subroutines of the Pearl program violated Competition's copyright. *Held:* The copyright was violated. The court noted that courts protect more than just subject and object codes. While subroutines may perform an idea (e.g., the par time for shots fired), how the subroutine is structured as software is the expression of the idea. The court found the structure of the subroutine to be nearly identical in Competition's and Pearl's programs.

[Pearl Sys., Inc. v. Competition Elecs., Inc., 8 USPQ2d 1520 (SD Fla. 1988)]

¶ 1.06 COPIES OF PROGRAM STRUCTURE AND SEQUENCE

Structure of computer program is copyrightable. Elaine Whelan developed a program for use by dental labs for Jaslow. The program was written for the mainframe used by Jaslow. Whelan and Jaslow together marketed the program to other labs. Jaslow decided that personal computer users would benefit from the program, and it created a program for PCs. Whelan claimed her copyright in the program was infringed. Jaslow contended that since no literal elements or codes were copied, there was no infringement. *Held:* A copyright in a computer program can be violated when its structure is misappropriated. The court noted that the structure of a program is the most time-consuming and costly part of development. The court differentiated the structure of a program from an idea, which is not protected by copyright. The Court noted that Jaslow could have developed another dental program that would not have violated the copyright; it would have just had to develop another structure. Structure is part of the expression of the program, which is copyrightable.

[Whelan Assocs., Inc. v. Jaslow Dental Lab., Inc., 797 F2d 1222 (3d Cir. 1986), cert. denied, 479 US 1031 (1987)]

Absent compelling justification, there must be direct competition between parties for finding of misappropriation. The U.S. Golf Association (USGA) developed a formula for computing an amateur golfer's handicap. St. Andrews developed a computer program that used the USGA formula. St. Andrews made the computer program easily available to golfers, including those who were not USGA members. The USGA claimed that St. Andrews misappropriated its formula, but Andrews countered that a mathematical formula cannot be misappropriated. *Held:* There was no misappropriation. The court held that absent some compelling justification, there must be a direct competition between parties for a finding of misappropriation. Here, there was no competition since the USGA's function was not to supply handicaps, but rather to promote the game of golf. Although the court stated that St. Andrews might have been trying to capitalize on the USGA's goodwill by using the formula, the court found uniformity to be a more compelling reason for using the formula since it had become the generally accepted method for handicapping golfers.

[United States Golf Ass'n v. St. Andrews Sys., Data Max, Inc., 749 F2d 1028 (3d Cir. 1984)]

Structure of program is an idea not protected by copyright.   Plains developed a program for use with mainframes for the cotton industry. Several employees eventually left Plains and went to work for Goodpasture, where they developed a substantially similar program for use with personal computers. Plains sought injunctive relief, but Goodpasture contended that there was no direct copying. *Held:* The court rejected Plain's contention that an injunction could be granted for "organizational copying." The court stated that the structure of the program was dictated by the cotton market. Since the market dictated the structure, the structure could only be realized with one expression. The structure then was more an idea than an expression, and only expression can be copyrighted.

[Plains Cotton Coop. Ass'n of Lubbock, Tex. v. Goodpasture Computer Serv., Inc., 807 F2d 1256 (5th Cir. 1987)]

Computerization of scoring system for psychological test violates copyright on test.   The University of Minnesota (UM) held a copyright on a psychological test, including material used in scoring the test. Applied Innovations developed a computer program for scoring the test that incorporated the copyrighted scoring materials: testing data, correlations, and classifications used to interpret test results. In UM's suit for copyright infringement, Applied contended that the analytical formats were facts or discoveries not protected by copyright. *Held:* The unauthorized computerization of the test infringed the copyright of the basic test. The court held that the program was based on the insights, choices, and selections of the developers of the test and that these insights, choices, and selections constituted protected expression. A method of analysis cannot be protected, but expression can exist in the way in which personal choices and discretion are exercised in analyzing and categorizing data.

[Applied Innovations v. Regents of Univ. of Minn., 876 F2d 626 (8th Cir. 1989)]

Program structure, sequence and organization, and user interface are protected by copyright.   Johnson had developed a program for water treatment plants. After hiring several Johnson employees, Phoenix developed a similar program. Johnson alleged copyright violation. Phoenix contended that since other companies had similar programs, Johnson's copyright was not original and therefore not valid. *Held:* The court held that whether a program is protected by copyright depends on whether it qualifies as expression or idea. If it is an expression, it is protected. While copying codes is clearly copyright infringement, copying structure, sequence and organization, and user interface are fact-based inquiries. Here, however, the court believed the structure was clearly expression.

[Johnson Controls, Inc. v. Phoenix Control Sys., Inc., 886 F2d 1173 (9th Cir. 1988)]

Wholesale copying of program violates copyright even though expression elements of program could become part of idea in future.   Nintendo, a maker of home video games, held a copyright on a program that allowed only Nintendo game cartridges to be played on its game system. Atari wanted to develop games that would be played on the Nintendo system, but needed to break the security program. Atari received an unauthorized copy of the source code and lifted the binary code from a Nintendo game cartridge. Nintendo sued for copyright infringement. Atari claimed that the security program could not be copyrighted, because the expression and idea merged as one. *Held:* The program could be protected by copyright. The court noted that Atari copied the whole security program, not just those features needed to make Atari cartridges usable on the Nintendo system. Although Atari claimed that this complete copying was to allow Atari games to be played even if Nintendo were to change the base system, the court believed that this would allow wholesale copyright infringement. Atari's rationale would allow any copier to allege that the expression is also an idea because of possible future changes by the copyright holder.

[Atari Games Corp. v. Nintendo of Am., Inc., 18 USPQ2d 1935 (ND Cal. 1991)]

Structure of prompting program is not protected by copyright because idea for program dictated its structure.   Hoffman and others developed a prompting program for Q-Co for use in Atari computers. After leaving Q-Co, Hoffman developed a prompting program for use with IBM computers. The Atari graphics hardware facilitated the writing of the original program. Because IBM did not have the same hardware, a much longer and complicated program needed to be written. Q-Co sued for copyright infringement, but Hoffman contended that a prompting program does not constitute copyrightable expression. *Held:* Hoffman's IBM program did not violate the Q-Co copyright. Although Hoffman's team worked on both programs and the programs had substantially similar features, the court determined that these features would be in any prompting program. Since the features would not be unique to the Q-Co program, they could not be classified as expression, but rather ideas, which are not protected by copyright.

[Q-Co. Indus., Inc. v. Hoffman, 625 F. Supp. 608 (SDNY 1985)]

Copy of program for another operating system can be derivative work in violation of Copyright Act.   SAS developed a statistical program for use with IBM computers. Believing that Vax computer users would also benefit from the program, S&H acquired a copy of the program, printed out its source code, and began work developing the program for Vax. Once it developed the program, SAS sued for copyright infringement. *Held:* The S&H work violated SAS's copyright. Although there were many original programming instructions, much of the program was copied. Furthermore, even if not a direct copy, the work clearly qualified as a "derivative work" under the Copyright Act. Such a work is one "based upon one or more pre-existing work. . . ." Since the S&H program was derived from the SAS work, it violated the copyright.

[SAS Inst., Inc. v. S&H Computer Sys., Inc., 605 F. Supp. 816 (MD Tenn. 1985)]

Program that cannot be substantially varied is not copyrightable.   Secure Services Technology manufactured fax machines that were capable of sending and receiving government faxes. These faxes were sent under a special protocol. Various makers used the protocol, which was subject to slight variations. TS later developed a fax machine that operated under a substantially similar protocol as Secure. Secure contended that TS violated its copyright. *Held:* A fax protocol is not protected by copyright. The court held that a protocol lacked the originality needed for copyright protection. The variations that could be made from the protocol were too limited to constitute an original work.

[Secure Servs. Technology, Inc. v. Time & Space Processing, Inc., 722 F. Supp. 1354 (ED Va. 1989)]

PART C.   DISPLAYS, OUTPUT, AND USER INTERFACE

¶ 1.07 DISPLAYS DISTINGUISHED FROM CODE

Copyright on audiovisual display of program extends to underlying program.
Kramer acquired and further developed a video poker game. Andrews, a distributer of the Kramer game, later developed its own poker game. Kramer alleged copyright infringement. Kramer sought to introduce the underlying program of the two games to show the infringement, and the district court would not allow this evidence. *Held:* The audiovisual copyright protected not only the display but also the underlying program. According to the court, the computer memory was a copy of the audiovisual display, which is protected by the copyright. Therefore, the district court could consider the implementing program when determining whether there had been an infringement.

[M. Kramer Mfg. Co. v. Andrews, 783 F2d 421 (4th Cir. 1986)]

¶ 1.08 VIDEO GAMES AND INTERACTIVE OUTPUT

[1] Copyrightable Expression in Computer Games

Look and feel of audiovisual component of video game is protected. Atari owned the rights to the Pac-Man video game. Phillips, through an independent contractor, developed the K.C. Munchkin game. Both games used maze structures and a central character that devours dots and is pursued by monsters. Atari sued for copyright infringement. Phillips countered that the games were not similar for the purpose of copyright. *Held:* The games were similar for copyright purposes. The look and feel of the Pac-Man characters were a distinctly created portion of the game showing a unique expression. The court noted that Phillips could create a game where characters served the same purpose and not violate the copyright, but they could not be the same or substantially similar in appearance.

[Atari, Inc. v. North Am. Phillips Consumer Elecs. Corp., 672 F2d 607 (7th Cir.), cert. denied, 459 US 880 (1982)]

Displays that ROM chips create are copyrightable even though images change. Williams developed a video game machine that incorporated a ROM chip. On this chip was stored the programs for the games. Artic developed a game using a substantially similar program also on a ROM chip. In response to Williams's claim of copyright infringement, Artic contended that the ROM chip was a part of the machine that could not be copyrighted, and furthermore that since the program created constantly changing images, the program was not "fixed" as per the mandate of the Copyright Act (17 USC § 102). *Held:* A program chip's information can be copyrighted and this program material was suitably fixed. The court noted that Artic was not being enjoined from using the ROM chip, only the program on the chip. It is the program not the chip itself that was copyrighted. The court then noted that the program was fixed, since the same images in the game could repeat. The fact that the game could have numerous outcomes was not deemed to materially affect whether the program was fixed.

[Williams Elecs., Inc. v. Artic Int'l, Inc., 685 F2d 870 (3d Cir. 1982)]

Replacement of distributed video game programs is not required to cure improper copyright notice. Kramer manufactured and marketed a computer video game entitled "Hi-Lo Double Up Joker Poker." Andrews subsequently marketed a substantially similar video game using the same name. When Kramer sued for copyright infringement, Andrews contended that the game was not copyrightable. *Held:* Kramer's computer poker game was copyrightable. The court explained that the idea of computerizing a popular game cannot be protected by copyright, but the manner in which it is carried out may be protectible. For example, the game of draw poker itself cannot be copyrighted and its basic elements are inherent in the idea of the game. But, a computer author who adds visual images of flashing cards, split screens, and other sights and sounds not required by the basic game produces a copyrightable work. Kramer's computerized poker game, the court concluded, demonstrated more than "a taint of originality."

[M. Kramer Mfg. Co. v. Andrews, 783 F2d 421 (4th Cir. 1986)]

[2] Infringement of Computer Games

Where idea and expression are entwined, computer program cannot be copyrighted.   Data East developed an arcade and home computer karate game. Epyx was the U.S. distributer for an English karate computer game. The games had many of the same features. Data East alleged copyright infringement, but Epyx contended that there was no infringement because the idea of a karate game is inseparable from its expression. *Held:* There was no copyright infringement. There must be a substantial similarity for a copyright infringement, which is shown when the ideas and expression are substantially similar. The court used an extrinsic test for ideas and an intrinsic test for expression. The ideas were substantially similar. If the expressions were found to be driven by idea, there could be no copyright. Here, the court found the expression of a karate game is limited by the actual sport and capabilities of the computer; therefore, the expression of the karate game was so entwined with the idea as to be uncopyrightable.

[Data East USA, Inc. v. Epyx, Inc., 862 F2d 204 (9th Cir. 1988)]

Video game similarities are based on idea, not expression.   Atari claimed that Amusement World's video game "Meteors" infringed Atari's copyrighted video game "Asteroids" because "Meteors" was substantially similar to Asteroids. Numerous design similarities existed between the two video games since each was based on a similar plot: a player locked in mortal combat with rocks while in space. Additionally, the idea for Meteors was based on Asteroids. *Held:* Although the video games were similar in idea, no copyright was infringed because each game's expression was sufficiently dissimilar from the other. First, the court defined the idea, not the expression, of both games as players battling rocks in space. Second, the court distinguished the games' expressions in a number of ways, including each game's feel, degree of realism, and degree of difficulty. Finally, similarities in game design were inevitable given the computer video game format.

[Atari, Inc. v. Amusement World, Inc., 547 F. Supp. 222 (D. Md. 1981)]

Animated toy's program is protected.   Worlds of Wonder marketed Teddy Ruxpin, an animated toy bear that operated on a two-track, cassette tape program that controlled

Teddy's sound and movement functions. Subsequently, Vector International produced a cassette tape marketed for replacement use in Teddy Ruxpin bears. *Held:* Applying the ordinary observer test, the court concluded that Vector's cassette tapes infringed Worlds's tapes because they were substantially similar. First, the Teddy Ruxpin toy was copyright protected as an audiovisual work that produced images and other expressions. The court then concluded that the two tapes were generally and specifically similar in their feel and concept, particularly noting the similarity in their voices and animated movements.

[Worlds of Wonder, Inc. v. Vector Int'l, Inc., 1 USPQ2d 1645 (ND Ohio 1986)]

[3] Animated Toys and Machines

Public performance of video game is protected. Red Baron imported and installed used video-game circuit boards into coin-operated video arcades for public performance. Taito, holder of the copyright for its video game called "Double Dragon" and its circuit board, claimed that Red Baron had infringed Taito's copyright since Red Baron was not licensed to use the circuit boards for public performances of the video game. *Held:* Red Baron infringed Taito's copyright of Double Dragon when it installed the circuit boards in video arcade units for public performance. Although Red Baron could legally purchase the circuit boards on the used market, Taito, as author of Double Dragon, held the exclusive right to make or license public performances of the game. Red Baron's purchase of the circuit boards on the used market did not extend that right to it. Public performance occurred when the video game was activated by coin and displayed its images and sounds in Red Baron's video arcades.

[Red Baron–Franklin Park, Inc. v. Taito Corp., 883 F2d 275 (4th Cir. 1989)]

¶ 1.09 USER INTERFACE OF DATA-PROCESSING PROGRAMS

Look and feel of program are not copyrightable where these elements express features that would be standard to type of program. John Friend created a computer outlining program that he sold to TR. He later developed another outlining program that was sold to Symantec. TR claimed that the later program was substantially similar to its program on which TR held the copyright. In particular, TR claimed that the look and feel of the Symantec program—pull-down menus and similar functions—violated the copyright. *Held:* There was no copyright infringement. The court noted that the features and functions that TR alleged had been copied were standard features of an outlining program. The court noted that standard features like these were clearly ideas, which are not copyrightable as a matter of law.

[Telemarketing Resources v. Symantec Corp., 12 USPQ2d 1991 (ND Cal. 1989)]

Audiovisual displays are protected artistic expression. Bronderbund developed for use on an Apple computer a program that creates greeting cards and is menu driven. Unison later developed a similar program for IBM computers. Both programs used similar menu screens and visual displays. Bronderbund claimed Unison infringed its copyright, but Unison countered that the sequence and arrangement of display screens are not copyrightable. *Held:* The screens are protected. The court stated that copyright protection extends beyond source and object codes, to overall program structure including audiovisual displays. The court noted that the Copyright Act requires that the pictorial design features must be separable from their utilitarian nature to be copyrightable. The court noted that the programmers' decisions for screen layout and appearance were driven by aesthetic concern rather than utilitarian requirements.

[Bronderbund Software, Inc. v. Unison World, Inc., 648 F. Supp. 1127 (ND Cal. 1986)]

Computer screen display is protected. Digital's predecessor invented a program for use in computer communications. The program had a status screen, which allowed the user to see the program's parameters and functions. This status screen was eventually copyrighted. Softklone's predecessor developed a program with a very similar status screen. Digital sued for copyright infringement, but Softklone claimed the screen could not be protected because it did not constitute expression, but was more like a blank form, which is not copyrightable. *Held:* The screen was protected. The court first noted that copyright of a program does not extend to the screen output, but once the screen is copyrighted, protection will extend to the screen if the screen is an expression rather than an idea. A screen constitutes expression if it can be differentiated from the idea. Here the court found the screen to be expression, stating that the screen was not like a blank form, because it was innovative and the form itself supplied information.

[Digital Communications Assocs., Inc. v. Softklone Distrib. Corp., 659 F. Supp. 449 (ND Ga. 1987)]

Program's menu structure, organization, and first letters of command names are expressive aspects of compilation entitled to copyright protection. Lotus, the holder of a copyright for the computer program Lotus 1-2-3, brought an action alleging that the macro-translation feature entitled "Key Reader" of Borland International's program infringed copyright. Borland's program used a file with phantom menus consisting of a virtually identical copy of the Lotus menu tree that Borland used for its emulation interface, but with only the first letter of each menu command name where the complete menu command name previously appeared. Borland argued that the copying of the 1-2-3 menu tree structure and first letters of command names was a necessary part of any system for interpreting Lotus 1-2-3 macros and that the Lotus copyright could not extend to Borland's phantom menus. Lotus responded that Borland had not proved that copying of any part of the menu tree was necessary for running or translating macros. *Held:* Copyright protection extended to Lotus 1-2-3's menu structure, organization, and first letters of command names copied by Borland; Borland's Key Reader infringed Lotus's copyrights in its 1-2-3 programs. Title 17 USC § 102(b) provides that "copyright protection for an original work of authorship does not extend to any idea, procedure, process, system, method of operation, concept, principle, or discovery, regardless of the form in which it is described, explained, illustrated, or embodied in such work." However, copyright protection does extend to the expressive aspects of a compilation. Here, the court held that the menu structure, organization, and first letters of the command names were part of the protectable expression found in the Lotus 1-2-3 program, and did not fall within the definition of "idea", "system", "process", "procedure", or "method" of the Lotus 1-2-3 program.

[Lotus Dev. Corp. v. Borland Int'l, Inc., 831 F. Supp. 223 (D. Mass. 1993)].

¶ 1.10 EXPRESSION IN THE USER INTERFACE

Interactive display screens are protected. Manufacturers Technologies produced, marketed, and copyrighted an interactive computer software program for estimating manufacturing costs, called "Costimator." Manufacturers claimed that Cams, which had subsequently produced several similar cost-estimating programs with similar screen displays, had infringed Manufacturers's copyright. Cams argued that the screen displays were uncopyrightable blank forms and conveyed no information to the user. *Held:* Manufacturers's copyright extended to the program's screen displays because, as a composite, the screen displays conveyed important information in analyzing cost-estimating problems. The displays dodged the blank forms rule since the displays conveyed information by expressing Manufacturers's cost-estimating process and the related manufacturing and engineering decisions of the program.

[Manufacturers Technologies, Inc. v. Cams, Inc., 706 F. Supp. 984 (D. Conn. 1989)]

¶ 1.11 COMPUTER-ASSISTED WORKS

Player participation does not vary originality of video games. Stern copyrighted and distributed a coin-operated video game known as "Scramble." Meanwhile, Omni Video Games, a competitor, released a video game also using the name "Scramble," which was virtually identical in sight and sound to Stern's game. Stern claimed copyright and trademark infringement against Omni and other defendants. Omni challenged the validity of the audiovisual copyright, claiming that it was not a fixed or original work since player participation varies the sequence of sights and sounds of the game. *Held:* Stern's copyright of Scramble as an audiovisual work was infringed because Omni's video game was substantially similar to Stern's game in its display images, sounds, and the sequence of those images. The effect that a player's participation has on the exact sequence of images during a particular play of the game does not create an original display for each play, since the game's author predetermined the sequence of images and sounds in the game program.

[Stern Elecs., Inc. v. Kaufman, 669 F2d 852 (2d Cir. 1982)]

¶ 1.12 MASKS AND CHIP TOPOLOGY

Substantially identical test is used when reverse-engineering defense is established. Brooktree developed a microchip to convert digital graphics information into analog information at high frequencies. Because Advance subsequently developed a microchip similar to Brooktree's, Brooktree sued under the Mask Work Act. Advance asserted that it used reverse engineering and design to develop its chip, and thus was not liable for infringement. *Held:* Since Advance established that it used reverse engineering and design, the court's infringement test was whether the chips were substantially identical to one another. The court justified this test as a balance between fostering independent product development and protection against infringement. Because the chips contained some dissimilarities in design, no infringement occurred.

[Brooktree Corp. v. Advance Micro Devices, Inc., 705 F. Supp. 491 (SD Cal. 1988)]

PART D.   END USERS, MODIFICATIONS, AND FAIR USE

¶ 1.13 DERIVATIVE WORKS AND PERSONAL MODIFICATIONS

Right-of-use license does not convey right to make derivative work. Payday contracted with SOS for SOS to provide computer payroll and accounting programs. Payday was allowed to use these programs only through a remote-access system and was not provided a copy of the programs. Under the contract terms, Payday acquired only the "right of use," while SOS retained "all rights of ownership." Payday subsequently copied the computer programs and made some modifications to them. SOS sued for infringement while Payday maintained that it had a right to make a personal-use modification to the programs. *Held:* Payday infringed SOS's copyright, since the contract licensed only a "right of use" where Payday could use the software only by a remote-access system. SOS did not convey to Payday a right to make a derivative work from the software.

[SOS, Inc. v. Payday, Inc., 886 F2d 1081 (9th Cir. 1989)]

"Derivative work" is defined.   Freeman gave Select a nonexclusive, revocable license to certain computer programs. Select subsequently made numerous modifications to the programs, and Freedman revoked the license. While Freedman claimed that Select infringed his copyright on the programs, Select asserted that it owned the derivative programs. *Held:* While a derivative work is one where the second work incorporates some or all of the expression of the underlying work, development and distribution of the derivative work does not imply an exclusive right in the preexisting work. Ownership of the derivative work is irrelevant where there is an infringement of the underlying work.

[Freedman v. Select Info. Sys., 221 USPQ 848 (ND Cal. 1983)]

¶ 1.14 OWNERS OF COPIES OF PROGRAMS

Copying program onto computer to examine its codes so the program can be overridden is not violation of copyright.   Vault developed a program that made it impossible for any program put on one of its disks to be used in a computer other than the one owned by the purchaser of the program. Although a program could still be copied, it would not be usable. Quaid developed a program to defeat the Vault program. In its development of this program, Quaid copied the Vault program onto its computer and examined it. Vault claimed Quaid violated its copyright. *Held:* There was no violation of copyright. The court stated that the Copyright Act explicitly allows computer programs to be copied onto the purchaser's computer where the copy is for the use of the program. The court refused to interpret this provision narrowly: It would not limit the use to only that contemplated by the software creator. Here, Quaid copied the program for a use associated with the program—its defeat. This was a legitimate use according to the court.

[Vault Corp. v. Quaid Software, Ltd., 847 F2d 255 (5th Cir. 1988)]

Statutory damages are set at a minimum because willful infringement is not demonstrated.   Banbury admitted its unauthorized use of Bly's "Finefont" computer program when it loaded the program onto its computer and subsequently used it to produce some correspondence and marketing materials. Bly sought statutory damages in the sum of $50,000, claiming that Banbury's infringement was willful. *Held:* Since Bly failed to provide sufficient evidence to establish that Banbury's infringement was willful or that Bly suffered any serious harm from the infringement, statutory damages were assessed at the minimum.

[Bly v. Banbury Brooks, Inc., 638 F. Supp. 983 (ED Pa. 1986)]

¶ 1.15 MODIFICATION KITS AND SUPPORT SYSTEMS

Copying cable descrambler program does not meet fair-use exception.   Cable/ Home developed a scrambler and descrambler chip to be used in the broadcast and reception of subscriber television broadcasts. Network developed a chip to enable satellite dish owners to descramble without Cable/Home's chip. Network copied 86 percent of Cable/Homes's chip programming and taught others how to sell and market these chips. Cable/Home sued for copyright infringement. Network alleged that it was subject to the fair-use exception. *Held:* There was no exception for Network. The four factors for the fair-use exception weighed against Network.   (1) nonprofit use: Network made substantial profits from selling the chips; (2) nature of the work: Network's chip allowed users of the chip to violate the broadcasters' copyrights; (3) amount copied: More than 86 percent of Cable/Home's program had been copied—an amount the court found significant; and (4) effect on the copyright holder's market: Because Cable/Home depended on the ability to protect its customers' broadcasts, any copying of its program undermined its relationship with those customers.

[Cable/Home Communications Corp. v. Network Prods., Inc., 902 F2d 829 (11th Cir. 1990)]

Enhancement of operating system infringes copyright.   Management distributed operating systems for its computers with various levels of performance related to the price charged for the license. The different performance levels were generated by limiting features in the operating systems. Hubco developed a software program and manual to remove the limiting features, and Management sued for infringement. *Held:* Hubco's software and manual infringed Management's copyrighted operating system by producing a direct copy of that program; namely, by copying Management's higher level operating codes.

[Hubco Data Prods. Corp. v. Management Assistance, Inc., 219 USPQ 450 (D. Idaho 1983)]

Plaintiff must establish factors of direct, vicarious, or contributory copyright infringement on part of defendant.   Joan Napoli, a computer programmer, sued her former customer, Sears, Roebuck and Company, and her competitor, Keane, alleging, among other things, copyright infringement. Keane moved to dismiss for failure to state a claim on infringement counts; Napoli filed a motion for partial summary judgment as to her ownership of a valid and enforceable copyright. *Held:* The copyright infringement claim against Keane was dismissed; Napoli's motion for partial summary judgment was denied. To establish a prima facie case of direct copyright infringement, Napoli had to prove that (1) she owned a valid copyright; (2) her work was original; (3) Keane copied the work; and (4) a substantial degree of similarity existed between the two works. Napoli failed to allege that Keane ever copied the system or that Keane created a system that was substantially similar to Napoli's. Accordingly, Napoli failed to state a claim for direct copyright infringement. Napoli also failed to state a claim for vicarious or contributory infringement. To state a claim for vicarious infringement, the complaint must allege that (1) the defendant had the right and the authority to supervise the infringing activity of another; and (2) the defendant had an obvious and direct financial interest in exploitation of the copyrighted materials. Here, the allegations in Napoli's complaint failed to satisfy either of these elements. Napoli made no claim that Keane could supervise any activities of Sears, nor did she allege that Keane stood to benefit financially as a result of the infringement. To establish a claim of contributory infringement, Napoli had to demonstrate that Keane (1) had knowledge of Sears's act of infringement and (2) induced, caused, or materially contributed to that infringement. Napoli failed to allege that Keane was involved in any actual infringement by Sears or that Keane induced such infringement. On the contrary, the complaint suggested that Keane only became involved after any infringement by Sears took place. Finally, the court denied Napoli's motion for partial summary judgment because a genuine issue of material fact existed as to whether Sears and Napoli were joint authors of the system.

[Napoli v. Sears, Roebuck & Co., 835 F. Supp. 1053 (ND Ill. 1993)]

Inducing others to violate data base license is contributory infringement. Telerate licensed customers to access its copyrighted, financial information data base using a Telerate-provided remote-access terminal. The license further stipulated that no other equipment was to be interfaced with the Telerate terminal Caro developed and marketed a software program called "Excel-A-Rate" that allowed users to access and analyze Telerate's financial information data base without using a Telerate terminal. Caro claimed that he did not infringe the data base and that accessing and copying the data base using Excel-A-Rate constituted a fair use. *Held:* Caro was vicariously liable for contributory infringement by inducing others to violate Telerate's copyright by copying the Telerate data base with Excel-A-Rate. Such access exceeded the applicable data base license and resulted in an unauthorized copy of the data base not protected by fair-use doctrines, since Telerate would be financially harmed.

[Telerate Sys., Inc. v. Caro, 689 F. Supp. 221 (SDNY 1988)]

PART E.   NOTICE, DEPOSIT, AND REMEDIES

¶ 1.16 COPYRIGHT NOTICE

Video game's registrability is predicated on its total sequence of images.   Atari filed for an audiovisual copyright on its video game, "Breakout." The Copyright Office refused to grant the copyright, claiming that the video game's components, its screen displays and sounds, did not contain sufficient original or musical authorship to warrant registration. *Held:*   The court remanded the case to the Copyright Office with instructions to reconsider Atari's application. Since Section 101 of the Copyright Act defines "audiovisual work" as a "series of related images," the Copyright Office was required to consider the total sequence of images displayed as the game is played, rather than isolating some of the video game's potentially noncopyrightable component images.

[Atari Games Corp. v. Oman, 888 F2d 878 (DC Cir. 1989)]

Unit-publication rule covers computer manuals and tapes.   Koontz developed and copyrighted a manual containing compiled data for estimating electrical construction contracts and later transferred that data onto computer tapes not containing a copyright notice. The manual and tapes were sold as a package. Jaffarian, a former employee of Koontz, used Koontz's computer tape data to produce a similar manual for estimating electrical construction contracts. Koontz sued for copyright infringement, while Jaffarian asserted that the computer tapes were not copyrighted. *Held:* Koontz's copyright was infringed because under the unit-publication doctrine, the copyright notice provided on the computer tape's user manual was also sufficient to protect the accompanying computer tapes. Application of the unit-publication doctrine was fair in this case because Jaffarian was not an innocent infringer when he was aware that Koontz held the copyright for the manual and its data.

[Koontz v. Jaffarian, 787 F2d 906 (4th Cir. 1986)]

Correcting future distributions is reasonable effort to cure improper copyright notice.   Forry developed, copyrighted, and marketed a computer program for an automatic voltage control device (AVC). Neundorfer, a former sales agent for Forry, also began to market its own AVC computer program, which was substantially similar to Forry's. Forry sued for infringement. Neundorfer contended that Forry had failed to provide proper copyright notice on its distributed programs and thus was not entitled to copyright protection. *Held:*   Under Section 405(2) of the Copyright Act, Forry had made a reasonable effort to cure its improper notice, and thus retained copyright protection for its AVC program. Forry was not required to affix proper notice to those copies that had already been distributed, but was required only to affix proper notice on those copies distributed after the improper notice was discovered.

[Forry, Inc. v. Neundorfer, Inc., 837 F2d 259 (6th Cir. 1988)]

Registration prior to infringement is necessary for award of attorney fees and punitive damages.   Evans contracted with CSS for CSS to write a classroom-management computer program, entitled "Project Basic," and accompanying user manual. Although CSS agreed that Evans was to retain the copyright for Project Basic, CSS subsequently marketed its own version of the program and user manual, which were substantially similar to Project Basic. Evans sued for copyright infringement. *Held:* Although CSS infringed Evans's copyright on the computer program and user manual, Evans was not entitled to punitive damages or attorney fees under Section 412 of the Copyright Act because Evans did not register its copyright prior to CSS's act of infringement.

[Evans Newton, Inc. v. Chicago Sys. Software, 793 F2d 889 (7th Cir. 1986)]

Copyright notice on manual is sufficient to establish unit-publication rule.   Lasercomb licensed Holiday to use its copyrighted computer-automated-design software entitled "Interact" for Holiday's manufacturing business. Lasercomb thoroughly trained Holiday's personnel to use the software. Subsequently, Lasercomb discovered that Holiday began marketing a virtually identical program and sued Holiday for copyright infringement. Holiday countered that Lasercomb failed to place any copyright notice on the software, and thus was not liable for infringement. *Held:* Lasercomb's copyright was infringed under the unit-publication doctrine since the software's user manual provided proper copyright notice on its first page. Since Holiday admitted that it received a complete set of Interact manuals when it received the software, Lasercomb was not required to establish that the software and manuals formed a single commercial unit in order to advance the unit-publication rule.

[Lasercomb Am., Inc. v. Holiday Steel Rule Die Corp., 656 F. Supp. 612 (MDNC 1987)]

¶ 1.17 REMEDIES

Similarities derived from common sources or dictated by function of program are insufficient to establish "substantial similarities between the structure, sequence and organization of the programs" necessary to establish infringement. CTI brought an action for, among other things, copyright infringement against former employees and the corporation formed by the former employees. CTI contended that "Transcend", a computer program developed by the former employees, infringed on the copyrights CTI held in its "Claims Express" and "EDI Link" computer programs. On appeal, CTI contended that the district court failed to apply the correct test to determine substantial similarity, and therefore erred in concluding that the structure, sequence, and organization of Transcend were not substantially similar to that of Claims Express and EDI Link. CTI contended that the correct test was the "abstraction-filtration-comparison" analysis, first announced in *Computer Associates International, Inc. v. Altai, Inc.*, 982 F.2d 693 (2d Cir. 1992). *Held:* The district court's finding that Transcend was not substantially similar to either Claims Express or EDI Link was affirmed. A plaintiff can establish infringement by showing substantial similarities between the structure, sequence, and organization of programs. Here, the district court found that although the programs shared some characteristics, the similarities were either derived from common sources available to the average programmer or were dictated by the function of the program. The district court also found that former employees had not copied any of CTI's proprietary algorithms. Therefore, the district court held that CTI had not met its burden of proof on the substantial similarities issue. The court of appeals noted CTI's argument must fail because CTI failed to identify any evidence in the record that indicated that the requisite similarities needed to satisfy the abstraction-filtration-comparison analysis were proved at trial.

[Comprehensive Technologies Int'l, Inc. v. Software Artisans, Inc., 3 F3d 730 (4th Cir. 1993)]

Material in public domain is copyrightable where programmer makes additions that are unique and not trivial. EF Johnson developed a mobile radio system using software imbedded on a ROM chip. Uniden developed a compatible system. EF alleged copyright infringement, noting that the Uniden program was substantially similar to the EF program, even including the same errors as the EF program. Uniden contended that the EF program was not copyrightable because it was not original, and that certain password functions and matrixes were in the public domain and as such were not copyrightable. EF contended that it had made changes in the public domain material so that it was original. *Held:* The program was copyrightable. The court noted that the test for originality is not stringent: Only a "faint trace" of originality is required. The court stated that even material in the public domain could be protected by copyright if changes by the author are not trivial addition. Here, EF created new permutations of basic password programs and used matrixes that were unique to EF. The program then was recognizably new and original material.

[EF Johnson Co. v. Uniden Corp. of Am., 623 F. Supp. 1485 (D. Minn. 1985)]

University enjoyed Eleventh Amendment immunity from copyright infringement allegations only before November 15, 1990; moreover, *ex parte Young* doctrine does not bar suit against Regents. Unix brought an action against the University of California and its Board of Regents, alleging copyright infringement. The university moved to dismiss the claim, arguing that it was immune from the suit because it benefited from the State of California's immunity under the Eleventh Amendment. The Regents further argued that the copyright claim against them should be dismissed because Unix had an available remedy against the university. *Held:* The copyright claim against the university was dismissed to the extent that it stated a claim for violations before November 15, 1990, when states enjoyed immunity under the Eleventh Amendment; the copyright claim against the Regents was not dismissed. As to violations after November 15, 1990, the court found that Unix had alleged facts sufficient to state a cause of action. As to the claim against the Regents, the defendants argued that under *ex parte Young*, Unix could bring an action against the Regents only if it had no cause of action against the university. Since there was a statutory remedy against the university for violations after November 15, 1990, they argued, there was no justification for naming the individual Regents as defendants. The court found that Unix could state a cause of action for any act within the limitations period against the Regents. Moreover, it was conceivable that Unix could succeed against in its claims against the Regents yet fail against the university.

[UNIX Sys. Labs., Inc. v. Berkeley Software Design, Inc., 832 F. Supp. 790 (DNJ 1993)]

CHAPTER 2

PATENT LAW: SOFTWARE AND SYSTEMS PROTECTION

PART A.   CLAIMS AND SCOPE

¶ 2.01 PATENT SYSTEM OVERVIEW

Mathematical algorithm is process within meaning of Patent Act and is therefore unpatentable.   Applicants filed in the Patent Office an application for an invention described as being related "to the processing of data by program and more particularly to the programmed conversion of numerical information" in general-purpose digital computers. Specifically, the applicants claimed a method of converting binary-coded decimal numerals into pure binary numerals, which claims were not limited to any particular art, technology, apparatus, machinery, or end use. At issue was whether the method described and claimed was a "process" within the meaning of the Patent Act. *Held:* The applicants' method was not a patentable process within the meaning of the Act. The procedures set forth in the applicants' claims were an algorithm or a generalized formulation for programs to solve mathematical problems of converting one form of numerical representation to another. One may not patent an idea, and that is what applicants sought in this case. The applicants' mathematical formula had no substantial practical application except in connection with a digital computer and, if a patent were granted, the patent would wholly preempt the mathematical formula and in practical effect would be a patent on the algorithm itself.

[Gottschalk v. Benson, 409 US 63 (1972)]

¶ 2.02 CLAIMS

Licensee's authorized "first sale" of patented chips deprives patent owner of any claim of infringement against purchaser.   A patent owner developed a line of math coprocessors covered by the patent. The patent owner entered into a cross-licensing agreement with a manufacturer under which each granted to the other irrevocable, nonexclusive, royalty-free licenses under all patents having an effective date prior to January 1, 2000. Under an agreement with a purchaser, the manufacturer agreed to manufacture coprocessors for the purchaser according to the purchaser's proprietary design specifications. The patent owner brought suit against the purchaser, alleging patent infringement. The purchaser maintained that, under the manufacturer's licensing agreement with the patent owner, the sale of coprocessors by the manufacturer to the purchaser was a "first sale" that extinguished the patent owner's rights with respect to those products. The patent owner argued that the "first sale" or "patent exhaustion" doctrine did not apply because the manufacturer never sold a product to the purchaser, but actually sold its fabrication services to the purchaser with an ancillary sale of chip wafers. Furthermore, the patent owner contended that, in order for there to be a "sale" of the product, the manufacturer would have to have owned intellectual property rights to the product. *Held:* The coprocessors were insulated from the patent owner's claim of infringement because they were sold to the purchaser by the manufacturer, which was authorized to do so under its licensing agreement with the patent owner. The patent owner's characterization of the manufacturer's agreement with the purchaser as one in which the manufacturer merely provided fabrication services to the purchaser was incorrect. That agreement was replete with references to the sale of semiconducter wafers that incorporated the coprocessor design and recited prices for the chips. Moreover, the manufacturer was authorized under the broad terms of its licensing agreement with the patent owner to sell the chips. To the extent that the patent owner had a patent covering the chips, the manufacturer's right to sell the chips deprived the patent owner of any claim of infringement.

[Intel Corp. v. ULSI Sys. Technology Inc., 27 USPQ2d 1136 (Fed. Cir. 1993)]

Patent is invalidated because inventor failed to disclose the best mode of practicing the invention. A patentee sued a competitor for infringement of its patent. The competitor counterclaimed that the patent was invalid because the patentee failed to comply with 35 USC § 112, which requires a patentee to set forth in its patent application "the best mode contemplated by the inventor of carrying out his invention." *Held:* The patent was invalidated for failing to satisfy the "best mode" requirement. Section 112 is designed to prohibit concealment of the best mode of practicing the claimed invention. A best mode analysis under Section 112 has two components. It must first be determined whether the inventor, at the time of filing a patent application, knew of a mode of practicing the claimed invention that the inventor considered to be better than any other. If the inventor did contemplate a preferred mode, there must be a comparison between what the inventor knew and what is disclosed in the application. In this case, the inventor failed to disclose the only mode of carrying out the invention ever contemplated, and the best mode requirement was thus violated.

[Chemcast Corp. v. ARCO Indus. Corp., 913 F2d 923 (Fed. Cir. 1990)]

"Best mode" disclosure requirement is not met where objective of invention is the use of standard audiotape in data capture and patentee knew that standard tape was not the best mode. A patentee filed suit, charging Datapoint with infringement of its patent, which related to a mode of "batch processing" of data. Datapoint argued that the patentee's application concealed the best mode of carrying out the invention. *Held:* Certain claims under the patentee's patent were invalid on the basis that the best mode of carrying out the invention was concealed. One of the objectives of the disclosed invention was to capture data "on magnetic tape cassettes of the general type presently finding extensive and widespread usage in audio entertainment equipment, but never heretofore used in data-handling apparatus." However, there was evidence that the patentee knew, in advance of filing its patent application, that the standard audiotape was not the best mode for carrying out the invention, and that the patentee purchased tapes and cassettes of its own design and specifications that were different from standard audiotapes. Even if, as the patentee argued, there was tape on the market that met its specifications, it was this tape that had to be disclosed to satisfy the best mode requirement of 35 USC § 112.

[Northern Telecom, Inc. v. Datapoint Corp., 908 F2d 931 (Fed. Cir. 1990)]

Since specification provided information sufficient to require only application of routine skill to produce digital computer program contemplated by patent application, there is no concealment of best mode.   An applicant filed certain patent claims for an automated digital processing system and method for a "Continuous Automatic Migration of Seismic Reflection Data with Waveform Preservation." The claims were rejected under 35 USC § 112 for being based on a specification that failed to disclose the best mode. The patent examiner rejected the claims on the basis that the applicant had not described the best mode in "sufficient detail to enable a person of ordinary skill in the art" to make and use the invention. Specifically, the examiner found that the applicant had failed to disclose any computer hardware, flow charts, algorithms, or programs with which the best mode would operate. At issue was whether the applicant's failure to disclose a listing of a known computer program was fatal to the application. *Held:* The specification in the application delineated the best mode in a manner sufficient to require only the application of routine skill to produce a workable digital computer program and, therefore, the applicant's disclosure was not a concealment of the best mode. The specification did provide the general mathematical equations used and did teach the further "trick" of chopping the physical input seismic traces into segments via mathematical manipulation.

[In re Sherwood, 613 F2d 809 (CCPA 1980)]

Claims that did not essentially recite a method of computing one or more numbers from a different set of numbers but that were "merely ancillary to a more encompassing process" are not classified as nonstatutory mathematical algorithms.   Logan applied for a patent relating to an apparatus and method for detecting a patient's inspiration. The examiner rejected all the claims under 35 USC § 101 as directed to nonstatutory subject matter. According to the examiner, the method and apparatus disclosed and claimed resided solely in the operation of a computer program; i.e., the pseudo-code that would operate on a variety of computers. The examiner further explained that the claims indirectly recited mathematical algorithms. *Held:* The patent claim incidentally required, either directly or indirectly, the performance of some mathematical computations, but essentially recited another type of method, and did not recite a mathematical algorithm, and was therefore patentable. A claim should be considered as reciting a nonstatutory mathematical algorithm only if it essentially recites a method of computing one or more numbers from a different set of numbers by performing a series of mathematical computations. Consequently, a claim that essentially recites another method does not recite a mathematical algorithm, even though it incidentally requires the performance of some mathematical computations. The approach should focus on what the claimed method steps do rather than how the steps are performed. Here, the Board concluded that the claims in the case were "merely ancillary to a more encompassing process" and declined to sustain the Section 101 rejection.

[Ex parte Logan, 41 Pat. Trademark & Copyright J. (BNA) 481 (PTO Bd. App. 1991)]

PART B.   SUBJECT MATTER ISSUES

¶ 2.03 COMPUTER PROGRAMS AND PATENT SCOPE

Process that includes use of mathematical formula and programmed digital computer is patentable.   Applicants filed a patent application for a process for molding raw, uncured synthetic rubber into cured precision products, claiming that their contribution to art resided in the process of constantly measuring the actual temperature inside the mold. The patent examiner rejected the application on the ground that the claims were drawn to nonstatutory subject matter. At issue on appeal was whether the process for curing synthetic rubber, which included in several of its steps the use of a mathematical formula and a programmed digital computer, was patentable subject matter under 35 USC § 101. *Held:* The process was patentable subject matter. A process is patentable subject matter under Section 101 if it is a new and useful act or series of acts performed on the article to be transformed and reduced to a different state or thing. While a mathematical formula cannot be the subject of a patent, applicants here sought protection for a process that employed a well-known mathematical equation. Applicants were not seeking to preempt the use of the equation, except in conjunction with all the other steps in their claimed process. When a claim containing a mathematical formula in a structure or process that, when considered as a whole, is performing a function that the patent laws were designed to protect, the claim satisfies the requirements of Section 101.

[Diamond v. Diehr, 450 US 175 (1981)]

The fact that claimed apparatus operated according to an algorithm does not make it nonstatutory.   The applicants' invention related to an autocorrelation unit for use in pattern recognition to obtain autocorrelation coefficients as for stored signal samples. The patent application specification stated that state-of-the-art units for calculation of autocorrelation coefficients had the disadvantage of requiring expensive multipliers and complicated circuitry. The principal object of the invention was to provide an autocorrelation unit for pattern recognition that evaluated autocorrelation coefficients by means of simple circuitry without the need for an expensive multiplier. The application was rejected on the sole ground that the subject matter claimed was nonstatutory under 35 USC § 101 because it was merely a mathematical algorithm. *Held:* The claim was directed to statutory subject matter. Although the claim recited a mathematical algorithm, what was claimed was an apparatus with specific structural limitations. The claim as a whole defined apparatus in the form of a combination of interrelated means, and there was no logical reason why it should not have been deemed statutory subject matter as either a machine or a manufacture as specified in Section 101. The fact that the apparatus operated according to an algorithm did not make it nonstatutory.

[In re Iwahashi, 888 F2d 1370 (Fed. Cir. 1989)]

Applicant claimed mathematical algorithm and is therefore unpatentable even though most of the claims limited use of the algorithm to a particular art or technology. The examiner rejected the applicant's claims for an invention used in seismic prospecting and surveying. The sole ground for rejection was that the claims were directed to nonstatutory subject matter under 35 USC § 101. Specifically, the examiner found that the claims were directed to a mathematical procedure outlined in the specifications. *Held:* The applicant's claims were unpatentable. Once it is found, as in this case, that a claim recites a mathematical algorithm, the claim as a whole must be further analyzed. If it appears that the mathematical algorithm is implemented in a specific manner to define structural relationships between the physical elements of the claim (in apparatus claims) or to refine or limit claim steps (in process claims), the claim being otherwise statutory, the claim passes muster under Section 101. If, however, the mathematical algorithm is merely presented and solved by the claimed invention and is not applied in any manner to physical elements or process steps, no amount of postsolution activity will render the claim statutory. In this case, the applicant claimed the mathematical algorithm itself, even though most of his claims limited its use to a particular art or technology. The applicant's claims were therefore unpatentable.

[In re Walter, 618 F2d 758 (CCPA 1980)]

Hardware elements that contained microprogrammed information are patentable since no mathematical formula was claimed or was essential to vitality of the claims. Applicants filed an application for an invention related to the internal operation of a computer and its ability to manage efficiently its operation in a multiprogrammed format. Specifically, the invention related to altering or repositioning information in the computer's system base. The patent examiner rejected the applicants' claims, and the Patent and Trademark Office Board of Appeals affirmed the rejection. The Board stated that, although the claims did not directly recite a mathematical formula or algorithm, the claims were nevertheless mathematical in nature, and they were for an improved method of calculation, which was unpatentable subject matter under 35 USC § 101. *Held:* The decision of the Board was reversed. The Board's analysis confused *what* the computer did with how it was done. While it is true that a digital computer manipulates data by performing mathematical operations, the significance of the data and their manipulation in the real world are important. In this case, the applicants were claiming a new and unobvious combination of hardware elements. No mathematical formula or mathematical method of calculation, improved or otherwise, was claimed or was essential to the vitality of the claims. Rather, the invention was a combination of tangible hardware elements—a machine—including some hardware elements contained microprogrammed information.

[In re Bradley, 600 F2d 807 (CCPA 1979)]

¶ 2.04 PARTICULAR SOFTWARE-RELATED INVENTIONS

[1] Conversion and Simulation Programs

Applicant's method of updating alarm limits during catalytic conversion processes is not patentable where only novel feature of method was a mathematical formula.   An applicant filed an application for a method of updating "alarm limits" during catalytic conversion processes. Alarm limits are numbers or values used to signal abnormal operating conditions during the processes. The only difference between conventional methods of changing alarm limits and the method described in the applicant's application was the use of a mathematical algorithm or formula. Although the computations can be made by pencil and paper calculations, the application's disclosure made clear that the formula was primarily useful for computerized calculations producing automatic adjustments in alarm settings. At issue was whether the identification of a limited category of useful, though otherwise conventional, post-solution applications of such a formula made the applicant's method eligible for patent protection. *Held:* The applicant's method was not patentable under 35 USC § 101. But for the mathematical algorithm, all aspects of the applicant's method were conventional. The processes in catalytic conversion were well-known, as were the practice of monitoring process variables, the use of alarm limits, the notion that alarm limit values must be recomputed, and the use of computers for automatic alarming-monitoring. An applicant simply provided a new and presumably better method for calculating alarm values. The notion that the use of the formula's results, no matter how conventional or obvious, could transform an unpatentable principle into a patentable process exalts form over substance.

[Parker v. Flook, 437 US 584 (1978)]

Claims are unpatentable where all but one of the types in the process were in essence a mathematical algorithm and the remaining step merely provided for collection of data.   The patent examiner rejected the applicants' application for an invention that provided a method of testing complex systems to determine whether the condition of a given system was normal or abnormal and, if abnormal, to determine the cause of the abnormality. The claims limited the disclosed invention to the diagnosis of individuals. Although the applicants agreed that their claims included a mathematical algorithm, they contended that the mere recitation of an algorithm did not automatically render the claims nonstatutory. At issue was whether the algorithm-containing claims were drawn to statutory subject matter. *Held:* The applicants' claims were unpatentable under 35 USC § 101 as being drawn to a nonstatutory mathematical algorithm. Although the mere presence of a mathematical exercise, as a step or steps in a process involving nonmathematical steps, should not preclude approval of an application, the analysis of the application requires careful interpretation of each claim in light of its supporting disclosure. That analysis is facilitated somewhat if the only physical step involves merely gathering data for the algorithm. In this case, the sole physical process step was the performance of clinical tests on individuals to obtain data, and the specification focused on the algorithm itself. From the specification and the claim, it was clear that the applicants were, in essence, claiming the mathematical algorithm, and the presence of a physical step in the claim to derive data for the algorithm did not render the claim statutory.

[In re Grams, 888 F2d 835 (Fed. Cir. 1989)]

Claims that included application of algorithm within context of a process that was otherwise statutory are proper subject matter for patenting.   The applicants' invention was in the field of image processing, particularly as applied to CAT scans. The invention was directed to an improvement in computed tomography whereby the exposure to X-rays was reduced while the reliability of the produced image was improved. The examiner rejected the applicants' claims and the Patent and Trademark Office Board of Appeals affirmed, finding that the claims did no more than present and solve a mathematical algorithm and were thus unpatentable. *Held:* Certain of the applicants' claims were patentable subject matter. If a claim would otherwise meet statutory requirements, even if inoperative or less useful without an algorithm, the claim presents statutory subject matter when the algorithm is included. If the claimed invention is a mathematical algorithm, it is improper subject matter for patent protection; whereas, if the claimed invention is an application of the algorithm, 35 USC

§ 101 will not bar the grant of a patent. In this case, certain of the applicants' claims were directed solely to the mathematical algorithm portion of the invention. These claims presented nothing more than the calculation of a number and thus were not statutory subject matter under Section 101. However, other claims of the applicants involved an improvement to a process through the application of a mathematical formula within the context of a process that encompassed significantly more than the algorithm alone. The applicants discovered an application of an algorithm to process steps that themselves were part of an overall process that was statutory, and therefore these claims met the requirements of Section 101.

[In re Abele, 684 F2d 902 (CCPA 1982)]

Applicants' claims, which recited an algorithm, set forth a process and are statutory within the meaning of Section 101. The applicants' invention related to a method of seismic exploration by which substantially plane or substantially cylindrical seismic energy waves were simulated from substantially spherical seismic waves. According to the applicants' specifications, the combining of signals to simulate plane or cylindrical wavefronts made possible a reduction in data correction and thereby reduced the expenditures of time and money required for seismic exploration. In sustaining the examiner's rejection of the applicants' claims, the Patent and Trademark Office Board of Appeals found that the claims directly recited a mathematical algorithm and that, since there was no close relationship between the algorithm and the other process steps except that the signals to be summed were generated by the precedent process steps, the claims preempted the algorithm. The Board therefore concluded that the claims were nonstatutory under 35 USC § 101. *Held:* The decision of the Board was overruled. The applicants' claims were not merely directed to the solution of a mathematical algorithm. The applicants' claimed process involved the taking of substantially spherical seismic signals obtained in conventional seismic exploration and converting those signals into another form. Thus, the claims set forth a process and were within Section 101.

[In re Taner, 681 F2d 787 (CCPA 1982)]

[2] Internal Operation Programs

Claim for method of controlling internal operations of computer does not recite a mathematical algorithm. Applicants characterized their invention as a method for controlling the internal operations of a computer. The invention was designed to convert a computer from a sequential processor to a processor that did not depend on the order in which it received program steps. The application's specification described the invention as involving an algorithm of a compiler program. In affirming the examiner's rejection of the applicants' claims, the Patent and Trademark Office

Board of Appeals found that the claims, in light of the specification, were directed in their entirety to the algorithm of the compiler, or variations thereof and, hence, the claims did not pass muster under 35 USC § 101. *Held:* The applicants' claims did constitute statutory subject matter, and the Section 101 rejection was reversed. The applicants' claims were directed to executing programs in a computer. The method operated on *any* program and *any* formula that may have been input, regardless of mathematical content. That a computer controlled according to the invention was capable of handling mathematics was irrelevant to the question of whether a mathematical algorithm was recited by the claims. There was no mathematical formula, calculation, or algorithm either directly or indirectly recited in the claimed steps of examining, compiling, storing, and executing.

[In re Pardo, 684 F2d 912 (CCPA 1982)]

[3] Artificial Intelligence and Expert Systems

Claims drawn to a mathematical algorithm not applied to physical elements or process steps and not limited to otherwise statutory matter are properly rejected. The applicants' invention was a process and an apparatus for carrying out the testing of a complex system by dividing the complex system into a plurality of elements and associating a factor of function or malfunction with each of the elements. The claims were related to replacing, in part, the thinking processes of a neurologist with a computer. In sustaining the examiner's rejection of the application, the Patent and Trademark Office Board of Appeals found that the claims were drawn to a technique of statistical analysis by which data was accumulated from a series of test operations and conclusions were drawn in accordance with a mathematical algorithm, and therefore the claims failed to satisfy the requirements of 35 USC § 101. *Held:* The claims were not patentable subject matter under Section 101, and hence the decision of the Board was affirmed. The applicants' specification indicated that the invention was concerned with replacing the thinking processes of a neurologist with a computer, and the claims recited a mathematical algorithm that represented a mental process that a neurologist should follow. Since the applicants' claims were to a mathematical algorithm representing a mental process that had not been applied to physical elements or process steps and was not limited to any otherwise statutory process, machine, manufacture, or composition of matter, the claims were properly rejected.

[In re Meyer, 688 F2d 789 (CCPA 1982)]

[4] Applications Programs

Since claimed method of translating from one language to another did not involve a mathematical problem and there was no recitation of an algorithm, claims

are not nonstatutory under Section 101.   The applicant's invention involved a method of operating a digital computer to translate from a source natural language (e.g., Russian) to a target natural language (e.g., English). The method involved three phases—the look-up phase, the syntactical analysis phase, and the synthesis phase. An important aspect of the invention was the separate treatment given high-frequency-use words versus low-frequency-use words, whereby the translation information for frequently used words was held in an easily accessible place in the computer. The decision of the Patent and Trademark Office Board of Appeals sustained the examiner's rejection of the claims under 35 USC § 101 as being directed to nonstatutory subject matter. According to the Board, the applicant's claimed invention was an algorithm or rule having no substantial application except in connection with a digital computer. In reaching its decision, the Board concluded that the term "algorithm" was not limited to expressions in mathematical terms, but rather included expressions in natural language. *Held:* The claims were not nonstatutory and the decision of the Board was reversed. The term "algorithm" in this context refers to a procedure for solving a given type of *mathematical* problem. A review of the claims in this case revealed that there was no direct or indirect recitation of a procedure for solving a *mathematical* problem. Translating between natural languages is not a mathematical problem in the context of Section 101, and none of the steps recited in the claims in this case were mere procedures for solving mathematical problems. Since the claims did not directly or indirectly recite an algorithm, the claims could not preempt an algorithm and, therefore, the claims were not nonstatutory.

[Application of Toma, 575 F2d 872 (CCPA 1978)]

Accounting method that requires only entering, sorting, debiting, and totaling expenditures as necessary preliminary steps to issuance of expense analysis statement is "method of doing business" outside scope of Section 101 patentability. Murray appealed the rejection of a patent claim for an "accounting method utilizing a financial institution's documents" and yielding an expense analysis statement for customers. The examiner rejected the claim under 35 USC § 101 as nonpatentable subject matter. *Held:* Murray's claimed accounting method was not proper subject matter for patent protection under Section 101 because it constituted a method of doing business and/or it preempted an algorithm. A series of steps is a "process" within the meaning of Section 101 unless it falls within a judicially determined category of nonstatutory subject matter exceptions. Methods of doing business fall within the category of nonstatutory subject matter exceptions. Here, the court found that the claimed accounting method, requiring no more than entering, sorting, debiting, and totaling expenditures as necessary preliminary steps to issuing an expense analysis statement was a vivid example of the type of "method of doing business" contemplated by the courts as outside the protection of the patent statutes. Moreover, in determining whether a claim reciting mathematics and/or computer programming is in compliance with Section 101, the court must examine, first, if the claim directly or indirectly recites an algorithm, or "[a] procedure for solving a given type of mathematical problem." If so, the court must determine whether the claimed method, as a whole, merely recites the algorithm such that it wholly preempts that algorithm. Here, the claimed method included the steps of subtotaling and totaling a variety of entered and sorted debits on an account; therefore, the claims defined a procedure for solving a mathematical problem, or an algorithm. As to the next step of the analysis, although the claims required a number of steps preceding subtotaling and totlaing, i.e., entering, coverting, sorting, correlating, storing, these preliminary gathering steps did not affect the "subject matter as a whole" determination. Similarly, the claimed concluding step, "printing and issuing said expense analysis statement to said user," amounted to no more than displaying the result of the calculations and was an insignificant postsolution activity that did not qualify the claimed system for patent protection. Therefore, the claims also preempted an algorithm for calculating expenses.

[Ex parte Murray, 9 USPQ2d 1819 (PTO Bd. App. 1988)]

¶ 2.05 DESIGN PATENTS

Patent claim for display screen icon is properly rejected as not being an ornamental design for an "article of manufacture."   Applicants filed a patent application, the sole claim of which was for an "ornamental design for an information icon for the display screen of a programmed computer system or the like. . . ." The examiner rejected the claim as unpatentable under 35 USC § 171, which allows for the patentability of an "ornamental design for an article of manufacture." The examiner concluded that the design as claimed was not an ornamental design for an article of manufacture, but was merely a picture or surface ornamentation per se rather than a design applied to an article. The examiner noted that no programmed computer system was either depicted or described. *Held:* The applicants did not present a design for an article of manufacture as required by 35 USC § 171. Consistent with Section 171, a design must be shown applied to an article. Although the applicants' specification, claim, and title expressly stated that the claimed design was for the display screen of a programmed computer system, they did not show an applied design. Specifically, they did not show the design applied to the asserted article as required by Section 171. If the applicants had properly presented and claimed the intended design as not merely a displayed picture, but as an integral and active component in the operation of a programmed computer, the subject matter would have constituted statutory subject matter under Section 171.

[Ex parte Strijland, 26 USPQ2d 1259 (BPAI 1992)]

PART C.   NOVELTY, UTILITY, AND OBVIOUSNESS

¶ 2.06 NOVELTY

Distribution of computer chip specification sheet to interested public constitutes "printed publication" for purposes of Section 102(b).   The patentee sued AMD for infringement of his patent for an invention that provided integrated circuit chips that could be interconnected in a computer with fewer wires (leads). The claimed novel invention was the use of transmitter and receiver means on a chip in order to transform incoming and outgoing signals so as to reduce the number of pads on a chip and the number of interconnecting leads between chips. The patentee had filed his application for patent on October 14, 1980. He asserted that AMD's chip infringed his patent. AMD argued that a specification sheet for its chip, which it had distributed to the public in September 1979 (more than one year before the patentee's filing), anticipated all of patentee's claims under 35 USC § 102(b). The patentee countered that AMD's specification sheet was not a printed publication for purposes of Section 102(b) because (1) there was no evidence in the record to prove that it was actually received by the public before October 14, 1979 and (2) the specification sheet was not "enabling" because it did not describe a computer program to make AMD's chip operational. *Held:* AMD's specification sheet was an enabling printed publication for purposes of Section 102(b). The statutory phrase "printed publication" has been interpreted to mean that, before the critical date, the reference must have been sufficiently accessible to the public interested in the art. Evidence of routine business practice can be sufficient to prove that a reference was made accessible before a critical date. Here, AMD presented extensive, uncontroverted evidence of business practice sufficient to prove availability and accessibility to the interested public before October 14, 1979. Furthermore, AMD presented uncontroverted evidence that a kit for programming its chip was available to the public and on sale before the critical date, and therefore there was an enabling publication. Moreover, the patentee's specification did not disclose any specific computer programs and did not suggest that a computer program was part of the invention and, therefore, specific computer programs were irrelevant to the claimed invention.

[Constant v. Advanced Micro-Devices, Inc., 848 F2d 1560 (Fed. Cir. 1988)]

Anticipation under Section 102 is established only when a single prior art reference discloses, expressly or under principles of inherency, each and every element of claimed invention.   A patent owner sued its former licensees for infringement of its patent for a system for decoding digital symbol codes representing a message and converting them into video control signals for display of the message on a tele-

vision screen. The device was designed to operate with standard television moni-
tors. The licensees argued that, under 35 USC § 102, the patent was invalid as anticipated by the disclosure in prior patents. *Held:* The patent was not invalid for
anticipation. Anticipation is established only when a single, prior art reference discloses, expressly or under principles of inherency, each and every element of a claimed
invention. Furthermore, with an element expressed in terms of a means plus function,
absent structure in a prior art reference that is capable of performing the functional
limitation of the means, the prior art reference does not meet the claim. In this case,
the prior patents failed to disclose all elements of the claim. Specifically, the prior
patents did not disclose any type of digital generating means as required by the patent's
specification limitation—"generating means . . . for *digitally* generating a video signal." While the prior patents covered a system that produced a digital output signal,
it did so in an *analog* fashion. The prior inventions had no digital generator, an element that was necessary to make the reference an anticipation.

[RCA Corp. v. Applied Digital Data Sys., Inc., 730 F2d 1440 (Fed. Cir. 1984)]

¶ 2.07 TIMELY APPLICATION

**Patent is invalid where system that is subject of patent was "on sale" more than
one year before filing patent application.**   TRW brought a patent infringement suit
against Unisys. The case involved a patent for a video document processing system
that was originally applied for by Teknekron, Inc., the predecessor-in-interest of TRW,
on March 21, 1977. The March 1977 patent application was subsequently declared
abandoned following the filing of a "continuation-in-part" application (CIP) on July
3, 1978. In its motion for summary judgment, Unisys argued that the patent was invalid or unenforceable because of the statutory "on-sale bar" provisions of 35 USC
§ 102(b). Specifically, Unisys claimed that an offer for sale of the invention occurred more than a year before the filing of the original patent application. *Held:* The
system that was the subject of the patent was "on sale" more than one year before
the filing of the patent application; therefore, by application of Section 102(b), the
patent-in-suit was invalid. Section 102(b) sets forth what is commonly known as
the "on-sale bar" rule. That section provides in pertinent part, "A person shall be entitled to a patent unless . . . (b) the invention was . . . on sale in this country, more
than one year prior to the date of the application for patent in the United States. . . ."
The ultimate determination of whether a patent is rendered invalid by the Section
102(b) "on-sale bar" calls for application of a two-pronged test: First, the court
must decide whether there was a for-profit "sale" or "offer for sale" made outside
the one-year grace period provided in the section. If the court finds that there was
such a "sale" or "offer for sale," it must decide, from the totality of circumstances,
whether, at the time of the sale or offer for sale, there had been sufficient development
of the invention to render it a tangible, marketable product. Here, the court found that

Teknekron made a concrete "offer for sale" of the system to the Philadelphia National Bank on January 19, 1976. At this time, the system was sufficiently developed to take the invention out of the "concept" sphere and place it squarely within the tangible developed "product" sphere. The patent application was filed on March 21, 1977, more than 14 months later. Therefore, since the invention was on sale more than one year prior to date of the application for patent, the "on-sale bar" rule was applicable, and the patent was invalid.

[TRW Fin. Sys., Inc. v. Unisys Corp., 835 F. Supp. 994 (ED Mich. 1993)]

¶ 2.08 NONOBVIOUSNESS IN GENERAL

Patent is invalid when it does not meet the "nonobvious" test of Section 103 of Patent Act.   Graham and others brought an infringement suit against John Deere of Kansas City and others alleging infringement of a patent, consisting of a combination of old mechanical elements, for a device designed to absorb shock from a plow shank in rocky soil to prevent damage to the plow. In 1955, the Fifth Circuit held the patent invalid, ruling that a combination is patentable when it produces an "old result in a cheaper and otherwise more advantageous way." The Eighth Circuit held that since there was no new result in the combination, the patent was invalid. The Supreme Court granted certiorari. *Held:* The patent did not meet the test of the "nonobvious" nature of the "subject matter sought to be patented" to a person having ordinary skill in the pertinent art, set forth in Section 103 of the Patent Act of 1952, and was therefore invalid. The Supreme Court announced the traditional test for Section 103 nonobviousness. It provides that under Section 103, the scope and content of the prior art are to be determined, differences between the prior art and the claims at issue are to be ascertained, and the level of ordinary skill in the pertinent art are to be resolved. Against this background, the obviousness or nonobviousness of the subject matter is determined. Such secondary considerations as commercial success, long felt but unsolved need, failure of others, and others, might be used to give light to the circumstances surrounding the origin of the subject matter sought to be patented. As indicia of obviousness or nonobviousness, these inquiries may have relevancy.

[Graham v. John Deere Co., 383 US 1 (1966)]

To establish obviousness, there must be some teaching, suggestion, or incentive to make the combination made by inventor; the fact that prior art disclosed the components of the device is insufficient evidence.   A patentee filed suit charging Datapoint with infringement of its patent, which related to a mode of "batch processing" of data. The invention of the patent, a programmable processor-based batch data-entry terminal, provided an improved way of entering, verifying, and storing data. Datapoint argued that the patent claims were obvious and therefore invalid under 35 USC § 103. Specifically, Datapoint argued that the differences between the patentee's invention and an earlier invention were trivial and merely represented routine design choice. The patentee asserted that its invention was a new combination of known steps and elements that provided a new and commercially successful solution to problems of batch data entry. Furthermore, the patentee contended that this combination was not taught or suggested by the prior art. *Held:* Datapoint had not established by clear and convincing evidence that the patentee's claims were invalid because of obviousness under Section 103. To establish obviousness, it was insufficient that prior art disclosed the components of the patented device, either separately or used in other combinations; a teaching, suggestion, or incentive to make the combination made by the patentee had to be established. Even if the changes from prior art were minor, the changes had to be evaluated in terms of the whole invention. In this case, the prior art failed to teach the combination and its use as set forth in the patentee's patent, and the invention's commercial success, although not determinative of the issue, was some indication that the patent would not have been obvious.

[Northern Telecom, Inc. v. Datapoint Corp., 908 F2d 931 (Fed. Cir. 1990)]

¶ 2.09 HARDWARE TECHNOLOGY AND OBVIOUSNESS

Claim of patent application that combines video display with display of other information is obvious to a person of ordinary skill and, therefore, is unpatentable. Raynes appealed the decision of the Board of Patent Appeals and Interferences of the U.S Patent and Trademark Office, to hold all claims of his patent application unpatentable for obviousness, or the failure to meet the requirements of 35 USC 103. The Raynes invention was a computer-processed interactive automobile service station, wherein the fuel pumps were equipped with means for display of video programming as well as fuel price and quantity and other electronically recorded information. *Held:* The Board correctly held that the combination of video display with the display of other information at the fuel pump would have been obvious to a person of ordinary skill. When determining whether a new combination of known elements would have been obvious in terms of Section 103, the analytic focus is on the state of knowledge at the time the invention was made. The Commissioner bears the burden of showing that such knowledge provided some teaching, suggestion, or motivation to make the particular combination that was made by the applicant. This determination is made from the viewpoint of the hypothetical person of ordinary skill in the field of invention. Here, the court pointed out that the Raynes display at the fuel pump merely performed the known function of video display of price/quantity data, in combination with the known functions of video programming. As such, the combination of video display with the display of other information at the fuel pump would be obvious to a person of ordinary skill.

[In re Raynes, 7 F3d 1037 (Fed. Cir. 1993)]

Where claim for method of manufacturing magnetic recording heads satisfies long-felt need for improvement of the manufacturing technology and employs a process that differs materially from that previously used, claim is not invalid for obviousness under Section 103. Philips, as assignee of the Peloschek patent, brought an action for infringement of the patent. The Peloschek patent subject matter was a process for the manufacture of a magnetic recording head, which was part of a tape recorder or computer that translated electrical impulses into magnetic patterns on a tape for the purposes of storage. The district court entered a judgment that held valid certain claims of the patent and held that the defendant, NMI, had infringed the patent. NMI appealed, challenging the validity of the Peloschek patent under Section 103 for obviousness. *Held:* The invention was not obvious within the scope of Section 103; therefore, the patent was valid. To resolve the issue of whether the invention was obvious within the meaning of Section 103, a court must examine the scope and content of the prior art, the differences between the prior art and the claims at issue, and the level of ordinary skill in the pertinent art. Here, the court found that the Peloschek patent was significantly different from the prior art and represented a distinct advancement in the level of skill of the art. The court noted that the existence of an important problem in the art that has remained unsolved for a long period, despite continued efforts and series of refinements of the art, until a new combination of concepts produces a solution, is evidence that the combination was not obvious. Where those skilled in the art are working in a given field and have failed after repeated efforts to discover a particular new and useful improvement, the person who first makes the discovery does more than make the obvious improvement that would suggest itself to a mechanic skilled in the art, and is entitled to protection as an inventor. Here, the Peloschek patent produced a result unobtainable with the prior processes in the field and cured a problem that had existed in the field. Accordingly, the claims were not obvious and the patent valid.

[US Philips Corp. v. National Micronetics, Inc., 550 F2d 716 (2d Cir. 1977)]

¶ 2.10 OBVIOUSNESS AND APPLICATION TECHNOLOGY

In determining whether patent covering implantable electronic pacer is invalid by reason of obviousness, scope of prior art to be considered is not limited to biomedical implants, but includes field of electrical engineering in general. CPI filed an action seeking, among other things, a declaration that the U.S. patent to Terry was invalid, unenforceable, and not infringed by reason of obviousness under 35 USC § 103. The Terry patent was held by Cordis. CPI claimed that the invention claimed by the Terry patent was previously made by others and that any difference between it and the prior art was obvious to those having ordinary skill in the art. The invention at issue was an implantable electronic pacer to control irregular human heart beats. *Held:* The Terry patent was invalid and not infringed by CPI under Section 103. The earliest date of conception of invention claimed in the Terry patent was July 1, 1970, the date that the entire conception was complete. In determining the issue of obviousness under Section 103, the court examined the scope and content of the prior art, the level of ordinary skill in the art as of July 1, 1970, and the differences between the Terry patent claims and the prior art. The court rejected Cordis's contention that the scope of prior art be limited to biomedical implantable stimulators. The court, noting the principle that the concept of scope of the art must be afforded a wide latitude, found that the scope of pertinent art in this instance included the field of electrical engineering in general, and more specifically, the use of both digital and analog circuitry. Based on the testimony of CPI's expert, an electrical engineer with extensive experience in microelectronics and circuit design techniques, and the scope and content of the prior art, including other patents, the court found that differences between the prior art and the subject matter of the Terry patent as a whole would have been clearly obvious to one with ordinary skill in the art of electrical engineering. Accordingly, under Section 103, the Terry patent was declared invalid and not infringed by CPI because of the making, selling, or using of any apparatus made, sold, or used by CPI.

[Cardiac Pacemakers, Inc. v. Cordis Corp., 215 USPQ 604 (D. Minn. 1981)]

PART D. INFRINGEMENT

¶ 2.11 INFRINGEMENT

Where accused device does not perform the identical function stated in means limitation of claim and does not use structure taught in the specification or equivalent structure, no infringement of claim of patent occurs. Carroll, the assignee of a patent for photoelectric touch input panel for use over computer display device, sued its competitor, EMS, for alleged infringement of claim 24 of Carroll's U.S. Patent 4,267,443. *Held:* The EMS device did not infringe claim 24 of Carroll's patent. In determining whether a claim has been infringed, the courts must undertake a two-step analysis. First, the claim must be properly construed to determine its scope and meaning. Second, the claim as properly construed must be compared to the accused device or process. To meet a means-plus-function limitation, an accused device must (1) perform the identical function recited in the means limitation and (2) perform that function using the structure disclosed in the specification or an equivalent structure. In construing claim 1, on which claim 24 relied, the court focused on the term "spaced apart" found in a means-plus-function limitation of claim 1. The court found the term to mean that the light beams were spaced apart and did not intersect over the entirety of their respective surface areas. In comparing the claim with the accused EMS devices, the court found that all the accused devices had beam surfaces that intersected to some degree. It held that the accused devices, by having beam surfaces that intersected, did not perform the identical function stated in the means limitation of claim 1 and did not use a structure taught in the specification or an equivalent structure. Accordingly, the accused EMS devices did not literally infringe claim 24 of Carroll's patent because they did not meet the means limitation of claim 1. In addition, the accused devices did not perform in substantially the same way to obtain substantially the same result as the claimed invention. Therefore, the accused devices did not infringe claim 24 based on the doctrine of equivalents as well.

[Carroll Touch, Inc. v. Electro Mechanical Sys., Inc., 3 F3d 404 (Fed. Cir. 1993)]

Literal infringement claim is reviewed considering totality of technology employed in the accused device, even though all elements of the patent claim were present in the alleged infringer. Texas Instruments, the holder of an electronic calculator patent (the '921 patent), brought an action against foreign manufacturers for alleged unfair methods of competition and unfair acts in importation and sale of portable electronic calculators, based on the manufacturers' alleged infringement of patent. The U.S. International Trade Commission found no infringement, and the patent holder appealed. *Held:* The total of technological changes made in the imported calculators required a finding of noninfringement under 35 USC § 112; the imported calculators did not infringe the properly construed claims when the invention and the imported calculators were viewed as a whole. Analysis of patent infringement entails two inquiries: determination of the scope of the claims, as a matter of law, and the factual finding of whether the properly construed claims encompass the accused structure. When the claimed invention is a novel combination of steps, all possible methods of carrying out each step of the combination are not required to be described in the specification. Correctly construed claims cover "equivalents of the described embodiments". Here, the court stated that it was not appropriate in this case, where all the claimed functions were performed in the imported calculators by subsequently developed or improved means, to view each such change as if it were the only change from the disclosed embodiments of the invention. It was the entirety of the technology embodied in the accused devices that had to be compared with the patent disclosure. The court held that, taken together, the accumulated differences between the invention and the imported calculators distinguished the imported calculators from that contemplated in the '921 patent and transcended a fair range of equivalents from the '921 invention. Texas Instruments did not sustain its burden of proving infringement by the imported calculators under Section 112. *Note:* In a later opinion, the court noted that it was the totality of the combination of elements that made the first invention patentable; thus, it was the totality of the technology in the accused infringing device to which it must be compared.

[Texas Instruments v. US Int'l Trade Comm'n, 805 F2d 1558 (Fed. Cir. 1986), reh'g denied with opinion 851 F2d 1327 (Fed. Cir. 1988)]

Claim for sample and hold circuit is not restricted to preferred analog embodiment referenced in narrower claims, but includes digital and hybrid circuits according to common understanding in the art at the time application was filed. The patent owner's patent claimed an invention for a data transducer position control system for rotating disk data-storage equipment. The patent owner alleged that certain rotating disk data-storage product lines, manufactured and sold by the defendant infringed claim 2 of its patent. At issue was whether the "sample and hold circuit" referred to in claim 2 was restricted to include only the analog sample and hold circuits of the preferred embodiment referenced in other claims, and not digital or hybrid circuits. *Held:* The sample and hold circuit of claim 2 could not be restricted to include only analog sample and hold circuits of the preferred embodiment, but include digital and hybrid circuits as well. The proper focus of inquiry for claim interpretation, whether questions of validity or infringement are involved, is what one skilled in the art would have understood the claim to mean at the time the application for the patent containing the claim was originally filed. When interpreting a broad claim by reference to other claims in a patent, it is a fundamental axiom of patent law that the limitations of the narrower claims are not read into the broad claim. Nor is a claim limited to the preferred embodiment. Individuals skilled in the art use the phrase a "sample and hold circuit" to refer to more than one specific type of circuit. In this case, since there was no statement in the specification or the file history that restricted it to one particular type of circuit, the phrase a "sample and hold circuit" was to be afforded its broad common meaning held at the time the application supporting the claim was filed. Therefore, the phrase referred to a circuit that could be either an analog circuit, a digital circuit, or a hybrid circuit.

[Quantum Corp. v. Mountain Computer Inc., 5 USPQ2d 1103 (ND Cal. 1987)]

Where accused device does not meet every limitation of patent claim exactly or by a substantial equivalent, infringement cannot be found. Lockwood, the holder of patents for self-service travel reservation terminals, filed an infringement action against American Airlines based on the airline's computerized reservation system. American moved for summary judgment on noninfringement grounds, arguing that Lockwood patents did not cover its SABREvision system because the claims in Lockwood's patents recited a type of self-contained, self-service computerized vending machine designed to replace travel agents or other sales personnel through advanced automation. In contrast, American claimed that the SABREvision system was an in-office computer system used exclusively by travel agents. Furthermore, American argued that Lockwood was estopped from arguing that the SABREvision system was "equivalent" to that which his patents could cover. American further claimed that the arguments Lockwood made when prosecuting the patents were inconsistent with the equivalency arguments he urged in this proceeding. Lockwood responded that summary judgment was not proper because material issues of fact existed relating to the definition of several of the terms in the claims. *Held:* Because Lockwood failed to carry his burden of coming forward with sufficient evidence in support of his proposed claim construction to warrant a trial, American's motion was granted. Infringement is found only when each and every limitation of a patent claim is met by the accused product exactly or by a substantial equivalent. The claims at issue contained several elements that were lacking in the accused SABREvision system, including a self-contained apparatus, audiovisual means, customer-operated means, and means for accepting payment. Moreover, the doctrine of equivalents could not be applied because Lockwood asserted no equitable facts or circumstances that would justify its application. Even if the doctrine had applicability to the case, Lockwood would have had to establish that the SABREvision system performed substantially the same function, in substantially the same way, to obtain substantially the same result as the claimed inventions. Lockwood could not meet his burden under this argument because of the missing elements in the claims. Furthermore, the court found that the doctrine of prosection history estoppel limited the doctrine of equivalents here. Lockwood's prior amendments and arguments to the patent examiner prevented him from contending that any of the claims of his patents covered the accused SABRE-vision system. Finding no indication that Lockwood intended the terms in the claimed patents to mean anything different than their ordinary meaning, the court granted American's motion for summary judgment.

[Lockwood v. American Airlines, Inc., 834 F. Supp. 1246 (SD Cal. 1993)]

¶ 2.12 REMEDIES

Award of damages for patent infringement based on royalty is vacated and remanded where evidence is presented that would enable district court to determine damages based on patentee's lost profits. Del Mar brought an action for patent infringement against Quinton. The district court found infringement and awarded double damages based on a 5 percent royalty and attorney fees and costs. Both parties appealed. *Held:* The measure for damages was vacated and remanded for a determination of damages based on Del Mar's lost profits. The district court's doubling of damages, and the refusal to triple them, based on the finding of willful infringement, was not unreasonable and was sustained; its finding that this was an exceptional case in terms of 35 USC § 285 and that attorney fees and costs were award-able to Del Mar was also affirmed. The statutory instruction of 35 USC § 284 for awarding damages for patent infringement is that the award must be "adequate to com-pensate for the infringement." The general rule for determining the actual damages to a patentee that is itself producing the patented item is to determine the sales and profits lost to the patentee because of the infringement. Although the statute states that the damage award shall not be "less than a reasonable royalty," the purpose of this alternative is not to provide a simple accounting method, but to set a floor below which the courts are not authorized to go. To recover lost profits, a patentee must show a reasonable probability that, but for the infringement, it would have made the sales that were made by the infringer. Here, Del Mar presented evidence showing the demand for the product, the absence of acceptable noninfringing substitutes, and its ability to meet the demand. Del Mar also offered a computation of its lost profits using an incremental income analysis. Moreover, the district court considered evi-dence as to the number and selling price of the accused models. Finally, the court held that the finding of willful infringement was legally sufficient to meet the criterion of "exceptional case" under Section 285. Consequently, the district court had discre-tionary authority to award attorney fees and costs to Del Mar based on the "excep-tional case" provision of Section 285.

[Del Mar Avionics, Inc. v. Quinton Instrument Co., 836 F2d 1320 (Fed. Cir. 1987)]

Defendant's motion for summary judgment is granted on laches claim where plaintiff cannot establish that its delay in filing lawsuit was reasonable; defen-dant's motion for summary judgment on estoppel claim granted is where de-fendant proves misleading conduct on part of plaintiff. ABB, the patent holder and exclusive licensee of a robotic wrist, brought suit against Fanuc, the manufacturer of robotics, for alleged infringement of the patent covering the robotic wrist. Fanuc moved for summary judgment on the grounds of laches and estoppel. *Held:* Because ABB could not put forth evidence sufficient to raise a genuine issue of material fact with respect to the elements of laches, Fanuc's motion for summary judgment was granted on this ground. Furthermore, because Fanuc established the three elements of estoppel, Fanuc's motion for summary judgment was granted on this ground as well. To prove laches, Fanuc had to show that (1) ABB's delay in filing suit was un-reasonable and (2) that to permit ABB to proceed with the suit would materially, i.e., economically or evidentiarily, prejudice Fanuc. The burden was on ABB to come for-ward with evidence sufficient to support a finding of the nonexistence of fact as to these two elements, because the court found the delay in filing suit was longer than six years. The court found that the only explanation offered for the delay in filing suit, that ABB did not want to sue one of its best customers, was not reasonable. More-over, the court found that to permit ABB to proceed with the suit would materially prejudice Fanuc. ABB could not overcome the presumption that the delay caused eco-nomic prejudice to Fanuc, as the court found that Fanuc enjoyed a significant expansion in sales of the product at issue during the period of delay. As to Fanuc's motion for summary judgment on the ground of estoppel, Fanuc successfully proved (1) misleading conduct by ABB, (2) reliance on that conduct, and (3) material prejudice. ABB's misleading conduct was found to be misleading inaction that followed its initial charge of infringement. Furthermore, the court held that Fanuc relied on this inaction; the only inference that could have been drawn from this inaction was that ABB would not pursue Fanuc. Finally, the court held that Fanuc would be materially prejudiced if the suit was allowed to continue. Because of the great expansion of Fanuc's sales during the period after ABB discovered the possible infringement, Fanuc would be inflicted with "damages which would likely have been prevented by an earlier suit."

[ABB Robotics, Inc. v. GMFanuc Robotics Corp., 832 F. Supp. 1386 (ED Wis. 1993)]

CHAPTER 3

TRADE SECRETS AND CONFIDENTIALITY

¶ 3.01 DEFINING PROTECTED INTERESTS

No taking of property occurs when researcher voluntarily submits confidential data in exchange for anticipated new product registration.   In developing pesticides, Monsanto, complying with FIFRA, provided the EPA with certain health, safety, and environmental data in its application for new product registration. Monsanto then argued that (1) the data-disclosure and data-compliance provisions of FIFRA effected a taking of property without just compensation; (2) Section 10 of FIFRA authorizes public disclosure of submitted trade secret "property" to the public; i.e., business competitors; and (3) the taking is for a private rather than public purpose. *Held:*   Monsanto's health, safety, and environmental data is trade secret "property" within Fifth Amendment protection. However, after the 1978 amendments to FIFRA, a data-submitting company cannot have a reasonable, investment-backed expectation that the EPA will keep data confidential beyond the statutory limit requirements. Since Monsanto was exchanging voluntary information for new registration, no taking occurred. Prior to the 1972 amendment, FIFRA was silent as to confidentiality of data; therefore, Monsanto had no reasonable investment-backed expectation of nondisclosure. During the period between FIFRA amendments (1972–1978), when Monsanto was given the opportunity to designate information as "trade secrets" at the time of disclosure, there was a possibility of a taking. However, any taking in this six-year period was a "public use" taking, in the interest of avoiding duplicative research by companies and permitting products to reach consumers more quickly. If a taking had occurred during that period, the proper forum for Monsanto was the Court of Claims.

[Ruckelshaus v. Monsanto, 467 US 986 (1984)]

[1] Trade Secrets as Property

No private right of action to enjoin disclosure by federal agency of information protected by Trade Secrets Act exists where decision of federal agency to disclose is reviewable under Administrative Procedure Act.   As a government contractor, Chrysler was required to furnish employment practice records to the Defense Logistics Agency (DLA), which informed Chrysler that third parties had made FOIA requests for disclosure of these records. Chrysler sought to enjoin release of its records, contending disclosure was barred by the Trade Secrets Act, which precludes government employee disclosure of trade secrets and confidential data "not authorized by law." *Held:* Information protected by the Trade Secrets Act is not subject to disclosure. Both the DLA and FOIA in this case are subject to federal agency regulation; and, neither theories of agency, executive order, nor legislative authority may compel disclosure. However, since the DLA's decision to disclose was reviewable under the Administrative Procedure Act, there was no private right of action to enjoin disclosure of such information under the Trade Secrets Act.

[Chrysler Corp. v. Brown, 441 US 281 (1979)]

PART A.   SECRECY

¶ 3.02 NOVELTY

Misappropriated technical data and pricing information may be considered trade secrets.   SI Handling manufactured material transport systems, in particular one called CARTRAC, which was used in the automotive industry. Heico was formed by former employees of SI, who endeavored to create a competing system, ROBOTRAC, and target it for sale to General Motors, an SI client. SI alleged violations of the Sherman Act, RICO, and various common-law contract and tort claims as well as misappropriation of trade secrets. SI also argued that price lists and customer lists were also protected subject matter. Heico argued that many of the technical points of design of the CARTRAC system (which had only one patent) were accessible technical data. *Held:* Heico had misappropriated numerous components and dimensions as well as the cost and pricing information and the contents of three pending patents. The court ordered a "lead-time" injunction, whereby the injunction would last only as long as necessary to negate the time advantage caused by the misappropriation, which would otherwise have taken longer to be completed by independent development.

[SI Handling Sys., Inc. v. Heisley, 753 F2d 1244 (3d Cir. 1985)]

Business's customer data base used by competitor to solicit new customers is considered misappropriated trade secret.   MAI Systems, a designer and manufacturer of computers and software, also serviced its product after sale for its customers. A competitor for the service business, Peak Computer, hired an MAI service manager, who brought to Peak technical servicing information as well as a customer data base. In its suit for copyright infringement and misappropriation of trade secrets, MAI claimed Peak was copying and using MAI software in violation of the Copyright Act and that the customer data base with which Peak was acquiring new service customers was a trade secret. Peak argued that its use of the software did not extend beyond diagnostic necessity and that the customer data base was neither a secret nor improperly used. *Held:* For purposes of copyright, improper loading of software by Peak into a service customer's computer RAMs constitutes infringement, a "copy" under the Copyright Act. Also, the customer data base has potential economic value; competitors should have to expend their own resources to solicit customers already using the MAI computer system; moreover, the employee who brought these trade secrets to Peak was in breach of his confidentiality agreement with his former employer.

[MAI Sys. Corp. v. Peak Computer, Inc., 991 F2d 511 (9th Cir. 1993)]

No valid claim for misappropriation exists where computer system does not attain trade secret status and where former employee's nondisclosure agreement is found unenforceable. Former employees of Jostens developed a class ring, computerized mold-making system for National Computer Systems. Jostens claimed trade secret status for this system on the basis of a proprietary clause in its contracts with its vendors. It also claimed a breach of confidentiality by its former employees, who had signed nondisclosure agreements. National claimed that Jostens' system was not unique and was similar to other systems in the public domain. Also, since some Jostens employees were not required to sign nondisclosure agreements, there was inadequate consideration to bind those who did. *Held:* There was no misappropriation, since the Jostens system did not attain trade secret status. The former employees merely used general experience and skills in developing the system for National; and, even if there were any special expertise involved, Jostens had failed to adequately insist on secrecy. The court found that the promise of future or continued employment is not adequate consideration for a nondisclosure agreement, especially where some employees with similar access to the information were not asked to sign nondisclosure agreements; therefore, the employment agreements were unenforceable.

[Jostens, Inc. v. National Computer Servs., 318 NW2d 691 (Minn. 1982)]

¶ 3.03 SECURITY AND DISCLOSURE

Action for misappropriation may be brought although manufacturer made merely perfunctory efforts at protection. Former employees of manufacturer allegedly stole trade secrets from their former employer, which in the course of enterprise had made only a moderate effort to protect the secrets. The employer sued for misappropriation and argued that "reasonable precaution" is a factual issue that precludes summary judgment. The employees claimed that failure to adequately protect trade secrets is tantamount to having no secrets, and therefore there was no theft by improper means since the information falls in the public domain. *Held:* The amount of effort industry uses to effect secrecy is a question of fact that precludes summary judgment. Manufacturers must be allowed to weigh the cost of precautions against added security benefits and not be placed continually in the position of having to overinsure themselves against theft, as such overattention to protective measures could become impairing to productivity.

[Rockwell Graphics Sys., Inc. v. DEV Indus., Inc., 925 F2d 174 (7th Cir. 1991)]

[1] Internal Procedures

Where there is no federal statutory patent protection, states may not enact laws that give patent-like rights that interfere with federal patent law system. After six years in the market, Bonito Boats was given state statutory protection for its boat hull design, which was federally unpatented; under Florida law, no duplicate molds could be taken from it and used by competitors. Competitor asked that Bonito's claim for damages be dismissed, arguing that the statute conflicted with federal patent law, which allows for creative freedom and activity in unprotected areas (in this case, the reverse-engineering method of creating new boat hulls from molds of boats already in the market). *Held:* The Florida statute was preempted by federal law. State law may not prohibit copying objects in the public domain. A state law seeking to give patent-like protection cannot undermine the carefully developed guidelines of federal patent law. A boat hull design in circulation for six years cannot seek patent protection from imitations under a state statute that alters the balance between protection and competitiveness developed under the federal scheme. States do have limited regulatory powers, but they cannot overstep these limits or they will be preempted by the Supremacy Clause of the federal Constitution.

[Bonito Boats v. Thunder Craft, Inc., 489 US 141 (1989)]

Where no nondisclosure agreement exists, former employee may bring unprotected information, which does not attain trade secret status, to new employer. Fairchild, in the business of semiconductor research, hired several Motorola employees, and Motorola sued for misappropriation of trade secrets and breach of contract. Fairchild claimed that all the alleged trade secret information was either fully disclosed by patents or was generally known in the trade. Motorola also claimed that its former employees were bound by a share option agreement; the employees argued that this option agreement was not an employment contract and that they were free to leave. *Held:* The employees were not wrongfully recruited by Fairchild and they had not breached any duty of confidentiality. Motorola had never advised them, either generally or specifically, which production processes, know-how, or other things it considered proprietary. Motorola established no lists or records as to what it considered proprietary trade secrets, and neither had it made a real effort to keep the claimed secrets secret. Moreover, its claimed secrets were in the public domain.

[Motorola, Inc. v. Fairchild Camera & Instrument Corp., 366 F. Supp. 1173 (D. Ariz. 1973)]

In presence of reasonable nondisclosure agreement provision, software developments supplied in confidence between agreeing parties may not be shared with third party following termination of agreement.   Com-Share entered into a mutually beneficial agreement with Computer Complex wherein they would share, in confidence, software research and technology. After termination of the agreement, and contrary to its two-year (subsequent to termination) nondisclosure clause, Computer Complex began sharing Com-Share–supplied software developments with a third party. Computer Complex argued that the fundamental concepts of this allegedly confidential information were in the public domain. Com-Share claimed that it had spent $2 million on developing the information and had carefully protected the concepts developed. *Held:* Under the Technical Exchange Agreement between the principals, Computer Complex was precluded from disclosing software technology to the third party. The purpose of the nondisclosure provision is self-evident, and for Computer Complex to supply Com-Share's competitor with confidential information prior to expiration of the two-year term would unjustly enrich Computer Complex at the expense of Com-Share.

[Com-Share, Inc. v. Computer Complex, Inc., 338 F. Supp. 1229 (ED Mich. 1971)]

[2] External Secrecy

Commercial news reporting does not necessarily fall within fair use exception to owner's exclusive right to use.   Section 107 of the Copyright Revision Act provides a "fair use" exception to the owner's exclusive use to reproduce as provided under Section 106. *Time* magazine made an agreement with Harper & Row to excerpt a portion of the soon-to-be-published memoirs of President Ford. *Nation* scooped *Time* by publishing an article with 300 words excerpted from the manuscript. *Time* then cancelled its planned article and did not complete payment to Harper & Row, which then sued *Nation* for this remaining $12,500 payment. *Nation* argued that under the fair use provision of Section 107, comment and news reporting are not infringements of copyright. *Held:* Nation's article did not fall within the fair use exception. It undermined the author's right to control first publication; moreover, its timing was such that *Nation* fully intended to supplant this valuable right for its own commercial gain. News reporting, in this case, was not a good faith fair use, and did not overcome the Copyright Act's main purpose, which is to protect the economic incentive to create and disseminate ideas. *Nation*'s article directly resulted in *Time*'s cancellation of its article; thus, causing Harper & Row actual damages of $12,500.

[Harper & Row Publishers, Inc. v. Nation Enters., Inc., 471 US 539 (1985)]

Cause of action for misappropriation exists if design information is unfairly obtained even where it could have been lawfully obtained.   Dravo Corp., builder of freight boxes, through a confidential relationship, obtained knowledge of Smith's secret designs, plans, and prospective customers, and then breached that confidence by using the information to its advantage and to Smith's detriment. By making its own boxes smaller and impossible to use interchangeably with Smith's, Dravo rendered Smith's product obsolete. Dravo argued that (1) Smith's business knowledge was no longer a secret; (2) it had been publicly disclosed; (3) no customer lists existed; and (4) Smith's patents were invalid, as many of the devices were in widespread use in the trade. *Held:* Dravo secured possession by unfair means, even though it was possible that Dravo could have discovered the information lawfully. Dravo, as a prospective purchaser of Smith's business, was in a position of trust and confidence when given access to the secret information.

[Smith v. Dravo Corp., 203 F2d 369 (7th Cir. 1953)]

Trade secret status sustained even where secret element is written in object code, unintelligible to humans. Trandes owned a set of computer programs used to design and construct rapid transit systems. Trandes issued a license to the Washington Metropolitan Area Transit Authority, which subsequently violated the strict confidentiality provisions of the agreement by allowing Atkinson access to the system. Atkinson contended that since the programs were written in object code, unintelligible to humans, they could not contain trade secrets. *Held:* The design use and interrelationship of the program's components were original and provided Trandes with a competitive advantage and were protectable trade secrets, even though the program was written in object code.

[Trandes Corp. v. Guy F. Atkinson Co., 798 F. Supp. 284 (D. Md. 1992)]

Imitator is liable for misappropriation where drawings are obtained for purpose of manufacturing new minicomputer. Digital, a minicomputer manufacturer, used diagrams containing the design of Data General's novel model to create its own device. Digital claimed that the designs were public knowledge; Digital further argued that a patent on part of the device supported its public disclosure claim. Data General countered that the diagrams were available only to its customers for self-maintenance purposes and that there were sufficient precautions taken to ascribe confidential status. *Held:* Use of the diagrams for other than maintenance purposes was a pirating by Digital and therefore a misappropriation of trade secrets. Also, the granting of a patent on a part of the device was not a full public disclosure of Data General's total logic design of the minicomputer. Digital did not lawfully reverse engineer the product, but in fact designed and thereafter manufactured through reliance on the misappropriated and misused drawings.

[Data Gen. Corp. v. Digital Computer Controls, Inc., 387 A2d 105 (Del. Ch. 1975)]

PART B.   CONFIDENTIALITY

¶ 3.04 THE MARKETPLACE AND REVERSE ENGINEERING

Competitor's disassembly of computer object code may be fair use of copyrighted work if such disassembly provides only means of access to unprotected elements of code.   Accolade was a video game competitor of Sega, which makes the Genesis console. Accolade reverse engineered Sega's video game programs in order to discover the requirements for compatibility with the Genesis console. In defense to Sega's suit, Accolade raised Section 107 of the Copyright Act, which provides that particular instances of copying that otherwise would be actionable are lawful, and sets forth the factors to be considered in determining whether the defense applies. Sega maintained that Congress did not intend that disassembly of object code be considered fair use, and that Accolade copied protected expression. Accolade argued that humans cannot gain access to the object code without disassembling the code, and that under the "nature of the copyrighted work" factor provided by Section 107, it could disassemble the code in order to discover the functional requirements for compatibility with the Genesis console. *Held:* Disassembly of copyrighted object code is a fair use, since Sega's programs contain unprotected aspects that cannot be examined without copying. Not all copyrighted works are entitled to the same level of protection, and computer programs pose unique problems in determining the extent of protection.

[Sega Enters., Ltd. v. Accolade, Inc., 977 F2d 1510 (9th Cir. 1992)]

Action for misappropriation is not preempted by federal copyright law in claims involving breach of confidentiality owed under license agreement.   UCR, a rent-to-own store, entered into a licensing agreement with Computermax wherein UCR obtained a specialized computer software program and service. UCR then began a careful in-house duplication of Computermax's program. By copying files, screens, and reports, UCR was able to develop its duplicate system in a fraction of the time required in independent research and development, and UCR also attempted to hide the new system from Computermax. *Held:* There was misappropriation by UCR, and because of the element of breach of fiduciary duties the action could not be preempted by copyright law. UCR was also found in breach of various contract provisions. Computermax made considerable efforts to maintain secrecy in its program and service. The license agreements strictly prohibited disclosure, restricted any reproduction by UCR, and prohibited assignment to third parties.

[CMAX/Cleveland, Inc. v. UCR, Inc., 804 F. Supp. 337 (MD Ga. 1992)]

Concealment of identity when purchasing competitor's product for research purposes is not misappropriation of trade secrets. Aloka, a manufacturer of ultrasonic imaging equipment, bought a machine, the Acuson 128, from its competitor Acuson, took it to Japan, and studied the Acuson 128 for 11 days. Acuson claimed that Aloka had misappropriated trade secrets, arguing that since it sold the Acuson 128 only to hospitals and doctors, the Acuson 128 was not in the public domain. It further claimed that Aloka breached the licensing agreement that Acuson required of all buyers when Aloka broke the machine's internal padlock. Acuson also argued that since the machine was purchased by an agent of Aloka who did not identify his affiliation to Aloka, it was improperly acquired. *Held:* Under California law, a trade secret loses protection either when disclosed to the relevant public or when its owner does not make "efforts that are reasonable under the circumstances to maintain its secrecy." Disclosure to physicians and hospitals is sufficient disclosure to the world. Moreover, Aloka's use of the machine falls outside the language of the licensing agreement and the padlocks belong, at any rate, to the person who buys the machine; Aloka was, therefore, free to cut them. Concealment of identity to obtain a publicly available product does not create liability under trade secret laws.

[Acuson Corp. v. Aloka Co., 209 Cal. App. 3d 425, 257 Cal. Rptr. 368 (1989)]

¶ 3.05 CONTRACTORS: MARKETING AND MANUFACTURE

After termination of relationship, either party may use general trade information gained through association. Automated developed a data-processing method of inventory control for automobile parts. It entered into an agreement with Service wherein they would jointly sell this system to dealerships, with a provision in their contract for a four-month trial period. Service terminated the relationship after the test period, but then immediately entered into an arrangement with Chevrolet to develop a similar system. Automated sued for breach of duty, arguing that Service used confidential information it had gained while in their relationship. *Held:* There was no showing that information at issue came within the New York definition of "trade secrets." After the termination of their agreement, Service was entitled, even though the appointment to meet with Chevrolet was made during the test period, to use general information gained through its association with Automated to develop an entirely different system, which it sold to the car manufacturer.

[Automated Sys., Inc. v. Service Bureau Corp., 401 F2d 619 (10th Cir. 1968)]

¶ 3.06 PRETRANSACTION DISCLOSURES

Nondisclosure agreements are binding when confidential information is shared for proposed joint venture.   EHC was an investment analyst that had an impressive track record bidding on Xerox copying machine lease portfolios. Sumitomo, in an attempt to delete EHC-type middlemen in such bidding, engaged EHC, signed EHC's nondisclosure and noncircumvention agreement, then dismissed EHC; and, although employing a new middleman, Sumitomo in effect independently pursued and won the portfolios. EHC claimed breach of contract and asserted that the new investor Sumitomo used was merely a "stalking horse," and that the bid was won by Sumitomo on the basis of EHC's information, which was protected by the nondisclosure and noncircumvention agreement. Sumitomo claimed that it gained all its information from the new investment analyst. *Held:* Sumitomo breached its agreement with EHC. Nondisclosure and noncircumvention agreements are closely parallel to employer-employee agreements that enable an employer to expose its employees to trade secrets. Similarly, a noncircumvention agreement enables potential joint venturers to share confidential information regarding a possible deal. Armed with such an agreement, EHC may protect its information by merely showing breach, and need not prove that Sumitomo was actually using EHC's confidential information. EHC was awarded equitable damages to the extent of Sumitomo's benefit, and a constructive trust was created over Sumitomo's profits from the purchase of the Xerox portfolio.

[Eden Hannon & Co. v. Sumitomo Trust & Banking Corp., 914 F2d 556 (4th Cir. 1990)]

¶ 3.07 EMPLOYEES

Misappropriation and use of distinctive computer software utility programs by former employees may result in liability in tort.   ICM, a large computer software developer and marketer, produced a generic program "system" for the personal computers of bank clients. Digital Transactions was formed by two former ICM programmers, who had signed nondisclosure and noncompetitive agreements, and a lawyer who had been a consultant to ICM. ICM maintained secrecy in its research, and when the former employees left ICM, they took files, diskettes, and a source code with them. They reconstructed, within two weeks after leaving, the program they had created for ICM. ICM argued that Digital had benefited from the trial and error research that ICM had subsidized and that the components of the program fit together in a particular and unique way. Digital did not contest the validity of the nondisclosure domain. *Held:* Trade secrets existed, the technology was created by the former employees when they were employed by ICM, and although no direct copying occurred, Digital benefited from their specific knowledge of the architecture and detail of the ICM program in creating substantially similar programs. Digital's lawyer, as well as the technicians, were aware of their confidential duty to ICM. Digital was enjoined from using the program for six months, the time ICM had invested in the original research.

[Integrated Cash Management Servs., Inc. v. Digital Transactions, Inc., 732 F. Supp. 370 (SDNY 1989), aff'd, 920 F2d 171 (2d Cir. 1990)]

Information may be considered secret, and therefore protected, even in absence of nondisclosure agreement, if employer took reasonable precautions aimed at confidentiality. Innovative was a manufacturer of simulated brick paneling and its only customer was Bowen Supply, which distributed the product nationwide. Bowen lured away an Innovative employee for the purpose of manufacturing the paneling for itself by using Innovative's formula. Innovative was forced out of business and sued Bowen for misappropriation of trade secrets. Bowen argued that the formula was inadequately protected and that it had modified the formula. Innovative claimed that its employees were pledged to confidentiality although it did not require nondisclosure agreements of them. *Held:* Although Innovative required no nondisclosure agreements of its employees, it still took reasonable precautions to protect the secrecy of its formula. Also, a modification or improvement by one's own effort does not remove liability if the basic formula is derived from another's secret. However, there was no demonstrated wanton, willful, or reckless disregard of Innovative's rights, so there was no award of punitive damages.

[In re Innovative Constr. Sys., Inc., 793 F2d 785 (7th Cir. 1986)]

[1] General Knowledge and Trade Secrets

Former employee's mere act of accepting employment by competitor is not sufficient for former employer to claim indirect competition. Kinder was formerly employed as a processor of medical claims by EDS, where he had signed a noncompetitive employment agreement; he left EDS and was engaged by a competitor of EDS to do similar work. EDS sued for breach of contract, claiming that Kinder was using methods developed by EDS, and that he was competing in violation of the agreement. Kinder argued that the agreement was unreasonably broad and violated state antitrust law, and that he was not, as an employee of a competitor, competing indirectly with EDS. *Held:* The mere act of entering into an employment relationship with an existing competitor is not sufficient by itself to constitute indirect competition with EDS by Kinder. Moreover, Kinder's work for the new employer was in an area of data processing distinct from that practiced by EDS, and he did not promote or solicit business from EDS. The noncompetitive provision was unreasonably broad as to coverage (forbidding competition "within 200 miles of any city in the United States in which EDS or any subsidiary or affiliated company does business"), and was therefore unenforceable and void.

[Electronic Data Sys. Corp. v. Kinder, 360 F. Supp. 1044 (1973), aff'd, 497 F2d 222 (5th Cir. 1974)]

Former employee bound by nondisclosure and anticompetitive clauses in employment contract may not use employer's computer program in new enterprise. J&K Computer was a former employer of Parrish, who had signed an employment contract with nondisclosure and noncompetitive provisions. Parrish made an electronic copy of an accounts receivable program of its previous employer and engaged two clients. J&K detected the similarity of Parrish's program to its program and filed suit. Parrish argued that the program was not a trade secret and that the anticompetitive agreement was unenforceable as too broad. *Held:* The anticompetitive agreement was enforceable at least as it related to a current customer of J&K. The accounts receivable program was a trade secret because although customers had access to it, J&K was attempting to keep it secret, and the program was not available to the computer trade as a whole. The nondisclosure provision allows Parrish to use general knowledge and experience upon leaving employ, but not to use a secret program.

[J&K Computer Sys., Inc. v. Parrish, 642 P2d 732 (Utah 1982)]

[2] Nondisclosure Agreements

Employee-developed secrets are protected information when employee bound by nondisclosure agreement leaves to develop similar technology elsewhere. SDRC and EMRC were both engaged in structural analysis testing. EMRC had been formed by several former employees of SDRC. These employees had signed nondisclosure agreements; however, at EMRC they continued research and effectively developed programs similar to those of SDRC. While still employed by SDRC, the individuals who were to soon become EMRC tried to lure a client away from SDRC. SDRC claimed breach of confidentiality and unfair competition. EMRC argued that the information did not rise to the level of protectable information. *Held:* EMRC was liable for breach of contract, as it had misappropriated SDRC's confidential and proprietary information. The court ordered EMRC to pay a royalty to SDRC for the period necessary for a competitor to duplicate the program by independent research rather than by the shortcut afforded by the use of confidential information. As to the luring of a client, EMRC and each individual were liable in tort for contract interference.

[Structural Dynamics Research Corp. v. Engineering Mechanics Research Corp., 401 F. Supp. 1102 (ED Mich. 1975)]

[3] Noncompetition Clauses

One-year, 50-mile noncompetitive agreement found reasonable in employer's action against former employees for breach of contract. In the presence of a one-year, 50-mile limit noncompetitive agreement, employees left Basicomputer. Basicomputer sued for breach of contract. The former employees argued that they were forced to sign the covenants under duress and that Basicomputer did not provide adequate consideration. They also claimed that the covenants were overbroad. Basicomputer argued that employees were required to sign as a condition of employment before beginning work. *Held:* The noncompetitive covenant was reasonable; it had not been signed by employees under economic coercion and it was not overbroad.

[Basicomputer Corp. v. Scott, 973 F2d 507 (6th Cir. 1992)]

Noncompetition clause does not apply where former employee's services were not unique or extraordinary and where alleged secrets were in the public domain. Several employees left Modern Communications, a telecommunications and teleproduction enterprise, to work for a competitor. Employees, computer graphics technicians, had signed contracts containing noncompetitive clauses. Modern sued for breach of the restrictive covenant and unfair competition clauses in its employment agreements, claiming the employees solicited Modern clients while still in its employ. The employees argued that their skills did not fall within the covenant. *Held:* No convincing evidence was found to prove that the employees' skills were unique or that they had divulged trade secrets to their new employer. The equipment they operated was available on the open market, and the equipment's operating techniques were not secret. The list of Modern customers was also in the public domain.

[Modern Telecommunications, Inc. v. Zimmerman, 12 AD2d 217 (NY App. Div. 1988)]

Overbroad restrictive covenants may be unreasonable restraints of trade. Former employees created a new company, General Data Systems, and began performing computer-related services for a bank that was a client of their former employer, Trilog. Trilog argued that while in its employ, the former employees had gained confidential information, and that by engaging the bank as a client, General Data had practiced unfair competition. The former employees claimed that they were not using confidential information, even though they did have knowledge of the client bank from their prior association with Trilog, and that they had a right to compete with Trilog for business because the restrictive covenants in Trilog's employment contract were unreasonable and posed undue hardship on them. *Held:* The covenants were too restrictive and not necessary to protect any valid interest of the former employer. For instance, one former employee was prohibited, in effect, from practicing his profession anywhere for anyone. The other two former employees were prohibited from working for any competitor of Trilog or for those employers by which they had gained contact through Trilog. The court distinguished general information from confidential, and found that the former employees were possessed of general trade information about banks, or information about where they could find such information, and they did not rely on or divulge confidential information.

[Trilog Assocs., Inc. v. Famularo, 314 A2d 287 (Pa. 1974)]

¶ 3.08 NEW COMPANIES AND COMPETITIVE HIRING

Luring away key employees may be actionable as misappropriation of trade secrets.   Facing competition in its "plug compatible peripheral device" market, IBM instituted merchandising programs and leasing plans that drove down prices. Telex sought relief under the Sherman and Clayton Acts, claiming predatory and anticompetitive practices by IBM. IBM counterclaimed that Telex misappropriated its trade secrets by luring away key IBM employees. The trial court awarded Telex $359 million in damages, a figure reduced after reevaluation of the market and further reduced by the finding in favor of IBM in its counterclaim against Telex. *Held:* The appeals court reversed the lower court's decision and held that IBM did not use monopoly power, even assuming it possessed such power. Its schemes followed ordinary marketing practices typical of those used in a competitive market, and there was no use of power to "foreclose competition, gain a competitive advantage, or destroy a competitor." However, Telex did misappropriate trade secrets when it lured away valuable IBM employees. The court also dismissed Telex's alternative claim that IBM was barred from recovery by the "unclean hands" doctrine, since the court's disposition of Telex's antitrust violation claim rendered this argument unavailing as to the trade secret misappropriation.

[Telex Corp. v. IBM, 510 F2d 894 (10th Cir. 1975)]

Former employees may not use confidential information to compete against former employer in bidding for contract when information was gained while in former employ.   C-E-I-R was a consultant firm engaged by a federal bureau to analyze its processing methods. It then bid on a project to implement its own recommendations. One of its competitors in this bidding was Computer Dynamics, a company formed by former employees of C-E-I-R who had been involved with the earlier consulting work. C-E-I-R sued to enjoin its former employees from bidding on the project, claiming that they had obtained confidential information while in its employ and that by bidding they were breaching fiduciary duties. *Held:* Computer Dynamics could not bid; its employees, before the termination of their employment with C-E-I-R, had gained highly valuable information from working on the consulting project. Moreover, recruiting key employees without C-E-I-R's knowledge further reduced C-E-I-R's ability to compete and gave Computer Dynamics an advantageous position in bidding. Consequential damages were awarded to C-E-I-R.

[C-E-I-R, Inc. v. Computer Dynamics Corp., 183 A2d 374 (Md. 1962)]

PART C.   REMEDIES AND MISAPPROPRIATION

¶ 3.09 MISAPPROPRIATION AND PROOF

To avoid claim of conversion, copies of files where originals were missing must be returned to owner even where there is no valid misappropriation claim.   ABC news obtained copies of confidential documents relating to FMC's pricing policy in contracts with the U.S. government. After FMC discovered some files missing, and did not have copies of them, it requested that ABC return the documents in its possession. ABC refused, claiming First Amendment protection, and FMC brought suit for conversion and misappropriation of confidential business information. ABC claimed that mere copies could not be converted. FMC argued that since there were no originals, ABC's refusal to return the documents amounted to the deprivation of the possession or use of its property. ABC claimed it could not have misappropriated the material because it is not a business competitor of FMC, nor was its use a business use. *Held:* Under the First Amendment, ABC was free to retain the copies of the FMC documents in its possession. However, to avoid liability in tort, ABC must return to FMC either the originals, if it had them, or a copy of any of FMC's documents of which FMC no longer has a copy. ABC was not a fiduciary of nor a competitor with FMC, so FMC failed to state a valid claim as to the misappropriation of confidential business information.

[FMC Corp. v. Capital Cities/ABC, Inc., 915 F2d 300 (7th Cir. 1990)]

Former employees may not use research and technology developed while working for former employer to create competing company.   Rothlein developed Sperry Rand's semiconductor research over a number of years before he left to form his own company, Semiconductor Division, composed of a number of former Sperry employees. Sperry sued the former employees for breach of their employment agreements and for misappropriation of trade secrets. The former employees claimed that they had modified well-known Sperry processes, and that much of their work was done from memory. *Held:* The former employees were found liable for breach of a confidential relationship and misappropriation of Sperry's trade secrets. They were entitled to use general knowledge and skills gained while in Sperry's employ, but they were not entitled to use their knowledge of Sperry processes and manufacturing specifics, the very secrets of Sperry's success that it had secretly developed at its own plant at great expense.

[Sperry Rand Corp. v. Rothlein, 241 F. Supp. 549 (D. Conn. 1964)]

Under "work for hire" doctrine of Copyright Act, for ownership right, employer has burden to prove that employee-creator was working within scope of employment.   Peiffer, a former employee of Avtec Systems, marketed with a third party a computer program that he had developed at Avtec. Avtec brought suit for copyright infringement under the "work for hire" doctrine of Section 201(b) of the Copyright Act. Avtec also claimed breach of fiduciary duty. Avtec had labeled the program a trade secret, maintaining reasonable efforts at secrecy. Peiffer claimed that he created the program in his spare time, not in the scope of employment. Peiffer also argued that the program was developed from information in the public domain. *Held:* Avtec failed to overcome the presumption that the creator is the owner unless acting within the scope of employment. However, Peiffer did breach contractual duties of loyalty and noncompetition as he misappropriated trade secrets.

[Avtec Sys., Inc. v. Peiffer, 805 F. Supp. 1312 (ED Va. 1992)]

¶ 3.10 THIRD PARTIES AND NOTICE

Third party is not liable for misappropriation of secret process if there was no confidentiality requirement in original relationship.   Ferroline Corp. of Louisiana licensed Ferroline Corp. of California to use a process it had developed to produce an industrial chemical called Carbonyl. The licensee then shared this alleged secret process with a third party, General Aniline & Film Corp. The developer sued the third party, claiming that there had been a confidential relationship between itself and its licensee at the time the third party obtained the process, and that use of this process by the third party was to the detriment of the developer. The third party claimed that the secret process was not secret, but merely an infringement of earlier European developers that held various foreign and domestic patents, and therefore, the process had become part of the public domain. Also, the third party argued that the misappropriation claim should be barred by laches, in that as early as 10 years before the suit, the developer was aware that the third party had purchased the process from the licensee. *Held:* The licensee's disclosure to the third party was not in breach of confidence since the disclosure was not in confidence—even though the developer had a valid process maintained in secrecy and disclosed to the licensee. Moreover, the suit was barred by laches.

[Ferroline Corp. v. General Aniline & Film Corp., 208 F2d 912 (7th Cir. 1953)]

¶ 3.11 DAMAGES

Where joint venture agreement is unilaterally breached in bad faith, breaching party's appropriation of computer service is wrongful conversion of protected trade secret. University Computing Company and LYC jointly created a new corporation, Lykes/UCC, which was to sell computer services. The new company deteriorated over management disputes and LYC unilaterally terminated the joint venture agreement. LYC then created a subsidiary to replace Lykes/UCC, seized the assets of Lykes/UCC and entered into the business that had been planned for the joint venture. LYC's subsidiary obtained a computer system belonging to University and began to market it. *Held:* LYC breached the joint venture in bad faith and misappropriated the computer service, a protected trade secret. However, LYC's subsidiary was ineffective in marketing the stolen computer service to any buyers, so the specific measure of damages was difficult to ascertain. The court found that proper damages could be determined by calculating what the parties would have agreed to as a fair price for licensing the trade secret to LYC; i.e., a "reasonable royalty" standard of measurement.

[University Computing Co. v. Lykes-Youngstown Corp., 504 F2d 518 (5th Cir. 1974)]

¶ 3.12 INJUNCTION

Even where there is clear breach of confidentiality, breaching party may still prevail on antitrust claim where noncompetitive clause in agreement is found too restrictive. EDS applied for a patent on a communications device called a Portable Remote Terminal and engaged Sigma to build 10 prototypes. EDS included in its contract with Sigma stringent nondisclosure and noncompetitive clauses. Subsequently, Sigma began manufacturing and selling a similar device. EDS claimed breach of confidentiality, and Sigma argued that all nondisclosure agreements were the result of duress, coercion, and undue influence on the part of EDS toward Sigma. Sigma counterclaimed for alleged violations of the Sherman and Clayton Acts. *Held:* Sigma infringed on EDS's patent and wilfully and maliciously used confidential information, thereby entitling EDS to recover damages. Sigma's counterclaims alleging antitrust violations could be upheld because EDS's anticompetitive clause, which had precluded Sigma from entering the computer service business, was too severe; therefore, Sigma was entitled to damages on its counterclaim.

[Electronic Data Sys. Corp. v. Sigma Sys. Corp., 500 F2d 251 (5th Cir. 1974), cert. denied, 419 US 1070 (1975)]

Covenant not to compete may be binding even when entered into ancillary to initial employment agreement. A physicist who worked for Modern Controls for one year developed a flat panel discharge display device for computers. Nine weeks after being hired by Modern, he signed a nondisclosure agreement and an agreement not to compete for two years subsequent to termination. Upon leaving, he went to work for a competitor and began developing for it a device similar to the one he had developed at Modern. Modern sought to enforce the covenants of the nondisclosure agreement. The physicist argued that the restrictive covenants lacked consideration, as they were entered into ancillary to the initial employment agreement; that he had divulged no trade secrets; and that Modern should not be allowed equitable enforcement because of its "unclean hands." *Held:* The covenants were binding, for there was sufficient consideration in the physicist's continued employment. Neither were they overrestrictive or unreasonable. The physicist's technical knowledge of Modern's computer device project qualified as protected information in that a competing device would eliminate Modern's competitive edge. He was not misled by Modern in their agreement.

[Modern Controls v. Andreadakis, 578 F2d 1264 (8th Cir. 1978)]

PART D.   FEDERAL LIMITS ON STATE-CREATED RIGHTS

¶ 3.13 PATENT LAW PREEMPTION

In matters of confidentiality and protected relationships, extension of trade secret protection by states to clearly patentable inventions does not conflict with federal patent policy of disclosure.   Employees of Kewanee Oil developed a type of synthetic crystal that was useful in the detection of ionizing radiation. They left to work for Bicron, a competitor, and in a relatively short time produced a similar crystal. Kewanee sued for misappropriation of trade secrets. Bicron argued that the state could not grant monopoly protection to processes and manufacturing techniques that were appropriate subjects for a federal patent, but that had been in commercial use for more than one year and so were no longer eligible for patent protection. *Held:* States may regulate the kinds of intellectual property that may be the subject of trade secrets, and they may regulate with respect to discoveries, as long as the regulation in the area of patents and copyrights does not conflict with the operation of federal law. Patent law does not explicitly endorse or forbid the operation of trade secret law. And, in matters of confidentiality and protected relationships, the extension of trade secret protection to clearly patentable inventions does not conflict with the patent policy of disclosure.

[Kewanee Oil Co. v. Bicron Corp., 416 US 470 (1974)]

State unfair competition laws may not prohibit copying a product where product is not novel and does not attain protected status under federal copyright law.   Stiffel secured a design and technical patents for a lamp that Sears copied and began selling. Stiffel sued under a claim of copyright infringement on the design and under the state's unfair competition act, claiming that Sears had created confusion in the trade as to the lamp's sources. Sears argued that the lamp was not entitled to protection since it was in the public domain and could be made and sold by anyone who chose to do so. *Held:* The lamp patents are invalid for want of invention; therefore, Sears had every right to copy Stiffel's design and to sell lamps almost identical to those sold by Stiffel. Moreover, to allow state unfair competition laws to prevent copying of articles that represent too slight an advance to be patented would conflict with federal law, which provides that such articles are in the public domain. Where there is no misuse of distinctive trademarks, labels, or packaging, mere consumer confusion is not enough to prevent copying by competitors.

[Sears, Roebuck & Co. v. Stiffel Co., 376 US 225 (1964)]

When article is unprotected by patent or copyright, state law may not prohibit copying of that article.   Having secured a design patent, Day-Brite began marketing a fluorescent lighting fixture. Compco then began making and selling a similar product. Day-Brite sued for patent infringement and unfair competition, claiming Compco was confusing the public. *Held:* The patent was invalid; therefore, the light fixture design was unprotected by federal patent or copyright, was in the public domain, and was freely accessible for copying. Compco had taken care to prevent customer confusion, clearly labeling both fixtures and containers and not selling through Day-Brite representatives. Compco did not attempt to represent the copy as the original, and absent proven attempts at deception, the state unfair competition law may not preclude a competitor free access to copy whatever the federal patent and copyright laws leave in the public domain.

[Compco Corp. v. Day-Brite Lighting, Inc., 376 US 234 (1964)]

Former employees who wrongfully misappropriate former employer's trade secret to develop similar product are subject to state trade secret laws and cannot seek preemption by federal patent law and policy.   Analogic hired employees during the development of an unpatented, high-speed data acquisition module. The employees left Analogic, formed their own company, and developed a similar module in only a fraction of the time they had spent on the earlier project. Analogic sought to enjoin the sales of the similar model, claiming the former employees had violated their employment agreements with Analogic in using data and documents belonging to it. The former employees argued that the state, in permanently enjoining the public sale of an item that could be duplicated by reverse engineering, was preempted by federal patent policy. *Held:* The former employees' success in producing the similar module was not the result of skill and intelligence acquired or increased and improved through experience acquired in the course of employment by Analogic or other employers, but from misappropriation of Analogic's trade secrets and in violation of their employment agreement with Analogic. Addressing the claim of preemption, the court found that the state may properly protect the holder of a trade secret against the unauthorized use of the trade secret by those to whom the secret has been confided under the express or implied restriction of nondisclosure.

[Analogic Corp. v. Data Translation, Inc., 358 NE2d 804 (Mass. 1981)]

¶ 3.14 COPYRIGHT PREEMPTION

Conversion action based on a theory of unauthorized publication may be preempted by federal copyright law. Taverns used satellite dishes to intercept signals that were intended only for direct receipt by a cable company operator. The cable company claimed that the transmissions were bought and sold, the cable company having an exclusive right to retransmit and therefore a right to the "possession" of the transmissions. The taverns sought to dismiss the cable company's claim for conversion, and argued that any conversion claim must be preempted in this case by federal copyright law. *Held:* A proprietary interest in the transmissions was found; however, the conversion claim was preempted by federal copyright law. A state cause of action is preempted if (1) the work of authorship in which rights are claimed falls within the subject matter of copyright—motion pictures and other audiovisual works are subject to protection; and (2) the state law has created legal or equitable rights that are equivalent to any exclusive rights within the general scope of copyright as specified in the Copyright Act; i.e., rights of exclusive production, performance, distribution, and display. The cable company's conversion action seeks to protect its rights of distribution, performance, and display in regard to the video signals that the taverns were intercepting and presenting to bar patrons. These rights are guarded by the Copyright Act, and this particular conversion action, which is based on a theory of unauthorized publication, is preempted.

[Quincy Cablesys., Inc. v. Sully's Bar, Inc., 650 F. Supp. 838 (D. Mass. 1986)]

[1] Claims Not Involving Special Relationships

Where product is not sufficiently original to merit copyright protection, state unfair competition law is preempted by federal copyright law. Financial Information, a financial reporting service, charged Moody's Investors Service with copyright infringement and unfair competition. Financial claimed that Moody's was publishing Financial's data, specifically its Daily Bond Cards. Moody's argued that collecting and publishing bond redemption data required no special knowledge or skill, and that the Daily Bond Cards were not copyrightable. *Held:* Financial's product was not protected. Although facts may not be copyrighted, there is protection for comprehensive compilations; however, Financial fell short of the "sufficiently original" standard, in that there was in the Daily Bond Cards little independent creation involved. Financial failed to place the material into any of the narrowly defined exceptions to federal law preemption. There had been no "immoral" misappropriation, or any sufficient characterization of the material as "hot news."

[Financial Info., Inc. v. Moody's Investors Serv., Inc., 808 F2d 204 (2d Cir. 1986)]

Baseball players' state law rights of publicity preempted by federal copyright law. In attempting to maintain its grip on television revenues, Major League Baseball Clubs filed an action in which it sought a declaratory judgment that it, not the Major League Players Association, possessed exclusive rights to broadcast games. Players Association claimed that the property rights in its names, pictures, and performances were misappropriated, and that it had rights of publicity in the performances. Clubs claimed that the telecasts fell within the "work for hire" provision of Section 201(b) of the Copyright Act, and therefore any state contract or tort claims by Players were preempted. Clubs also maintained that the telecasts were within the scope of employment. *Held:* The statutory presumption that the employer owns the copyright in a work made for hire was not rebutted and Players' state law rights of publicity were preempted by federal copyright law.

[Baltimore Orioles, Inc. v. Major League Baseball Players Ass'n, 805 F2d 663 (7th Cir. 1986)]

Federal copyright law does not preempt state laws that protect different interests of plaintiff. Stillman created a successful silent commercial for Eastern Airlines and sought to sell a similar commercial to United Airlines, providing in his pitch some ideas of how the silent commercial could be used. United did not hire Stillman, but it did air a silent commercial similar to the one Stillman had created for Eastern. The creator of United's commercial, Burnett, claimed that the commercial was the result of "lucky inspiration." Stillman copyrighted his silent commercial and sued for fraud. Burnett filed a motion for summary judgment, arguing that the fraud claim was preempted by federal copyright law. *Held:* The claim was not preempted. Federal copyright laws protect Stillman's right to reap the benefits of the particular expression he employed in creating the Eastern silent commercial. The state law, by contrast, protects his right to prevent others from fraudulently taking credit for, and presumably benefiting in the future from, Stillman's ability to develop novel ideas.

[Stillman v. Leo Burnett Co., 720 F. Supp. 1353 (ND Ill. 1989)]

Common-law tort claims that are not equivalent to one of the exclusive rights provided by federal copyright law are not preempted.   Data General, a software manufacturer, accused Grumman Systems Support of infringement by Grumman's use and copying of certain software that was developed by Data General. Data General also made state law claims in conversion, unfair competition, unjust enrichment, and misappropriation of trade secrets. Grumman moved for summary judgment, arguing that Data General's claims are preempted by federal copyright law. *Held:* The conversion and the misappropriation claims were not preempted, as they are not equivalent to one of the exclusive rights created by the Copyright Act. Both the unfair competition and unjust enrichment claims were preempted, as both are equivalent to the copyright infringement claim.

[Data Gen. Corp. v. Grumman Sys. Support Corp., 795 F. Supp. 501 (D. Mass. 1992)]

[2] Contractual or Special Relationships

State court retains jurisdiction where cause of action by former employer sounds in contract and there is no substantial question of patent law sufficient to confer removal.   AT&T sued INC and four INC employees for breach of contract and misappropriation of proprietary information. INC removed the case to federal court, and AT&T appealed, arguing that its claims did not arise under federal patent law, but were state contract and tort claims based on its former employees' breach of their employment contract. INC claimed that in spite of the language of the employment agreement between AT&T and its former employees (now the defendant INC employees), federal patent issues were necessary to AT&T's claims of misuse and misappropriation. *Held:* The circuit court transferred the case to state court, finding that since every theory of a claim as pled must depend on patent law if there is to be federal jurisdiction, and since the language of the employment agreement was constructed as to have both patent and general law meanings, there was no federal jurisdiction.

[American Tel. & Tel. Co. v. Integrated Network Corp., 972 F2d 1321 (Fed. Cir. 1992)]

Use of copyrighted expression violates state law duty of confidentiality, rendering state right qualitatively distinct from federal rights, and foreclosing preemption under Copyright Act.   Altai hired a former employee of Computer Associates who, with expertise gained at Computer, promptly duplicated a computer program for his new employer. When Computer filed copyright and trade secret misappropriation claims against Altai, Altai rewrote the program. There remained virtually no lines of code that were identical to Computer's program, and therefore the lower court denied Computer's infringement claim and held that the trade secret claim was preempted by federal law. On appeal, Altai argued that Section 301 of the Copyright Act preempted Computer's state law cause of action. Computer argued that when its former employee stole its program's code and incorporated it into Altai's design, he breached his confidentiality agreement, a distinctly state cause of action, and that Altai's rewritten program still embodied many of Computer's trade secrets. *Held:* The district court's finding that Computer's trade secret claims were preempted by federal law was vacated and remanded with direction to address more fully the factual and theoretical bases of Computer's trade secret claims. The court found that the new program was created because of the employee's breach of duty, and since it was based on the first duplicate, raised a trade secret claim against Altai.

[Computer Assocs. Int'l, Inc. v. Altai, Inc., 982 F2d 693 (2d Cir. 1992)]

Restrictive language in licensing agreement may be preempted by federal Copyright Act. Vault developed computer diskettes under the trade name PROLOK, which were designed to prevent unauthorized duplication of programs placed on the diskettes by software companies. Vault also asked the buyers of its diskettes to adhere to a licensing agreement, thereby seeking to give further protection to the companies that placed their software programs on PROLOK diskettes, as they, not Vault, owned the copyrights to these programs. Quaid produced COPYWRITE, which contained a feature called RAMKEY, which "unlocked" Vault's protective device. Vault claimed that, in violation of the Copyright Act, Quaid in developing RAMKEY (1) directly copied Vault's program into the memory of Quaid's computers, (2) contributed to the unauthorized copying of Vault's program and the programs of Vault's customers, and (3) created derivative works of Vault's program. *Held:* Even though Quaid copied Vault's program with the intention of defeating its protective function, such use is not precluded by the Copyright Act. Using RAMKEY to make archival copies is also allowable; therefore, Quaid's sale of COPYWRITE diskettes with the RAMKEY feature does not constitute contributory infringement. RAMKEY is not a "derivative work," incorporating in some form a portion of the copyrighted work and the restriction in Vault's licensing agreement is preempted and unenforceable.

[Vault Corp. v. Quaid Software, Ltd., 847 F2d 255 (5th Cir. 1988)]

State breach of contract action may not be preempted by federal copyright law where contract provides rights not equivalent to exclusive copyright right. Computer Associates licensed software programs to National Car Rental, which contrary to their agreement used the programs to process the data of third parties. National argued that Computer's action for breach of contract sought to protect rights equivalent to exclusive copyright rights, and therefore was preempted by federal copyright law. Computer argued that National, in its distribution to third parties, exceeded the uses allowed under the license, and that beyond the copying of the programs, National's processing of data was the prohibited act in violation of a contract right not existing under the copyright law. *Held:* Computer's contract claims were not equivalent to exclusive rights under copyright, and were not preempted. Under federal copyright law, the distribution right, even with respect to computer software, is only the right to distribute *copies* of the work.

[National Car Rental Sys., Inc. v. Computer Assocs. Int'l, Inc., 991 F2d 426 (8th Cir. 1993)]

Without written agreement for display rights to work of art, there is no requirement for written memorandum of sale as to underlying property right.   A sculptor sought to regain possession of a sculpture from a restaurant where it was displayed. The sculptor contended that the work was merely loaned to the restaurant, and he sought recovery under a state statute that leaves ownership of a work of art in the artist whenever a conveyance of any right to publicly display the art is made, unless such right of ownership is transferred in writing. The restaurant argued that, although there was no writing, there had been an outright sale, there was no transfer of intangible rights, and the statute never came into play. *Held:*   The dispute of whether there had been a sale or loan was remanded. As to the construction of the statute, the court found that where there is an express, written conveyance of one or more of the limited rights listed in the statute, there can be no accompanying transfer of ownership unless the transfer is also in writing. Since in this case there was no written transfer rights, there was no requirement for a written memorandum of sale of the underlying property rights.

[Chamberlain v. Cocola Assocs., 958 F2d 282 (9th Cir. 1992)]

Breach-of-contract claims involving misappropriation of trade secrets and breach of confidential duty found viable even where "unauthorized use" claims are preempted by federal copyright law.   Brignoli entered into an agreement with BHS, which provided for BHS's use of Brignoli's computer programs. Brignoli claimed breach of contract and misappropriation of a trade secret, in that BHS was paying him less than the agreed-on compensation, and further argued that BHS continued in the unauthorized use of his computer programs. BHS argued that Brignoli's computer programs fell within the scope of subject matter protected by federal copyright law. *Held:*   Brignoli's "unauthorized use" claims were preempted. Computer programs are entitled to protection under copyright law, even where portions of the programs may be uncopyrightable as "ideas" rather than "expressions." However, Brignoli was allowed to pursue the breach-of-contract, "promise to pay" claims because of Brignoli's allegations that the programs are trade secrets, which makes the claims qualitatively different from copyright claims. Moreover, neither claims alleging breach of an agreement of confidentiality nor duty of confidentiality are equivalent to copyright claims. The court dismissed the preempted claims and found the breach-of-contract claims viable.

[Brignoli v. Balch Hardy & Scheinman, Inc., 645 F. Supp. 1201 (SDNY 1986)]

CHAPTER 4

RESEARCH, DEVELOPMENT, AND OWNERSHIP

PART A.   EMPLOYEE OWNERSHIP

¶ 4.01 EMPLOYEE DEVELOPERS

Employee owns invention even if employer resources are used absent contract or circumstances indicating duty to assign.   Rowland was hired as general engineer with neither written contract, nor understanding that he would design new equipment, nor oral agreement to assign inventions he designed. Later, without an increase in pay, he was placed on a project to design a table. After completion of the design, Rowland signed the patent application as joint inventor of the table with a co-worker. After laying off Rowland, Aetna-Standard requested that he assign interest in the patent to it, and he refused. Aetna-Standard argued that it should own the patent because it assigned Rowland to devote time and skill to solve specific design problems, for which he was compensated. *Held:* Aetna-Standard was not entitled to assignment of Rowland's invention. Rowland had no contract, written or oral, to assign any inventions created during his employment. Rowland signed the patent application as joint-inventor, and Aetna-Standard asked for assignment only after discharging Rowland. Further, Rowland was not specifically recruited to design the table, and received no additional compensation. Although Aetna-Standard has no right to Rowland's patent interest, it did have shop right to royalty-free, nonexclusive use of the table designed at its place of business using its resources.

[Aetna-Standard Eng'g Co. v. Rowland, 493 A2d 1375 (Pa. Super. Ct. 1985)]

[1] Works for Hire and Particularity

Employee hired to devise or perfect instrument or means for accomplishing prescribed result has sold individual rights in advance to his employer.   Solomon, a government employee, was assigned the duty of devising a stamp. The subsequent invention was accomplished wholly at government expense according to specifications that Solomon recommended. He notified the government that he would not charge for use of his stamp if adopted. After receiving the patent, Solomon assigned the rights to a third party, who sued the government for infringement. *Held:* The government owned the rights in the invention. When an employee in a specific line of work devises an improved method for accomplishing that work and uses the resources of his employer to develop and perfect that work, a jury or court would be warranted in finding that the employee had granted to such employer an irrevocable license to use that invention. The general rule is that any employee performing all the duties assigned to him may exercise his inventive faculties as he chooses with the assurance that whatever invention he may conceive or perfect is his individual property. An employee hired to invent or perfect a specific instrument or means for accomplishing a prescribed result has no claim to title after successfully accomplishing the work for which he was hired. Solomon had already received payment by performing the work for which he was hired. Whatever rights he may have had as an individual he had sold in advance to his employer.

[Solomon v. United States, 137 US 342 (1890)]

[a] Patent and Copyright Ownership

Rules of patent ownership are determined by state law. An inventor went bankrupt and a third party, X, acquired the patent by assignment from an assignee claiming title to the patent through the trustee in bankruptcy. Meanwhile, the inventor had assigned the patent to a third party, Y. X sued the inventor and Y in district court, requesting declaratory judgment of ownership, injunction against infringement, and imposition of constructive trust. The inventor moved to dismiss for lack of federal subject matter jurisdiction. *Held:* A suit seeking a declaratory judgment of patent ownership does not fall within patent laws; however, a complaint that alleges patent ownership and seeks appropriate relief sets forth a patent law question sufficient to confer federal jurisdiction. That a nonfederal issue (patent ownership) must be resolved before the federal issue (infringement) is immaterial in determining whether there is federal jurisdiction.

[Vink v. Schijf, 839 F2d 676 (Fed. Cir. 1988)]

Baseball players' contract for live performance conveys ownership of television broadcast rights. Players claimed live game telecasts misappropriated their property rights in their names, pictures, and performances, thereby unjustly enriching the Clubs. The Clubs claimed copyright in telecasts as works made for hire and that its rights preempted players' rights of publicity in their performances. *Held:* Telecasts are copyrightable audiovisual original works of authorship fixed in a tangible form because they are simultaneously recorded when transmitted. Since players are employees and their performances before broadcast audiences are within the scope of their employment, the telecasts, which consist of players' performances, are works made for hire under copyright law. Absent an express written agreement to the contrary, the Clubs are presumed to own all rights encompassed in the telecasts of games. The Clubs' ownership of copyright preempts Players' equivalent common and state law rights of publicity in their game-time performances under 17 USC §§ 106, 301(a). Players remain free to bargain for a joint or exclusive interest in the copyright of telecasts.

[Baltimore Orioles v. Major League Baseball Players, 805 F2d 663 (7th Cir. 1986)]

If employer ignores its own rules in dealing with its employee, employee may claim ownership of invention despite written agreement to the contrary. Cole, an employee of a CDC subsidiary, developed a software program on his own time using his own materials. When Cole initially offered the program to CDC, CDC declined to support development. Later, a CDC manager made an oral agreement with him on behalf of CDC; Cole was to complete testing and be responsible for updating the software while CDC would market it. Cole perfected the program working on the company computer and deleted copies of the program from his home computer. Subsequently, CDC, unbeknownst to Cole, attempted to sell the software to one of its major clients. Later, when the program was ready for marketing, Cole's manager ordered him to destroy the program on CDC premises or be fired. The manager refused to allow Cole to make a copy of the program for his home computer. Cole sued CDC for breach of contract and conversion. CDC alleged that the software belonged to it since Cole had signed a disclosure and assignment agreement stating that any software employees developed, either on their own time or company time, belonged to the company. *Held:* CDC breached its contract with Cole. Cole did not need to show that he was entitled to *exclusive possession* of the program; rather, he only needed to show a *right* to the property in question. CDC acted outside any established company procedures, including the assignment and disclosure agreement. Further, in forcing Cole to destroy all copies of the program other than those in the possession of CDC, a claim of conversion was proper.

[Cole v. Control Data Corp., 947 F2d 313 (8th Cir. 1991)]

Employee owns invention even if employer hires him to do similar work; however, a constructive trust may be imposed if employee breaches fiduciary duties. Peiffer, an employee of Avtec, worked for several years using computer programs and developing simulations for use in satellite orbital analysis. On the basis of that proprietary knowledge, Peiffer developed a software program, "Orbit," to demonstrate satellite orbits. Avtec awarded him a bonus and had him use the program as a marketing device to Avtec customers. Other Avtec employees suggested changes that Peiffer incorporated into the program. Four years later, Peiffer developed, with another company, KKI, a new version of Orbit (O2) as a standalone program with independent abilities. A full-time employee of Avtec, Peiffer deliberately refused to use a newer version of the Orbit demonstration program in marketing to Avtec's customers, despite specific requests from Avtec. When Avtec learned that Peiffer had created O2 with KKI and was marketing it to Avtec's customers, it sued for copyright infringement, misappropriation of trade secrets, and breach of fiduciary duty. *Held:* Copyright of the Orbit and O2 programs belonged to Peiffer, not to Avtec. The Orbit program was not work for hire. Avtec had to show that the program was within the scope of Peiffer's employment under agency law principles mandated by *CCNV v. Reid*, 490 U.S. 730 (1989). While Avtec did show that this was the sort of work Peiffer was employed to perform for it, it was unable to prove that development of the Orbit program occurred "substantially within Avtec authorized time and space limits" or that Peiffer was "motivated, at least in part, by a purpose to serve Avtec." However, because Peiffer made use of Avtec's proprietary information to develop the program and used the Orbit program as a demonstration program and marketing device, Avtec gained an interest in it as a trade secret in a similar manner as an employer may possess shop rights to an employee's patented inventions. KKI violated Avtec's trade secret because it knew or should have known that the Orbit program was a protected trade secret. Furthermore, Peiffer's frequent demonstration of the program to customers constituted the granting to Avtec of a license to use it for similar purposes. Finally, because of Avtec's trade secret rights in the Orbit program, KKI's misappropriation of trade secrets in marketing the O2 program, and Peiffer's intentional sabotaging of various business opportunities for Avtec, a constructive trust was imposed on Peiffer and KKI forcing them to remit 15 percent of the gross revenues from the O2 program to Avtec.

[Avtec Sys., Inc. v. Peiffer, 805 F. Supp. 1312 (ED Va. 1992)]

Expectations of parties are relevant to determination of ownership. Amoco sued former employee Lindley over ownership rights to a software computer program that he developed while working for Amoco. Lindley had written a contract agreeing to disclose promptly "all inventions or discoveries" capable of use in connection with Amoco's business and not to disclose such matter to others without Amoco's consent. Lindley argued that the computer program was not an "invention" and therefore not property under the contract. *Held:* The software program was not patentable under current law, and therefore, it was neither invention nor discovery under the contract. Further, Amoco formally denied Lindley in writing the right to develop software, never took steps to protect software or the software manual as confidential, to indicate exercise of dominion over the software, and never approached Lindley as to ownership prior to bringing suit. While a computer program conceived and developed using a company's resources may qualify for trade secret protection, courts look to the equities of the set of circumstances from which the claimed trade secrets arise. Factors to be considered include how many of the innovative elements in the newly developed process are available in the prior art; whether the company treated the innovation with requisite secrecy so as to place others on notice of its claim; and time, money, and company facilities used in its production and the employer's knowledge thereof. In the instant case, evidence of trade secret was inconclusive, especially since Amoco did not divulge such secret to Lindley and Amoco needed Lindley's expertise to use software.

[Amoco Prod. Co. v. Lindley, 609 P2d 733 (Okla. 1980)]

[b] Trade Secret Ownership

Trade secret protection granted to enjoin use of specific, nonstandard formulas, but not with respect to employee's knowledge of suppliers and customers.   SI was granted a preliminary injunction enjoining a company headed by former employees from the use and disclosure of certain trade secrets. *Held:* Trade secret protection was properly granted to specific matters such as processes of manufacturing tubes, dimensions, tolerances and method of fit between tubes, and efficiency factors gained from component experience. But, such protection was inappropriate for knowledge of the existence of alternate suppliers of parts at lower prices. This knowledge would be protectible only if dependent on knowing the secret specifications of such parts, but granting protection would place an undue burden on innocent vendors and an artificial restraint on trade. Nor was SI's knowledge of key decision makers in customers' companies protectible as falling in the category of "customer lists"; while such information is valuable, it can only be protected through reasonable covenants not to compete. Finally, "know-how" in systems engineering is not protectible, since it is not specific enough; it covers too many matters that belong to an employee's general knowledge and skill. An employer may not, after employees leave, assert proprietary rights over their problem-solving ability or knowledge of mistakes to be avoided.

[SI Handling Sys., Inc. v. Heisley, 753 F2d 1244 (3d Cir. 1985)]

Equitable factors favor employer ownership of trade secrets when employees conceal an invention or mislead employer so it will not support it.   Disgruntled employees formed a rival corporation. In the course of setting up the rival corporation, the employees took confidential documents and dissuaded their employer, Sperry Rand, from entering a potentially lucrative field monopolized by a rival, where they intended that their new corporation would profit. After leaving, they took other trade secrets, including manufacturing processes and customer lists. Sperry sued for breach of duty of loyalty and fidelity, as well as misappropriation of trade secrets and wrongful removal of confidential documents. The former employees claimed that all information and processes taken were commonly known in the trade or readily discernible; therefore, they were neither patentable nor protectible as trade secrets. *Held:* Sperry's processes were trade secrets because they provided it with competitive advantage. Further, it is no defense to misappropriation of trade secrets to claim that the process or information could have been developed independently, without resort to information gleaned from the confidential relationship; while anyone may discover a trade secret and thereafter use it with impunity, that does not excuse obtaining a trade secret by improper means or the inequitable use of it. Were the information so easily discovered, why had the employees marked documents "confidential" and taken strict security measures to preserve secrecy of drawings virtually identical to those of Sperry? The employees were entitled to make use of skills learned and knowledge acquired in developing trade secrets for their former employer. But, they were not entitled to breach their fiduciary duty to Sperry by using or imparting to others their knowledge of the end products, processes, and procedures that gave the Sperry corporation its superior product, and which Sperry had maintained scrupulously as trade secrets. Further, the employees' breach of loyalty was revealed when they discouraged Sperry from competing with a rival at the same time they intended their own company to do so.

[Sperry Rand Corp. v. Rothlein, 241 F. Supp. 549 (D. Conn. 1964)]

Employee developers of structural analysis program are barred from using similar program because their contract contained restrictive covenants. Structural Dynamics sued former employees for unfair competition, misappropriation and misuse of confidential and trade secret material, and breach of confidential disclosure agreements with respect to structural design of computer program. The employees responded that the information was not novel or subject to protection as confidential information or trade secrets. *Held:* The employees were liable on all counts. An employee who shares in the creation, innovation, or development of the subject matter of a trade secret has no duty not to use or disclose such knowledge, absent an express contractual obligation not to use or disclose such information obtained during his or her employment adverse to the employer's interest. The employee's interest in the subject matter may be at least equal to that of the employer or, in any event, such knowledge is part of the employee's skill and experience. Although the employees did not obtain the claimed trade secrets through improper means, they had all signed explicit agreements of confidentiality and not to compete, the clear terms of which did not exclude information, technology, or knowledge that the employee himself discovers, developes, or contributes. Such contracts were valid and enforceable. Both Structural Dynamics and the employees acknowledged the value, uniqueness, and confidentiality of the computer program. Structural Dynamics acted at all times in a manner consistent with the preservation of the program's confidentiality. Finally, novelty and uniqueness are not required to afford trade secret protection, as they would be in patent applications; but, a unique and valuable software program, such as the instant one, falls within the definition of confidential information.

[Structural Dynamics Research Corp. v. Engineering Mechanics Research Corp., 401 F. Supp. 1102 (ED Mich. 1975)]

Presence of nondisclosure agreement supports holding developer of software program had violated trade secret law by developing similar program for another

company.   Integrated Cash Management sued former employees for misappropriation and use of trade secrets after they formed a rival company that competed with it in creating generic software programs for the banking industry. The employees maintained that none of the information was novel, nor in any event, secret information. *Held:* The employees were liable for misappropriation and use of trade secrets, and were enjoined from using any versions of Integrated programs for six months. Integrated made reasonable efforts to maintain secrecy of software source code, required programmers to sign nondisclosure agreements, and kept doors to premises locked. The elements of the software modules may have been generally known, but their specific construction to fit and work together in a particular combination gave Integrated a competitive advantage, and thus entitled it to protection from misappropriation. Further, the large expenditures of time and money in investigating alternatives that ultimately proved unworkable were also protectible as a trade secret. While it is difficult to balance the interests of skilled employees and former employers, the presence of a nondisclosure agreement put the employees on notice that the programs were considered trade secrets. Although the employees good faith was not in doubt, they failed to meet their burden of showing that they developed their software from scratch, not relying on Integrated's protected trade secrets.

[Integrated Cash Management Servs., Inc. v. Digital Transactions, Inc., 732 F. Supp. 370 (SDNY 1989)]

Absent enforceable noncompetition agreements, employee is entitled to use his general skill and expertise, even in competitive employment.   A skilled employee, who was in part hired because he came with prior knowledge of Dynamic Research Corporation's management system, informed Dynamic that he was leaving and would work for a competitor. Dynamic did not object. Dynamic sued to enjoin the employee and new company from using trade secrets. *Held:* The nature of the information, which was public and obvious, and the conduct of the parties—Dynamic took no appropriate precautions to protect information as trade secrets—militated against a finding that Dynamic was entitled to restrain the employee from working for a competitor; therefore, the nondisclosure agreement only affirmed the intent of the parties to be bound by the common law of trade secrets. Upon termination of employment, an employee may carry away and use the general skill or knowledge acquired during the course of employment. In circumstances where an employee enters a job with extensive experience, the employer has a heavy burden in isolating the secrets for which it claims protection. Dynamic failed to meet this burden. The employer's interest in the secret must be crystal clear to justify restraint. Although the employee signed a nondisclosure agreement when hired, he was never put on notice that the obvious notions with which he was working were trade secrets. Again, when he left and stated that he would work for a competitor, Dynamic did not object or mention the nondisclosure agreement. A nondisclosure agreement cannot make secret that which is not secret, and it is for the courts to determine whether an alleged trade secret is in fact such.

[Dynamic Research Corp. v. Analytic Sciences Corp., 400 NE2d 1274 (Mass. App. Ct. 1980)]

Designing application for employer in one industry does not bar subsequent employment to design improved system for another company, even if in direct competition. Jostens, Inc., sued former employees and computer firm for misappropriation of trade secrets and proprietary data in Jostens' CAD/CAM computer system to design and manufacture rings. *Held:* To merit trade secret protection, the matter involved could not be generally known or readily ascertainable, and the owner must have intended to keep it confidential. But, in this case, Jostens failed to identify specifically its trade secret claims; i.e., whether it was to the entire CAD/CAM system or something less. The computer firm never accepted Jostens' proposed proprietary clause, and had even stated expressly in contract that no variation from the terms of the contract would be incorporated without its specific approval in writing. The Jostens CAD/CAM system consisted of standard vendor products; the assertion that a trade secret resides in some combination of otherwise known data is insufficient to establish trade secret status. In addition, Jostens failed to take reasonable steps to maintain secrecy: It allowed employees to make public presentations and write articles on the ring production system and components; also, it only recently took security measures to bar potential customers from its plant. Jostens' failure to take reasonable precautions to protect confidentiality did not put employees on notice as to what information was confidential. When an employee departed and stated he would work in area of CAD/CAM development, Jostens voiced no objection. Finally, the confidentiality agreement signed after the employee had been working for the firm for four years without an increase in wages, promotion, or greater access to information was not binding. The promise of continued employment is not adequate consideration.

[Jostens, Inc. v. National Computer Sys., Inc., 318 NW2d 691 (Minn. 1982)]

In absence of contractual restrictions, an employee developer has a co-equal right to use intellectual product under trade secrecy law. Greenberg, a skilled chemist, went to work for Wexler's customer and helped the customer develop a product similar to one sold by Wexler. Although Greenberg had no written or oral contract of employment or other restrictive agreement, Wexler sued Greenberg and the former customer for breach of duty of nondisclosure of trade secrets arising from a confidential relationship with Wexler and misappropriation of trade secrets. *Held:* Greenberg owed no duty to Wexler, absent a contractual obligation not to use or disclose secret formulas. Greenberg never engaged in research nor conducted any experiments nor created nor invented any formula; rather, the products were the fruits of Greenberg's own skill as a chemist, without appreciable assistance, expenditure, or supervision by Wexler. Greenberg's knowledge of the value of these formulas and that their disclosure would be harmful merely indicates that Greenberg knew the value of his finds and the harmful effects that competition could bring. His knowledge by itself does not support a finding that he was never to compete. Therefore, Greenberg had an unqualified privilege to use the technical knowledge and skill acquired by virtue of his employment. Finally, customers are entitled to compete with suppliers, even in the use of identical goods, provided that they behave equitably. Facts show that customers did not entice Greenberg away in order to obtain trade secrets; rather, they sought his expertise.

[Wexler v. Greenberg, 160 A2d 430 (Pa. 1960)]

[2] Joint Use and Shop Rights

Shop right gives employers a nonexclusive license to use invention patented by employee. Government employees sought patents for items invented with the aid of government resources. Their inventions were not within the scope of their employment, but rather the result of their scientific curiosity. The government opposed claiming exclusive rights to the patents or that the patents, by being the result of government research, had been dedicated to the public available for all to use. *Held:* An employer that has employed a skilled workman for a stated compensation to devise and make improvements in articles manufactured is not entitled to a conveyance of patents obtained for inventions made by him while so employed, in the absence of express agreement to that effect. The rule is that employment merely to design, or construct, or devise methods of manufacture is not the same as employment to invent (where the employee accomplishes that which was the precise subject of the contract of employment). This rule, based on a distinction between an idea and its application in practice, defines the limit of the "shop right": Where a servant, during his hours of employment, working with his master's materials and appliances, conceives and perfects an invention for which he obtains a patent, he must accord his master a nonexclusive right to practice the invention. While equity requires that the employer receive that right in compensation for the use of his materials, time, and facilities to attain a concrete result, equity does not require that the employee convey to the employer the rights to an invention that is the original conception of the employee alone.

[United States v. Dubilier Condenser Corp., 289 US 178 (1933)]

¶ 4.02 ASSIGNMENTS OF INVENTIONS IN EMPLOYEE CONTRACTS

Implied license to use preexisting copyrighted material arose in favor of partnership as against partner. Ries and Oddo entered into a partnership to publish a book that Oddo would write and Ries would finance. Oddo delivered to Ries a manuscript that consisted partly of reworkings of previously published articles written by Oddo and partly of new material also written by Oddo. Ries was dissatisfied and gave the manuscript to another writer to complete. Eventually, Ries published a book that contained substantial quantities of Oddo's work along with the new writer's contribution. Oddo sued Ries for copyright infringement. *Held:* With respect to the copyright in the book, as a partner, Ries is co-owner of the partnership's assets, including the copyrights. A co-owner cannot be liable to another co-owner for infringement of the copyright, even when that co-owner is not a joint author of the work. However, in respect to the copyright in the articles, Ries did infringe Oddo's rights. While Oddo granted Ries an implied license to use the articles as incorporated in the manuscript, this license did not give Ries or the partnership the right to use the articles in any other work than the manuscript itself. A particular license does not permit the licensee to use the underlying work in any other derivative work. Ries exceeded the scope of the partnership's license.

[Oddo v. Reis, 743 F2d 630 (9th Cir. 1984)]

[1] Reasonableness and Statutory Limitations

In employment contracts, agreements not to compete are judged on reasonableness standards similar to those used in noncompetition agreements. When Ciavatta started working for IR, he signed a clause stating that he would assign the right, title, and interest in any patent he might invent within one year after termination of employment if related to the business or research of IR. Nine months after being fired by IR, Ciavatta applied for a patent on a mining device competitive with a device sold by IR. IR sued to force Ciavatta to assign his patent rights to IR in accord with the contract. *Held:* The agreement was unreasonable and unforceable in this case. Here, Ciavatta was not hired to invent products, and his invention was not based on trade secrets nor on IR's proprietary knowledge, nor the result of expenditures of IR's resources; rather, he invented it, months after being fired, as a product of his general skill, expertise, and knowledge. Courts will enforce holdover agreements if they are reasonable. The test for reasonableness for "assignment clauses" parallels that used in interpreting holdover agreements. Agreements will be enforced to the extent that they (1) would be limited and reasonably necessary to protect the employer's legitimate interests (e.g., trade secrets, proprietary information), (2) would cause no undue hardship to the employee (i.e., future employment), and (3) would not impair the public interest (e.g., competition, inventiveness). Courts must evaluate such agreements in light of the individual circumstances of the employer and employee.

[Ingersoll-Rand v. Ciavatta, 542 A2d 879 (NJ 1988)]

[2] Interpretation of Assignment Clauses

Time-limited assignment clauses narrowly drafted to protect employer's trade secrets are enforceable.   MAI required employees to sign two agreements: a patent waiver agreement requiring assignment to MAI of "any developments, inventions and improvements made while . . . employed by . . . [MAI] and for 90 days thereafter"; and a confidentiality agreement to refrain from disclosing trade secrets to others. Within 90 days of being terminated by MAI, employees formed a rival company marketing competitive software products "markedly similar" to MAI's products. MAI sued for breach of the two contracts and specific performance of the patent waiver agreement to assign rights in software. *Held:* These agreements could not be characterized as restrictive covenants not to compete, since they served distinctly different purposes. The confidentiality agreements protected and preserved MAI's trade secrets and other valuable confidential information. The patent waiver agreements assured MAI, which had hired employees and supported their research, that it would benefit from inventions resulting from their employment activities. Such agreements are necessary to ensure commercial viability in a highly competitive market of developing technology, and are properly characterized as necessary incidents to employment contracts in that field.

[MAI Basic Four, Inc. v. Basis, Inc., 880 F2d 286 (10th Cir. 1989)]

Ambiguous employment contracts may leave material issues of fact unresolved. In 1985, Lieberam, a German student, came to GP on a temporary, six-month contract. Lieberam never signed the employee confidentiality agreement that would have transferred the legal ownership rights to GP for any invention conceived or made by him "during" his term of employment at GP. While at GP, Lieberam conceived of a design for a condenser system. Some of this inventing was done at the expense of GP. GP invited Lieberam back as a permanent employee in 1987 and asked him to sign an invention agreement, which he did. In 1988, Lieberam became concerned that GP considered itself owner of the rights to the condenser system and filed a patent application. GP then brought suit against him, claiming the invention agreement had retrospective effect and that Lieberam had misappropriated trade secrets. Both sides moved for summary judgment. *Held:* Factual issues relating to the contract remained because it was ambiguous: The term "during" (in the phrase "during my employment") could have retrospective effect. Therefore, summary judgment was inappropriate, although a consideration of the contract as a whole could reasonably construe it to have only prospective effect. Finally, GP could have a claim against Lieberam for breach of contract and misappropriation because Lieberam distributed copies of the invention to non-GP recipients. While the invention may have been conceived before the invention agreement became effective, the subsequent activities of Lieberam and GP employees may have effectively converted it into a joint project.

[Georgia-Pac. Corp. v. Lieberam, 959 F2d 901 (11th Cir. 1992)]

Employment contracts to disclose inventions are construed strictly. Goldwasser sued SCC for patent infringement and IBM intervened, claiming it owned the patent. Goldwasser, while still an employee of IBM, invented and obtained patents for a word processing program, PointWriter, and related spell-checking applications. As a condition for employment with IBM, Goldwasser signed an agreement to assign to IBM "all right, title and interest in any invention or idea, patentable or not" relating in any manner to IBM's business that is "made or conceived" while "working [for] IBM." Goldwasser disclosed the PointWriter program to IBM while still employed, but IBM declined to market it. In 1985, with his wife, he obtained a patent on the software. The spell-checking application was also conceived and reduced to practice while Goldwasser was working for IBM, but patent applications were filed after Goldwasser left IBM, and were issued in 1990. In his exit interview, Goldwasser signed a document stating he had disclosed all his inventions and ideas to IBM; however, he never disclosed the existence of the PointWriter patent or the spell-check patent to IBM. Goldwasser claimed that IBM was barred by laches or the statute of limitations from asserting its rights with respect to the second invention. *Held:* IBM owned the spell-check patent. The employment agreement that Goldwasser signed was valid and enforceable because it did not violate public policy against unreasonable restraint of trade. Goldwasser clearly breached that contract. At no time did Goldwasser actually own the program because, pursuant to the agreement, the program belonged to IBM, as it was conceived and reduced to practice while Goldwasser was working at IBM. IBM was under no obligation to demand assignment of the program at a specific time. Even if IBM had been given notice of the program or patent application, IBM was free under the contract to demand an assignment at any time it pleased. The contract was breached when Goldwasser refused to convey the patent when requested.

[Goldwasser v. Smith Corona Corp., 817 F. Supp. 264 (D. Conn. 1993)]

Employment contracts to disclose inventions are construed strictly. Key employees left Science Accessories and formed a company with a third-party inventor, who conceived a superior competitive product. Science sued the employees for equitable relief for breach of fiduciary and contractual duties on the theory that the employees had known of the inventor's concept and kept information secret from their employer while developing a working model of it. Science contended that it should be granted a property interest in the invention, since the employees had signed contracts to disclose "any invention or discovery which I may make or conceive, either alone or jointly with others, while employed by the Company" and that such invention or discovery would become property of Science. *Held:* The employees' employment contracts did not contain covenants not to compete; therefore, the employees were free to make reasonable preparations to compete while still employed by Science and after quitting. The law of agency does not impose a duty on agent to disclose to his or her principal information obtained in confidence, the disclosure of which would be a breach of duty to a third person. Here, the inventor disclosed the invention to employees on a confidential basis. Further, uncontroverted trial evidence indicated that Science was not interested in or able to develop new products, and hence invention did not constitute corporate opportunity for Science. Finally, the employees did not breach their contract to disclose inventions "made or conceived" by them during their employ, since they invented nothing and contributed nothing to the invention. Science's construction of the contract would have the effect of enabling an employee without a property interest in an invention to confer property rights on his employer merely by undertaking the physical act of assembling a working model— in disregard of the rights of the owner/inventor.

[Science Accessories v. Summagraphics, 425 A2d 957 (Del. 1980)]

¶ 4.03 FACULTY-DEVELOPED SOFTWARE

University faculty contract does not make faculty publication work for hire.
A university professor wrote an article with two other colleagues, but objected that his name appeared last in the list of authors, rather than first, since he claimed to be the principal author. Weinstein sued his co-authors and the university for deprivation of property. *Held:* Weinstein did have a property interest in the copyright to the article; and, by publishing a jointly written work, his co-owner did not deprive him of his "property," since each co-owner of a copyright may revise the work and publish the original or revision. Although the standard university contract here addressed work-for-hire issues raised by the 1978 revision of the copyright laws, the clause in question granting copyright in the university for "works created as a specific requirement of employment or as an assigned University duty" read more naturally when applied to administrative duties than to professorial ones. That a university requires all its faculty members to write does not mean that their publications fall within the ambit of the aforementioned clause. There is a long academic tradition since copyright law began that faculty own the copyrights in their writings, a tradition that the university's policy purports to retain.

[Weinstein v. University of Ill., 811 F2d 1091 (7th Cir. 1988)]

Faculty authorship is exception to work-for-hire doctrine.   Two high-school teachers wrote a manual for DEC word processors. The school district asked Sony to rewrite the manual to apply to Sony word processor. Sony did so, unaware of the teachers' copyright claim. The teachers sued for infringement. *Held:* In the instant case involving high-school teachers, whose employment does not contemplate producing books and articles as part of their employment duties, there was a stronger presumption in favor of their claims to authorship and that the manual was not a work for hire. There is a well-recognized and largely unchallenged "teacher exception" to the work-made-for-hire doctrine of the 1976 Copyright Act. Basically, a university does not supervise its faculty in the preparation of books and articles and it is poorly equipped to exploit their writings. Thus, although one might conclude from a literal reading that the Act inadvertently abolished the teacher exception, in consideration of the havoc that such a conclusion would wreak on settled practices of academic institutions, and the ill-suitedness of the work-for-hire doctrine to the conditions of academic production, in the absence of express congressional language to the contrary, the exception might be deemed to have survived the enactment of the Act.

[Hays v. Sony Corp. of Am., 847 F2d 412 (8th Cir. 1988)]

Joint authorship is not found where no intent to merge contributions exists. Respect Inc. and Coleen Mast (the author) brought a copyright infringement action against the Committee on the Status of Women, d/b/a Project Respect. The Committee had obtained federal funding from the Department of Health and Human Services (DHHS) for the texts. As a result of previous litigation, the author was provided with renewed control over the manuscripts, and Respect with the assigned copyrights to the books. Hence, the Committee ordered books directly from Respect, until it obtained permission from the DHHS to begin printing the books itself. Both parties moved for summary judgment on the issue of ownership of the copyrightable work. *Held:* The Committee had no copyright rights stemming from the work-made-for-hire statute or from the joint-authorship statute. Moreover, the DHHS exceeded its authority when it gave the Committee permission to print and distribute the books to the economic detriment of Respect as the copyright owner. Under the Copyright Act, if the creator of a work is an independent contractor, Section 101(2) applies. Under that provision, the organization owns the copyright only if the work fits within one of a group of nine specifically enumerated groups and if the parties expressly agree in a signed, written instrument that the work shall be considered a work made for hire. After considering such factors as composition control, where the author performed most of her work, and the nonbusiness nature of the Committee, the court determined that the author was an independent contractor as a matter of law. Moreover, although the texts, classified as "instructional texts", did fall within one of nine enumerated categories of Section 101(2), the parties never expressly agreed in a signed, written instrument that the works would be considered works made for hire. Hence, the Committee had no rights stemming from the work-made-for-hire statute. In addition, the works were not found to be joint works. Joint authors are "co-owners of copyright in the work" under the Copyright Act. Here, the requisite intent was missing; the author never intended to make anyone else a joint author, including two authors who assigned their rights of joint authorship, if any existed, to the Committee. Finally, the court held that 45 CFR § 74.145(c) and 5 USC § 301 did not grant the Committee, derivatively through DHHS, an unrestricted right to reproduce and distribute the books itself. Section 301 did not authorize the DHHS to adopt a regulation such as

Section 74.145(c), which permitted the DHHS to grant the Committee rights so directly at odds with the author's copyright.

[Respect, Inc. v. Committee on Status of Women, 815 F. Supp. 1112 (ND Ill. 1993)]

PART B.   JOINT AND SEQUENTIAL OWNERSHIP

¶ 4.04 JOINT DEVELOPMENT AND OWNERSHIP

Discovery of fiscal matters may not be obtained for cause of action seeking an accounting until the accounting is established.   Alexander Tsigutkin brought suit against Brian Scanlan and others seeking a share of profits from the sale of a computer program. In each of the causes of action asserted by Tsigutkin, he demanded an accounting of all monies earned by the corporate defendant since his association with the corporation was terminated and of all profits derived from the computer program. Scanlan brought a motion for a protective order with respect to an item of Tsigutkin's motion to produce, in which Tsigutkin sought to have the defendants produce for his inspection copies of all executed contracts with the corporate defendant's customers, including maintenance contracts. *Held:* Discovery of fiscal matters may not be obtained for causes of action seeking an accounting until the right to an accounting is established. Here, receipt of the contracts in question would permit Tsigutkin to calculate the corporate defendant's gross profits on each computer program sold. Therefore, the contracts constituted fiscal matters to which Tsigutkin was not entitled prior to establishing his right to an accounting. The lower court erred in denying Scanlan's motion for protective order.

[Tsigutkin v. Scanlan, 599 NYS2d 262 (App. Div. 1993)]

[1] Joint Invention and Patent Law

Patents are issued to all inventors of a particular invention by statute.   Assignee of rights of joint inventor, whose name was inadvertently omitted from the patent application, sought to intervene in an infringement suit and to correct the patent certificate to reflect the assignor's rights, pursuant to 35 USC § 256. The district court allowed intervention but denied authority to grant certification of assignor's rights as joint inventor. Sperry Rand argued that the statute required joinder and permission of all parties. *Held:* The statute does not require the joinder of all parties for court to correct an error in the patent certificate because of an inadvertent omission of the joint inventor. Patents have the attributes of personal property. While the Commissioner of Patent requires the consent of all parties to institute such a change, after issuance, it is for the courts to determine property rights in judicial proceedings that afford due process of law. The statute merely requires that all interested parties have notice and an opportunity to be heard.

[Iowa State Univ. Research Fund, Inc. v. Sperry Rand, 444 F2d 406 (4th Cir. 1971)]

[2] Copyright and Joint Software Development

Joint authorship in prior work is insufficient to make one a joint author of derivative work. Two doctors, Freeman and Weissmann, who authored numerous scholarly articles over a number of years, became embroiled in a copyright dispute after Weissmann published a 1985 article, "P-1," derived from prior joint works, listing herself as the sole author. In 1987, Freeman prepared copies of P-1, in which he replaced Weissmann's name with his own and added three words to the title for use in a medical school course. Before using the materials, Weissmann asked that P-1 not be used and it was removed from the course materials. Weissmann then sued for copyright infringement. *Held:* The doctors' joint authorship of prior works did not make them joint authors and co-owners of all derivative works. To hold otherwise would stand copyright law on its head, and eviscerate the copyright protection that attaches to a derivative work that is wholly independent of the protection afforded the preexisting work. Joint authorship requires that each author *intend* to contribute to the joint work, to which another will or already has contributed, *at the time* the contribution is made; in short, it requires collaboration. A co-author has no property rights in a new work prepared without his involvement. Thus, inclusion in P-1 of an independently authored 1984 article by Freeman did not constitute a contribution on his part, since he could not have formed the requisite intent at that time to contribute to the 1985 article. Joint authors are joint owners of copyright with respect to the joint work—they have independent rights to reproduce their work in whole or in part. They may not bring infringement actions against one another, although they do have a duty to one another to account for profits.

[Weissmann v. Freeman, 868 F2d 1313 (2d Cir. 1989)]

One who suggests to programmer that he invent program, and that the program should perform several specific functions, is not co-author of resulting program designed, developed, and coded (written) by other party. Jaslow hired Whelan to design software for his dental lab. The agreement provided that Whelan's company would maintain ownership of the "Dentalab" program and pay Jaslow a 10 percent royalty on all connected sales of software to other dental labs. Jaslow in his spare time wrote a PC-compatible program, "Dentcom" ("a new version of the Dentalab computer system"), canceled the royalty agreement, and sought to prevent Whelan from marketing the program to dental labs. When Whelan refused, Jaslow sued in state court for misappropriation of trade secrets, while Whelan countersued in district court for copyright (and trademark) infringement. Jaslow claimed that Whelan's copyright in the program was invalid since he had been co-author of the program, and his omission from the copyright registration form rendered the copyright defective. *Held:* Whelan alone was author of the program; it was her expertise and creativeness that designed the methods by which the raw information would be stored, held in memory, collated, assembled, updated, incorporated, and the like. Jaslow had no claim to co-authorship since his instructions and contributions (including designing the language and formats of some of the visual screens) to Whelan's program were not sufficient to constitute him as a co-author of the system. Finally, Jaslow did not own the copyright as a "work for hire" under 17 USC §§ 101 and 201(b), and since Whelan as author of the entire system was an employee of an independent contractor. In addition, the express contract between Jaslow and Whelan's company provided that the software developed for the system would "remain under [Company's] ownership." The contractual provision superseded any potential work-for-hire rights.

[Whelan Assocs. v. Jaslow Dental Lab., 609 F. Supp. 1307 (ED Pa. 1985), aff'd, 797 F2d 1222 (3d Cir. 1986)]

Copyright ownership excludes authorship for persons whose contributions consisted merely of general statements or ideas that they did not translate into fixed, tangible expressions.   Ross and Wiggonton agreed to design a MacCalc spreadsheet program for Macintosh computers with Ross working on a computational component and Wiggonton on a user interface component. Wiggonton and Ross had no formal contract other than a nondisclosure of proprietary information agreement. Ross gave Wiggonton a list of user commands he thought interface should contain. After a disagreement, Wiggonton went to work for Ashton-Tate and developed an interface for the "Full Impact" spreadsheet. Ross sued Ashton-Tate for copyright infringement in respect to the user interface of the spreadsheet. *Held:* Ross's contributions to the interface of the program in the form of ideas or directions were insufficient to award him joint-authorship status for copyright purposes. The general rule is that a person must translate ideas into copyrightable expression to receive copyright protection as author of a work. The Ninth Circuit held that for joint authorship, each author must make an independently copyrightable contribution. Further, assuming that Ross had a one-half interest in the entire jointly authored MacCalc, this would be insufficient to make him a joint author of a derivative work. Ross may have a claim for compensation for use of the original joint work, but such claim sounded in equity, not copyright, and, in any event, would have to be brought against Wiggonton, not Ashton-Tate.

[Ashton-Tate Corp. v. Ross, 916 F2d 516 (9th Cir. 1990)]

Parties' conduct may implicitly authorize derivative work, even when contract states the contrary.   DSI provided training software that PCI marketed to various clients. The program was written in FORTRAN and designed to run on time-sharing mainframes maintained by DSI. A 1975 agreement composed by PCI provided that DSI "expressly disclaims any and all claims of ownership, proprietorship or partnership or other interest of any nature" in "new [simulation] products . . . that may be developed at any time in the future." In the 1980s, DSI created simulation software for microcomputers based on the prior FORTRAN source code. A pay dispute arose, and DSI copyrighted its microcomputer software and source code and brought suit for copyright infringement. PCI alleged ownership of the software based on the 1975 agreement and that, in any event, it was an unauthorized derivative work. *Held:* The parties' conduct showed that the software was treated as DSI's. The contract clause was not so broad as to cover the creation of microcomputer programs, a situation not contemplated or anticipated by the agreement. PCI turned over to DSI all license fees from the disputed software. Indeed, DSI billed some of PCI's clients directly for license fees, without objection from PCI. This was in contrast to the fees paid under the mainframe licenses, where DSI received "royalties." Further, the software did not constitute unauthorized use of PCI's preexisting materials. Again, PCI's conduct showed that it implicitly authorized and condoned them: When it became aware of the programs, it welcomed them, accepted them, and put them to profitable use.

[Dynamic Solutions, Inc. v. Planning & Control, 646 F. Supp. 1329 (SDNY 1986)]

[a] Coauthorship Based on Ideas and Intent

Authorship vests solely in the person who develops ideas, not in the person who merely suggests them. Geshwind, a producer, hired Digital to make a computer graphics animation based on a storyboard he provided. Digital worked closely with Geshwind to produce a suitable animation. Garrick exhibited a film that included the Digital animation without crediting Geshwind's contribution, although with Digital's permission. Geshwind filed a copyright registration for the film listing himself as author and then brought suit against Garrick for copyright infringement. *Held:* Digital as creator of the computer software data base and computer-animated film was the author and owner of the copyright here, not Geshwind. Digital's employee was like a painter who learned his techniques from other artists and teachers, while Geshwind was like the agent for the person whose portrait is painted. The fact that the agent "wanted changes in details and aspects of the portrait and even made suggestions, the compliance with which may or may not have improved the effect, does not make him the creator." Alternatively, Digital and Geshwind were joint authors. Since a joint author does not need the other's permission to use or license the work, and since the film was exhibited with Digital's permission, Geshwind's infringement claim was without merit.

[Geshwind v. Garrick, 734 F. Supp. 644 (SDNY 1990), aff'd, 927 F2d 594 (2d Cir. 1991)]

Supplier of an idea is no more the author of program than is the supplier of disk on which program is stored.   SOS provided accounting software services to Payday. Pursuant to a written agreement, the programs were SOS's property and all hardware and software were located at SOS's place of business; while Payday acquired the "right of use" of the programs, SOS retained "all rights of ownership" in the programs. Two former SOS employees pirated the software and installed it on Payday computers with the intention of translating it into a new computer language and revising programs so as not to infringe. SOS sued for copyright infringement; Payday maintained it was a licensee and joint author, based on contributions of its employee. *Held:* A person who merely describes to an author what the commissioned work should do or look like is not a joint author under the 1976 Copyright Act. Authorship is a question of fact. Payday's employee only told programmers what tasks the software was to perform and how it was to sort data; she did none of the coding and did not even understand computer language. "The supplier of an idea is no more the author of a program than is the supplier of the disk on which the program is stored." Further, a licensee may infringe the owner's copyright if its use exceeds the scope of its license. The license is construed in accordance with the purposes of copyright law, while state law canons of contractual construction are relevant to the extent they do not interfere with federal copyright law and policy. So construed, Payday's "right of use" in the contract did not refer to copyright. The provision that "SOS retains all ownership rights" clearly encompassed copyright ownership.

[SOS, Inc. v. Payday, Inc., 886 F2d 1081 (9th Cir. 1989)]

Mere ideas and suggestions are insufficient to justify coauthorship.   MGB sued Ameron for copying the floor plan of an MGB "Islander II" home from a copyrighted advertising flyer. *Held:* MGB could not sue for copyright infringement because it was not the owner of the copyright in the advertising flyer. In the absence of a contract stating that the drawings would be considered work for hire, MGB was not the author of the drawings under the work-for-hire doctrine. Under the work-for-hire doctrine of the 1976 Copyright Act, the author of the flyer was the drafting service that, acting as independent contractor, produced the flyer. MGB employees exercised insufficient control and direction over the finished product to make it a work for hire. Indeed, drafting was not part of the regular business of MGB, which always used an outside drafting firm. The language of 17 USC § 101(2) does not include "architectural drafting" as one of the activities that may be done by independent contractors as work for hire. Finally, MGB had no rights as a co-author of the plans because of the control and discretion it exercised over the content of the final product. Its employee's noncopyrightable contributions to the final drawings and the sketch it provided did not form an "inseparable or interdependent" part of them.

[MGB Homes, Inc. v. Ameron Homes, Inc., 903 F2d 1486 (11th Cir. 1990)]

¶ 4.05 JOINT VENTURE RELATIONSHIPS

[1] Joint Ownership

Joint ventures may exist in absence of formal contracts. IMCO entered into a "business relation" with three individuals to develop an optical scan system to read stenotype and translate it into English. After development of the prototype and two working models, the individuals left, taking certain property and equipment, and formed TSI. IMCO sought return of property through requesting a writ of replevin. TSI claimed that the equipment belonged to a joint venture and that an action for replevin would not lie against joint venturers. *Held:* In this case, no joint venture existed because, among other things, there was no agreement to share costs or risk of loss. A joint venture can exist even without a formal contract if the course of conduct of the parties establishes an implied contract to that effect. Further, the roles played by defendants and the manner in which they functioned was more characteristic of an employee or independent contractor relationships than joint venturer status. Another factor to be considered was that IMCO maintained exclusive control over funds for the project; no joint account was ever established and no funds were commingled.

[Institutional Management Corp. v. Translation Sys., Inc., 456 F. Supp. 661 (D. Md. 1978)]

[2] Collateral Research and Development

Competition is permitted between former partners in joint venture after end of project, absent indicia of bad faith or agreement to the contrary. Automated Systems developed software for an automobile parts inventory control system and entered into a sales agreement with IBM subsidiary, SBC, for a "test-sell period," during which SBC acquired the exclusive right, as Automated's agent, to market and sell the system. When the results of the test-sell period proved disappointing, SBC refused to extend it, and canceled the agreement. SBC, which had no prior knowledge of application of IBM systems to automobile parts distributors, went on to develop a rival system and obtained a contract to provide that system to Chevrolet, which it had contacted during the test-sell period. Automated sued SBC for wrongful use of trade secrets and business opportunity. *Held:* Subsequent competition by SBC was permissible since it had performed the sales agreement in good faith. Once the contract ended, SBC was free to compete. Chevrolet was no more a customer or business opportunity to Automated than SBC. In fact, Chevrolet rejected Automated's proposal presented after the end of the test-sell period. The information that SBC's employee gained about Automated's business during the sales effort was general information not protected by trade secret law. The system that SBC sold to Chevrolet differed substantially from the one that was the subject of the agreement, and thus SBC did not violate any of Automated's trade secrets. Contrary to Automated's assumptions, the contract did not contemplate the joint development of an inventory control system, but only a sales contract for a particular system then in existence.

[Automated Sys., Inc. v. Service Bureau Corp., 401 F2d 619 (10th Cir. 1968)]

[3] Preexisting Works

At outset of joint venture, partners must identify jointly developed work from other technology used.   A joint venture partnership was formed between a Bedford subsidiary with BEHR to finance Bedford's development of four new products. A clause in the contract provided that all new research and development prepared for the partnership would become partnership property. When Bedford filed for bankruptcy, BEHR filed for a declaratory judgment for title to "new" software developed during the period of funding. *Held:* Neither party attempted to establish any "baseline" to define the existing technology as of the closing date on the research and development contracts. Because of the way that Bedford operated and the vague language of the partnership agreement, it was impossible to determine what source code and object code embodied the old technology as opposed to the similar embodiment of the new technology. If the partnership had identified and segregated the relevant source and object codes, and given appropriate notice (e.g., filing a UCC financing statement) of its interest in the software, it would have been protected from the assertion of creditors' rights in any subsequent bankruptcy proceeding. But, failing to define its interest, the partnership must stand in line with its general claims along with the other unsecured creditors to the company.

[In re Bedford Computer Corp., 623 Bankr. 555 (Bankr. DNH 1986)]

At outset of joint venture, it is not generally known which element of a work will be incorporated in ongoing research or eventual product development.   Textron hired TOS to help design robots for mass production of industrial tools for TIGER technology. While there was no separate contractual document, Textron sent a letter to TOS stating that TOS would have rights to apply developed technology to "noncompetitive applications," namely, manipulator. TOS responded to that letter stating the costs of the project and did not object to the proprietary clause of the prior letter. TOS never stated it would claim rights to inventions or technology developed, while Textron paid TOS huge amounts in development and cost overruns. TOS prepared, without objection, designs on Textron drawing paper with a proprietary legend claiming all TIGER designs as property of Textron. When TOS announced it was claiming TIGER technology as its property and that it planned to file patent applications, Textron removed all designs and drawings in TOS's possession and canceled the contract. Two months later, TOS announced it would compete in fields of industrial robots. Textron sued for injunction. *Held:* There was a valid and enforceable contract between the parties with respect to the TIGER technology. TOS manifested its assent to Textron's offer by its silence in respect to the terms of the letter, coupled with its performance with the offer. The exchange of letters clearly stipulated that the technology developed would belong to Textron and that TOS would acquire only a nonexclusive license to use it in noncompetitive applications. However, the agreement only contemplated application to technology developed under the TIGER contract. Thus, TOS technology developed *before* the agreement, in the absence of a document initialed by both sides, belongs to TOS. This is true because TOS's conduct during the agreement was not such as to constitute acquiescence to that prior technology belonging to Textron. Finally, Textron was entitled to injunctive relief with respect to the technology developed under the contract.

[Textron, Inc. v. TeleOperator Sys. Corp., 554 F. Supp. 315 (EDNY 1983)]

Copyright may be transferred either by written conveyance or operation of law. Bates had his own software company, Knowledge Engineering (KE), but was in need of capital. Bates formed a close corporation with Brooks called KEI, where Brooks supplied capital, while Bates supplied computer expertise. Brooks copyrighted software in the name of KEI listing Bates as the author. Brooks then brought a derivative shareholder suit (he owned 49 percent of the stock) against Bates for marketing the KEI software on behalf of his old company KE to KEI's customers, in violation of his fiduciary obligation to KEI and infringement of KEI's copyrighted software. Bates moved for dismissal, claiming Brooks had fraudulently registered the software in KEI's name. *Held:* There is nothing in the record to support a finding that Bates transferred his copyrights to Brooks or KEI by a written instrument or by operation of law. The Copyright Act of 1976 (17 USC § 204(a)) clearly states that there can be no transfer of copyright ownership except pursuant to a written instrument unless there is a transfer by operation of law. Transfers of copyright by operation of law are limited in number and depend on circumstances that establish the author's express or implied consent. While the parties negotiated, they were unable to reach any agreement about transfer of copyrights. Bates's conduct in placing copyright notices on his software in the name of his old company, KE, taken in conjunction with formation of the new corporation with a similar name, KEI, fell well short of constituting a transfer of Bates's copyrights to the new corporation, KEI. This was not a case of a corporate owner of a copyright merging with another or dissolving so that its copyrights pass to the corporations' shareholders by operation of law. Rather, it was a case of two individuals negotiating with each other, agreeing and then disagreeing in circumstances that cannot be said to give rise to a transfer of copyrights by operation of law.

[Brooks v. Bates, 781 F. Supp. 202 (SDNY 1991)]

¶ 4.06 CONTRACTORS AND CONSULTANTS

[1] Works for Hire and Commissioned Works

Copyrighted works prepared under contract generally remain property of independent contractor rather than employer or hiring party.   CCNV hired Reid to make a sculpture depicting homeless people in a Nativity scene. Reid agreed to sculpt three figures while CCNV provided a metal grating for the pedestal. CCNV paid Reid for the materials used, while Reid agreed to donate his services. There was no written contract or agreement as to copyright. After a dispute, Reid filed for copyright. CCNV filed a competing copyright registration claiming it was a "work made for hire" under 17 USC § 101. *Held:* There was no employment relationship here; the copyright belonged to Reid. Copyright law distinguishes between works by employees and works by independent contractors. In determining whether a work is for hire under the Copyright Act, a court first should ascertain using principles of general common law of agency whether the work was prepared by an employee or an independent contractor. In making such a determination, it is crucial to examine the hiring party's right to control the manner and means by which the product is accomplished. Other relevant factors include the skill required, source of instrumentalities and tools, work's location, duration of the relationship between the parties, hiring party's right to assign additional projects to the hiree, method of payment, payment of employee benefits, tax treatment of the hired party, and the like. Here, although CCNV gave Reid direction as to the sculpture's specifications, other factors weighed heavily against finding an employment relationship: Reid's skill as a sculptor; Reid supplied his own tools; Reid's work was not supervised by CCNV; Reid only worked for two months; CCNV had no right to assign Reid additional projects; apart from the deadline, Reid decided how and when to work. CCNV was not in the business of creating sculptures and it did not pay Reid any employment benefits such as Social Security or workmen's compensation. CCNV may, however, be a joint author if CCNV and Reid prepared the work with the intention that their contributions be merged into a unitary whole (17 USC § 101).

[Community for Creative Non-Violence v. Reid, 490 US 730 (1989)]

Payment of Social Security taxes and benefits is of crucial importance in determining worker's status as employee or independent contractor for copyright purposes.   Bonelli hired Aymes to work as a computer programmer. Under the direction of Bonelli, who was not a programmer, Aymes created CSALIB, an accounting and inventory software. Aymes left after a dispute over time and wages; Bonelli insisted that Aymes sign a release of his rights to CSALIB, but Aymes refused. Aymes subsequently obtained a copyright for CSALIB in his own name, and sued Bonelli for infringement, in using the program in multiple locations, and for back pay. *Held:* Aymes was entitled to the copyright. Applying the "work-for-hire" test articulated in *CCNV v. Reid*, 490 U.S. 730 (1989), a court must weigh the various *Reid* factors according to their significance in the case and not apply them in a wooden manner. Of primary importance are (1) the hiring party's right to control the manner and means of creation, (2) the skill required, (3) the provision of employee benefits, (4) the tax treatment of the hired party, and (5) whether the hiring party has the right to assign additional projects to the hired party. While the first factor weighs in Bonelli's favor, the other factors tip the balance in favor of Aymes. Aymes was a highly skilled programmer. Bonelli did not provide him with any benefits nor did he pay Aymes's Social Security taxes. This is highly significant because every case since *Reid* that has applied the test has found the hired party to be an independent contractor where the hiring party failed to extend benefits or pay Social Security taxes. A company cannot treat a worker as an independent contractor when it is financially beneficial, and then claim that the worker was its employee when such treatment is no longer to its benefit. It must adhere to its original choice. Therefore, Aymes was entitled to the copyright. It was not disputed, however, that Aymes sold the program to Bonelli, and that he therefore had a clear right to use that program within his company (and, by implication, at multiple locations within the company, absent a written agreement to the contrary), although it remains to be determined whether Bonelli made unlicensed derivatives of the program for external corporations. Finally, the issue remains whether Bonelli was a "joint owner" of the program because of his contribution to its creation.

[Aymes v. Bonelli, 980 F2d 857 (2d Cir. 1992)]

Agency principles regarding apparent authority may be inapplicable in determining copyright ownership under work-for-hire rules. MacLean was a highly paid employee of MMH. As part of his duties, he directed a study on designing a job evaluation system for the New York Stock Exchange (NYSE). After he left MMH in 1985, he formed his own company but continued providing the same services to the NYSE on MMH's behalf without alerting it that he was no longer employed by MMH. In 1986, MacLean wrote a job evaluation software program (JEMSystem) for NYSE on his own using his own equipment. He delivered the equipment to NYSE with a note on MMH stationery stating "we've written" to administer your system. In 1987, MacLean gave copies of JEMSystem to MMH employees for the purpose of transferring data from the MMH mainframe to NYSE's data base. Later, MacLean learned that MMH had incorporated his software into its own competing CompMaster program. MacLean obtained a copyright registration and brought suit against MMH for infringement. The district court granted MMH a directed verdict on the grounds that MMH owned the system as a work for hire, that it had an implied license to use it, and that the claims were barred by laches. *Held:* MacLean owned the copyright. First, a consideration of the nine factors articulated in *CCNV v. Reid*, 490 U.S. 730 (1989), could lead a reasonable jury to conclude that MacLean was not an actual servant of MMH when JEMSystem was created. MacLean worked on the NYSE project for a brief period before leaving MMH. MacLean was a skilled worker, working with his own software at his own company facility; he had absolute discretion over when and how long to work. MMH paid him as a consultant and did not pay his Social Security taxes or provide any benefits such as worker's compensation or health insurance. Further, MacLean's "apparent agency" could not create an employment relationship for copyright purposes. The work-for-hire doctrine focuses on the relationship between the alleged employer and employee. Here, MacLean and MMH knew the status of their relationship; any apparent employment relationship perceived by third parties was immaterial. Second, MMH had a nonexclusive implied license to use the program to service its client, NYSE. MacLean's delivery of a copy of the software to MMH employees did not constitute a conveyance of any rights in the copyrighted work embodied in the object. However absent a written contract to the contrary, MMH did not have the right to exploit the software beyond the scope of the implied license and incorporate it into its own competitive software. Finally, the facts did not establish the existence of laches on MacLean's part.

[MacLean Assocs., Inc. v. William M. Mercer-Meidinger-Hanson, Inc., 952 F2d 769 (3d Cir. 1991)]

Issues of credibility may determine employee's status as independent contractor or employee.   Graham, a CD-ROM disk publisher, hired James to cure deficiencies and add certain features to a file-retrieval program in "Quickbasic" that Graham had authored with someone else. James denied using a preexisting program, and maintained he started from scratch. Graham published the disk in 1991, acknowledging the contributions of all three programmers. Later, James informed Graham that he knew "C" language and could write the program in C language. Graham bought copies of the program and James worked on it at Graham's place of business. James included a copyright notice naming himself as the author of the program. James worked for Graham during September 1991, but when he refused to remove the copyright notice from the disk, Graham fired him. After leaving Graham, James began to distribute the retrieval program under his own name. Graham then sought a preliminary injunction against James, claiming copyright infringement. *Held:* Graham was entitled to an injunction since the balance of hardships tipped in his favor. The risk of damage to his competitive edge in the CD-ROM publishing business outweighed any loss James might suffer if barred from commencing distribution of the program on his own. As far as the merits of the case, Graham had to show that he owned a valid copyright and that James engaged in unauthorized copying. The central question as to copyright ownership turned largely on the credibility determination of whether Graham was a paid employee charged with writing the retrieval program or an independent contractor who accepted license fees from Graham for allowing him to use the program.

[Graham v. James, 1992 WESTLAW 10844, Copy. L. Rep. (CCH) ¶ 26,892 (WDNY 1992)]

[2] Contracts and Property Rights

In an infringement action, it is a valid defense to assert that plaintiff does not own work that is the basis of the suit. Koontz wrote a manual containing a compilation of data for estimating bids for electrical construction contracts. In 1976, Koontz entered into an agreement with HP where HP would develop a computerized version of his system while Koontz would supply the manuals to be used in conjunction with the program. The program contained significant portions of the data compilations from Koontz's 1975 copyrighted manual. When the product did not sell, HP and Koontz terminated their relationship. Koontz later updated the program. When two former employees formed a competitive company, copied the HP software, and used its information to write a competing manual, Koontz sued for copyright infringement. Defendants claimed that Koontz's assertion of copyright in the data compilation contained in the software was invalid since it was transferred under the 1976 agreement with HP, and since it lacked a copyright notice. *Held:* The evidence indicated that Koontz did not transfer his rights in the data compilation contained in the software to HP. Further, the absence of a copyright notice affixed to the software did not invalidate Koontz's copyright, since under the "unit publication doctrine," affixing the copyright notice to one element of a publication containing various elements gives copyright protection to all elements of the publication.

[Koontz v. Jaffarian, 787 F2d 906 (4th Cir. 1986)]

Express contract terms determine ownership in works developed under contract. A software developer sold TR a software program. The sales contract granted the developer the right to use "the non-application-specific libraries and routines" specified in an attached schedule, which included pull-down screens and menu bars. Later, the developer sold another similar program to SC that used pull-down screens and menu bars. TR sued SC for copyright infringement, claiming SC's program was substantially similar and that its visual screens infringed on the "look and feel" of TR's program. *Held:* There was no infringement here. The use of menu bars, pull-down windows, and the color scheme of the programs were unprotectable features under the copyright laws or were licensed to developer pursuant to the written contract. Although TR owned the program, the developer maintained ownership and control of the elements specified in the agreement.

[Telemarketing Resources v. Semantec Corp., 12 USPQ2d 1991 (ND Cal. 1989), aff'd in part 1992 WESTLAW 67204 (9th Cir. 1992)]

Under the terms of Copyright Act of 1909, no transfer of copyright ownership of works of art is found where evidence fails to show oral agreement to transfer or conduct implying transfer; moreover, no transfer of ownership is found under Copyright Act of 1976 based on legend-endorsement found on checks issued to

artist by magazine.   Playboy Enterprises, Inc., and its subsidiary, Special Editions Ltd. (SEL), brought a declaratory judgment action against the artist's widow (Dumas) and her corporation (JDI) seeking a declaratory judgment that Playboy was the sole owner of all right, title, and interest in all copyrights of works of art created by the artist that appeared in Playboy's magazine. Playboy and SEL claimed that the copyrights in question were transferred to Playboy, or in the alternative, that the works were "works made for hire," thereby giving Playboy the copyrights outright. Dumas and JDI counterclaimed, alleging, among other things, copyright infringement. *Held:* Playboy and SEL's claim for declaratory judgment was dismissed; Dumas and JDI's counterclaim for infringement was granted, with an award of $42,357.95 for profits Playboy and SEL gained from their infringing activities. Because the works in question were created between 1974 and 1984, the court reviewed theories of ownership under the Copyright Act of 1909 (1909 Act) and the Copyright Act of 1976 (1976 Act). Under the 1909 Act, the transfer of the common-law copyright could be oral or inferred from conduct. Based on expert testimony as to industry practice, the prices paid for the works by Playboy, the lack of proof of any oral agreements, and Playboy's lack of evidence of any underlying oral negotiations with the artist, the court found that only one-time rights were transferred to Playboy in the paintings created prior to 1978. Moreover, pre-1978 California law provided that when a work of fine art was transferred, the right of reproduction was reserved to the artist unless the right was expressly transferred by a document in writing. Because the legend-endorsement stamped on the back of checks issued to the artist, which read "PAYEE AC-KNOWLEDGES PAYMENT IN FULL FOR THE ASSIGNMENT TO PLAYBOY ENTERPRISES, INC. OF ALL RIGHT, TITLE, AND INTEREST IN AND TO THE FOLLOWING ITEMS . . . ," failed to specify rights of reproduction that were to be transferred with the alleged transfer of ownership of the artist's works of art, those transfers were invalid under California law. The court found that the legend was insufficient, by itself, to transfer copyright ownership of the artist's works under the 1976 Act. Moreover, two other legend-endorsements used on checks issued to the artist, which referred to "work-made-for-hire", were also insufficient to transfer copyright ownership of the artist's works under the 1976 Act. Finally, the court found that under both the 1909 Act and the 1976 Act no "work made for hire" relationship actually existed between Playboy and the artist; therefore, Playboy and SEL could not claim ownership in the artist's works based on this theory.

[Playboy Enters., Inc. v. Dumas, 834 F. Supp. 295 (SDNY 1993)]

Title to copyright in computer program does not pass because agreement was rescinded.   BBS, a software marketer, contracted with Amica, a software developer, to sell its PCH software. While BBS represented itself as a viable and solvent company capable of actively and aggressively promoting PCH, it was in fact neither financially sound nor solvent at the time of the negotiations, nor did it have a sales department, as alleged. Relying on these material misrepresentations on the part of

BBS, Amica discontinued marketing its PCH software for several months. BBS also breached its warranty to use best efforts to market PCH and related products. BBS requested and agreed to pay for certain modifications to the PCH software. Although Amica sent BBS several modified versions, BBS refused to accept them, and never paid for modifications. The final version of the modified software was never shipped because Amica grew anxious because of prior defaults by BBS. When BBS fell farther behind in its payments, Amica offered to return funds paid if BBS would rescind the agreement, but BBS refused. To mitigate damages, Amica later canceled the contract and resumed selling its PCH software. BBS's assignee sued for breach of contract and copyright infringement, pointing to the agreement, which stated that Amica "irrevocably transfers to BBS all its rights, title and interest to the *program* and *its* documentation including copyright in the programs. . . ." *Held:* Amica was entitled to maintain its copyright. Applying principles of contract interpretation and in light of the evidence, it was clear that the parties did not intend for title to pass before Amica completed modifications of the PCH program that were accepted and paid for by BBS. The modifications were materially completed but BBS never accepted or paid for them. BBS failed to make substantial payments due under the contract, and admitted inability to do so. Before title to the program or any part of it ever passed, Amica rescinded the agreement, as was its right under California law. Because of its timely rescission, title would belong to Amica even were it found that title had passed on the signing of the agreement; in that case, title would have reverted back to Amica by virtue of its lawful cancellation of the contract. Title, in addition, could not pass prior to delivery. In light of the material misrepresentations, bad faith, and breaches of BBS, Amica was entitled to maintain its copyright. The agreement, drafted by BBS, was ambiguous; the term "program" was not defined. California UCC applied to the interpretation of this contract since computer programs are goods. Goods must both exist and be identified before any interest in them can pass; goods that are not identified or nonexistent are "future" goods. The purported present sale of any interest in future goods operates as a contract to sell.

[In re Amica, 135 BR 534 (Bankr. ND Ill. 1992)]

Implied license cannot imply conveyance of ownership rights in computer program. EMS, a metal repair company, hired Professor McPhate as a consultant on one of its jobs in 1972. McPhate wrote a computer (engine analysis) program to solve the problem, based on public domain software. Although he continued providing consulting services to EMS until 1977, he never signed an employment contract or confidentiality agreement. EMS claimed the program as its own because it had hired McPhate to perform a specific task. McPhate claimed that the program was his, since he never billed them for the software, but only for the use of the software. McPhate always retained physical possession of the program and never wrote a manual for the program. Without such a manual, the program was useless to EMS. *Held:* Despite the absence of an agreement between EMS and McPhate concerning ownership of the program, the evidence clearly established McPhate did not intend to vest ownership of the program in EMS. That McPhate did not sign a confidentiality agreement was of lesser import than the conduct of McPhate with respect to the program. Even in the absence of a restrictive covenant not to disclose confidential information, trade secrets will be protected where a confidential relationship exists.

[Engineered Mechanical Servs. v. Langlois, 464 So. 2d 329 (La. Ct. App. 1984)]

Express contract terms are determinative of ownership in works developed under contract. SCC bought an IBM computer and hired Shauers to develop appropriate software. SCC entered into a written agreement with Shauers that stated that Shauers was not required to keep confidential any ideas, concepts, or techniques developed in the course of the agreement. It also stated that the programs could not be assigned or otherwise transferred without Shauers's prior written consent. Later, SCC filed a complaint seeking a declaratory judgment that, under the contract, it had the sole proprietary right of ownership in the software as a work for hire. *Held:* In view of the explicit terms requiring Shauers's prior written consent to transfer the programs, the only question here was whether the written agreement was orally waived or modified by subsequent sales assented to by Shauers without her written consent. There are three aspects of ownership rights. First, the work-for-hire doctrine does not determine ownership rights to the physical objects in which the computer programs are embodied. Although not specifically stated in the contract, the material object embodying the programs was owned by SCC, the hiring party, since the contract was both for services and sale. Second, Shauers reserved the ownership rights to use the ideas and concepts incorporated in the program. Finally, there was the ownership right to transfer the programs.

[Shauers v. Sweetwater County Comm'rs, 746 P2d 444 (Wyo. 1987)]

¶ 4.07 END-USER MODIFICATIONS

Reverse engineering insulates an end user from trade secret liability, but not copyright or patent liability. Bonito developed a highly successful but unpatented fiberglass boat. TCB manufactured a duplicate vessel in violation of a Florida statute. Bonito sued for damages under the Florida statute. TCB contended that the Florida statute was invalid under the supremacy clause. *Held:* The Florida statute was invalid. Federal patent law reflects a balance between the need to encourage innovation and to avoid monopolies that stifle competition. To a limited extent, federal patent laws must determine both what is protected and what is free for all to use. Trade secret law is not incompatible with patent law since the public remains free to exploit the trade secret through reverse engineering or independent creation. Congressional control over patent and copyright does not deprive the states of the power to adopt rules to promote intellectual creation within their own jurisdiction, as long as they do not impermissibly interfere with the federal scheme. Here, the Florida statute impeded the public use of otherwise unprotected design and utilitarian ideas embodied in an unpatented, and now, unpatentable boat by offering Bonito patent-like state law protection. The statute conflicts with the strong federal policy favoring free competition in ideas that do not merit patent protection.

[Bonito Boats v. Thunder Craft Boats, 489 US 141 (1989)]

PART C.   ANTITRUST LAW AND INNOVATION

¶ 4.08 SINGLE PRODUCT AND PRICE INNOVATION

[1] Predatory Pricing

To prevail in antitrust action, plaintiff must prove that rival is likely to recoup the costs of its predatory behavior.   Liggett (the Brook Group) pioneered sale of generic cigarettes. Liggett brought suit against BWT, charging it engaged in predatory pricing by selling generic cigarettes below cost. Liggett claimed it was being squeezed by BWT offering, prior to selling a single generic cigarette, discriminatory volume rebates to wholesalers to force Liggett to raise its own prices (to enable it to match the rebates without cutting profits), thus diminishing the list-price gap between generic and name-brand cigarettes. The alleged object of this scheme was to eliminate competition from generic cigarettes, which at the time represented 4 percent of the cigarette market. *Held:* Liggett was unable to prove that BWT had a reasonable prospect of recovering its losses from below-cost pricing. A plaintiff seeking to establish competitive injury resulting from a rival's low prices must prove two things: first, that "the prices complained of are below an appropriate measure of its rival's costs" and, second, that the competitor had a reasonable prospect, or that there was a "dangerous probability," of recouping its investment in below-cost prices. Recoupment, the ultimate object of an unlawful predatory pricing scheme, is the means by which a predator profits from predation. Without it, predatory pricing produces lower prices, and thus enhances consumer welfare. That below-cost pricing may inflict painful losses on its target is irrelevant if *competition* is not injured; antitrust laws were passed to protect competition, not competitors. For recoupment to occur, the below-cost pricing must be capable of producing the intended effects on the firm's rivals. The threshold inquiry turns on whether, given the aggregate of losses caused by the predatory pricing, the rival would likely succumb. If circumstances indicate the latter to be the case, the plaintiff must prove that the predatory scheme alleged would cause a rise in prices sufficient to compensate for the amounts expended on the predation. A determination of likelihood of recoupment requires an estimate of the cost of the alleged predation and a close analysis of both the scheme alleged by the plaintiff and the structure and conditions of the relevant market. While difficult to establish, the preceding factors are prerequisites to recovery since they are the essential components of real market injury.

[Brook Group, Ltd. v. Brown & Williamson Tobacco Corp., 113 S. Ct. 2578 (1993)]

Predatory pricing conspiracy is by nature highly speculative. Zenith and other U.S. firms brought suit against Japanese manufacturers of consumer electronics products (CEPs) on the theory that they illegally conspired to drive U.S. firms from the CEP market. The gist of the scheme was to charge artificially high prices for CEPs sold by them in Japan, while at the same time fixing and maintaining low prices for CEPs sold in the United States. This pricing conspiracy allegedly produced substantial losses for the Japanese firms. The Japanese did set minimum prices for CEPs and did agree among themselves to sell their products through five U.S. distributors but claimed they were compelled to do so by the Japanese Ministry of International Trade & Industry (MITI), and that they were therefore not liable. *Held:* Zenith was unable to show it suffered an antitrust injury from the Japanese companies' (1) pricing below the level necessary to sell their products or (2) pricing below some appropriate measure of cost. The evidence indicated rather that the conspiracy was to raise prices, not lower them. That result would not help Zenith; for, although it would violate the Sherman Anti-Trust Act, Zenith would stand to benefit from such a conspiracy. A predatory pricing conspiracy is by nature speculative, since the agreement to price below the competitive level requires the conspirators to forgo profits in the hope of recouping losses in the form of later and greater monopoly profits. The success of such schemes is inherently uncertain because the short-term loss is definite and the long-term gain is indefinite, dependent on successfully neutralizing the competition and maintaining monopoly power long enough to harvest the profits. Predatory pricing conspiracies are generally unlikely to occur and the alleged conspiracy's failure to succeed in more than 20 years of operation is strong evidence that the conspiracy does not in fact exist.

[Matsushita Elec. Indus. Co. v. Zenith Radio Corp., 475 US 574 (1986)]

¶ 4.09 INTEGRATED SYSTEMS INNOVATION

[1] Integrated Product Superiority

In antitrust cases, the market determines product superiority, not the technical experts, but joint ventures involving monopolies have sufficient anticompetitive potential that they must be scrutinized closely. Berkey Photo sold cameras and Kodak film to its customers, as well as provided them with photofinishing services. It also bought other supplies and equipment from Kodak. Berkey charged that a Kodak conspiracy with flash lamp manufacturers caused it to lose sales in the camera and photofinishing markets and to pay excessive prices for Kodak film and equipment. It also charged that Kodak introduced the Kodak 110 camera along with Kodacolor II film in order to cut into Berkey's sale of cameras, since Kodacolor X film in 110-size cartridges would have done just as well. Berkey introduced the testimony of two Kodak technicians, who testified that Kodacolor X film would produce "satisfactory pictures, satisfactory customer results." *Held:* Kodak did not violate Section 2 of the Sherman Anti-Trust Act. Kodak was under no obligation to predisclose information of its new film and format to its competitors. The attempt to develop superior products is an essential element of lawful competition. Thus, Kodak did not violate antitrust law merely by introducing the 110 product with an improved film. There was considerable technical evidence that Kodacolor II film was inferior to its predecessor in several respects; however, it was not disputed that the "grain" of Kodacolor II was superior. In the context of antitrust law, the question of product quality has little meaning. A product that commends itself to some users because of certain superiorities may be rendered unsatisfactory to others by flaws they consider fatal. No one person is the arbiter of superiority, since preference is a matter of individual taste. The only question that can be answered with any certainty is whether there is sufficient demand for a particular product to justify its production; the answer is supplied by the reaction of the market. Further, Berkey was not able to show injury in fact. However, there is merit to the charge that Kodak colluded with the flash-bulb makers, in violation of Section 1 of the Sherman Act. There is a vast difference between what a monopolist can do with the power that it has acquired legally in respect to charging any nonpredatory price and what competitors may conspire to do to raise prices. Joint ventures involving a monopolist must be scrutinized with care lest they fortify barriers already in place. Here, Kodak agreed to a joint venture with Sylvania to develop its Magicube flash bulb with Kodak cameras. Over Sylvania's protests, Kodak insisted that details of the new device be withheld from the public. When GE came to Kodak with a proposed piezoelectric crystal flash, Kodak put GE off temporarily, not wishing to introduce two new flash systems at approximately the same time. After discussions over the course of three years, Kodak agreed to market the bulb for its camera, and again extracted a secrecy agreement to prevent disclosure to other lamp and camera manufacturers before the new camera was marketed. The camera appeared on the market more than two years later. While GE and Kodak were not direct competitors, and Kodak and Sylvania were only potential competitors, because of Kodak's market power over cameras, it effectively excluded the development of competing joint ventures. In effect, Kodak delayed without any technological justification the introduction of GE's desirable improvements into the marketplace for two years solely to suit Kodak's convenience. GE and Sylvania were unlikely to go to other camera manufacturers that lacked independent development potential. The alternative to joint development with Kodak was no development.

[Berkey Photo, Inc. v. Eastman Kodak Co., 603 F2d 263 (2d Cir. 1979)]

Introduction of new superior product is free of antitrust liability. Telex brought suit against IBM, charging it with antitrust violations. Telex manufactured IBM-compatible computer peripherals. But, IBM assumed an aggressive posture to drive Telex out of business through a strategy of price cuts, marketing format changes (fixed and extended-term leasing), and CPU design changes to control the compatible peripherals market. *Held:* The record clearly demonstrates that rather than behaving in a predatory manner, IBM engaged in the type of competition prevalent throughout the industry. The use of monopoly power to control prices or to exclude competition violates antitrust laws. But, not all monopoly power is unlawful or must be involuntarily acquired to be licit. Such a holding would require a competitor to stand idly watching its market share, acquired by dint of research and technical innovations, eroded by competitors that market copies of its products. The Sherman Anti-Trust Ac⁺ was not legislated to inhibit or penalize technical attainments, or to prohibit the adoption of legal and ordinary marketing methods already current in the marketplace, or to prohibit price changes, however reasonable. To interpret it otherwise would amount to outlawing ordinary competition.

[Telex Corp. v. IBM, 510 F2d 894 (10th Cir. 1975)]

CHAPTER 5

INTERNATIONAL INTELLECTUAL PROPERTY ISSUES [RESERVED]

PART II

TRANSACTIONS AND THIRD-PARTY LIABILITY

CHAPTER **6**

COMPUTER AND SYSTEMS SALES CONTRACTS

¶ 6.01 NATURE OF TRANSACTION

Where mixed contract is predominantly for management and computer consulting services, UCC does not apply.   Faberge, Inc., and Ernst & Young (E&Y) had a computer management consulting agreement, which Faberge subsequently assigned to Conopco's parent, Unilever United States. Faberge previously had acquired Arden from Eli Lilly and Company; E&Y had been retained by Faberge to migrate Arden off Lilly's system. Conopco sued the partners of E&Y, alleging, among other things, breach of implied warranty of fitness for use under the UCC. Conopco claimed that E&Y provided the Arden computer system to Faberge in a condition that breached the implied warranty of fitness for the purpose for which it was intended. This claim relied on Section 2-315 of the UCC, codified in New Jersey at N.J. Stat. Ann. § 12A:2-315. Conopco claimed that E&Y agreed to assume responsibility for delivering the entire Arden computer system, and that this was the "good" that brought the transaction within the ambit of the UCC. E&Y moved for summary judgment, arguing that the transaction did not involve goods and that, even if it did, there was no sale. Therefore, E&Y argued, its engagement was not governed by the UCC. *Held:*   The contract entered into by the parties was predominantly one for services, and therefore the UCC did not apply. Section 2-102 of the UCC provides that "Unless the context otherwise requires, this chapter applies to transactions in goods. . . ." The contract between Faberge and E&Y was a mixed goods and services contract. To determine whether goods or services predominate, the court must look to the "essence" or purpose of the contract. In the written and oral agreements, E&Y did not agree to sell or provide any computer hardware or accessories to Faberge. The agreement between

Faberge and E&Y was not one for a turnkey computer system. Moreover, E&Y was not compensated on the basis of goods provided, but rather on the basis of professional services rendered. Faberge did not pay separately for any of the customized software produced by E&Y employees or by contract programmers under the supervision of E&Y. The contract was one for management and computer consulting services, pure and simple, with all of the hardware bought from another company, and most of the software purchased from a computer software vendor.

[Conopco, Inc. v. McCreadie, 826 F. Supp. 855 (DNJ 1993)]

Where contract's predominant factor is a transaction of sale, with labor incidentally involved, UCC applies. Design Data brought action against Maryland Casualty seeking recovery under a commercial policy for damages to computer equipment that occurred during the shipment of the equipment to Design Data's customer. On appeal, Maryland Casualty contended, among other things, that the lower court erred in finding that Design Data had an insurable interest in the computer equipment at the time the damage was discovered. In determining this question, the Nebraska Supreme Court examined whether the transaction was covered by the Nebraska Commercial Code, because the transaction was a mixed contract involving the performance of services and the sale of goods. *Held:* The sale of goods was the predominant factor in the contract; therefore, the provisions of the Nebraska UCC applied to the contract. The test for inclusion in or exclusion from the sales provisions is not whether a contract is mixed; but, granting it is mixed, whether the predominant factor is the rendition of service, with goods incidentally involved, or whether it is a transaction of sale, with labor incidentally involved. Here, the hardware and software, sold as a bundled unit, were the essential terms of the sale. The installation and training, which were also included in the purchase price, were incidental to the sale.

[Design Data Corp. v. Maryland Casualty Co., 503 NW2d 552 (Neb. 1993)]

[1] Goods or Services

Mixed contract for wastewater treatment system involving both the sale of goods and installation services is governed by UCC despite long installation period. The purchaser of a wastewater treatment system brought suit against the seller, alleging, among other things, breach of contract. The purchaser argued that the UCC and its statute of limitations did not apply to this case because the equipment purchased did not meet the UCC's definition of goods. The UCC defines "goods" as "all things . . . which are movable at the time of identification to the contract for sale. . . ." The purchaser argued that the enormous size of the wastewater treatment system and its integration into the manufacturing facility itself precluded its treatment as a good under the UCC. *Held:* The court held that the wastewater treatment system was a good under the UCC. Here, the court noted that the proposal listed 88 separate items to be provided by the seller; those items were moveable at the time of identification to the contract of sale. Additionally, the court noted that the fact that the contract also called for installation services did not preclude applying the UCC. Mixed contracts involving the sale of goods and services are, the court stated, generally governed by the UCC.

[Cambridge Plating Co. v. Napco, Inc., 991 F2d 21 (1st Cir. 1993)]

Where contract's main objective is to transfer "products" under the "predominant purpose" standard, transaction to provide software, hardware, sales, marketing, and technical components relating to a document management system falls within scope of Pennsylvania UCC.   A computer software producer brought an action against a computer manufacturer, alleging (1) fraud, (2) breach of contract, and (3) wrongful interference with contractual relations. The jury found for the manufacturer on the fraud count, but awarded damages to the software producer on the breach-of-contract and wrongful interference claims. The district court granted judgment n.o.v. to the manufacturer on the interference claim, but did not disturb the jury's decision awarding damages for breach of contract. The court determined that the services provisions in the contract predominated, and thus the arrangement was not one primarily for the sale of goods governed by the UCC. Both parties appealed. *Held:*   Computer software is a "good" within the meaning of Pennsylvania's version of the UCC. The court of appeals determined that computer programs—while the product of an intellectual process—are goods rather than intellectual property. The court noted that while a computer program may be copyrightable as intellectual property, it does not change the fact that once that same program is in the form of a floppy disk or other medium the program is tangible, moveable, and available in the marketplace. Thus, the UCC applies to computer programs rather than common law. Where, as here, the contract calls for the sale of goods and services, the applicability of the UCC depends on an examination of the predominance of goods or services called for by the contract. In this case, the parties contemplated the sale of computer hardware and software—both goods within Pennsylvania's version of the UCC—and services by various technical and marketing personnel. Because the projected sales figures showed that the sale of goods clearly predominated over the sale of services, the UCC applied to the contract as a whole under the "predominant purpose" rule.

[Advent Sys. Ltd. v. Unisys Corp., 925 F2d 670 (3d Cir. 1991)]

Contract providing for software and data-processing development, as well as modification services, is a "good" pursuant to UCC under New Hampshire law. Colonial Life entered into a contract with Electronic Data Systems for the license of computer software and data-processing services. Furthermore, Electronic Data contracted to provide Colonial with four years of customization to fit the system to Colonial's particular needs. At the end of the modification period, Electronic Data was to grant Colonial a license to use the software. Electronic Data and Colonial entered into subsequent letter agreements stemming from their inability to adhere to the original contractual obligations. Electronic Data never delivered a fully functional product to Colonial. *Held:* The court found that the UCC was applicable to this contract. In its analysis, the court noted that a contract for computer data-processing services is neither a contract solely for services nor a contract entirely for the sale of goods. Whether the UCC applied to the contract depended on the predominant purpose of the contract. Here, the court reasoned that—despite the contemplated years of service support in the contract—the main purpose or thrust of the contract was for the software product (called the Insurance Machine by the parties). Furthermore, the court noted that under New Hampshire's version of the UCC, the UCC is applicable to any "transaction in goods," and not limited solely to sales of goods. Thus, the licensing agreement fell within the ambit of the UCC.

[Colonial Life Ins. v. Electronic Data Sys. Corp., 817 F. Supp. 235 (DNH 1993)]

Contract to develop and beta-test software is treated as services contract. The plaintiff brought an action alleging breach of an oral contract to develop a computer software accounting and business package tailored specifically for the defendant's distributors and franchisees. Furthermore, the plaintiff alleged that he had performed all of his obligations pursuant to the oral contract. The defendant filed a motion to dismiss the complaint because, among other things, the contract was not enforceable under the Illinois statute of frauds. The court and the parties did not deal specifically with the issue of whether the sale of the software was potentially a sale of goods under the UCC; instead, the court's analysis dealt with the Illinois general statute of fraud. *Held:* The plaintiff's full performance of his obligations under the contract precluded the application of the statute of frauds. The court noted that it is well settled that complete performance on the part of one of the parties to an oral agreement bars application of the statute of frauds.

[Noesges v. Servicemaster Co., 598 NE2d 437 (Ill. App. Ct. 2d Dist. 1992)]

Contract for sale of customized microprocessors is treated as contract for the sale of services, and not as sale of goods governed by UCC. Teletron contracted with TI for the manufacture and sale of customized microprocessors to be used in computerized energy management systems. TI failed to timely deliver the microprocessors, and Teletron lost distributors, credibility, and the chance to market its energy management system. The court analyzed the contract as one for sale of services, and not as a sale of goods. On appeal, Teletron sought the reinstatement of the jury's award of lost profits and additional damages under the Texas Deceptive Trade Practices Act, or, alternatively, a new trial. *Held:* The court affirmed a jury verdict finding that TI was not grossly negligent in failing to produce the microprocessors. Also, the court reinstated the jury's award of lost profits, plus prejudgment and postjudgment interest.

[Teletron Energy Management, Inc. v. Texas Instruments Inc., 838 SW2d 305 (Tex. Ct. App., Houston 14th Dist. 1992)]

[2] Tangibles or Intangibles

Whether software will be governed by product liability law could potentially depend on whether the software is considered an intangible or tangible item. Mushroom enthusiasts picked, cooked, and ate mushrooms after relying on information contained in a book. They became severely ill and brought suit against the book's publisher, alleging, among other things, that the book contained misleading and erroneous information regarding the identification of deadly species of mushrooms. One of enthusiasts' claims alleged liability based on product liability theory. *Held:* The court of appeals held that product liability is geared toward the tangible world and does not take into consideration the unique characteristics of, among other things, ideas, and expression. As such, ideas contained within a book are intangible items and are, accordingly, not subject to product liability claims. Thus, the court affirmed the lower court's decision and held that the enthusiasts could not recover against the book's publisher under a product liability theory. However, in dicta, the court noted that the enthusiasts' argument was stronger when analogized to aeronautical charts. Several jurisdictions have held that such charts are "products" for product liability purposes when they depict geographic features or instrument approach information for airplanes. The Ninth Circuit noted that aeronautical charts are highly technical tools that graphically depict mechanical and technical data.

[Winter v. GP Putnam's Sons, 938 F2d 1033 (9th Cir. 1991)]

PART A.   DEFINING THE BARGAIN

¶ 6.02 RESOURCES AND SOLUTIONS CONTRACTS

Turnkey computer system is one that is "pre-packaged and can be virtually plugged right in and ready to function immediately." Triangle Underwriters bought a computer system from Honeywell. Subsequently, Triangle brought an action, alleging, among other things, breach of contract in order to recover damages from an alleged failure of performance of the computer system sold by Honeywell. The computer system was represented as being a turnkey computer system. Triangle argued that the contract was one for services rather than for the sale of goods. *Held:* The contract was for the sale of goods; accordingly, the UCC statute of limitations was applied. Triangle's breach-of-contract claim was time barred.

[Triangle Underwriters, Inc. v. Honeywell, Inc., 604 F2d 737 (2d Cir. 1979)]

Solutions, as opposed to resources, contracts impose dissimilar performance obligations. A purchaser bought a computer and other related equipment. It then brought suit against the computer manufacturer for, among other things, rescission of the contract based on breach of an implied warranty of fitness. The district court rescinded the contract and awarded damages. The computer manufacturer appealed. It knew of the purchaser's particular purposes for the equipment. More specifically, the purchaser wished to improve its system of paperwork and produce its records faster and more efficiently. Furthermore, the computer manufacturer knew of the buyer's reliance on it to fulfill these needs. *Held:* The court held that the rule that there is no implied warranty of fitness where a known, described, and definite article is purchased by its trade name was not applicable to the purchase of 10 business machines, including a computer, that were to be incorporated into a system intended to be tailored to the purchaser's needs. In so doing, the court accepted the lower court's determination that the equipment was not fit and suitable for the intended purpose and that it did not perform the required functions in accordance with the known purpose.

[Sperry Rand Corp. v. Industrial Supply Corp., 337 F2d 363 (5th Cir. 1964)]

Presumption of general contract law restricting vendor's obligation to provide workable resources stimulates commercial fraud litigation with respect to computer acquisitions. Financial Timing Publications bought computerized typesetting equipment. After the purchase, it brought action against Compugraphics alleging, among other things, fraud. On appeal, the Eighth Circuit considered Compugraphic's motion for summary judgment on the fraud claim wherein all of the elements of fraud were stipulated to be in existence except for reliance. Compugraphics argued that language in the contract itself was tantamount to an admission by Financial Timing that it did not rely on any representations made on behalf of Compugraphics. *Held:* The court held that the contractual provision did not preclude the jury from considering other evidence that Financial Timing relied on Compugraphics's representations regarding the capabilities of the computerized typesetting equipment. As such, the court reversed the trial court's order granting summary judgment on Financial Timing's fraud claim, and remanded it for further proceedings consistent therewith.

[Financial Timing Publications, Inc. v. Compugraphics Corp., 893 F2d 936 (8th Cir. 1990)]

¶ 6.03 REQUESTS FOR PROPOSAL

Malpractice standard of liability is used for consultant assisting client in finding, purchasing, and implementing turnkey computer system. Diversified Graphics hired a big-six accounting firm to assist it in obtaining a computer system to fulfill its data-processing needs. Diversified requested a turnkey computer system that would fully perform its in-house data-processing needs and not require the hiring of computer programmers or extensive training for its personnel. Instead, Diversified received a computer system that was difficult to operate and failed to meet its data-processing needs. *Held:* The court of appeals held the accounting firm to a professional standard of care. There was sufficient information in the record for a jury to determine the applicable standard of care and whether or not the firm met that standard; thus, Diversified's claim for damages was properly submitted to the jury. Diversified's judgment, based on a theory of negligence, was affirmed.

[Diversified Graphics, Ltd. v. Groves, 868 F2d 293 (8th Cir. 1989)]

¶ 6.04 ACCEPTANCE STANDARDS AND TESTING

After computer system satisfies elaborate standards and rigorous testing relating to its acceptance, other deficiencies in performance may be construed as a risk borne by buyer and not a breach of contract by seller if contract does not state otherwise. Sha-I Corporation, a designer and installer of a sophisticated clinical laboratory computer system, sued the City and County of San Francisco, as the operator of a hospital in which the computer system was installed, for breach of contract. Sha-I agreed to design and install a computer system for the hospital in three successive phases described as "systems". After each installation, each system was to be subjected to a 30-day acceptance test. If the system met certain design specifications, the City and County of San Francisco were to accept and pay for the system. The dispute arose with respect to the third and final system, which was found by the trial court to have been tested and accepted by the City and County of San Fransisco. *Held:* Sha-I's system met the standards set forth in the contract, and any subsequent problems that developed with the system were deemed to be irrelevant. The court noted that in developing state-of-the-art computer systems, there is the inherent risk that the system will not function as originally hoped. The parties to such contracts are free to allocate the risk of this in their contract as they so mutually choose. Here, once the computer system passed the acceptance tests, the City and County bore the risk and became obligated to pay the contract price and suffer the consequences if the system were to subsequently not perform up to expectations.

[Sha-I Corp. v. City & County of San Francisco, 612 F2d 1215 (9th Cir. 1980)]

¶ 6.05 SOFTWARE AND HARDWARE CONTRACT INTERDEPENDENCE

The term "bundling," in accordance with computer industry usage, means only the computer system and operating system at no additional cost. Graphic Sales entered into a lease agreement with Sperry, a manufacturer of computer hardware and software. Graphic brought suit against Sperry, alleging fraud in the inducement, common-law fraud, and violation of the Illinois Consumer Fraud and Deceptive Business Practices Act. Essentially, Graphic claimed that Sperry misrepresented that application programs would be offered at no additional cost based on, among other things, the manufacturer's brochures. Both parties agreed that the lease of the computer equipment involved a "bundled" product, but they disagreed as to the meaning of that term within the context of their contract. *Held:* In accordance with the custom and usage in the computer industry, the only software included in the bundled product was the operating system, and any application software was to be leased separately. Thus, the court found that the application software was not included in Graphic's lease of the bundled computer system.

[Graphic Sales, Inc. v. Sperry Univac Div., Sperry Corp., 824 F2d 576 (7th Cir. 1987)]

Lease of computer hardware and software by single vendor is viewed as interdependent for breach-of-contract purposes. A leasor of computer software and hardware brought breach-of-contract action against the lessee. A default judgment was entered against the lessee, and the lessee attempted to demonstrate a meritorious defense to the default. Here, the lessee asserted that it had leased computer hardware and software as a package, and the failure of the software constituted a failure of the entire system to perform. *Held:* The lessee demonstrated a meritorious defense. The default judgment was vacated.

[Olivetti Leasing Corp. v. Mar-Mac Precision Corp., 459 NYS2d 399 (Sup. Ct. 1983)]

PART B.   WARRANTIES AND REPRESENTATIONS

¶ 6.06 EXPRESS WARRANTIES

Express warranty is possibly created where parties to contract discuss a computer system's ability to integrate and interchange programs and data but do not include such provisions in their contract. Both Management and McDonnell Douglas were providers of computerized hospital accounting systems. McDonnell's products previously consisted of mainframes while Management's systems were minicomputer based. McDonnell planned to market a minicomputer system and bought a minicomputer hardware manufacturer in furtherance of that goal. Furthermore, McDonnell entered into a licensing purchase agreement for minicomputer software from Management. McDonnell claimed that Management falsely warranted that its system was integrated; i.e., able to interchange programs and run as a single system. McDonnell allegedly was told by Management's officers that the system was integrated. Management was granted a directed verdict at the trial level on this issue. *Held:* The court reversed and remanded this issue for retrial. The court noted that it was a question of fact whether the system could be integrated and the trial court was in error by granting Management a directed verdict.

[Management Sys. Assocs. v. McDonnell Douglas Corp., 762 F2d 1161 (4th Cir. 1985)]

Breach of express warranty may be found where a promise that a product has a certain quality is not fulfilled. In 1984, L.S. Heath & Sons decided that its current computer system was becoming outmoded and resolved to upgrade and enhance its computer and telecommunications capabilities. Heath agreed to purchase a new system from AT&T, and a master agreement was signed by the parties in September and October 1984. By the end of 1987, after an abundance of trouble, the system was not working as Heath had anticipated. Heath sued for breach of implied and expressed warranties. *Held:* AT&T's statement in the recommendation to Heath that AT&T's "completed intregated [sic] processing and voice/data communications network [will] satisfy all of your [Heath's] aforementioned objectives" could amount to an express warranty, and consequently the district court's finding, ruling in favor of AT&T on the breach of express warranty count, was reversed. A statement can amount to a warranty, even if unintended as such by the seller, "if it could fairly be understood . . . to constitute an affirmation or representation that the product possesses a certain quality or capacity relating to future performance." Evidence suggested that "complete integration" was not provided as promised and that the AT&T system did not have the ability to expand as promised in the recommendation.

[LS Heath & Son v. AT&T Info. Sys., 9 F3d 561 (7th Cir. 1993)]

UCC parol evidence rule standard does not hinge exclusively on presence or absence of merger clause; instead, intent of the parties to make a written contract the sole and exclusive expression of their agreement is used. Sierra Diesel, a family owned business, bought computer software and hardware from Burroughs Corporation in order to do inventory, receivables, and invoicing functions. Prior to the sale of the computer system, Burroughs sent Sierra a letter that made various express representations about the system, including that it "can put your inventory, receivables and invoicing under complete control." The computer did not properly perform the invoicing and accounting functions for which it had been purchased and Sierra brought an action against Burroughs. The agreement between Sierra's owner, an unsophisticated businessman, and Burroughs involved at least four different writings purported by Burroughs to be the contract in question. Burroughs moved for summary judgment on the grounds that the contracts were fully integrated and the letter was not a part of the contract. *Held:* The court held that the printed form contracts supplied by Burroughs did not represent a final integrated contract despite a merger provision to the contrary. In its analysis, the court noted that in deciding whether a writing is the final integration of two parties' agreement, it is necessary to look to the intent of the parties. One relevant factor the court used here was the sophistication of the parties. The court noted that Sierra's owner was not a sophisticated businessman and had little knowledge of computers or contract terms. Moreover, he fully expected the representations made to him in the letter to be part of the contract. As such, the court allowed the letter to be introduced into evidence despite a merger clause and general warranty disclaimer clause in the form contracts.

[Sierra Diesel Injection Serv. v. Burroughs Corp., 874 F2d 653 (9th Cir. 1989)]

Written specifications relating to technical specifications of computer system component relied on by purchaser create enforceable express warranty despite general warranty disclaimer clause. A distributor of computer terminals brought an action against the manufacturer, alleging, inter alia, breach of warranty and interference with prospective business relations. The manufacturer represented in written specifications that cathode-ray computer terminals would operate at 19,200 baud (1,920 characters per second). Moreover, in promotional literature, the manufacturer claimed that those terminals were "inherently reliable." In fact, the computer terminals did not operate at 19,200 baud, were plagued by various manufacturing problems, and failed to perform according to specifications. *Held:* Because the distributor relied on the representations made by the manufacturer regarding the specifications of the terminals (i.e., 19,200 baud transmission rate), this statement constituted an express warranty. The court further held that the warranty disclaimer clause in the relevant contracts did not override the highly particularized warranty created by the specifications.

[Consolidated Data Terminal v. Applied Data Sys., 708 F2d 385 (9th Cir. 1983)]

Alleged verbal express warranties are excluded where warranty disclaimers in contract directly refute claimed warranty. The plaintiff sued a computer vendor, alleging, among other things, breach of an express warranty allegedly verbally given to him by the vendor's salesman. The sales receipt contained a handwritten comment "30 day return, 90 day warranty" on its face. The computer software and owner's manuals contained the full text of the warranty. The plaintiff alleged that the vendor's salesman stated that a 90-day refund policy was in place. Moreover, the plaintiff did not read the sales receipt, but instead relied on the alleged representations of the salesman. *Held:* The court held that the 30-day return policy, as indicated on the sales receipt and manuals was in force. It noted that a party may not benefit from his failure to use common prudence and diligence.

[McCrimmon v. Tandy Corp., 414 SE2d 15 (Ga. App. 1991)]

¶ 6.07 IMPLIED WARRANTIES

Implied warranty of merchantability is not breached when product covered by warranty is not used for the ordinary purpose for which it was intended.   Right Weigh Scale Company sold and installed various types of scales and associated equipment, including scales for weighing trucks. Right Weigh agreed to become a distributor for Eaton digital weight indicators. Eaton introduced a new indicator, the UMC 600. Distributors could purchase two varieties of this indicator, shielded or unshielded. Eaton's unshielded indicators were not legal for trade per Handbook 44, published by the National Bureau of Standards and adopted by the State of Mississippi, because they did not perform properly in the presence of radio frequency interference (RFI). Pursuant to Right Weigh's purchase orders, Eaton shipped Right Weigh a number of unshielded UMC 600 indicators. Eaton did not know how Right Weigh intended to use the indicators; Right Weigh used a number of the indicators in applications that required them to be legal for trade. Right Weigh also failed to test the scales at the time of installation to determine whether they operated properly in the presence of RFI, although Handbook 44 required such testing for all installations where radios were likely to be used. Eaton's warranty policy limited the customer's remedy to repair and/or replacement of the defective product. A separate clause stated that Eaton was not liable for any special or consequential damages of any kind. Even after Eaton provided Right Weigh with shielded replacement units free of charge, a $6,000 credit to offset additional expenses, and allowed Right Weigh to keep the unshielded UMC 600 indicators, Right Weigh demanded additional expenses and lost profits related to the replacement of the unshielded indicators. When Eaton refused, Right Weigh filed suit for breach of implied warranty of merchantability, breach of express warranty, and breach of warranty of fitness for a particular purpose. The jury awarded Right Weigh $62,700 in damages for breach of an implied warranty of merchantability and rejected the two remaining claims. *Held:* No reasonable jury could have found that Eaton breached the implied warranty of merchantability; the verdict was not supported by substantial evidence. For goods to be merchantable, they must, among other things, "pass without objection in the trade under the contract description" and be "fit for the ordinary purposes for which such goods are used." No evidence in the record established that the unshielded indicators were defective when used for the ordinary purposes for which they were intended. The evidence also established that the vast majority of applications did not require legal for trade, RFI-resistant indicators; no reasonable jury could conclude that all digital weight indicators must be shielded from RFI to be fit for ordinary use in Mississippi. Right Weigh simply chose to use an unshielded indicator in applications requiring shielding; such a use was not an ordinary use and did not make the unshielded indicator unmerchantable.

[Right Weigh Scale Co. v. Eaton Corp., 998 F2d 287 (5th Cir. 1993)]

Implied warranties in commercial sales settings can be disclaimed by conspicuously displaying such limitation on remedies if such disclaimers are valid under state law. The subsequent buyer of various computer equipment brought an action against the intermediate buyer and manufacturer, alleging breach of sales and service contracts. The sales contract between the buyer and the intermediate buyer contained, in a conspicuous way, a limitation on the remedies that precluded liability for breach of any implied warranty of merchantability. Under Ohio state law, this disclaimer was valid. *Held:* The intermediate buyer and the manufacturer did not breach any implied warranties with respect to the computer equipment because, among other things, the sales contract between the buyer and the intermediate buyer contained the conspicuous disclaimer. Furthermore, in this case, there were factual uncertainties regarding whether the computer equipment was actually defective.

[Leson Chevrolet Co. v. Oakleaf & Assocs., Inc., 796 F2d 76 (5th Cir. 1986)]

Merchantability warranty and implied warranty of fitness are breached where medical accounting computer system has numerous "bugs" in its program that are beyond reasonable and acceptable flaws. A neurologist entered into a contract with Neilson Business Equipment Center, Inc., to lease computer hardware, software, and related services. Neilson knew at the time of contracting with the neurologist that he desired to use the system for, among other things, billing purposes. Furthermore, as part of the agreement, Neilson agreed to customize the computer system to meet the doctor's specific needs. The computer system failed to adequately perform the intended billing functions. *Held:* Neilson breached the implied warranties of merchantability and fitness for a particular purpose by delivering a computer system that did not perform its functions. The court stated that to be merchantable, the computer system had to have been capable of passing without objection in the trade under the contract description and be fit for the ordinary uses for which it was intended. In this case, because of its various flaws, the computer system failed to meet this standard. For example, the system produced bills that were not compatible with the doctor's records. Furthermore, the court noted that an implied warranty of fitness for a particular purpose was applicable because the seller knew at the time of contracting the particular purpose for which the buyer purchased the goods and that the buyer relied on the seller's skill or judgment to select or furnish suitable goods. This warranty was similarly breached because of the computer system's operational flaws.

[Neilson Business Equip. Ctr., Inc. v. Monteleone, 524 A2d 1172 (Del. Super. 1987)]

¶ 6.08 COMPUTER VIRUSES

Releasor of "worm" into the INTERNET is criminally prosecuted pursuant to Section 2(d) of Computer Fraud and Abuse Act.   This case involved the well-publicized criminal prosecution of Robert Tappan Morris, a graduate student in Cornell University's computer science Ph.D. program. Morris released a "worm"—a program that travels from one computer to another but does not attach itself to the operating system of the computer that it "infects"—into the INTERNET national computer network, subsequently causing various computer systems to cease functioning for a certain period. Morris was convicted of violating the Computer Fraud and Abuse Act of 1986 (18 USCA § 1030(a)(5)(A) (1989)) at the trial level, and he appealed. Morris raised two statutory construction issues on appeal. First, whether the government must prove that Morris intended to prevent authorized use of the computer's information and thereby cause loss. Second, what satisfies the statutory requirement of "access without authorization." *Held:* The appeals court held that the scienter requirement "intentionally" applied only to the "accesses" section of Section 1030(a)(5)(A) and not to the "damages" phase. Thus, Morris's first argument on appeal failed. Next, the court analyzed what satisfies the statutory requirement of "access without authorization." Here, Morris was authorized to use computers at Cornell, Harvard, and Berkeley, all of which were on INTERNET. The court, in finding for the government, noted that Congress did not intend an individual's authorized access to one federal-interest computer to protect him or her from prosecution for accessing other federal-interest computers.

[United States v. Morris, 928 F2d 504 (2d Cir. 1991)]

¶ 6.09 COMPATIBILITY AND COMMUNICATIONS

No breach of implied warranty of merchantability is found where software and computer terminals are incompatible with various popular computer software systems.   A purchaser of software and computer terminals brought suit against the seller, alleging, inter alia, breach of the implied warranty of merchantability. The manufacturer showed that it had sold more than 1 million of the terminals since their introduction. Additionally, the plaintiff "bench-tested" individual terminals prior to the installation of terminals at customer locations. The only defect alleged was incompatibility with certain software programs, including Multi-Link Advanced, Benchmark, and WordPerfect. *Held:* The court found that the manufacturer had not breached an implied warranty of merchantability. The plaintiff introduced no evidence proving that compatibility with those programs was a criterion of merchantability in the computer terminal trade.

[Step-Saver Data Sys., Inc. v. Wyse Technology, 752 F. Supp. 181 (ED Pa. 1990)]

Intermittent adequate performance of computer system, both internal and external, does not preclude claim for breach of express warranty of capability. Crickett Alley had a Wang computer, which was located in its main office, and wished to purchase computerized cash registers compatible with its existing computer. Data Terminal represented to Crickett that its cash registers were compatible with Crickett's Wang computer. Crickett purchased 10 cash registers from Data Terminal and difficulties occurred when the equipment was being programmed. The court found that the fundamental problem was the inability of the Wang computer to communicate with the computerized cash registers; however, occasionally the Wang computer and the cash registers could communicate. Crickett ultimately brought this action, alleging breach of an express warranty of capability relating to its purchase of computerized cash registers from Data Terminal. *Held:* Data Terminal breached its express warranty of compatibility. The court found that the warranty of compatibility carried with it the necessity that such communication be reliably regular and consistent.

[Crickett Alley v. Data Terminal Sys., Inc., 732 P2d 719 (Kan. 1987)]

¶ 6.10 RESPONSE TIME

Dealings of two parties, viewed as a whole, create express warranty as to response time of computer system that survives warranty limitation in contract. The parties to this action entered into a contract for a turnkey computer system for the plaintiff's shoe-making equipment business. The defendant represented that the computer system would have a response time of under three seconds and, in a worst-case scenario, eight or nine seconds. In fact, the response time of the delivered system exceeded 30 seconds. The contract of sale contained a warranty limitation clause; however, the contract itself did not contain any response-time specifications. Those specifications were in an attachment to the contract, the "Performance Analysis," which was completed prior to signing the contract. USM brought this action, alleging, among other things, breach of contract and commission of unfair or deceptive acts. *Held:* The court found that there was an express warranty as to the response time of the computer. Here, the court noted that the parties always regarded response time as being significant. Thus, while the Performance Analysis was phrased in terms of goals and estimates, the court found a promise by the defendant that the response time would not exceed the worst-case scenario of eight or nine seconds. Since the response time was far in excess of that parameter, the court found that the express warranty was breached despite warranty limitation language in the contract itself.

[USM Corp. v. Arthur D. Little Sys., Inc., 546 NE2d 888 (Mass. App. Ct. 1989)]

¶ 6.11   AUTOMATION AND HUMAN INVOLVEMENT

Software system that is allegedly burdensome to operate, but has no other "defects," is found not defective.   Family Drug Store purchased a computer software system from GSCS for approximately $2,500, as compared with similar systems costing between $10,000 and $15,000. During training sessions for the software, Family Drug Store found that the system was relatively difficult to operate. Family Drug sought to avoid the sale or, in the alternative, have the contract declared unenforceable. *Held:* The contract was enforceable. The court noted that there were no misrepresentations as to the computer software system's capabilities; in fact, the system functioned as intended. In this case, Family Drug measured the effectiveness of a $2,500 system against that of $10,000 and $15,000 systems. Family's enforceable expectations were viewed in light of the computer system's expense. The fact that the system was cumbersome and difficult to operate was not cause to void the contract or render it unenforceable in that light.

[Family Drug Store of New Iberia, Inc. v. Gulf States Computer Servs., Inc., 563 So. 2d 1324 (La. Ct. App. 1990)]

PART C.   OBLIGATIONS RELATED TO THE SALE

¶ 6.12   COLLATERAL OBLIGATIONS

Computer software company is not required to provide design documentation of legal research software.   A debtor and former supplier of computer services to legal researchers appealed an order of the district court affirming a referee's order allowing the claim of a creditor. The creditor's claim concerned computer hardware and software delivered to the debtor. The debtor argued that it did not owe money because the creditor had not delivered the entire software package for which the debtor had contracted. The contract incorporated a letter in which the creditor agreed to "provide the initial software to enable you [debtor] to operate your prototype system." The creditor did not provide documentation regarding the computer software's source code or actual design of the software. However, the creditor did provide the debtor with operator's and programmer's manuals. *Held:* The manuals were sufficient "system documentation" to enable the debtor to operate the computer system. Neither the contract, custom, nor usage required the creditor to provide any further documentation.

[Law Research Serv., Inc. v. General Automation, Inc., 494 F2d 202 (2d Cir. 1974)]

Negligent installation claim is treated as separate, viable cause of action. AIB contracted with Baldwin to provide computer programs and systems for AIB. After repeated attempts to get the computer programs and systems working had failed, AIB brought suit, alleging, among other things, breach of contract and negligent installation of the computer system. The jury returned a general verdict for AIB on its claims and for Baldwin on his counterclaim for unpaid purchases. Baldwin appealed, contending that the jury's verdict for AIB was not supported by a preponderance of the evidence. *Held:* There was sufficient evidence to sustain the jury's verdict; as such, the appellate court affirmed the jury's verdict.

[Baldwin v. Alabama Ins. Brokers, Inc., 599 So. 2d 1196 (Ala. Civ. App. 1992)]

PART D. DISPUTES AND REMEDIES

¶ 6.13 DEFINING A BREACH OF CONTRACT

Reasonable secondary cause is sufficient proof for breach of warranty in sale of high-technology product. Altronics, security businesses that bought radio-operated security systems, sued Repco, the manufacturer/seller of the systems. Altronics, which was composed of two Pennsylvania corporations involved in the business of selling and servicing electronic security and alarm systems to subscribers in Eastern Pennsylvania, bought three wireless, radio-operated security systems from Repco. The first system was operational. The second system malfunctioned, in that it allegedly received substantial interference from other frequencies that rendered it an unreliable alarm system for Altronics's customers. Moreover, Altronics received a notice of violation from the FCC arising from the interference created by the second system. The third system was never installed. Altronics sued to recover the purchase price of the two systems and all incidental and consequential damages. *Held:* The court found that Repco breached the implied warranties of merchantability and fitness for a particular purpose with respect to the second system despite Altronics's lack of identifying any specific defect in the equipment. Here, the court noted that to establish a breach of either of these warranties, Altronics had to prove that the equipment was defective. The court noted that to prove that the product was defective in light of the absence of any specific, identifiable defect, Altronics was required to show that: (1) the product malfunctions; (2) it used the product as intended or reasonably expected by the manufacturer; and (3) other reasonable secondary causes were absent. In this case, the system clearly malfunctioned. Also, Repco did not contend that Altronics misused the system. As such, the court focused on the third element—absence of other reasonable, secondary causes. Altronics met its burden regarding the third element by showing that it properly installed the system. In refuting other arguments by Repco as to why the system malfunctioned, the court noted that Pennsylvania law does not require plaintiffs to refute all possible explanations offered by defendants.

[Altronics of Bethlehem, Inc. v. Repco, Inc., 957 F2d 1102 (3d Cir. 1992)]

Supreme Court of Connecticut does not require expert testimony to establish breach of warranty for sale of computer systems.   The parties entered into two contracts for the delivery of two computer systems. The purchaser did not fully pay license fees or software support charges because it was unhappy with the output performance of the systems. The seller brought suit to recover money allegedly due it pursuant to a contract for sale. The buyer counterclaimed to recover damages as well as a return of money already paid. Among other things, the court examined whether a buyer of computer systems may recover money under a theory of breach of express warranty without expert testimony identifying the cause of the computer system's generation of inaccurate data. *Held:* The court found that expert testimony was not required in this case. Importantly, the court noted that there were three significant factors bolstering its and the lower court's decision here. First, the buyer's burden of proof was attenuated because the trial court found that the buyer's right to return of the computer software's price was grounded in its right of rejection under Article 2 of the UCC. Under Connecticut law, a rejecting buyer need only show that "the tender of delivery fail[s] in any respect to conform to the contract. . . ." Second, the purchaser introduced some expert testimony at the trial level about the software's deficiencies. Finally, the buyer relied on the seller's representations.

[Latham & Assocs. v. Raveis Real Estate, 589 A2d 337 (Conn. 1991)]

¶ 6.14 PERFORMANCE ISSUES

[1] Rejection and Debugging New Systems

Buyer or licensee of computer software that waits four months after installation to reject does so on timely basis.   The purchaser of accounting software for a supermarket brought an action to recover the purchase price of the software. Prior to the purchase, the software had not been used with the operating system that the purchaser had on its computer system; however, Contemporary Computer assured the purchaser of the compatibility of the software with the operating system. The parties amended the contract of sale, adding that the buyer had the right to return the software for any reason within 90 days of purchase. The 90-day remedy did not expressly state that it was an exclusive remedy. Evidence at trial showed that there were problems with the software from the date of installation. *Held:* The purchaser timely rejected the software. The court found that the 90-day return remedy was not the purchaser's exclusive remedy and did not preclude it from rejecting the system at a later date. Instead, the court noted that the 90-day return addendum was simply an additional, nonexclusive remedy. The court noted that the buyer, absent a specific provision in the contract, had a reasonable amount of time in which to determine whether or not the goods were defective. Here, the purchaser's numerous complaints were met by assurances from Contemporary that those problems would be corrected. Thus, the purchaser acted reasonably in keeping the goods while Contemporary attempted to remedy the defects.

[David Cooper, Inc. v. Contemporary Computer Sys., Inc., 846 SW2d 777 (Mo. App. SD 1993)]

[2] Revocation

Revocation of computer sales contract is disallowed where, among other things, defects do not substantially impair value of system and timely notice of revocation is not given. Iten Leasing purchased a computerized accounting system from Burroughs Corporation consisting of, in part, an accounting machine, internal memory for the system, data-save device, reader/feeder/stacker attachment (R/F/S), and computer software. The magistrate at the trial level found that the R/F/S never worked satisfactorily; adjustments to this device worked only temporarily. Additionally, the data-save device only worked properly on two occasions. Iten brought suit, alleging misrepresentation, fraud, and breach of express warranty; additionally, Iten sought rescission of the contract. The magistrate found that the misrepresentations regarding the two defective devices were not material to the purchase of the accounting system as a whole, and limited damages accordingly. *Held:* The court affirmed the magistrate's finding that the failure of the R/F/S and data-save devices did not substantially impair the value of the system and, thus, under Minnesota law, revocation was not a proper remedy. The court noted that the system, as a whole, worked despite the malfunctioning of the two devices. Furthermore, under Minnesota law, Iten, by waiting four months within which there was no contact with Burroughs seeking correction of the defects or replacement of the devices, did not timely give notice of revocation.

[Iten Leasing Co. v. Burroughs Corp., 684 F2d 573 (8th Cir. 1982)]

Buyer of computer system is able to revoke contract for sale more than two years after initial delivery where seller assured buyer during that period that software problems would be remedied. A seller of a computer system brought suit to recover the full purchase price for the system plus maintenance and service charges. The buyer counterclaimed, seeking a refund of the purchase price based on his alleged revocation of the acceptance of the system. *Held:* The purchaser's use of the computer system for more than two years after its initial delivery did not preclude his revocation of acceptance. The court noted that a party's revocation of acceptance depends on the facts and circumstances surrounding the revocation, and is usually a question for the trier of fact. In this case, the buyer relied on repeated assurances by the seller that the software and hardware problems would be resolved. On the basis of that evidence, the court held that the jury could reasonably conclude that the buyer's revocation was seasonably given.

[Triad Sys. Corp. v. Alsip, 880 F2d 247 (10th Cir. 1989)]

Nine-month delay does not preclude revocation of contract relating to sale of computer equipment where that period was characterized by continued attempts by the seller to rectify problems with the equipment. Aubrey's R.V. Center purchased a computer system from Tandy Corporation in order to perform various business functions, including point-of-sale/inventory control functions. Tandy furnished the computer hardware and chose a third-party vendor for the point-of-sale/inventory control functions. From the time of delivery, the computer system failed to adequately perform some of the contracted-for business functions; specifically, the system would not act as a point-of-sale recorder. Aubrey's and Tandy attempted to get the computer hardware and software systems to work together as contracted for, but were unable to do so. Approximately nine months after Aubrey's accepted Tandy's proposal, Aubrey's sent a letter to Tandy requesting rescission of the sales contract. Several months thereafter, after Tandy stopped its attempts to rectify the problems, Aubrey's brought an action seeking rescission of the sales contract. *Held:* Aubrey's had seasonably given notice of rescission despite the fact that approximately nine months elapsed between acceptance of the computer system and the letter requesting rescission. In this case, the court noted that the initial two-month delay was possibly attributable to the fact that the buyer's lack of computer experience prevented it from understanding problems with the computer system. Once Aubrey's understood the extent of the computer system's problems, the other seven months were characterized by the court as "a continuing series of complaints, negotiations, promises, and repeated attempts by Tandy [seller] to adapt the software to the hardware." The court noted that the buyer should not be penalized for its patience with Tandy's efforts to rectify the computer system's problems.

[Aubrey's RV Ctr. v. Tandy Corp., 731 P2d 1124 (Wash. App. 1987)]

¶ 6.15 LIMITED WARRANTIES AND REMEDIES

Manufacturer's warranty limitations made in original contract of sale apply to subsequent buyer of computer equipment. A purchaser of used computer equipment brought an action to recover purely economic losses resulting from alleged defects in computer equipment. The original computer sales contract contained warranty limitations restricting the manufacturer's liability. Both the used-equipment buyer and the original buyer were commercially sophisticated. *Held:* A warranty limitation that is legally operative against the original purchaser of computer equipment is effective against all successive buyers. The computer purchaser was entitled to recover only as much as its predecessor could have recovered.

[Datamatic, Inc. v. International Business Mach. Corp., 795 F2d 458 (5th Cir. 1986)]

Manufacturer's warranty disclaimer of implied warranties of fitness and merchantability made in dealer's contract is effective even though manufacturer is not a party to contract. The buyer of a computer system brought a third-party action against the manufacturer of computer equipment based on breach of, among other things, the implied warranties of fitness for a particular purpose and merchantability. Specifically, the buyer alleged that the computer was inadequate for its intended use and that its malfunctioning caused him to lose profits and clients. On appeal, the buyer argued that the district court erred in instructing the jury regarding the disclaimer of warranties, and that the warranty disclaimer was unconscionable and inconspicuous. *Held:* The manufacturer's disclaimer or limitation of remedy was part of the basis of the bargain and was not ineffective merely because the manufacturer was not a party to the contract between the dealer and the buyer. The court noted that, among other things, the disclaimer was conspicuous in that it appeared in large print on the front of the contract form directly above the line for the buyer's signature. Also, that large print on the front of the form directed the buyer to the controlling terms on the back of the form. The court noted that the warranty disclaimer was not unconscionable under Arkansas law where the buyer was a well-educated buyer with some background in commercial law and who shopped extensively for computer equipment to suit his needs. Moreover, the buyer was aware of the disclaimer and testified that he understood it.

[Hunter v. Texas Instruments, Inc., 798 F2d 299 (8th Cir. 1986)]

Two-year statute of limitations period in contract bars claims brought more than two years after causes of action arose. Hyatt Corporation contracted with Encore Systems to install computer equipment at various Hyatt hotels. Hyatt later sued Encore, contending that Encore incorrectly calculated late-payment charges, improperly billed for 3B2 computer equipment, billed for printer cables that were never delivered, and charged excessive restocking fees. Encore filed a motion for summary judgment, claiming that most of Hyatt's claims were barred by a contractual statute of limitations. The applicable contract had a two-year limitation period; no action arising out of the agreement could be brought by either party more than two years after the cause of action arose or, in the case of nonpayment, more than two years from the date payment was due. Hyatt responded that the limitation period did not begin to run until after the contract concluded, which was less than two years prior to filing. *Held:* The claims were not one cause of action that arose at the conclusion of the contract; at the latest, the claims accrued at the time Hyatt became aware of the alleged overbillings, which it conceded was more than two years prior to filing suit. Nevertheless, a genuine issue material fact existed as to whether the parties' relationship was one of a mutual account and, if one existed, whether any reconciliation occurred. Equipment was being installed hotel by hotel and, in accordance with the agreement, was being billed, invoiced, and paid as it was being installed. Hyatt produced no evidence supporting its contention that the purchased equipment and software could only function after being installed at all the hotels; to the contrary, the agreement itself supports the view that the equipment was usable before being installed at all sites. A mutual account is based on a course of dealing wherein each party gives credit to the other on the faith of the indebtedness to itself. A statute of limitations begins to run when the last entry is made in the account. If there is a reconciliation of the mutual debts, the statute of limitations for claims up to that point will be measured from the point of reconciliation. Here, disputed evidence existed as to whether a mutual account relationship existed between the parties and as to whether any agreement or reconciliation was ever reached as to the balance in the account and the amount owed from one party to the other. Accordingly, summary judgment on this issue was denied.

[Hyatt Corp. v. Encore Sys., Inc., No. 92 C 8160, 1993 WL 338179 (ND Ill. Aug. 31, 1993)]

Buyers of computers have duty to mitigate damages when seller breaches contract. The parties to this action entered into a contract for the sale and installation of several computers. The defendant breached the contract by failing to install a system that met the needs of the Jewish Press, Inc. The Jewish Press made one half-hearted attempt to sell the computers and, later, donated them to a university. The trial court entered judgment for Jewish Press. *Held:* Jewish Press had an obligation to mitigate its damages, which it failed to meet. Here, the court noted that Jewish Press failed to exert reasonable efforts to mitigate its damages. As such, the court reduced the trial court's award by the market value of the computers at the time of trial.

[Jewish Press, Inc. v. Willner, 594 NYS2d 51 (App. Div. Dept. 2d 1993)]

[1] Failure of Purpose in Replacement and Repair Remedies

Contractual repair and replacement remedy does not restrict computer purchaser's right to recovery under breach-of-warranty theory where seller's breach is total and fundamental. A purchaser brought suit, alleging, inter alia, breach of warranty in connection with the sale of a computer system. The contract between the parties contained an express provision providing for a repair and replacement remedy. Additionally, the buyer let the seller know that time was of the essence and the seller represented that the system would be up and running by a date certain. One and one-half years after that date certain, the seller had not provided the buyer with a fully operational computer system. *Held:* The exclusive remedy of repair and replacement did not preclude the buyer's right to recovery of damages for the breach of warranty. The court noted that as long as the buyer has use of substantially defect free goods, the remedy should be given effect. However, where the seller is unable or unwilling to conform the goods to the contract, the remedy does not take effect. The delay made the correction remedy ineffective and, thus, that provision failed in its essential purpose.

[Chatlos Sys. v. National Cash Register Corp., 635 F2d 1081 (3d Cir. 1980)]

Replacement and repair remedy will not limit buyer's right of recovery if seller's breach is total and fundamental. The buyer of a computer software system brought an action alleging fraud and breach of contract against the seller based on defects in the system. The contract obligated Lab-Con to correct any malfunctions or "bugs" in the computer software system; conversely, the contract also limited Lab-Con's liability to the contract price. The district court awarded the buyer the amount paid under the contract and consequential damages and the seller appealed. *Held:* The default of the seller was so total and fundamental that the failure of the repair remedy expunged Lab-Con's liability limitation. Thus, consequential damages were properly awarded.

[RRX Indus., Inc. v. Lab-Con, Inc., 772 F2d 543 (9th Cir. 1985)]

[2] Consequential Damage Limitations

Manufacturer of integrated computer circuits is liable for lost profits as consequential damages where damages were reasonably foreseeable. Troxler entered into a contract for the manufacture and sale of custom-made microelectronic components by Solitron. Troxler advised Solitron of, among other things, its need for prompt production of the components to secure a competitive advantage in the marketplace through early introduction of its product that incorporated the component. The delivery dates fixed by the parties were not met. Solitron continually delayed delivery of the components, requested a price increase of 100 percent, and ultimately repudiated the contract by announcing it would no longer manufacture custom chips. Thereafter, Troxler brought an action to recover damages, including lost profits, arising from Soltron's breach of contract. *Held:* Under North Carolina law, a plaintiff in a breach of contract action may recover lost profits, as consequential damages, which the defendant could reasonably foresee arising from its breach of contract.

[Troxler Elecs. v. Solitron Devices, Inc., 722 F2d 81 (4th Cir. 1983)]

Computer contract specifying that lost profits are unrecoverable is enforced even though such profits would have been recoverable under UCC.   Three-Seventy Leasing was formed for the purpose of purchasing computer hardware in order to lease such hardware to end users. The parties to this action entered into a contract whereby Ampex was to deliver six computer core memory units to a third party. The contract contained a provision precluding consequential damages as a remedy. Three-Seventy sought lost profits under a breach-of-contract theory. *Held:* Three-Seventy was not able to recover lost profits as consequential damages. Section 2719 of California's Commercial Code provides that consequential damages may be limited or excluded unless such limitation or exclusion is unconscionable. The issue of unconscionability was not raised at the trial level, nor was there evidence to support such a claim. Thus, the court found that the limitation on consequential damages was valid and precluded recovery of damages for lost profits.

[Three-Seventy Leasing Corp. v. Ampex Corp., 528 F2d 993 (5th Cir. 1976)]

Warranty disclaimer clause provides for limited repair remedy, and exclusion of consequential damages is not enforced where breach of contract is total and complete.   Hawaiian Telephone Company contracted with Microform Data for the manufacture and installation of a computerized telephone directory system. The contract between the parties provided for express warranties in lieu of any liability on the part of the manufacturer for consequential damages. Specifically, the contract called for the manufacturer to make repairs to the equipment as necessary at no additional charge to Hawaiian. Microform failed entirely to deliver the computerized directory system, and Hawaiian brought this action for breach of contract. *Held:* The provision in the contract limiting the manufacturer's liability never became effective because Microform never installed a system. The court found that repair warranties were inextricably tied to the provision excluding consequential damages, and both depended on delivery of the system. Since the system was never delivered, consequential damages were not precluded pursuant to the contract. The court rejected Microform's argument that failure to deliver a system was equivalent to failure to remedy a defect in a delivered system.

[Hawaiian Tel. Co. v. Microform Data Sys., 829 F2d 919 (9th Cir. 1987)]

Consequential damages disclaimer in written equipment contract is inapplicable to associated oral contract for software.   Carl Beasley Ford, a Ford Motor Company dealer, bought electronic accounting equipment from Burroughs Corporation in order to produce records required under Beasley's franchise agreement with Ford. The contract did not include an oral agreement between the parties whereby Burroughs agreed to furnish 13 computer software programs. The price of the programs was included in the price of the equipment. Burroughs had problems installing and testing the programs by the date agreed on by the parties. Beasley eventually, through its counsel, sent Burroughs a letter rejecting the computer. Beasley brought action to recover the purchase price and consequential damages, alleging that the equipment failed to perform as warranted. *Held:* The consequential damages disclaimer in the written equipment contract was held to be inapplicable to the oral contract for the software. The court noted that Burroughs's own personnel noted that the computer was virtually worthless without the programs. Furthermore, the court noted that Burroughs sold the equipment at a "bundled" price; thus, although two separate agreements were used—one written and one oral—the two agreements were virtually inseparable insofar as the utility of the equipment was concerned.

[Carl Beasley Ford, Inc. v. Burroughs Corp., 361 F. Supp. 325 (ED Pa. 1973)]

¶ 6.16 UNCONSCIONABILITY

Computer lessee's computer naiveté is not, in and of itself, grounds to conclude that lessor's contractual limitations on liability and disclaimers of warranty are oppressive or unfair. Earman Oil, lessee of computer equipment, brought an action alleging breach of implied and express warranties and for tortious misrepresentation against a computer manufacturer. Burroughs Corporation asserted that exculpatory provisions of the contract shielded it from liability. The court considered, among other issues, whether the contract's exculpatory provisions were unconscionable. Earman contended that the actions of Burroughs were overreaching and unfair, thereby rendering the contract's exculpatory provisions unconscionable and, therefore, unenforceable. *Held:* Earman's mere inexperience with computers was not enough to prove unconscionability. The court noted that Earman based its unconscionability argument on (1) the relatively short negotiations period with only two or three meetings between the parties' representatives and (2) the fact that Earman was in the business of selling oil and therefore presumptively unfamiliar with computers. Furthermore, Earman argued that these allegations met the first three elements of unconscionability. Those elements, as enunciated by the court, are: (1) examination of the negotiation process as to length of time in dealing, (2) the length of time for deliberations, (3) the experience or astuteness of the parties, (4) whether counsel reviewed the contract, and (5) whether the buyer was a reluctant purchaser. Here, the court stated that the small number of meetings between the parties indicated nothing about the length, nature, or fairness of the negotiations. Next, it noted that the short duration of the negotiations indicated by Earman did not mean that Earman's deliberations were limited to that period. Finally, the court did not equate Earman's core business with a lack of experience or astuteness as a negotiator. Thus, Earman, by its inexperience, did not establish elements necessary to prove unconscionability.

[Earman Oil Co. v. Burroughs Corp., 625 F2d 1291 (5th Cir. 1980)]

Form agreement excluding consequential damages and limiting plaintiff's remedy to correction of computer software tax-preparation program is not per se unconscionable.　　The plaintiff bought a computer software program for the purpose of preparing 1982 tax returns. The contract, a preprinted form, provided for a specific, limited warranty—to correct the program. Consequential damages were expressly prohibited under the contract. The plaintiff argued that the damages limitation was unconscionable and, thus, unenforceable. *Held:* The contractual provision was enforceable; the plaintiff was not entitled to consequential damages. Under New York's version of the UCC, "limitation of consequential damages for injury to the person in the case of consumer goods is prima facie unconscionable but limitation of damages where the loss is commercial is not." Thus, the court noted, the contract's exclusion of consequential damages for breach of contract was not prima facie unconscionable. Next, the court noted that just because the contract was an adhesion contract—one of prespecified form and not negotiated—did not make it unconscionable. Here, the court noted that the nondrafting party had the choice of accepting or rejecting the contract as drafted.

[Harper Tax Servs., Inc. v. Quick Tax Ltd., 686 F. Supp. 109 (D. Md. 1988)]

¶ 6.17　MANUFACTURER LIABILITY

Purchaser of computer system is not third-party beneficiary of written dealer purchase agreement between manufacturer and dealer.　　The purchaser bought a computer system from a dealer to use for billing and accounts receivable purposes. The dealer had purchased the computer system from the manufacturer pursuant to a dealer purchase agreement. Because of software problems, the computer did not perform to the plaintiff's satisfaction. The purchaser then brought action for breach of contract, as a third-party beneficiary of a written dealer purchase agreement, against the computer manufacturer. *Held:* The purchaser was not a third-party beneficiary to the written dealer purchase agreement. The court noted that there are two types of third-party beneficiaries—donee beneficiaries and creditor beneficiaries. In this case, there was no evidence adduced to support recognizing the purchaser as either kind of beneficiary. First, the purchaser introduced no evidence to show that the dealer was under any duty or obligation to the purchaser that the dealer intended to discharge by entering into the dealer purchase agreement. Accordingly, the plaintiff was not a creditor beneficiary. Second, there was no evidence supporting the proposition that the dealer intended to make a gift to the plaintiff. As such, the plaintiff was not a donee beneficiary.

[Stayton Co-op Tel. Co. v. Lockheed Elec. Co., 717 P2d 1283 (Or. App. 1986)]

PART E. MASS-MARKET SOFTWARE CONTRACTS

¶ 6.18 DESIGN IMPOSSIBILITY

Practical impossibility does not relieve computer manufacturer from liability for liquidated damages under breach-of-contract theory. An electronics manufacturer, Wegematic, and the Federal Reserve Board of the United States contracted for an intermediate-type, general-purpose electronic digital computing system. Under the terms of the contract, Wegematic was obligated to deliver the computer nine months from the date of the contract. The contract contained a liquidated damages clause of $100 per day for any delay. The computer manufacturer was unable to deliver the computer as promised and the Fed ultimately procured another computer from another vendor. The United States brought action, seeking damages under a breach-of-contract theory. Wegematic sought to avoid liability under an argument that delivery was impossible because of "basic engineering difficulties" whose correction would have cost more than $1 million and taken anywhere from one to two years. Even then, the success of such a correction was uncertain. Thus, Wegematic argued that the "practical impossibility" of completing the contract excused its defaults in performance. *Held:* The court held that the alleged engineering difficulties did not relieve Wegematic of its liability to the government. In this case, the court noted that Wegematic chose to accept the risk of development of the computer system.

[United States v. Wegematic Corp., 360 F2d 674 (2d Cir. 1966)]

Although binding contract was not entered into by parties, manufacturer/seller of goods can recover reliance damages from intended purchaser based on doctrine of promissory estoppel. Cyberchron Corporation was a New York corporation engaged in the business of providing customized computer hardware for military and civilian use. Calldata Systems was a Florida corporation and a subsidiary of Grumman Data Systems Corporation. Grumman had a contract with the U.S. Marine Corps to build a combat command control system. The equipment at issue was a rugged computer workstation designed to operate under rough military and combat conditions in a command center. For two years, the parties were involved in extended negotiations as a result of which Cyberchron attempted to produce this "ruggedized" computer equipment. Although some equipment was produced by Cyberchron, no such equipment was actually delivered to Calldata or Grumman, nor was any payment made to Cyberchron. As a result, Cyberchron sued Calldata, alleging breach of contract, quantum meruit, and promissory estoppel claims. *Held:* Despite extensive negotiations, Cyberchron did not enter into a binding contract with Grumman; therefore, Cyberchron's breach of contract claim was dismissed. Moreover, Cyberchron was not to recover under the doctrine of quantum meruit because Grumman received no benefit from Cyberchron's actions, Cyberchron failed to fully perform, and Grumman was not unjustly enriched. However, Cyberchron established all the elements of its promissory estoppel claim and was entitled to reliance damages. In New York, the doctrine of promissory estoppel, a rule applicable only in the absence of an enforceable contract, has three elements: (1) a clear and unambiguous promise, (2) a reasonable and foreseeable reliance by the party to whom the promise is made, and (3) an injury, in some cases elevated to requirement of an unconscionable injury, sustained by the party asserting the estoppel by reason of its reliance. The doctrine of promissory estoppel is applicable to actions involving the sale of goods governed by the UCC. Cyberchron established all three elements of its promissory estoppel claim. First, Cyberchron established that Grumman made clear and unambiguous representations, promises, inducements, and directions to Cyberchron to proceed, manufacture, assemble, and deliver the ruggedized equipment, notwithstanding the lack of agreement by the parties concerning the weight of the equipment. Furthermore, there were promises that if Cyberchron produced the ruggedized equipment, it would be paid. As to the second element, Cyberchron established that it reasonably relied on Grumman's promises. As to the third element, Cyberchron established that it was "injured" as a result of these promises. Grumman's conduct, exerting pressure on Cyberchron to produce the units at great expense and then abruptly terminating the transaction to purchase inferior equipment from another company, was unconscionable. Accordingly, Cyberchron was awarded its direct out-of-pocket losses it incurred because of its unjustified reliance on Grumman's promises and inducements.

[Cyberchron Corp. v. Calldata Sys. Dev., Inc. 831 F. Supp. 94 (EDNY 1993)]

Where contract is one for design services relating to experimental computer software system, there is no breach of contract when the software is not successfully completed. A computer software company entered into a contractual relationship with an engineering firm endeavoring to produce a computer software program. The letter agreement provided that the computer software company was to be paid by the hour. Later, the plaintiff complained that the computer software had not been completed to its satisfaction. *Held:* The court determined that the contract was one predominantly for services; thus, the UCC did not apply. Here, the court noted that the terms of the contract spoke in terms of time, which connoted the rendition of services—and not a sales transaction. There was no breach of warranty because, under these facts, the engineering firm did not contract to deliver a working product; instead, it contracted to provide services in the attempt to develop a program.

[Micro-Managers, Inc. v. Gregory, 434 NW2d 97 (Wis. App. 1988)]

¶ 6.19 SHARED DESIGN RESPONSIBILITY

[1] Contingent Responsibilities

Hospital that accepted and paid for services of computer software developer for 18 months after objecting that services were inadequate is estopped from claiming damages or seeking a refund. A provider of computer software and management services and a hospital contracted for a computerized patient accounting and billing system. The system had many problems from its installation. At a luncheon meeting between the parties, the hospital expressed, among other things, its dissatisfaction with the system and its intention to obtain another computer system. The topics discussed at the meeting were entered in a letter written by a hospital representative. The hospital continued to make payments on the contract for 18 months while it sought out, procured, and installed a new computer system. When the other computer system became operative, the hospital disconnected the provider's computer system and ceased payments under the contract. The provider then brought suit against the hospital for breach of contract. The hospital counterclaimed, alleging, among other things, breach of warranty, negligent design and repair, negligent misrepresentation, and professional malpractice. *Held:* The hospital was estopped from contending that the computer management services were excessive for the 18-month period after the letter was given to the provider. The court noted that the hospital did not protest that the management service fees were excessive in light of the poor performance of the system, attempt to renegotiate those fees, or otherwise reserve its rights. Rather, the hospital continued to pay the management fees in full. Thus, the provider was led to believe that its management services were acceptable to the hospital.

[Hospital Computer Sys. v. Staten Island Hosp., 788 F. Supp. 1351 (DNJ 1992)]

Software vendor's failure to provide software is not breach of contract where buyer does not provide design specifications. H/R Stone purchased computer software and hardware from computer seller Phoenix. Phoenix promised to deliver computer hardware and software to Stone within 150 days. The contract provided for a forfeiture by Phoenix if the computer software was not timely completed. Phoenix subcontracted out the design of certain software for Stone. Stone did not provide the subcontractor with enough information for that subcontractor to complete its contractual provisions, which hindered Phoenix in fulfilling its obligations to Stone. *Held:* Stone's failure to provide the subcontractor with design specifications was a breach of contract that relieved Phoenix from all obligations under the software portion of the contract. The court noted that Stone's failure to supply necessary information to Phoenix's subcontractor was a breach of the implied covenant of good faith and fair dealing.

[H/R Stone, Inc. v. Phoenix Business Sys., Inc., 660 F. Supp. 351 (SDNY 1987)]

Buyer's alleged hindrance of seller's performance of contractual obligations does not repudiate contract where seller was denied access to facilities and individuals after its unsuccessful attempts to render performance. The parties to this action entered into a lease agreement for a computerized accounting system. Pursuant to the contract, Olivetti Corporation was to transfer a data base onto the computer system, train the lessee's employees, and make the computer system operational. Olivetti did not successfully complete any of these tasks, despite having one of its representatives make repeated visits to Diversified Environment's place of business. Apparently, Olivetti's representative spent time discussing his religious beliefs with Diversified employees and did not train the relevant employees or make the computer operational. Additionally, the data was not fully transferred to the computer system. Thereafter, Diversified, upon receiving complaints from its employees relating to the Olivetti representative's proselytism, refused entry to that representative. Diversified then brought action for breach of contract based on the allegation that the computer had never been made operational. Olivetti argued that its non-performance was excusable because it had been prevented from performing its contractual obligations. *Held:* Olivetti had no excuse for its nonperformance under the contract. The court noted that Diversified barred Olivetti's representative from its place of business only after attempts to perform had been allowed and unsatisfactorily performed.

[Diversified Env'ts, Inc. v. Olivetti Corp., 461 F. Supp. 286 (MD Pa. 1978)]

[2] Nonexpert End Users

Defense relating to failure to complete computer system because of plaintiff's requested design changes fails where plaintiff is an inexperienced end user to whom defendant owes a duty to advise. Napasco brought suit against a computer services company alleging breach of contract relating to the installation of an on-line computer inventory control and accounting system. In this case, Napasco sought to update its manual accounting and inventory control system via computerization. Tymshare contracted to sell Napasco a complete, "integrated" computer system for its accounting and inventory control needs. Napasco requested changes to the computer system. The installation of the computer system was plagued with delays and was never satisfactorily installed. Thereafter, Napasco elected not to proceed with the installation of Tymshare's computer system and brought suit. Tymshare argued that because of the changes in the computer system requested by Napasco, Napasco cannot now recover any damages for breach of contract. *Held:* Napasco's requested changes did not vitiate Tymshare's duty to perform under the contract. The court stated that Tymshare was the expert in this transaction as to how the computer system operated, its capabilities, and how long requested modifications would take. Here, the court noted that Tymshare—because of its greater expertise—should have focused Napasco on precisely how long modifications would take, their cost, and their feasibility.

[Napasco Int'l, Inc. v. Tymshare, Inc., 556 F. Supp. 654 (ED La. 1983)]

CHAPTER 7

TECHNOLOGY LICENSING AND COMPUTERS

PART A.   OVERVIEW OF LEGAL ISSUES

¶ 7.01 NATURE OF INTANGIBLES CONTRACTS

Nonexclusive license does not give broad rights including copyright to licensee.
MacLean was an employee of Mercer. After leaving Mercer, he continued as a consultant, but also formed his own company, which was in competition with Mercer. While a consultant for a Mercer client, MacLean developed software, which Mercer acquired. Both Mercer and MacLean tried to develop advanced versions of the program. Mercer and MacLean each claimed the other infringed its copyright. Mercer alleged that it had a nonexclusive implied license to MacLean's original program. *Held:* The nonexclusive license did not give Mercer rights to further develop the program. According to the court, only an exclusive license transfers ownership rights, and such a license must be in writing. Here, there was no writing transferring ownership rights. Mercer's rights arose from MacLean giving the program to Mercer for the client, for which MacLean worked. This transfer was limited to Mercer's continuing use in the relationship with the client. The transfer did not give Mercer the

right to develop or to sell the program. There was no evidence that MacLean gave a broad license for the exploitation of the program.

[MacLean Assocs., Inc. v. William M. Mercer-Meidinger-Hanson, Inc., 952 F2d 769 (3d Cir. 1991)]

¶ 7.02 ANTITRUST AND RELATED CONSIDERATIONS

Escrow account for royalties due, pending suit challenging validity of patent, is improper.   Cordic held licenses on two Medtronic patents. Cordic claimed that the patents were invalid. During the suit to prove the invalidity, Cordic sought a court order allowing it to place royalties due under the license into an escrow account and sought an order forbidding Medtronic from canceling the license. The district court granted both requests, and Medtronic appealed. *Held:* Order vacated. According to the court, the escrow order was improper because a licensee cannot be forced to pay royalties during the time that it is challenging the patent. The court believed that it was against public policy to force the party best able to challenge an invalid patent to pay royalties. However, the court noted that the licensee must bear the consequences of not paying the royalties; both a money judgment for royalties unpaid should the licensor prove the validity of the patents and loss of the license because of nonpayment of royalties. Should Cordic prevail on the merits, the court found no evidence that Medtronic would be unable to reimburse the royalties if Cordic were to pay them. Furthermore, there was no provision of law preventing such recoupment.

[Cordic Corp. v. Medtronic, Inc., 780 F2d 991 (Fed. Cir. 1985)]

Licensing agreement that grants licensor rights far greater than those given by Copyright Act is misuse of copyright.   Lasercomb developed a software program for the creation and manufacturing of certain machine tools. Holiday also manufactured machine tools and licensed software from Lasercomb. The licensing agreement provided that neither Holiday nor its employees would develop a similar program for 99 years. Reynolds, an employee of Holiday, copied the Lasercomb software to develop a program for Holiday. When Lasercomb sued for copyright infringement, Reynolds asserted the defense of misuse of copyright. *Held:* There was a misuse of copyright. The court first analogized the defense to misuse of patent. The defense arises when the copyright or patent holder tries to control a licensee's behavior; such control being beyond the scope of the patent or copyright. The court held that a copyright holder could not use the copyright to secure rights or a limited monopoly not granted by the copyright office. Here, the court found the licensing agreement to be an attempt to gain rights beyond the scope of copyright. The 99-year prohibition was longer than a copyright grant; furthermore, Lasercomb tried to use its copyright in a program to stop competition in a competing idea: certain machine tool production.

[Lasercomb Am. Inc. v. Reynolds, 911 F2d 970 (4th Cir. 1990)]

Reducing prices only for certain clients, who are being courted by competitor, may be violation of Sherman Act.   Control Data was a third-party servicer of certain IBM computers. CES, founded by several former Control Data employees, tried to engage in a comparable business. CES tried to woo several Control Data clients. Control Data responded by offering lower prices for the clients sought by CES. CES sued under the Sherman Anti-Trust Act, alleging predatory pricing. *Held:* There was sufficient evidence of predatory pricing for the matter to go to jury. The court noted that where prices are reduced only for certain clients rather than across the board, the prices could be seen as predatory. Here, Control Data only lowered prices to those clients sought by CES; therefore, with regard to CES, Control Data's pricing could be seen as a barricade to CES's entry into the market and as a sign of Control Data's attempted monopolization.

[CE Servs. v. Control Data Corp., 759 F2d 1241 (5th Cir. 1985)]

PART B.   INTEGRATED SYSTEMS AND LEVERAGE

¶ 7.03 TYING ARRANGEMENTS

Court announces three factors to examine before illegal tie can be found.   IBM developed an integrated disk driver and disk storage unit to replace what had been two separate units. This single unit offered increased storage space and on-line access to all materials saved. It also reduced the cost per megabyte of storage. Memorex sold separate drivers and storage units, and claimed that the IBM integration constituted an illegal tying arrangement. *Held:* There was no illegal tie. According to the court, three factors must be examined before a tie can be found. The court looked at: (1) the function of the aggregation; here, the function was to offer more storage at a lower price; (2) cost savings apart from savings associated with marketing two products instead of one; here, because the unit was integrated, certain components needed to tie the separate units and make them readily attachable and removable were not present, resulting in cost savings; (3) whether the tied products are normally sold as a unit; here, the unit was designed to be sold as one. In fact, the court noted that Memorex, seeing the superiority of such integration, had developed a similar unit. None of the factors led the court to find an illegal tie-in.

[ILC Peripherals Leasing Corp. v. IBM Corp., 448 F. Supp. 228 (ND Cal. 1978), aff'd sub nom Memorex Corp. v. IBM, 636 F2d 1188 (9th Cir. 1980), cert. denied, 452 US 972 (1981)]

[1] Product Differentiation

Integration of memory storage and central processing units are not illegal tying arrangement. IBM sold central processing units (CPUs) and various peripheral units including memory storage units. Telex sold peripheral units for IBM CPUs. When IBM developed a CPU with an integrated memory unit, Telex claimed that this was an illegal tying arrangement and was predatory on its sales of memory units. *Held:* IBM did not violate the Sherman Anti-Trust Act with its introduction of an integrated CPU. According to the court, IBM did not use monopoly power for advantage. The price of the new units gave IBM a 20 percent profit over costs. This wide a profit margin the court was not deemed predatory. Furthermore, the adaptation of the memory unit and CPU into one smaller, compact machine was a valid innovative adaptation rather than an attempt to monopolize.

[Telex Corp. v. IBM, 510 F2d 894 (10th Cir. 1975)]

[2] Bundling and Economic Power

No illegal tying arrangement exists where manufacturer charges software licensing fee and gives no warranty to purchasers that do not acquire manufacturer's whole system. Atex developed and manufactured hardware and software for use by newspapers and magazines. Xeta developed video screens and keyboards that could be used with the Atex system. Xeta claimed that Atex imposed an illegal tying arrangement on its customers by requiring them to use Atex screens and keyboards when acquiring an Atex system. In particular, Xeta pointed to the facts that users of Xeta equipment received no warranty on their Atex equipment and that Xeta users were charged a licensing fee for software. *Held:* There was insufficient evidence to show an illegal tying arrangement for a grant of a preliminary injunction. The court stated the first test for a tying arrangement is that there be a tie. According to the court, the fact that warranty was given only to those customers using only Atex equipment did not constitute a tie. This simply represented a common computer practice. The fact that Atex charged a licensing fee for software to Xeta users was also not evidence of an illegal tie. Since this fee represented a breakdown of costs charged to Atex users in their flat fee, it would include the software license.

[Xeta, Inc. v. Atex, Inc., 852 F2d 1280 (Fed. Cir. 1988)]

There is no illegal tying arrangement where manufacturer lacks sufficient market power and reasonable alternatives exist.   AI Root had licensed MAI hardware and software from CD. AI decided to purchase used MAI equipment, but continue to acquire MAI operating software from CD. CD would only license the software AI wanted if AI would agree to license certain other MAI software. AI claimed that this was an illegal tying arrangement, and cited the MAI copyright on its software to show MAI market strength. *Held:* There was no illegal tying arrangement. The court held that MAI lacked sufficient economic power for an illegal tying arrangement. The court looked to numerous other small-computer makers to show that MAI did not have substantial power. Furthermore, a copyright by itself does not evidence economic power, but rather great demand for a product evidences such power. There was no evidence of great demand or unavailability of substitutes for MAI products.

[AI Root Co. v. Computer/Dynamics, 806 F2d 673 (6th Cir. 1987)]

Power over price is requirement for illegal tying arrangement; uniqueness and market share may be surrogates for power over price.   Various individuals operated franchises of CAC. As part of the franchise agreement, they were required to have their data processed at CAC's data-processing center. If they did not, they had to have their data reports look exactly like CAC reports. When personal computers became inexpensive, the franchisees bought computers, which were unable to generate reports that had the exact CAC appearance. They nonetheless generated their own reports. When CAC terminated the franchise agreement, the franchisees alleged that the data processing and franchises were illegally tied. *Held:* There was no illegal tying. The court noted that power over price is a requirement for illegal tying. Market share and uniqueness can be used to show such power; but according, to the court, the franchisees established neither. There was no showing that CAC dominated the accounting field; in fact, CAC was a small player. As to uniqueness, plaintiffs failed to show that CAC had any power to stop competitors from entering the franchise accounting business or had any cost advantage over potential competitors. Although CAC's business was unusual, it was not unique.

[Will v. Comprehensive Accounting Corp., 776 F2d 665 (7th Cir. 1985)]

Manufacturer's requirement that its operating system software purchasers also buy its computers can be illegal tying arrangement regardless of manufacturer's marketing power.   Data General manufactures computers and operating system software for those computers. It sells the computers and software as a package. Digidyne sells comparable computers, which are capable of running the Data General operating system. Data General, however, refused to license its software to anyone but its computer buyers. Digidyne claimed this constituted an illegal tying arrangement. *Held:* A tying arrangement is illegal per se if the seller of the tying product has the capacity to force some buyers to purchase a tied product that they do not want or would have preferred to purchase elsewhere. The court stated that market dominance over all or many buyers was not required. All that was needed was a showing that the power existed over some buyers. A showing that the effect was not insignificant was sufficient to warrant antitrust consideration. Furthermore, since the Data General operating system was copyrighted, it could not use that government-given monopoly to force the purchase of another product—its computers.

[Digidyne Corp. v. Data Gen. Corp., 734 F2d 1336 (9th Cir. 1989)]

Court refuses to use "lock-in" analysis to determine relevant market in antitrust case. GBS marketed Phillips computers. Phillips computers used a memory card that it acquired from two German manufacturers that dealt exclusively with Phillips. GBS claimed that Phillips attempted to monopolize the market for memory cards through its agreement with the manufacturers. According to GBS, the relevant market for consideration of the antitrust claim was the market for the cards. *Held:* There was no monopoly. The court stated that the relevant market was not the market for memory cards, but rather the market for small computers generally. Looking to competing computer systems, the court pointed out that there was no market for the memory cards absent the Phillips computer. The two were integral parts of each other. The court refused to use a "lock-in" analysis in which the locked-in component by itself is deemed to be the relevant market. The court stated that the "lock-in" analysis would allow any plaintiff to point to a unique component of a manufacturer and claim that the manufacturer had a monopoly.

[General Business Sys. v. North Am. Phillips Corp., 699 F2d 965 (9th Cir. 1983)]

[3] Services and Systems

No illegal tie exists where software developer, not manufacturer, requires users of program to have most recent update of program. Prime Computer was the manufacturer of computer systems and software and the licensee of Ford Motor Company software. The Ford license required that users of the Ford software have the most current version. Prime supplied for an annual-fee hardware maintenance and software support services, which included software updates. The initial purchase of the Ford program did not require a hardware maintenance agreement, but the cost of support services and updates of the Ford program absent the hardware maintenance agreement was prohibitively expensive. Virtual Maintenance sought to perform hardware maintenance on Prime computers but discovered that the arrangement for software and hardware maintenance made entry into Prime repair service difficult. Virtual successfully claimed that the software support and hardware maintenance agreement constituted an illegal tying arrangement. Prime appealed, claiming that the jury was given too limited a market for its determination of the tying product market: The market for the Ford software. *Held:* The market was too narrowly defined at trial. The court stated that market definitions cannot be based on a single manufacturer's products, because such markets do not reflect interbrand competition. Ford's requirement that all users of the Ford program have the updated version of the software is not one imposed by Prime. The court felt that the trial court defined the market on the demand side alone; this definition is erroneous. The supply side must also be considered. According to the court, other suppliers could enter the market to supply Ford-type software. The fact that certain Ford users had already purchased Prime hardware did not lock those users into the Prime contracts. "Lock-in" theory only holds if the monopolizer has no fear of being replaced by competitors because of the substantial investment in equipment; however, Ford controls the Ford program, not Prime. Therefore, it lacks the power to control prices. If Ford believed the Prime prices were too high, it could choose not to renew its license.

[Virtual Maintenance, Inc. v. Prime Computer, Inc., 957 F2d 1318 (6th Cir. 1992)]

Computer maintenance firm that uses manufacturer's time-and-materials service to carry out its own service controls lacks standing to assert antitrust claim. Hewlett-Packard (HP) is the manufacturer of computers, and offers repair service options for those computers: (1) a service contract for a flat annual fee or (2) a time and materials (T&M) contract: a charge for each repair. Hypoint discovered that HP computers were very reliable and that it could sell service contracts for less than HP and use HP's own T&M personnel to execute the repairs for Hypoint's clients. HP discovered this and stopped its four-hour repair response time to T&M customers. Hypoint claimed that this constituted a violation of antitrust law. *Held:* Hypoint lacked standing to assert an antitrust claim, nor was there a requisite showing of antitrust injury. There was no showing of a requisite antitrust injury. According to the court, an injury to a competitor is not necessarily an antitrust violation. Furthermore, Hypoint depended on HP's services, which HP was free to change. According to the court, HP's termination of the four-hour response time had no anticompetitive impact. It was in fact beneficial to competing service organizations because the decision angered T&M customers and caused them to search for alternative service providers. The elimination of the four-hour response time also made it easier for new firms to enter the market, since it lowered the standard for service. The limitation in service without a corresponding decrease in price was the economic equivalent of an increase in price, which the court believed is clearly not anticompetitive.

[Hypoint Technology, Inc. v. Hewlett-Packard Co., 949 F2d 874 (6th Cir. 1991)]

Court adopts broad market definition in suit alleging illegal tying arrangement. Allen-Myland was in the business of installing upgrades in IBM mainframes, a service also provided by IBM. IBM provided for net-priced upgrades: If IBM had to remove a piece of the computer and replace it with a new component as part of the upgrade, IBM would bundle the cost of labor and of the new component. Myland contended that this bundling constituted an illegal tying arrangement. As part of its charges, Myland argued that the relevant market was for sales of new mainframe systems, a market in which IBM retained a substantial share. *Held:* There was no illegal tie. The court adopted a broad market definition. The market included the host of products that provide reasonable alternatives to purchases of large-scale mainframes and upgrades and that constrain IBM's ability to raise prices of these products or exclude competition. This included leased computers and lesser systems that could be linked to serve in distributed data-processing approaches. The court noted that the increasing overlap and interchangeability of large- and small-scale systems. The court's broad market definition led the court to reach the conclusion that IBM had insufficient market power to sustain a per se antitrust violation.

[Allen-Myland, Inc. v. IBM, 693 F. Supp. 262 (ED Pa. 1988)]

¶ 7.04 PACKAGE LICENSING

Licensing agreement that provides for royalties on package of patents, which royalties would continue until last patent expires, is not misuse of patent where agreement is not coerced. Beckman licensed a group of patents on instruments from Technical. In this package, it received a license on an instrument on which the patent was pending but not yet granted. The license provided for royalty payments until the last patent expired. When the patent was granted on the last instrument, Beckman alleged misuse of patent, claiming that Technical improperly extended the term of the patents beyond their expiration. *Held:* Absent a conditioning of the license upon receiving a package of all the patents, no misuse could be found. According to the court, a licensing agreement voluntarily entered will not be found a misuse of patent. The fact that the term of the license was extended by a patent granted after the agreement did not show a misuse of patent. Only coercion or conditioning of a license to cover unpatented products or procedures would be considered a misuse.

[Beckman Instruments, Inc. v. Technical Dev. Corp., 433 F2d 55 (7th Cir. 1970), cert. denied, 401 US 976 (1971)]

PART C.   PROVISIONS AND TERMS OF LICENSING

¶ 7.05 TECHNOLOGY SCOPE OF LICENSE

In broad sales agreement, copyright holder not only transfers its copyright but also any causes of action under copyright that arose before transfer. SAPC held a copyright on a spreadsheet program similar to one developed by Lotus. Lotus later bought the entire software business of SAPC. In the purchase agreement, it ac-quired all rights, tangible and intangible, in the SAPC programs and the copyrights to those programs. When SAPC tried to sue for incidents of copyright infringement and of misappropriation of trade secrets occurring before the transfer, Lotus alleged that the purchase agreement precluded such suit. *Held:* SAPC was prevented from suing. According to the court, the purchase agreement unambiguously transferred all rights under the copyright to Lotus. Therefore, the right to sue Lotus was trans-ferred to Lotus. The court noted that a party seeking to deviate from the terms of a broad and general conveyance such as the one between SAPC and Lotus has the burden of proving the asserted specific exception. SAPC failed to show any basis to conclude that there was a reservation of a prior right of action against Lotus and that any previously existing claims were not transferred by the agreement.

[SAPC, Inc. v. Lotus Dev. Corp., 921 F2d 360 (1st Cir. 1990)]

License that provides for reservation of ownership rights in licensor is synony-mous with reservation of copyright. SOS provided hardware and software for processing payrolls. Payday supplied payroll services for clients, and seeking to com-puterize its systems, licensed software from SOS. The licensing agreement stated that SOS allowed use of its program but retained ownership. Upon receiving unautho-rized copies of the SOS program, Payday terminated the agreement. SOS sued for copyright infringement, but Payday claimed that it could not violate the copyright since it had a license to use the program. *Held:* A licensee can violate copyright. Ac-cording to the court, if the licensee's use is beyond the scope of the copyright, the li-censee may be liable for copyright infringement. Although state contract law governs the interpretation of contract, such law cannot stand in the way of the federal policy designed to protect and encourage intellectual property rights. Therefore, although state law stated that ambiguities are interpreted against the drafter and here the license does not mention copyright, the fact that SOS retained ownership meant that it re-tained copyright. Furthermore, when interests in intellectual property are not expressly conveyed in the license, the interests are reserved to the licensor.

[SOS, Inc. v. Payday, Inc., 886 F2d 1081 (9th Cir. 1989)]

Court adopts broad use of parole evidence to determine whether licensing agree-ment transferred the copyright. Stacey developed a computer program for Fried-man, an attorney in the practice of debt collection. In their development contract, the parties agreed that the resulting program was to be Friedman's "property" although Stacey would have access to and use of parts of the program. Stacey, however, made superficial changes to the program and sold it to other debt collection lawyers, including Friedman's competitors. Friedman claimed that Stacey violated his copy-right. However, Stacey contended that Friedman had no copyright because the development agreement did not convey such an interest, and Stacey moved to dismiss. *Held:* The court refused Stacey's motion to dismiss. According to the court, the meaning of "property" in the development agreement was ambiguous as to whether it gave ownership of the copyright or just ownership of a copy of the program to Friedman. The court decided that it would need to use a liberal approach to the parole evidence rule to allow testimony as to what the ambiguous term meant. The court reasoned that extrinsic evidence could be used to interpret an existing term and that interpretation would not be inconsistent with the contract.

[Friedman v. Stacey Data Processing Servs., Inc., 17 USPQ2d 1858 (ND Ill. 1990)]

¶ 7.06 OBLIGATIONS OF GOOD FAITH AND BEST EFFORTS

Absent showing of unfair price, corporation does not breach its duty to minority shareholders by selling licenses to another corporation that later sells licenses for significantly more. MCS entered into a permanent and exclusive licensing agreement with PEI, in which PEI received the rights to two software programs for cash and the assumption of certain MCS debt. PEI also hired the MCS majority stockholder to manage the MCS software. PEI later sold the licenses for significantly more than that which it paid. Jones, a minority shareholder of MCS, sued MCS and PEI, claiming that they breached their fiduciary duty to the minority shareholders in the execution of their licensing agreement. *Held:* There was no breach of duty. The court noted that the licensing agreements were conducted at arm's length. The payments made thereunder were fair market value. The fact that the licenses appreciated in value did not affect the fact that at the time the license between MCS and PEI was executed the price was fair. Furthermore, there was no showing in the record that the majority shareholder compromised the value of the licenses in exchange for employment with PEI.

[Jones v. Management & Computer Servs., Inc., 976 F2d 857 (3d Cir. 1992)]

Court circumvents statute of frauds for nonexclusive requirements contract. Advent, an English company, developed a hardware and software system for placing engineering drawings into computer data bases. Unisys desired to market the system in the United States. Under an agreement with Unisys, Advent agreed to supply hardware and software needed by Unisys as well as manpower and technical assistance to Unisys for building and installing the system of any Unisys buyers. Unisys terminated the agreement. When Advent sued for breach of contract, Unisys claimed that the UCC statute of frauds provision (UCC § 2-201) applied. That section requires that there be a writing that specifies quantity for there to be a sales contract. Otherwise, the agreement is unenforceable. *Held:* The statute of frauds was inapplicable. The court said that the agreement between Advent and Unisys could be seen as a nonexclusive requirements contract. The court stated that Section 2-306 of the UCC lifts an exclusive requirements contract, which does not specify amount, out of the statute of frauds. The UCC's rationale for lifting the quantity requirement for a requirements contract was that such contracts were speculative and the UCC does not want to impinge on commercial development. Furthermore, the requirement that best efforts be used in a requirements contract gave the court reason to believe that there would be sales, and therefore the contract did provide for some definite sales. The court then found it easy to extend the rationale for exclusive requirements contracts to nonexclusive requirements contracts.

[Advent Sys., Ltd. v. Unisys Corp., 925 F2d 670 (3d Cir. 1991)]

Licensor, absent an explicit duty to act in licensee's best interest, is not fiduciary for licensee. Tel-Phonic contracted with TBS to purchase TBS hardware and to market TBS software. Subsequently, problems arose with hardware delivery and with the functioning of the software. Tel-Phonic claimed that TBS's representations were false, that TBS billed for charges not due, and that TBS was liable for other improprieties. As a result of such behavior, Tel-Phonic sued TBS, claiming that TBS had breached its fiduciary duty. *Held:* There was no breach of duty. According to the court, there was no breach because there was no duty. The relationship between TBS and Tel-Phonic was a contractual arm's length transaction. TBS made no assurances that it would act in Tel-Phonic's best interests. Without such assurances, Tel-Phonic could not rely on its own subjective trust that TBS would act as a fiduciary.

[Tel-Phonic Servs., Inc. v. TBS Int'l, Inc., 975 F2d 1134 (5th Cir. 1992)]

Court refuses to imply duty to use best efforts. Perkin-Elmer was the manufacturer of hardware that Kardios bought and adapted so that the hardware could "emulate" or "imitate" an IBM computer. Kardios had difficulties selling these modified computers and sought a licensing agreement with Perkin-Elmer in which Perkin-Elmer would market and sell the computers. The parties entered into an agreement in which Perkin-Elmer agreed to sell 100 computers per year—if not, Kardios could terminate the agreement. Furthermore, the agreement provided that two Kardios distributors were allowed to continue selling the adapted product. Although drafts of the agreement contained a "best efforts" clause, it was absent from the final agreement. Perkin-Elmer did not expend great effort to sell the product and was unsuccessful in its sales attempts. Kardios, therefore, terminated the agreement and sued for breach of contract, claiming Perkin-Elmer failed to use its best efforts. *Held:* There was no failure of best efforts on the part of Perkin-Elmer. The court stated that it would not imply a duty to use best efforts under the facts of this case. The court first looked at the ability of Kardios to terminate the agreement if Perkin-Elmer did not sell 100 units per year. This freed Kardios to market the units itself. Kardios, therefore, was not locked into an agreement with Perkin-Elmer. The court also looked to the fact that certain Kardios distributors could also sell the computers. Perkin-Elmer, therefore, lacked exclusive control over Kardios warranting best efforts. Finally, the court refused to imply a duty that had been clearly refused by the parties. The parties had included best efforts in draft agreements but not in the final agreement.

[Kardios Sys. Corp. v. Perkin-Elmer Corp., 645 F. Supp. 506 (D. Md. 1986)]

Duty of best efforts to sell and market product cannot be imposed on purchaser of product when purchaser made substantial upfront royalty payments. Para-Data sold to Telebit Corporation the Communications Products Division of Para-Data and exclusive rights to a computer-networking product known as ACS. The parties entered into a formal contractual agreement. Telebit paid ParaData $1 million as a technology licensing fee and $1 million in prepaid royalties on Telebit's future sales of ACS products. Telebit also agreed to pay royalties to ParaData on ACS sales over the next four years according to an agreed-on formula. Dissatisfied with the efforts made by Telebit to sell ACS products, ParaData brought suit against Telebit, alleging that Telebit breached its contract by failing to aggressively market and sell ACS products. Specifically, ParaData argued that the court should imply on Telebit as an exclusive licensee a duty of best efforts to market and sell ACS products. Para-Data also argued that Telebit's actions violated an implied covenant of good faith and fair dealing when Telebit failed to adequately support the sale and marketing of ACS products. *Held:* The court refused to imply a duty of best efforts on Telebit; the court also refused to imply a covenant of good faith and fair dealing on the enforcement of the contract. Here, ParaData received $1 million in upfront royalty payments in exchange for the exclusive rights to ACS products that it granted to Telebit. These prepaid royalty payments assured ParaData that it would receive something for its sale of the ACS products. The payments also gave Telebit an incentive to effectively market ACS to make up for the cost of acquiring the system. Since Telebit made a substantial upfront payment of royalties, the court found it unnecessary to imply a duty of best efforts. As to the action for breach of an implied covenant of good faith and fair dealing, the court noted that such an action is recognized only where "a party to a contract makes the manner of its performance a matter of its own discretion"—which depends on the nature of the agreement between them. Here, Telebit had no discretion in the performance of its duties under the terms of the contract. Specifically, Telebit had no express duties to market or sell ACS products under the contract.

[Paradata Computer Networks, Inc. v. Telebit Corp., 830 F. Supp. 1001 (ED Mich. 1993)]

Even though party does not expressly bind himself to use reasonable efforts to bring profits and revenues into existence, agreement executed by parties is "in-

stinct with obligation", and consequently is binding. Otis F. Wood and Lucy, Lady Duff-Gordon, a fashion designer, entered into an employment agreement. Under the terms of the agreement, Wood had the exclusive right to place Lucy's indorsements on designs of other manufacturers. Wood also had the exclusive right to place Lucy's designs on sale or to license others to market them. In return, Lucy was to receive one half of "all profits and revenues" derived from any contracts Wood might make. Wood sued Lucy for breach of contract, claiming that Lucy placed its indorsement on fabrics, dresses, and millinery without his knowledge, and withheld the profits. *Held:* A binding contract existed; it was not void for want of mutuality. Even though Wood did not expressly bind himself to use reasonable efforts to place Lucy's indorsements and market Lucy's designs, such a promise could fairly be implied. An express promise may be lacking; however, if the whole writing is "instinct with an obligation," a contract exists. The implication of a promise was apparent here. Lucy had given an exclusive privilege and was to have no right for at least a year to place its own indorsements or market its own designs except through Wood. Lucy's sole compensation for the granting of the exclusive privilege to Wood was one half of the profits produced from Wood's efforts. Wood promised that he would account monthly for all money received and that he would take out all necessary patents and copyrights. Wood's promises to pay Lucy one half of the profits and to render accounts monthly was a promise to use reasonable efforts to bring profits and revenues into existence.

[Wood v. Lucy, Lady Duff-Gordon, 222 NY 88, 118 NE 214 (1917)]

¶ 7.07 SECURITY INTERESTS IN INTANGIBLES

[1] Defining Collateral

Filing rather than possession is needed to perfect security interest in computer programs. The debtor was in the business of collecting and sorting legal information using its own programs and data base. The debtor owed money to its attorney. To secure its debt, the attorney pursuant to an oral security agreement took copies of the Information's computer programs and data bases. The trustee in bankruptcy claimed a priority in the program and challenged the attorney's security interest. *Held:* The attorney lacked a perfected security interest. The court noted that although possession was a means of perfection, this means was not available for intangibles. The court determined that the programs and data bases were intangibles because their value did not arise from the media on which they were stored but rather from the information stored. Information is an intangible, which can only be perfected through filing. Furthermore, since the attorney only possessed a copy of the program, his possession did not put others on notice that he held a security interest. Only a filing would provide such notice.

[In re Information Exch., Inc., 98 BR 603 (Bankr. ND Ga. 1989)]

Security interest in computer program does not extend to enhanced versions developed by licensee. The debtor granted a security interest to creditor in a software program. This interest was properly perfected. Later the debtor entered into a licensing agreement with Intelligent Investment Systems, which allowed Intelligent to develop advanced versions of the software for which debtor would receive royalties. When the debtor filed for bankruptcy, the creditor claimed to have an interest in the software, including advanced versions of the programs developed by Intelligent. *Held:* The court limited the creditor's lien to the version in existence at the time of its loan. The enhancements could be identified separately from the earlier version and were not, therefore, within the lien. The copyright in the derivative work material was in the licensee Intelligent, which was not a party to the loan agreement.

[In re C Tek Software, Inc., 127 BR 501 (Bankr. DNH 1991)]

Where there is no clear delineation of which party owns which computer program developments, court makes no decision on those programs. BEHR, a venture capital partnership, and Bedford entered into an agreement whereby BEHR would finance computer developments of Bedford. Under the agreement, BEHR would own all technology and new products developed after the time of the agreement. Any technology before the agreement remained the property of Bedford. However, no clear delineation of property rights was ever made. Computer codes in existence at the time of the agreement were not set down to establish a basis for Bedford's and BEHR's property rights. When Bedford filed for bankruptcy, BEHR claimed to be the owner of all Bedford codes since they were all developed subsequent to the agreement. *Held:* BEHR had no rights in the programs. According to the court, the software constituted tangible property, since it had no existence without the "actual hardware components to which it gives operational life" and since the software is also embodied in a tangible medium. To the extent that it is tangible, it is covered by the UCC. Under the UCC, a buyer of identifiable goods may replevy those goods. However, under the contract at issue, it was not clear which goods were identified and which goods actually belonged to BEHR since there was no basis at the time of the contract for what would constitute new developments. Even if the goods were intangible, the law would also require the ability to segregate and identify what belonged to BEHR, and under the vague basis of the contract this was not possible.

[In re Bedford Computer Corp., 62 BR 555 (Bankr. DNH 1986)]

¶ 7.08 FORUM SELECTION

Choice-of-law clause preempts claim of violation of Massachusetts statute, since the state's law does not govern the agreement. Northeast contracted with

Microdata to be the sole distributor of certain Microdata software in a defined terri-
tory. Several years into the agreement, Microdata terminated it. Northeast sued, claiming numerous improprieties by Microdata and brought suit on numerous claims
including a violation of the Massachusetts unfair trade practices statute. A magistrate
determined that the parties had stated that the contract claims would be settled under
California law; and analogizing unfair trade practices to a contract claim, he determined that California law applied. Since California had no unfair trade practices
statute, the claim was dismissed, and Northeast appealed. *Held:* Affirmed. The court
noted that the Massachusetts statute was designed to prevent a breach of contract accompanied by bad motive. Since the statute was essentially breach of contract, any
claim thereunder alleging violations related to the breach of contract would be a
contract claim. Such contract claims clearly fell within the choice-of-law provision
in the original agreement. Thus, since the choice-of-law clause provided for California law, the Massachusetts statute was inapplicable. The court noted, however, that
a claim of fraud in the formation of the contract would fall outside the contract's choice-
of-law provision and could be pressed under the Massachusetts statute.

[Northeast Data Sys., Inc. v. McDonnell Douglas Computer Sys. Co., 986 F2d 607
(1st Cir. 1993)]

PART D.   ROYALTY ISSUES

¶ 7.09 ROYALTY DURATION

**Royalty payment clause in licensing agreement is interpreted according to
behavior of parties and construction that seemed most logical.**   Management
System Associates and McDonnell Douglas Corporation entered into a licensing
agreement that provided for royalty payments by McDonnell for all of its sales or
leases of Management's software. For leases, the royalty payment was to be made
in full at the beginning of the lease period. Management sued for insufficient royalty payments, claiming that the royalty payment on the leases should be based on the
useful life of the software. McDonnell countered that the payment should be based
on the lease term. *Held:* Royalty payments were correctly calculated based on the
lease term. The court noted that the licensing agreement would be interpreted by the
conduct of the parties over time. Where the parties interpret a contract one way, the
court would not change that construction when one party later claims ambiguity.
The court noted for most of the contract period, McDonnell sent Management copies
of the leases with the royalty payments clearly based on the lease terms. MSA did not
object. Also, using the rules of contract interpretation, the court followed the interpretation of the contract that made more sense. The Management interpretation was

flawed because it called for McDonnell to make payments on a term to which the lessee had not agreed.

[Management Sys. Assocs. v. McDonnell Douglas Corp., 762 F2d 1161 (4th Cir. 1985)]

¶ 7.10 ROYALTY COMPUTATION

Court holds that patent holder of chip can base its royalty on whole semiconductor of which chip is just a part. Western held a patent on a process for manufacturing silicon chips for use in semiconductors. Stewart Warner Corporation violated the patent, but contended that Western misused its patent by charging royalties based on the price of the whole semiconductor that Western's licensees produced. Stewart alleged that royalties should have been based on the price of the chip alone, because by charging a royalty based on the whole semiconductor Western was receiving royalties on unpatented parts. *Held:* There was no misuse of patent. The court noted that misuse would occur if Western charged a royalty for semiconductors that did not use its chips. That was not the case here. According to the court, the semiconductor was easier to value than the chip; and therefore, it was easier to compute royalties. Furthermore, most of the value of a semiconductor is in the chips, not the plastic around it. Western was really not getting extra royalties from the unpatented parts, since those parts had little value. The court also believed that Western charged a lower royalty percentage than it would have if just the chip were the basis of the royalty payment.

[Western-Elec. Co. v. Stewart Warner Corp., 631 F2d 333 (4th Cir.), cert. denied, 450 US 971 (1980)]

PART E.   LICENSEE'S OBLIGATIONS AND RIGHTS

¶ 7.11 NONDISCLOSURE AND INFORMATION USE

Nondisclosure agreement is basis for finding that information is trade secret. Integrated Cash Management developed a combination of generic programs. It claimed this integrated combination as a protected trade secret. Several employees of Integrated, who had signed nondisclosure agreements, left Integrated to work for Digital Transactions. When Digital developed a similar combination, Integrated successfully sued for misappropriation of trade secrets by Digital and its former employees, who appealed. *Held:* Affirmed. According to the court, several factors weighed in favor of the finding of misappropriation. A trade secret can be any pattern known only to one business that gives that business a competitive edge. Although the programs were generic, Integrated's combination of them was a unique whole. Furthermore, Integrated guarded the secret; its promotional literature, while speaking of the combination, did not reveal its workings. The nondisclosure agreements clearly put employees on notice that the combination was protected information, and the architecture of the combination could not be duplicated without years of research or misappropriation.

[Integrated Cash Management Servs., Inc. v. Digital Transactions, Inc., 920 F2d 171 (2d Cir. 1990)]

¶ 7.12 NONCIRCUMVENTION AND COMPETITION

For preliminary injunction against employee who signed noncompetition agreement, corporation need only show that employee had access to confidential information; it need not prove that information is trade secret. Andreadakis while employed at Modern Control signed a noncompetition agreement whereby he agreed not to work for a competitor of Modern for two years, or if he did work for a competitor, not to work on the same types of projects on which he worked at Modern. Andreadakis left Modern, where he was working on computer display screens, and began work at a competitor doing the same. Modern sought to enjoin Andreadakis from such work, and the district court declined to grant an injunction finding the noncompetition agreement was probably unenforceable. *Held:* The injunction should have been granted. The court stated that the principal reason for the agreement was to protect confidential business information and trade secrets. The court then gave the standard for an injunction. Modern did not have to prove that it had any trade secrets; such a finding would be time-consuming and defeat the purpose of an injunction. Rather, Modern needed to show that there was confidential information and that Andreadakis had access to it. Here, the court found that there was such information, and he did have access thereto.

[Modern Controls v. Andreadakis, 578 F2d 1264 (8th Cir. 1978)]

¶ 7.13 MODIFICATIONS AND IMPROVEMENTS

[1] Licensee's Right to Adapt Technology

Licensees who purchase circuit board that changes nature of video game create derivative work in violation of licensor's copyright. Midway was the manufacturer of video game machines. Artic invented circuit boards for two of Midway's machines. These boards allowed for a faster rate of play and were sold to the licensees of the Midway machines. Midway sued for copyright infringement, but Artic contended that there was no infringement because the board just allowed for a faster rate of play. *Held:* Licensees are not authorized to use speeded-up versions of the game under copyright law. Copyright law allows the copyright holder the exclusive right to prepare derivative works. The licensees who used the Artic circuit board also created a derivative work. Although the court believed the definition of derivative work did not neatly encompass the Artic circuit board, there was a market for the speeded-up games because a fast rate of play would generate extra revenue that would be earned by licensees of the games. The court believed this factor tipped the balance in favor of Midway.

[Midway Mfg. Co. v. Artic Int'l, Inc., 704 F2d 1009 (7th Cir. 1983)]

Owner of program is allowed to develop enhanced versions of program for its own use but may not sell those versions to others. Foresight Resources sought a preliminary injunction against Pfortmiller to prevent him from selling or distributing an enhanced version of Foresight program. Pfortmiller had developed the enhanced program for the use of Hall-Kimbrell, a purchaser of the Foresight program. Foresight claimed that Pfortmiller's enhanced program violated Foresight's copyright. *Held:* Injunction granted. The court held that the owner of a copy of a program is allowed to make adaptations to a program if the adaptation is for the program owner's use only. The court noted that the Copyright Act allows the owner of a program to make adaptations if those adaptations are made in connection with the owner's use of the program. Although Hall-Kimbrell did not make the adaptations itself, the court found no violation of copyright when Hall-Kimbrell allowed an outsider with computer expertise to make the enhancements if those enhancements were solely for the use of Hall-Kimbrell. The court did forbid Pfortmiller from selling the enhanced program to third parties, however, since he would not be adapting the programs owned by those third parties but would rather be selling copyrighted material.

[Foresight Resources Corp. v. Pfortmiller, 719 F. Supp. 1006 (D. Kan. 1989)]

Licensing agreement that allowed enhancements to software does not allow enhancements that create whole new software that renders part of licensing agreement meaningless. PRC and the National Association of Realtors (NAR) entered an agreement in which NAR was granted a nonexclusive license to use PRC's on-line software. The PRC software allowed on-line access to real estate listings data bases. In return for the license, NAR was to use its best efforts to sell to its members books of complete real estate listings produced by PRC. Under the agreement, NAR was allowed to make enhancements to the on-line software. NAR developed an enhancement in which information called up on the PRC service could be manipulated so that the product printed would be camera ready for a printer, thereby requiring no typesetting. Those with the enhancement, then, could produce their own real estate books. PRC believed that the enhancement violated the licensing agreement. *Held:* The enhancement violated the licensing agreement. According to the court, the agreement did not cover use of the system to produce a multiple-listing book that rendered the original system obsolete. The court indicated that the license to use and make further developments in an on-line computer system did not cover converting that system into an entirely different, "off-line" product. The court also believed that allowing NAR members to produce their own books would render the best-efforts clause in the agreement meaningless.

[PRC Realty Sys., Inc. v. National Ass'n of Realtors, Inc., 766 F. Supp. 453 (ED Va. 1991)]

¶ 7.14 RESALE AND USE OF LICENSED TECHNOLOGY

Absent broad conveyancing language, licensing agreement will not give licensee right to serve as foundry for parts. Intel sued to stop the importation of certain computers that it claimed violated patents that it held. One of the foreign makers, Atmel, claimed that it did not violate the Intel patent because it acquired its Erasable Programmable Read-Only Memories (EPROMs) from Sanyo. Sanyo and Intel had a licensing agreement whereby Sanyo could make, use, and sell any Sanyo products using Intel patents. Intel claimed that this agreement only extended to products made by Sanyo; it did not allow Sanyo to become a foundry for parts for others. Atmel countered that the Intel/Sanyo agreement was only limited to not allowing others to use the Intel patents to make their own products. *Held:* The agreement did not allow others to use Sanyo as a foundry for parts. According to the court, if Sanyo was a foundry, others could turn to Sanyo for parts using Intel patents. The court believed that the agreement was not that broad. It noted that the Sanyo license was royalty free. The court would not believe that Intel would grant so broad a license without a demand for money. The court also noted that the interpretation pressed by Atmel would allow any company in the world to get parts from Sanyo without paying a licensing fee to Intel.

[Intel Corp. v. US Int'l Trade Comm'n, 946 F2d 821 (Fed. Cir. 1991)]

Party to licensing agreement that treats it as continuing in the successor to the other party may not later claim that agreement lapsed because transfer did not comply with licensing agreement. Intel and Mostek entered into a cross-licensing agreement whereby they agreed to allow use of each other's patents. Under the agreement, Mostek was to pay a one-time royalty of $100,000 to Intel. The agreement also provided that the license would continue in any party that acquired all or substantially all of the assets of either Mostek or Intel. SBS-Thomson subsequently bought assets of Mostek, so that no operational business was left with Mostek. SBS informed Intel of the transfer. At Intel's request, SBS paid the $100,000 royalty, and for five years the parties operated under the licensing agreement. Intel then claimed that the agreement was not valid because SBS did not acquire substantially all of Mostek's assets. *Held:* The transfer of assets complied with the original licensing agreement between Intel and Mostek. The court noted that the appropriate standard under general corporate law is that a company sells all or substantially all of its assets when the sale is of assets quantitatively vital to the operation of the corporation and the sale is out of the ordinary and substantially affects the existence and purpose of the corporation. This occurred in the underlying transfer. Furthermore, Intel was prevented from contesting the transfer because it had reasons to know and a chance to investigate the transfer, accepted benefits from the transfer, and accepted performance for five years after the transfer.

[Cyrix Corp. v. Intel Corp., 803 F. Supp. 1200 (ED Tex. 1992)]

¶ 7.15 CUSTOM COMMERCIAL END-USER LICENSES

Buyer of patented product does not violate patent.   Intel and Hewlett-Packard (HP) entered into a cross-licensing agreement whereby each had access to the patents of the other. Intel held a patent on a certain co-processor. ULSI developed the same co-processor design, which it gave to HP. HP was to manufacture chips according to this design, which ULSI would then sell. Intel claimed that by causing others to use the ULSI design, ULSI infringed Intel's patent on the co-processor. Intel was granted a preliminary injunction. *Held:* Injunction lifted. The court noted that under the HP/Intel licensing agreements, HP was allowed to exploit Intel patents. According to the court, ULSI was a buyer of chips from HP, and a buyer of patented goods is insulated from a claim of patent infringement. Although Intel claimed that USLI was only purchasing services from HP (the ability to manufacture according to USLI design), the court looked to the UP/ULSI contract, which specified that it was for the sale of chips. The fact that HP was working from ULSI's design had no bearing for the court since HP was authorized to exploit the Intel patents. As long as HP sold the chips, Intel had no claim since the licensing agreement was broad, and in no way limited foundry arrangements.

[Intel Corp. v. ULSI Sys. Technology, Inc., 27 USPQ2d 1136 (Fed. Cir. 1993)]

[1] Licensee's Sole Use and Secrecy

Copyright law does not preempt similar state action if elements needed to prove state action are different or greater than those needed to prove copyright violation.   Trandes developed a computer program, which it licensed to the Washington

Metro Area Transit Authority (WMATA). WMATA allowed Atkinson to have access to and use of the program. Trandes claimed that WMATA and Atkinson misappropriated trade secrets and was awarded damages. Atkinson and WMATA appealed, claiming that the trade secrets claim was preempted by federal copyright law, and since Trandes lacked a valid copyright, it had no basis for a suit. *Held:* There was no preemption. According to the court, there is no preemption if the elements of the state action are different or greater than those of the federal action. The court concluded that it is not correct to focus on the violative acts alleged and whether those acts support both copyright and trade secret actions. Instead, the elements of the two causes of action—not the facts pled to prove those elements—should be compared. On this basis, the court found an extra element to the trade secret claim: abuse of confidence or other improper conduct involved in procuring a copy of the work. This distinctive feature is not necessary to a copyright action. Since breach of confidence was proved, the extra element sustained the action for misappropriation of trade secrets.

[Trandes Corp. v. Guy F. Atkinson Co., 996 F2d 655 (4th Cir. 1993)]

Copyright law does not preempt contract provision where elements needed to prove breach of contract differ from elements needed to prove violation of copyright.   CA licensed software to National for use by National alone. When National wanted to allow a third-party data processor to do its computing, CA allowed the third party the use of its software on the condition that it be used for National alone. CA eventually learned that National had been processing data for others using the CA software. CA claimed that National violated the licensing agreement, but National countered that the contract claim was preempted by federal copyright law. *Held:* There was no preemption. The court stated that if the contract claim was co-extensive to acts forbidden under copyright, the claim would be preempted. According to the court, copyright law forbids the distribution of a copyrighted work. However, CA did not allege distribution; rather, it alleged misuse of the program under the license. The court concluded that the alleged contractual restriction on National's use of the licensed programs constituted an extra element in addition to the copyright rights making this cause of action qualitatively different from an action for copyright. Unlike a claim of unauthorized distribution, the claim that the software was improperly used does not lie within the exclusive rights of the Copyright Act.

[National Car Rental Sys., Inc. v. Computer Assocs. Int'l, Inc., 991 F2d 426 (8th Cir. 1993)]

¶ 7.16 MASS-MARKET END USERS

Box licensing agreement disclaiming warranties is not part of parties' contract.
Step-Saver created integrated hardware and software packages for its customers. For

many of its packages, it used a TSL program. The packages had many uncorrectable problems, and Step-Saver was sued by its clients. Step-Saver in turn sued TSL, which claimed that it had no liability because the licensing agreement on the program boxes explicitly disclaimed all warranties. Step-Saver claimed that the box agreement was not the agreement, but rather the telephone purchase order constituted the agreement. *Held:* The disclaimer of warranty was invalid. The court found Section 2-207 of the UCC applicable; therefore, the additional terms of the box agreement would be incorporated only if explicitly accepted by Step-Saver. According to the court, the telephone order served as the offer to contract, since it was specific as to time, amount, and price. Although warranty is a major item, the UCC supplies default rules. Furthermore, TSL never expressed unwillingness to proceed with the contract if the terms of the Box agreement were rejected, nor did any course of dealing constitute an override of Section 2-207.

[Step-Saver Data Sys., Inc. v. Wyse Technology, 939 F2d 91 (3d Cir. 1991)]

State law that prohibits copying allowed by Copyright Act is preempted by Copyright Act. Vault developed a program that prevents copying material put on its disk. Quaid acquired the disk, disassembled the program, and learned how to defeat it. Vault then developed an advanced version of the program that the Quaid program could not defeat. Vault sought, under Louisiana licensing law, to prevent Quaid from copying and disassembling the new program. The Louisiana Software License Enforcement Act allows the prohibition of copying or disassembly of a program if those restrictions are clearly spelled out in the licensing agreement. *Held:* The Louisiana statute was preempted by federal copyright law. According to the court, the Copyright Act allows copying of software for archival purposes or adaptation and use of the program. The Louisiana law squarely conflicted with federal law. Where such a conflict exists with copyright law, state law may not deny the benefits granted by federal law. Accordingly, the license agreement was unenforceable.

[Vault Corp. v. Quaid Software, Ltd., 847 F2d 255 (5th Cir. 1988)]

PART F.   DISTRIBUTION LICENSES

¶ 7.17 EXCLUSIVE DEALERSHIPS

Licensing agreement should go no further than what is needed to effectuate agreement; otherwise, it may be restraint of trade.   Aetna and Doran entered into a licensing agreement whereby Doran would develop driving simulators (hardware and software) using Aetna film and using the Aetna name on the finished product. Under the agreement, Aetna would exclusively aid Doran in marketing the simulators, and Doran would no longer make its own simulator films. ISDC entered the simulator business. Although it bought films from Aetna, Aetna refused to aid in marketing ISDC simulators. When ISDC failed, it sued Aetna and Doran, claiming that their licensing agreement was an unlawful restraint of trade prohibited by the Sherman Anti-Trust Act. *Held:* There were sufficient facts alleged to go to trial. The Sherman Act requires that a licensing agreement go no further in its marketing requirements than is necessary to effectuate the rights granted. When Doran stopped making films, effectively giving Aetna a monopoly over simulator films, the parties went beyond what was needed to effectively market the simulators. ISDC alleged that the agreement that Doran stop producing films is what propelled the exclusive marketing agreement. The court held there was sufficient evidence for a jury to consider this motivation.

[Instructional Sys. Dev. Corp. v. Aetna Casualty & Sur. Co., 817 F2d 639 (10th Cir. 1987)]

¶ 7.18　MAIL ORDER AND TERMINATION

Computer manufacturer may terminate dealers that do not offer full service and that cut into profit margins of full-service dealers. Apple Computer told distributors that they would be terminated if they sold Apple products by mail. OSC claimed that this ultimatum was in response to complaints by non–mail-order dealers who wanted to keep prices higher. OSC sued for unfair price competition. Apple alleged that mail-order sales were incompatible with its products, which were to be tailored by the dealers to the consumer's individual needs. *Held:* Apple violated no antitrust law. According to the court, a showing of unreasonableness is needed to show a restraint is anticompetitive. The fact that there were complaints by some dealers about the lower prices of mail-order dealers was insufficient absent a showing of a common scheme or conspiracy to raise prices. The court accepted Apple's reason for terminating mail-order dealers and further noted that protecting the profit margins of full-service dealers was also a sufficient reason for termination.

[OSC Corp. v. Apple Computer Co., 792 F2d 1464 (9th Cir. 1986)]

¶ 7.19　FAIR-DEALER TERMINATION LAWS

There is no showing of irreparable harm necessary for preliminary injunction where distributor had other sources for hardware and software. Modern Computer was a distributor of MB computer software, and under the software agreement Modern Computer also agreed to purchase Texas Instruments hardware from MB. Modern Computer also distributed other software products. MB tried to convert all its distributors to licensees under new agreements. Modern Computer refused, and MB raised prices charged to Modern Computer. Numerous lawsuits were filed and Modern Computer sought a preliminary injunction to forbid MB from canceling the distribution agreement. *Held:* No preliminary injunction could be granted. The court stated that for a preliminary injunction to be granted, irreparable injury needed to be shown. According to the court, Modern Computer could fulfill its hardware needs directly from Texas Instruments and it could acquire alternative banking software. The court noted that Modern Computer's customer base did not depend totally on MB software (only 86 of almost 400 customers used MB products). The court stated if Modern Computer had any remedy, it would be at law for damages on the merits of the case.

[Modern Computer Sys., Inc. v. Modern Banking Sys., Inc., 871 F2d 734 (8th Cir. 1989)]

PART G. BREACH AND TERMINATION OF LICENSE

¶ 7.20 REMEDIES FOR EXCEEDING LICENSE TERMS AND SCOPE

Licensor's restrictions on licensee's international sales and production output are not violation of antitrust.   Nintendo was the inventor of a home video game system, which used game cartridges so that a multitude of games could be played on the system. The system had a patented security system so that only games developed by Nintendo or its licensees could be played on the system. Without a license, Atari developed games bypassing the security system. Nintendo threatened suit for patent infringement on the third-party distributors of the Atari games. In a request for a preliminary injunction, Atari sought to stop Nintendo from bringing suit against Atari distributors. Atari claimed that Nintendo could not sue for patent infringement, because it violated antitrust laws with its licensing agreements that restricted international sales and the number of games produced. *Held:* The injunction was denied. While a patent does not insulate against an antitrust claim, Atari needed to allege some violation of antitrust related to the patent. According to the court, attempted enforcement of an invalid or fraudulent patent, coercion of sales of unpatented goods with patented goods, or scheme to violate antitrust would violate antitrust law. Restrictions on international sales are not a violation of antitrust; and, absent any further evidence of wrongdoing, a restriction on the number of cartridges that could be distributed is also no violation.

[Atari Games Corp. v. Nintendo of Am., Inc., 897 F2d 1572 (Fed. Cir. 1990)]

Showing of monetary loss only is insufficient for grant of injunction. Hodge licensed certain computer billing programs to Comtel. Comtel was acquired by USA Mobile, which continued to use the Hodge programs for the billing clients acquired from Comtel. Mobile also allowed access to the source code of the Hodge programs to its consultants. When Hodge learned of this access, it successfully sued to enjoin Mobile from using the program. Mobile appealed, claiming that any loss suffered by Hodge would only be lost licensing fees, and this was no basis for an injunction. *Held:* The injunction was lifted. According to the court, a showing of irreparable harm is needed before it may grant an injunction. A showing of monetary damages only is insufficient for this purpose. Any lost licensing fees will be recoverable in a suit for damages. The court noted that harm would come from unauthorized dissemination of the program, but this was not at issue. Mobile had agreed not to disseminate the program; it only wanted to use the program. Hodge stated that not granting the injunction could lead other of its licensees to suspend payments. Those licensees could be led to believe that since Mobile was not paying licensing fees neither should they. The court noted, however, that Hodge would still retain a right of recovery under law against such breaching parties.

[Hodge Business Computer Sys., Inc. v. USA Mobile Communications, Inc., 910 F2d 367 (6th Cir. 1990), opinion withdrawn and appeal dismissed, 924 F2d 1058 (6th Cir. 1991)]

¶ 7.21 ELECTRONIC SELF-HELP REMEDIES

Remote deactivation of computer is held lawful when licensee fails to pay fees. American Computer Leasing leased computer equipment to JFI, which needed the equipment to maintain computer contact with one of its suppliers. The computer manufacturer, ADP, licensed software to JFI. The licensing agreement provided for continuing payments by JFI and access to the computer system by ADP. JFI became delinquent in its payments, and ADP entered JFI's computer by remote and deactivated the system. JFI sued both American and ADP, claiming that the deactivation was unlawful. *Held:* The deactivation was not unlawful. According to the court, remote deactivation is permitted for breach of payment obligations. The court first noted that since American was not responsible for the deactivation and absent any showing of a conspiracy, it could not be held liable for the deactivation. ADP was not liable for any damages for the deactivation either. The court noted that deactivation was not a form of extortion, since JFI was obligated to pay fees for the use of the computer system. Absent payment, ADP had a legal right pursuant to the licensing agreement to deactivate. The court next noted that under the governing law, trespass or nuisance involves damage to land; deactivation of a computer was in no way related to land. Furthermore, the court stated that JFI, under its agreement, allowed access to its computer to ADP; therefore, JFI could not claim the access was unlawful.

[American Computer Leasing v. Jack Farrell Implement Co., 763 F. Supp. 1473 (D. Minn. 1991)]

¶ 7.22 EFFECT OF BANKRUPTCY ON LICENSES

Court refuses to hold contested use of copyrighted intangible property a violation of automatic stay. The U.S. Department of Justice (DOJ) contracted with Inslaw to receive a legal case management program. The original program was in the public domain, but Inslaw also developed an enhanced version. Under an agreement, Inslaw provided the DOJ with copies of the object and source codes of the program and installed the program in 22 DOJ offices. After Inslaw filed for bankruptcy, a dispute arose as to whether the DOJ improperly disseminated the program to other offices. Inslaw sued in bankruptcy court, claiming that the dissemination was a violation of the automatic stay: The dissemination was an exercise of control by the DOJ over its trade secrets. *Held:* There was no violation of the stay. According to the court, the stay forbids the exercise of control of the debtor's property by others. Believing that Inslaw's interpretation of the stay was too broad, the court refused to extend the meaning of "exercise of control" to intangible property rights. The court stated that to interpret the stay, this broadly would turn every dispute as to property ownership into a violation of the automatic stay. The court noted that Inslaw retained remedies under contract or tort law, but it could not recover under the provisions of the stay.

[United States v. Inslaw, 932 F2d 1467 (DC Cir. 1991)]

Automatic stay prevents termination of executory contract. CCI was a manufacturer and developer of computer hardware and software. Codex manufactured computer networking equipment. As part of a joint venture, CCI and Codex entered into an agreement whereby Codex would buy over a period of years a minimum amount of CCI hardware and software. The agreement provided that it was terminable by either party if the other filed for bankruptcy. CCI filed for bankruptcy, and Codex stopped making its minimum purchases. CCI claimed Codex violated the automatic stay by repudiating the contract and was awarded damages. *Held:* Affirmed. According to the court, the purpose of the stay is to give the debtor time to reorganize; therefore, its property is handled by the court. The court determined that the contract rights here were property within the Bankruptcy Code, and that correct procedure to terminate the rights was through the courts. Codex claimed that because the contract was executory under state law, property rights did not automatically vest in the bankruptcy estate, and therefore Codex could not be automatically stayed for terminating the contract. The court, however, held that the contract became property of the estate upon filing despite language in the contract making bankruptcy a default provision. The court held this was in keeping with the meaning of 11 USC §

541(c)(1), which overrides the contract provision and any state law making the contract executory and therefore terminable.

[Computer Communications, Inc. v. Codex Corp., 824 F2d 725 (9th Cir. 1987)]

Exclusive license with warranties is held executory contract under Bankruptcy Act of 1898. Fenix licensed software from Select-a-Seat. Under the agreement, Fenix would make an up-front payment and annually pay a flat percentage of its income attributed to the software. Select agreed to grant an exclusive license to Fenix and warranted the programs. After Select filed for bankruptcy under the Bankruptcy Act of 1898, the receiver successfully rejected the licensing agreement as an executory contract. Fenix claimed that the contract was not executory because it had already paid the up-front fee and received the software. *Held:* The contract was executory. The court stated that an executory contract was one in which obligations are uncompleted so that breach by one party would justify breach by the other. According to the court, because Fenix was obligated to pay an annual percentage of fees and because Select was required not to license to others and to warranty the software, both parties had uncompleted obligations. If either party breached, the other would be excused. The court refused to see the exclusive license as an intangible right that vested at the time of contract. According to the court, it was a continuing right that could be breached. If Fenix suffered any damages as a result of the breach, it was positioned to file suit as a creditor.

[Fenix Cattle Co. v. Silver, 625 F2d 290 (9th Cir. 1980)]

Federal bankruptcy law rather than choice-of-law clause governs contract when debtor is undergoing Chapter 11 reorganization. EI agreed to supply software to Ontario Hydro. After filing for Chapter 11 bankruptcy reorganization, EI chose to reject its executory contract with Ontario Hydro, which sued for damages under the contract, claiming that Ontario law governed under the choice-of-law clause in the contract. EI claimed that federal bankruptcy law governed and that Ontario Hydro's damage claim was limited by that law. *Held:* Federal bankruptcy law governed. Since EI had filed for bankruptcy, the contract fell within EI's reorganization and federal bankruptcy law. Under applicable law, when EI rejected the contract, Ontario Hydro could elect to terminate the agreement or retain the rights of performance by EI. Since Ontario Hydro did not respond to EI's rejection of the contract, the court stated that Ontario Hydro terminated the software license. Once the license was terminated, the liquidated-damages clause thereunder was also terminated. Ontario Hydro could only claim actual damages proved and would be paid with other unsecured claims.

[In re EI Int'l, 123 BR 64 (Bankr. Idaho 1991)]

CHAPTER **8**

COMPUTER AND
SOFTWARE LEASING

¶ 8.01 CHOICE OF FORMAT

Fee to administrate leases must be amortized over life of leases for tax purposes. As part of a sale/leaseback, taxpayers bought interests in computer equipment and exchanged their notes. Taxpayers agreed to lease the equipment back to the seller for a 41-month period. Under the lease agreement, taxpayers agreed to pay over a 12-month period a management fee for the administration of the lease. The taxpayers deducted the whole of the management fee as an expense of carrying on a trade (IRC § 162(a)). The IRS contended that the fee should have been amortized over the whole of the 41-month lease agreement. *Held:* The management fees were capital expenditures that should have been amortized over the life of the lease. While the court noted that the fact that the benefits of the management agreement would last longer than a year was not dispositive, this one-year rule was still an appropriate factor for consideration. Noting that the management company would provide services over the life of the lease rather than performing most of the services during the payment period, the court determined that the management contract was a separate asset.

[Segilman v. Comm'r, 796 F2d 116 (5th Cir. 1986)]

Sale/leaseback using nonrecourse notes lacks economic substance for tax purposes. Taxpayers were all investors in a circular sale/leaseback of computers. Under the arrangement, the lessee would purchase the equipment with a secured note from a bank. The lessee then sold the equipment to Elmco, which issued the lessee a nonrecourse note and lease for the equipment. Elmco then sold the equipment and transferred the leases to the taxpayers for a recourse note. Elmco also guaranteed to the taxpayers the lease payments. The taxpayers claimed deductions based on the losses on their computer investments. *Held:* Deductions were denied. According to the court, there was no risk to the taxpayers of any real economic loss, and claimed losses are allowed only to the extent that the investments are at risk. The court first noted that Elmco guaranteed the rent, which covered the taxpayers noted to Elmco. It was as if Elmco guaranteed the amounts owed to itself. Next, the court found that taxpayers' recourse notes were shielded by Elmco's nonrecourse notes. The court believed that Elmco would not proceed against taxpayers because it had no liability to lessee since lessee only held a nonrecourse note. If Elmco were to sue on taxpayers' notes, Elmco would have a windfall because it would owe the lessee nothing. The court felt that it was not realistic to expect Elmco to sue, and stated that Elmco was a straw man allowing taxpayers to assume Elmco's nonrecourse liability.

[Young v. Comm'r, 926 F2d 1083 (11th Cir. 1991)]

Lessor of computer equipment is not third-party beneficiary under service contract between lessee and service provider. American Finance leased computer equipment to a lessee who contracted for computer maintenance and support services from CSC. The lease required that the lessee acquire such a service contract. The lessee filed for bankruptcy, and American tried to sue CSC for breach of the service contract under a third-party beneficiary theory, claiming that since the service contract was required, the parties should have known it was a beneficiary under the service contract. *Held:* AFC was not a third-party beneficiary of the service contract. According to the court, there must be implicit or explicit evidence in the contract that the parties intend the contract to benefit some third party. The court could only find unilateral intent toward a third-party beneficiary: The lessee may have known American was to benefit from the service contract, but CSC did not. Such unilateral knowledge was insufficient to bind CSC. The four corners of the contract expressed no language that would put CSC on notice that anyone other than the lessee was to have benefited from the agreement.

[American Fin. Corp. v. Computer Servs. Corp., 558 F. Supp. 1182 (Del. 1983)]

PART A.   TYPES OF LEASES

¶ 8.02 TRUE LEASE OR SECURITY INTEREST

Clear expression that document is a lease leads court to hold it is a true lease rather than a secured sale.   Brock and Tandy entered into an agreement whereby for 40 months Brock was to rent computer equipment, and at the end of that period Brock was to return the equipment. Upon Brock's bankruptcy, the trustee claimed that Brock did not have a lease, but rather entered a secured sale, and that Tandy as an unperfected creditor lost priority in the equipment to the trustee. Tandy claimed the agreement was a true lease giving it the right to repossess. *Held:* The agreement was a true lease. According to the court, the language of the agreement clearly indicated a lease, and evidence of a purchase option was contradicted by the requirement that the equipment be returned. Brock was required to return the equipment, with no duty or even option to purchase the equipment. While the court noted that the lease was for longer than the useful life of the equipment, that 85 percent of the time Tandy sold the equipment to the lessee at the end of the term, and that the lease had an acceleration clause, none of these factors overrode the clear expression of the agreement that it was a lease.

[Carlson v. Tandy Computer Leasing, 803 F2d 391 (8th Cir. 1986)]

A true lease will be found where title remains with supplier and there is no option to purchase.   Gulfview sought to obtain new computer equipment, but the supplier would not finance the purchase. The supplier did, however, introduce Gulfview to Growth, which agreed to buy the equipment and lease it to Gulfview. The lease provided that Gulfview would return the equipment at the end of the lease term and that title remained with Growth. The lease also provided that risk of loss was on Gulfview. Growth was not a dealer in computers, maintained no showroom, nor possessed the equipment at any time before the lease. In fact, Growth never came into possession of the equipment until Gulfview defaulted on the lease, and Growth repossessed the equipment. In defense to Growth's deficiency claim, Gulfview alleged the lease was in fact a usurious financing arrangement. *Held:* There was no usury, because there was no financing arrangement. The court first stated that it would look to the substance rather than the form of the transaction to determine whether the agreement was a true lease. According to the court, the parties did contemplate a true lease because title remained with Growth and because there was no option to purchase. The court believed that a purchase option was a vital component necessary for a financing arrangement.

[Growth Leasing Ltd. v. Gulfview Advertiser, Inc., 448 So. 2d 1224 (Fla. Dist. Ct. App. 2d Dist. 1984)]

True lease exists where lessor retains title and has right to retake the equipment at end of lease term.   Measurex leased computer hardware and software to three Maine paper companies. The systems were substantially similar. Under the 102-month lease agreements, the ownership of the systems was to remain with Measurex and at the end of the term the lessees could purchase the systems for 25 percent of cost. The state tax assessor claimed that as owner Measurex was subject to the state use tax. Measurex countered that lessees were the owners rather than Measurex because the leases were "in lieu of purchase" and exempt from the use tax. *Held:* These leases were true leases, and Measurex was subject to the use tax. According to the court, the state tax assessor is given discretion to determine which leases are in lieu of purchase. Under the assessor's interpretation, the lessee must acquire title and the equipment for all intents and purposes. Here no such facts were present. Under the clear terms of the lease, title remained with Measurex, which had the right to retake the equipment at the end of the lease term. Therefore, under the assessor's definition, the agreement was clearly a lease, not a purchase.

[Measurex v. State Tax Assessor, 490 A2d 1192 (Me. 1985)]

Lease is found a security interest subject to Article 9 of UCC where lessee has option to purchase for $1.   Lewis leased computer equipment under an agreement that provided for payments over 84 months and that granted an option to purchase the equipment for $1 at the end of the lease term. The lease was assigned to RFC. When Lewis stopped payment on the lease, RFC repossessed the equipment, sold it, and tried to proceed against Lewis for missed lease payments. Lewis claimed that the lease was really a sale with a security interest and that RFC was only entitled to deficiency payments if the sale of the equipment was commercially reasonable. *Held:* The lease was really a security interest. The court held as a matter of law that the lease was intended for security. Under UCC § 1-201, a lease is a security interest if the lessee "has the option to become the owner of the property . . . for a nominal consideration. . . ." Under the lease herein, the purchase option provided for a $1 payment: clearly nominal. Since the lease was a security interest, RFC was required under UCC § 9-504(3) to dispose of the repossessed equipment in a commercially reasonable fashion, which included proper notice of sale to Lewis.

[Reyna Fin. Corp. v. Lewis Serv. Ctr., Inc., 429 NW2d 380 (Neb. 1988)]

[1] UCC Standards

UCC Article 2 warranties not extended to lease where lessee was required to return the equipment and had no purchase option.   Rountree entered a purchase agreement with Shell Group, Inc. concerning computer equipment. Two weeks after delivery of the equipment, a Shell representative told Rountree, he could reduce his monthly payments by entering an agreement with Citicorp. Under this agreement, Citicorp would own the equipment and lease it to Rountree. Rountree would be responsible for all repairs and return the equipment at the end of the lease term. The equipment had problems and Rountree stopped payments, and Citicorp filed suit. Rountree claimed defenses under UCC Article 2. *Held:* UCC Article 2 is inapplicable. According to the court, Article 2 applies to sales. The clear language of the lease was that no sale was contemplated: Citicorp retained title and granted no purchase option. Even though a sale had been contemplated in the original agreement with Shell, that agreement was terminated when the lease was entered. The court would not read terms of the terminated sales agreement into the subsequent lease.

[Citicorp Credit, Inc. v. Rountree, 364 SE2d 65 (Ga. Ct. App. 1987)]

Where lessee has no purchase option and must return the equipment, true lease is found.   WL Scott leased computer equipment to Madra Aerotech. The lease provided that at the end of the lease term, Scott would regain possession of the equipment. After the lease was consummated, Scott filed a financing statement regarding the computer equipment with the Secretary of State pursuant to the UCC. When Madra became delinquent in its payments, Scott repossessed the equipment and successfully sued for deficiencies under the lease. On appeal, Madra contended a deficiency should not have been awarded. Because the lease was really disguised security interest, Scott was required to follow certain procedures. Since the procedures were not followed, a deficiency could not be allowed. *Held:* Judgment affirmed. According to the court, the lease was a true lease rather than a security agreement. The court noted that Madra was required to return the equipment at the end of the lease term. Furthermore, there was no evidence, either on the face of the lease or oral, that there was a purchase option at the end of the term. According to the court, the lessee must receive some equity in the equipment if the lease is to be deemed a security interest. Here, Madra received no equity.

[WL Scott, Inc. v. Madra Aerotech, Inc., 653 P2d 791 (Idaho 1982)]

[2] Tax Law Standards

Fact that computers in sale/leaseback had residual value and earn income does not preclude finding that sale/leaseback is sham.   A taxpayer bought computers and as part of the purchase was assigned the subleases on those computers. For the purchase, the taxpayer made a down payment, signed a full recourse note, and at closing paid almost $117,000 of prepaid interest. Under the agreement, he would make no loan payment until the seventeenth month and would receive minimal lease payments. After the seventeenth month, the loan and lease payments were essentially offsetting. At the end of the lease period, the leases were renewed and the taxpayer earned $87,000. The computers had some residual value at the end of first lease term, although the amount was in dispute. The taxpayer claimed deductions for interest payments and depreciation, which the IRS denied. The taxpayer claimed to have a business motive and challenged the denial. *Held:* Deductions denied. The court looked to whether the taxpayer had a business purpose and whether the transaction had any economic substance besides tax savings. The court first looked at the objective portion of the test and found no economic substance, as the transaction had no profits in the first eight years; profits would only come from re-leasing and residual value. Although there was a re-leasing and residual value, the court found the first a "fluke" that could not have been realistically expected at the time the transaction was entered into and the residual value even at its maximum amount was so low as to make the profits over eight years minimal (an eight-year yield of 14 percent). As to the subjective belief of the taxpayer, the court could not find any business purpose, since neither the taxpayer nor his investment adviser had any knowledge of computers, nor did they explore the residual value or the possibilities of reletting the computers.

[Hines v. United States, 912 F2d 736 (4th Cir. 1990)]

Court establishes two-pronged test to determine whether transaction is tax sham for tax purposes.   Rice's Toyota entered a sale/leaseback transaction with Finalco. Rice's bought computers from Finalco, which in turned leased them from Rice's for eight years. Finalco then subleased the computers for five years. Furthermore, payment to Rice's from Finalco after this five-year period was contingent upon Finalco finding a subsequent sublessee. Rice's financed its purchase with recourse and non-recourse notes. Because of its computer ownership, Rice's took depreciation deductions from its tax returns. Rice's also took interest expense deductions related to the notes. The IRS claimed and the tax court agreed that the transaction was a sham, and disallowed the deductions. *Held:* The transaction was a sham. According to the court, a two-pronged inquiry is used to determine whether a transaction constitutes a sham: (1) the taxpayer has no business purpose for the transaction other than tax avoidance and (2) the transaction has no economic substance because no possibility of profit exists. According to the court, Rice's only entered into the transaction for the tax benefit that it would derive. The court further noted that Rice's could have little profit motive, because the residual balance at the end of the five-year sublease was less than the balance owed to Finalco. Because that debt was nonrecourse, the court expected Rice's to simply walk away from the transaction. It would have no loss, but would have been able to take large deductions. Thus, the transaction was totally tax motivated without any profit expectations.

[Rice's Toyota World v. Comm'r, 752 F2d 89 (4th Cir. 1985)]

Two-pronged test to determine sham transactions is not rigid; a sham could be found under only one prong. A taxpayer entered into a sale/leaseback agreement. In his research for potential investment, the taxpayer, on the advice of his accountant, sought to purchase a computer system that could have high residual value after any lease. The taxpayer, therefore, entered a sale/leaseback transaction. The tax court found the transaction a sham because (1) it had no business purpose and (2) it had no economic substance. On appeal, the taxpayer conceded the second point but challenged the first. *Held:* Affirmed. The court noted that the two-pronged test was not rigid and cases could arise where a sham is found under only one prong of the test. The court noted, however, that the taxpayer's claim of a business purpose was self-serving and that the advice he received from his accountant was flawed because the accountant's analysis of the transaction was in error.

[Shriver v. Comm'r, 899 F2d 724 (8th Cir. 1990)]

Deductions denied where taxpayers cannot show investments were at risk. Finalco owned computer equipment financed by a nonrecourse note secured by the equipment. Finalco also received the leases and the right to lease payments on the equipment. Finalco sold the equipment to LeasePro for a full recourse note. Finalco also assigned the leases. LeasePro in turn sold the equipment and assigned the leases to taxpayers. The taxpayers financed their purchases with full, limited, and nonrecourse notes. Because the lease and note payments were offsetting, the taxpayer, who owed money to LeasePro, assigned its right to payment under the lease to LeasePro. Lease-

Pro and Finalco then only made offsetting entries in their books; no cash changed hands, since the LeasePro and Finalco payments were also offsetting. The IRS denied the taxpayers deductions for depreciation under the lease since their interests were not at risk. The taxpayers countered that the investments were at risk to the amount of the limited and full recourse notes. *Held:* Deductions denied. The court, looking to IRC § 465(a)(1), stated that taxpayers can only deduct amounts up to the investment at risk. If there is protection against loss, such as nonrecourse financing or "other similar arrangement," a deduction will not be allowed. The court, looking at the economic realities, believed that the limited recourse notes were a similar arrangement preventing risk. The court noted that since no money changed hands and all payments were offsetting, the taxpayers did not risk loss. Furthermore, since the original equipment loans to Finalco were nonrecourse, if Finalco were to default, no one in the Finalco, LeasePro, or taxpayer chain would be financially harmed. The court noted that neither Finalco nor LeasePro could collect against taxpayers on taxpayers' notes absent a showing of harm; and since the original loan was nonrecourse, no harm could be shown.

[Moser v. IRS, 914 F2d 1040 (8th Cir. 1990)]

Transactions established with no economic purpose besides tax deductions held to be sham. Taxpayers all entered into a sale/leaseback agreement. Under the agreement, the taxpayers would purchase the equipment and pay a management fee to the seller. The taxpayers were in no way bound by the seller's initial purchase of the equipment. The seller was to act as the taxpayers' agent with regard to the computers and would sublease them to the end users. The subleases were arranged so that no excess would be generated to distribute to the lessors. The taxpayers took deductions for depreciation and management fees, which both the IRS and the tax court denied. The taxpayers contended that since the seller was the taxpayers' agent, there was no sham transaction. *Held:* Affirmed. The court established a test whereby it would determine whether the transaction had any practical economic effects other than the creation of income tax losses. The court found no practical effects. The court denied any agency relationship, noting that the seller sold at a substantial markup and did nothing to enhance the value of the computers. Furthermore, the fact that the taxpayers were not bound by the seller's purchase of the computers even though the seller was the taxpayers' agent contradicted any agency relationship. The court also noted that the taxpayers seemed to have no concern for the equipment of which they were the ostensible owners. Given the structure of the sublease, the taxpayers would not receive any income from them. The taxpayers' only benefit was in the form of tax deductions. And given the facts, the transaction was established solely for those deductions and was therefore a sham.

[James v. Comm'r, 899 F2d 905 (10th Cir. 1990)]

PART B.   LEASE OBLIGATIONS AND RIGHTS

¶ 8.03 LESSOR WARRANTIES

Article 2 of UCC is not applicable where there is true lease.   Lockhead bought IBM computer equipment secured by a security interest granted to IBM. Lockhead then sold the equipment to OPM, which leased it back to Lockhead. The lease contained a "hell or high water" clause that provided that Lockhead would make all rental payments. OPM assumed Lockhead's payment obligation to IBM. Unknown to Lockhead and not in breach of the lease, OPM sold the computer equipment subject to the lease, which equipment was in turn sold. OPM never paid IBM. Lockhead stopped its rent payments and eventually settled with IBM for payment for the equipment. The ultimate purchaser of the equipment claimed title to the equipment and Lockhead was forced to settle with that party. Lockhead then sued OPM for recovery of attorney's fees in settling the suit with the purchaser, claiming that under UCC Article 2 OPM violated the title warranty. *Held:* Recovery of fees denied. UCC Article 2 was inapplicable, because it applies to sales not to leases. The clear intention of the parties was that the transaction was a lease, not a sale. Furthermore, the substance of the agreement clearly contemplated a lease. Lockhead was not the purchaser. OPM retained rights in the equipment and could assign the lease without Lockhead's consent. Lockhead was required to return the equipment at the end of the lease term. OPM clearly retained ownership, and therefore there was no sale to implicate UCC Article 2.

[In re OPM Leasing Serv., 61 BR 596 (Bankr. SDNY 1986)]

There are no warranties of merchantability and fitness for purpose where lease is simply a financing arrangement.   SPE sought to lease computer equipment. It, therefore, chose the computer system that it desired and contracted that Pacific American Leasing purchase the equipment from the supplier and lease it to SPE. The lease provided that there were no warranties and that the lease was a true lease rather than a sales agreement. SPE claimed, however, that there was an oral purchase option. After the equipment was delivered, SPE sent notice to Pacific that the equipment had been received and was operational. The equipment soon thereafter experienced problems, and after a year SPE notified Pacific of these problems and terminated lease payments. Pacific sued for payment, and SPE countered that Pacific had breached its warranties. *Held:* There was no breach of warranty. As a threshold matter, the court needed to determine whether the warranty provisions of UCC Article 2 apply to leases. The court stated that where a lease has elements of a sale, Article 2 would apply; however, if a lease were intended solely as security, Article 2 would be inapplicable. Here, the warranties of merchantability and of fitness for purpose were inapplicable even though the lease had indicia of sale. First, there was no warranty of merchantability because Pacific was not a merchant—one that deals in a kind of goods. Second, there was not warranty of fitness for purpose because Pacific knew neither the intended use of the equipment nor held itself out as an expert. In fact, SPE chose the equipment. Since the equipment did not meet its needs, SPE could blame only itself. Finally, the lease clearly disclaimed any warranties.

[Pacific Am. Leasing Corp. v. SPE Bldg. Sys., Inc., 730 P2d 273 (Ariz. Ct. App. 1986)]

[1] Common-Law Warranties

Software held part of computer system that breached UCC warranties. Monteleone leased computer equipment and software for his office from Neilson. The software did not work properly and Monteleone eventually terminated the lease for cause. Monteleone later successfully sued for breach of warranty under the UCC. Neilson contended that the computer software was an intangible, not goods, under the UCC and therefore the warranty provisions of the UCC were inapplicable. *Held:* Affirmed. The court first noted that Monteleone contracted for a computer system, both hardware and software. The software could not be seen as a separate entity. The court then stated that the system failed the warranty of merchantability and warranty of fitness for purpose. According to the court, the goods were not "merchantable" and this resulted in damages. Furthermore, Neilson knew the purpose for the lease and was to supply equipment tailored for that purpose. Since the equipment did not meet the purpose, it failed the warranty.

[Neilson Business Equip. Ctr., Inc. v. Monteleone, 524 A2d 1172 (Del. 1987)]

Vendor that arranges for lease financing and delivers worthless equipment is responsible for refunding all lease payments, even those parts constituting interest payments. Schatz sought to automate its accounting and inventory. It, therefore, entered into negotiations with Olivetti and presented an outline of its needs. Olivetti agreed to sell a system that would meet its requirements and specified in several letters that the computer equipment would perform as required. Schatz entered into a lease financing arrangement through a third party and took delivery of the equipment. Schatz hired a programmer, but the computer never did function even after several meetings between the programmer and Olivetti employees. Olivetti finally admitted that the equipment would not work as promised and offered to resell the equipment at a $10,000 loss to Schatz. Schatz sued to recover payments made on the lease. *Held:* Schatz could recover payments. The court found UCC § 2-714 applicable. Under that section, damages are measured by the difference between the value of the goods delivered and the value of the goods as warranted. The court said that the computer as delivered had no value because it could not perform any tasks. The court accepted the sales price as the value of the goods as warranted. Since the computer had no value and the sales price was the value as warranted, Schatz was entitled to receive all money paid. This also included the interest payments that were part of the lease payments. The court believed that since Olivetti arranged the lease financing, the interest payments were foreseeable, consequential damages that were covered under UCC § 2-714.

[Schatz Distrib. Co. v. Olivetti Corp., 647 P2d 820 (Kan. Ct. App. 1982)]

Where lease has indicia of sale, UCC Article 2 warranties will be found applicable. JL Teel leased equipment to Houston United Sales. Under the lease, Houston was to insure the equipment, pay taxes on it, and keep it in good operating condition. The equipment had serious problems within three months of delivery. Houston asked Teel to take the equipment away, but when Teel tried to do so it would not grant Houston a release from rental payments. Teel sued for payments and Houston claimed that the equipment did not meet UCC Article 2 warranties. Teel countered that Article 2 was inapplicable to a lease. *Held:* The court found Article 2 applied. Noting the commercial realities, the court stated that leasing had become a major way of transferring equipment. The transactions were mainly for tax benefits rather than warranty avoidance. Although the court would not analogize all leases to sales, it did note that the lease here had similar elements to a sale; the lessee had to pay taxes, insure the equipment, and returned the option to purchase the equipment for a nominal sum. Given commercial realities and the structure of the transaction, the court believed UCC Article 2 applied.

[JL Teel Co. v. Houston United Sales, Inc., 491 So. 2d 851 (Miss. 1986)]

Bailment for mutual benefit must be fit for its intended purpose where bailor knows of intended use of equipment. Lovely sought to lease computer equipment from Burroughs. A Burroughs representative met with Lovely and over time the representative became aware of Lovely's needs and recommended certain equipment. Although no formal lease was signed, the equipment was delivered and payments were made. The equipment, however, functioned poorly, resulting in damages to Lovely's business. He therefore sued for violation of express and implied warranties. Burroughs countered that there were no warranties because the transaction was a gratuitous bailment. *Held:* Burroughs breached its warranties. According to the court, the bailment was not gratuitous. Because the court refused to believe that Burroughs would part with an expensive piece of computer equipment without a profit motive, it classified the arrangement as a "bailment for mutual benefit." Equipment under such a bailment must be in a condition fit for its intended use where the bailor knows of its use and particularly where the bailee relies on the bailor's expertise. Here, there was ample evidence that Burroughs knew of Lovely's needs and represented that it had equipment that would adequately fulfill those needs.

[Lovely v. Burroughs Corp., 527 P2d 557 (Mont. 1974)]

[2] Warranty Disclaimers

Court refuses to extend UCC Article 2 warranties to "as is" lease.   Tolaram sought to obtain computer equipment for its business. Tolaram's controller went to a Tandy retail store and agreed to lease certain equipment after receiving assurances from two Tandy employees that the computer system would meet Tolaram's needs. The lease provided that Tandy retained title, Tolaram was to return the equipment at the end of the lease term, and Tolaram accepted the equipment "as is." Tolaram subsequently determined that the equipment did not work as well as desired, stopped making lease payments, and sued, claiming a breach of implied warranties of merchantability and fitness for purpose. *Held:* There were no implied warranties. The court stated that under UCC Article 2, the implied warranties only applied to the sale of goods not to leases. Pointing to the fact that nothing in the lease contemplated a sale, the court refused to see the lease here as a financing arrangement rather than a true lease. The lease provided for no purchase option or transfer of title. The court furthermore refused to extend the warranties to leases as a matter of public policy. The court stated that equitable concerns did not come to bear where Tolaram knew the lease was for equipment "as is."

[Tolaram Fibers, Inc. v. Tandy Corp., 375 SE2d 673 (NC Ct. App. 1989)]

¶ 8.04 MAINTENANCE AND REPAIR

Damages for unjust enrichment awarded to servicer of computer equipment after lessor terminates its agreement.   BSL leased computer equipment to FAI, a corporation later acquired by Foothills Automotive Plaza. Under the agreement, FAI was required to provide maintenance service for the computers. FAI entered a service and maintenance agreement with Display Data. Sometime after Foothills acquired FAI, a controversy over lease and maintenance payments developed. Foothills terminated both agreements and was sued by Display, which was awarded damages. *Held:* Award affirmed. The court noted that under the maintenance agreement, the system was supported and serviced. The court felt that these were benefits that supported an award against Foothills for unjust enrichment. Although the district court also based its opinion on a third-party beneficiary theory, the circuit court did not address that theory, since it believed that there was sufficient undisputed evidence to ground its opinion on a theory of unjust enrichment.   . .

[Business Sys. Leasing v. Foothills Automotive Plaza, Inc., 886 F2d 284 (10th Cir. 1989)]

Failure to maintain equipment under a lease is question for jury.   Schepps entered a lease with Burroughs for computer equipment. The lease provided for service to the equipment, and for a discount on monthly payments. However, if Schepps were to terminate the lease, the discount would need to be refunded to Burroughs. Schepps terminated the lease, and in defense to Burroughs's refund claim, Schepps alleged a failure of consideration. Schepps claimed that the service was inadequate and that the trial court should not have allowed the jury to determine otherwise. *Held:* The refund to Burroughs was proper. According to the court, the jury was asked to determine whether Burroughs failed to maintain the equipment, not whether consideration had failed. The latter inquiry would be made by the court after the former was decided. Here, there was sufficient evidence for a jury to determine that Burroughs did not fail to maintain the equipment. The court noted that Burroughs had a better than average response time to problems and kept the computer running longer than average. Since the jury determined that Burroughs maintained the equipment, the trial court could rule that there was no failure of consideration.

[Schepps Grocery Co. v. Burroughs Corp., 635 SW2d 606 (Tex. Ct. App. 1982)]

¶ 8.05 OBSOLESCENCE AND UPGRADES

Upgrades are not accessions to leased equipment. CSA leased a computer to Unum. Under the lease, any "replacements" or "substitutions" were to become part of the leased equipment by accession. However, any readily removable "additional equipment" was to remain with Unum. Unum upgraded the equipment by taking out one module and adding a new one. CSA claimed that under the lease or common law, the upgrade was accessed to the computer. Unum claimed that the lease was ambiguous, and looking to the lease as a whole, no accession occurred as a result of the upgrade. *Held:* There was no accession. According to the court, the terms "replacement," "substitution," and "additional equipment" were vague and the court looked to extrinsic evidence to find their meanings. The court interpreted "replacement" or "substitution" to include only that equipment that constituted a like-kind exchange. Any regular maintenance of the equipment that required a new part would fall under these terms. "Upgrades," however, were not like-kind exchanges, but rather "enhancements." These enhancements would not inure to the benefit of CSA, since they were readily removable and since CSA would receive at the end of the lease term the same type of equipment that it leased out. Under a common-law accession doctrine, the court looked to the intention of the party making the addition. If no accession was intended and the equipment was readily removable, the court would find no accession.

[Computer Sys. of Am., Inc. v. Unum Life Ins. Co., 975 F2d 922 (1st Cir. 1992)]

Neither obsolescence nor violation of statute invokes lease's casualty clause. CSA acquired the rights to purchase Data General computers and to lease them to

Southwestern Bell. The computers leased by Bell were for use in its telecommunications business. CSA subsequently discovered that Bell was not using the equipment. Bell claimed that it stopped using the equipment because it was obsolete, while CSA claimed Bell stopped using the equipment because it violated FCC regulations. Under CSA's theory, such discontinuation of use implicated the casualty clause of the lease. Under that clause, Bell was required to report any casualty ("loss or destruction") to CSA within 15 days. Because no such report was made, CSA alleged that Bell violated the lease. *Held:* There was no violation. Under the clear terms of the lease, only loss or destruction (i.e., theft or irreparable damage) constituted a casualty under the lease. According to the court, neither obsolescence nor violation of FCC statute would invoke the casualty clause using the clear meaning of that clause. Thus, under the contract, Southwestern Bell had no duty to return the unused equipment to CSA.

[Computer Sys. of Am., Inc. v. Data Gen. Corp., 921 F2d 386 (1st Cir. 1990)]

Upgrades do not include complete replacement of old equipment for new equipment.   Trust Company of New Jersey owned a Burroughs computer and leased peripheral equipment from STC for use with the computer. Under the lease, STC agreed to make "field installable model upgrades" of STC equipment at Trust's written request. Trust subsequently bought a new Burroughs computer that was not compatible with Trust's existing peripheral equipment. Trust, therefore, made a written request for model upgrades. Such upgrades were not forthcoming because STC was under an agreement with Burroughs not to sell or produce peripheral equipment for the type of computer acquired by Trust. Trust then acquired equipment from Burroughs directly and sued for breach. STC claimed that it was not required to supply the upgrades under the contract. *Held:* There was no breach. According to the court, "field installable model upgrades" are those upgrades that can be installed at the lessee's business site. Such upgrades would not include the complete removal of equipment and replacement by new equipment. Even if such complete removal were intended by the agreement, the Burroughs/STC agreement forbade STC from selling Burroughs equipment or from producing peripheral equipment for the Burroughs computer. Since the agreement with Trust provided that STC supply its own upgrades, STC was under no obligation to supply equipment exclusively owned by Burroughs.

[Storage Technology Corp. v. Trust Co. of NJ, 842 F2d 54 (3d Cir. 1988)]

Where computer memory is not material part of lease, any variation of memory is not a material alteration of lease.   Worthen Bank bought computer equipment and leased it to Telecompo through Worthen Bank's leasing agent. The lease was guaranteed by Meachum. When the equipment was delivered, an invoice accompanying the equipment stated that the computer system included 24K of memory when in fact it included only 16K of memory. The lease itself did not specify memory capacity. When Telecompo failed, Worthen Bank sought the lease payments from Meachum, who countered that the failure to deliver 24K of memory constituted a material alteration of the lease that excused his performance. *Held:* There was no material alteration of the lease. The court based its decision on three factors: (1) the lease never specified memory capacity; thus, the lease could not be altered in that regard; (2) even if the lease were altered, there was no evidence that Telecompo needed the extra 8K of memory, thereby making memory an immaterial factor of the lease; and (3) there was simply a mutual mistake regarding memory; neither party learned that the equipment did not match the invoice until after Telecompo had failed. Therefore, there was no alteration, because Worthen Bank did not intend to deliver nor Telecompo to receive any equipment other than that invoiced.

[Meachum v. Worthen Bank & Trust Co., 682 SW2d 763 (Ark. App. 1985)]

Where upgrading a system would require substantial downtime, system is held to be obsolete. Zayre leased a computer and peripheral equipment from CSA. The lease allowed Zayre to terminate any equipment that had become obsolete or surplus. After time, Zayre decided to upgrade its equipment, and sought to purchase a new system, believing it could more quickly convert to a new system than try to upgrade the existing system. Zayre then bought from another dealer and subsequently terminated the entire CSA lease, claiming that the equipment had become obsolete. CSA sued for payments due under the lease. *Held:* Zayre properly terminated under the lease. Although the entire system as individual components had not become obsolete, the system as a whole did. The court based this opinion on the substantial downtime that the system would experience during an upgrade. Zayre could only effectively continue its business by the purchase of a new system. Therefore, Zayre did not breach its lease with CSA, because the lease clearly allowed for termination under the circumstances.

[Zayre Corp. v. Computer Sys. of Am., Inc., 511 NE2d 23 (Mass. Ct. App. 1987)]

Obsolescence of one piece of equipment does not render whole computer system obsolete where other pieces of equipment can be successfully integrated. Western Reserve sought to lease computer equipment from CSA. Under the agreement, Western leased numerous pieces of equipment, which could be divided into two groups: the central processing unit (CPU) and the input/output unit (I/O). The lease provided that if any piece of equipment became "obsolete" or "surplus" in Western's reasonable estimation, Western could terminate the lease regarding that piece of equipment. Western decided that it needed a larger CPU to handle an increased volume of business, and eventually bought a CPU, but used the new CPU with the old I/O.

Western later bought a new I/O and terminated all lease payments, claiming that when the CPU became obsolete the whole system became obsolete and that when it bought the new units the leased units became surplus. *Held:* The lease was improperly terminated with regard to the I/O. According to the court, the contract term "obsolete" refers to "Western Reserve's technical or functional requirements." Here, it was obvious that the leased CPU could not handle the increased volume of business, but the I/O could, having been successfully used with the new CPU. There was no proof that the leased I/O was inadequate. Even if the leased CPU were inadequate, the lease clearly specified termination was only allowed for inadequate equipment, not for all equipment. To accept a complete termination would make the whole lease terminable whenever one piece of equipment failed. The court believed that this interpretation did not comport with the face of the agreement. The court also refused to find the I/O surplus. According to the court, "surplus" means "not needed or used" rather than "not wanted." Since Western clearly needed an I/O, the unit was not surplus.

[Computer Sys. of Am., Inc. v. Western Reserve Life Assurance of Ohio, 475 NE2d 745 (Mass. Ct. App. 1986)]

Where there are two reasonable interpretations of lease term, matter is properly left to trier of fact.   Taylor leased computer equipment from SMI. The 84-month lease provided for a termination with no penalty after 24 months if Taylor were to lease upgraded equipment from SMI. After 44 months, Taylor sought to lease upgraded equipment, but the leases that SMI sent to Taylor for consideration included penalty payments for early termination of the original lease. Taylor stated that there should be no penalty payments included in the new lease. Taylor then terminated its original lease, claiming the SMI was in breach. SMI then sued for damages, claiming that the upgrades could include a penalty payment because Taylor was required to exercise its option to upgrade without penalty within a reasonable time after 24 months. *Held:* There was sufficient evidence to sustain a jury finding accepting SMI's interpretation of the lease. According to the court, the phrase "at the end of 24 months without penalty" was ambiguous. It could mean at anytime between the twenty-fourth and the eighty-fourth month of the lease, or it could mean within a reasonable time after the twenty-fourth month. Because either meaning was reasonable, the trial court properly admitted evidence regarding the circumstances surrounding contract formation.

[Taylor Publishing Co. v. Systems Mktg., Inc., 686 SW2d 213 (Tex. Ct. App. 1984)]

¶ 8.06 SUBLEASE AND ASSIGNMENT

If parties do not explicitly state they intend a novation, court will not presume one.   Bayou leased computer equipment to SH. The lease allowed either party to assign its interest thereunder. SH sublet the equipment to Epic. The sublease was acknowledged by Bayou, which agreed to receive payments directly from Epic. Epic subsequently defaulted on its lease payments, and Bayou sued SH for payments due under the original lease. SH disclaimed liability, contending that the assignment to Epic was a novation that ended any of its liability. *Held:* There was no novation. Under the Louisiana Civil Code, there must be a clear indication of a novation by both parties. A novation will not be presumed from the circumstances. According to the court, there was no such clear indication. Bayou simply agreed to receive payments from Epic; it did not agree to release SH from liability. Without an explicit release, SH could not escape liability.

[Bayou Acceptance Corp. v. Superior Hydrolics, Inc., 446 So. 2d 558 (La. Ct. App. 1984)]

¶ 8.07 FINANCE LEASES AND THIRD-PARTY LIABILITY

[1] Warranties of Supplier

Disclaimer of warranties in sales agreement carries over to lease of same equipment.   Unable to purchase Burroughs computer equipment, Earman decided to lease the equipment. Under the transaction, Earman first signed a purchase agreement and 12 days later NER signed a lease and purchase order for the equipment. The equipment was subsequently installed but never worked properly. Earman sued for breach of warranty as a third-party beneficiary under the lease. Burroughs claimed that the Burroughs/Earman purchase agreement disclaimed all warranties of merchantability. Earman countered that since there was no sale directly to Earman, the purchase agreement was inapplicable. *Held:* There was no breach. The court first noted that the purchase order between Burroughs and NER incorporated the warranty terms of the Burroughs/Earman agreement. The NER agreement made reference to the Earman agreement, saying that those terms were incorporated. The NER agreement also provided that Earman had been informed of its warranty rights. Since the disclaimers of the Earman agreement were incorporated into the NER agreement, Earman as a third-party beneficiary could claim no greater rights than NER. The court also used the old contract rule of incorporating all agreements that involve one transaction and interpreting them as a group. Since the three agreements were virtually contemporaneous, the terms of all three could be used to interpret each one. The court stated similar reasoning would apply if the lease were instead viewed as a financing arrangement.

[Earman Oil Co., Inc. v. Burroughs Corp., 625 F2d 1291 (5th Cir. 1980)]

Failure to repair and replace defective equipment may lead to suit for damages when warranties are not disclaimed in sales agreement.   Kalil Bottling Company bought computer equipment from Burroughs. The equipment was delivered, but Kalil was unable to secure financing to pay for the equipment. The equipment was then sold by Burroughs to a financer, which leased it to Kalil. The sales agreement between Kalil and Burroughs disclaimed all warranties, but did provide for replacement or repair of defective parts. The sales agreement between Burroughs and the financer extended those same warranties to Kalil. When the computer failed to perform, Kalil sued for breach, but Burroughs contended that all warranties were disclaimed. *Held:* Burroughs did not disclaim all liability. Under the agreement, Burroughs was to replace all defective parts so that the equipment would conform with the equipment promised. If the equipment was not repaired so that it conformed within a reasonable time, the supplier is in breach of the repair and replace warranty. If the supplier does not repair and replace, this remedy is not exclusive and a party may sue for damages.

[Kalil Bottling Co. v. Burroughs Corp., 619 P2d 1055 (Ariz. Ct. App. 1980)]

Lease can be held to be a financing for sale from vendor to lessee, as lessee and vendor were in privity of contract.   Century sought to purchase a Burroughs computer, and the parties entered a purchase agreement. To facilitate the transaction, Burroughs sold the computer to a leasing company that leased it to Century. Under the lease, the lessor gave no warranties and disclaimed liabilities for damages and lateness of delivery. Under the lease, Century was required to pay all taxes and lease payments regardless of the equipment's performance. Burroughs sent the equipment late and the equipment never functioned properly. Century stopped payment on the lease and a judgment was entered for the lessor. Century then sought to recover the judgment from Burroughs, which claimed Century was not in privity of contract with it, and therefore had no standing to sue. *Held:* There was privity. According to the court, the lease agreement was a financing arrangement rather than a true lease. The transaction was really a sale by Burroughs to Century, with financing by the lessor. In making its determination, the court looked to the lease agreement, which put the risk of loss and all costs on the lessee, Century. Furthermore, the lessor had no contact with the equipment, which was installed directly by Burroughs. Therefore, the transaction was best defined as a purchase money financing.

[Burroughs Corp. v. Century Steel, Inc., 664 P2d 354 (Nev. 1983)]

Where agreement states that vendor's warranties are to pass to lessee, lessee and vendor are found to be in privity of contract.   Uniflex sought to lease computer equipment and met with an Olivetti official to determine Uniflex's needs. Uniflex eventually leased Olivetti equipment through a lease financing company. The financing company disclaimed all warranties, although its purchase agreement with Olivetti provided that all of Olivetti's warranties would pass through to Uniflex. When the equipment failed to operate properly, Uniflex sued Olivetti for breach of warranty. Olivetti disclaimed any liability to Uniflex, alleging that it was not in privity of contract with Uniflex. *Held:* There was privity of contract. According to the court, Uniflex was a third-party beneficiary of the Olivetti/financing company agreement. Under that agreement, the standard warranties were to pass to Uniflex. Since it was clear that Uniflex received warranties under this agreement as a third-party beneficiary, Olivetti could not deny privity.

[Uniflex v. Olivetti Corp., 445 NYS2d 993 (Sup. Ct. 1982)]

[2] Waiver of Defenses

Where lease clearly specifies that lessee's only recourse is against vendor, lessee may not sue lessor for breach of warranty. King bought computer equipment from Worlco. The purchase was financed with a lease from Copelco. The Copelco lease, in capital letters stated that Copelco was not the manufacturer or supplier and gave no warranties as to the equipment and that if any problems with the equipment arose, King was to bring suit against the supplier. When the equipment proved unsatisfactory, King sued Copelco. Copelco moved to dismiss, owing to the language in the lease. *Held:* Counts dismissed. According to the court, the clear language of the lease shielded Copelco from any liability. The court noted that state law required that disclaimers of warranty be in clear language and placed conspicuously. Here, the equipment was leased "as is" and the type disclaiming warranties was in capital letters. The court then noted that the lease clearly specified that King should seek remedies against the supplier. The court found no allegations that any other than Worlco was the supplier.

[King Indus., Inc. v. Worlco Data Sys., Inc., 736 F. Supp. 114 (ED Va. 1989), aff'd, 900 F2d 253 (4th Cir. 1990)]

Confessed-judgment clause upheld. IPM was the guarantor of payment to Atlantic Leasing, the lessor of computer equipment. The guarantee contained a confessed-judgment clause providing that should payments be in default, Atlantic could go to court, procure representation for IPM, and have a judgment entered against IPM. When the lessee ceased payments when the computer proved to be defective without hope of repair, Atlantic proceeded against IPM under the confessed-judgment clause. IPM then challenged the judgment. *Held:* Judgment affirmed. The court stated that one's right to a hearing could be waived if voluntarily, knowingly, and intelligently made. The court stated that IPM was a sophisticated party, not overpowered in bargaining strength, and with ready access to counsel. It therefore should have understood the terms of the agreement. The court also noted that no specific consideration was needed for the enforceability of such provision. The court noted that the confessed-judgment can be opened if there is a valid defense, but IPM had the burden of showing the defense beyond just a bald assertion that one existed.

[Atlantic Leasing & Fin. v. IPM Technology, 885 F2d 188 (4th Cir. 1989)]

"Hell or high water" clause upheld in lease between commercially sophisticated parties.   Colorado Interstate leased computer equipment from CMI. The lease was subsequently assigned to CIT. The lease provided that as long as rents were paid, Colorado's quiet enjoyment of the equipment would not be infringed. The lease also contained a "hell or high water" clause, stating rents would be paid. Colorado wanted computer upgrades, and CMI leased equipment from EDS; CMI in turn subleased the equipment to Colorado. The sublease incorporated the terms of the original Colorado/CMI lease. CMI defaulted on its lease payments to EDS, which threatened repossession. Colorado then began to pay EDS directly. Colorado claimed that the threatened repossession impaired its quiet enjoyment and sued for recoupment of rent. *Held:* There was no breach. The court stated that the "hell or high water" clause precluded any defense. The court stated that the quiet enjoyment clause was separate from the obligation to pay rent. The court refused to strike down the term where two commercially sophisticated parties went into the agreement knowing the terms. The court noted that the clause is often the only protection that the lessor has against the devaluation of the equipment because of obsolescence. The equipment will more readily hold its value to the lessor through the clause; according to the court, repossession may be substantially less valuable to the lessor.

[Colorado Interstate Corp. v. CIT Group Equip. Fin., Inc., 993 F2d 743 (10th Cir. 1993)]

Where there is "hell or high water" clause, lessee cannot assert defenses for nonpayment.   Farrell leased computer equipment from ACTL. The lease provided that rental payments would be made regardless of any defense by Farrell. Farrell subsequently defaulted on payments. The equipment was repossessed and sold. In defense to ACTL's claim for a deficiency, Farrell contended that it did not receive a stipulated loss value sheet and that the equipment was sold at less than it could have been sold for had it been sold more quickly after repossession. *Held:* Farrell was subject to damages. The court first noted that the "hell or high water" clause was strictly enforceable as a matter of law. Therefore, Farrell was required to pay the amounts due under the lease. The court stated that the fact that Farrell did not receive a stipulated loss value sheet was irrelevant to the damage calculation. However, a delay in the sale would reduce the damage award by the amount lost by the delay.

[American Computer Trust Leasing v. Jack Farrell Implement Co., 763 F. Supp. 1473 (D. Minn. 1991)]

[3] Warranties of Lessor

Lessee on notice that lessor has disclaimed all warranties only has recourse against vendor. Petroziello sought equipment that would communicate with his bank's computer so that he could ascertain his customers' credit ratings. Petroziello entered negotiations for such equipment. To facilitate the transaction, USL bought the equipment chosen by Petroziello and leased it to him. The lease disclaimed all warranties and stated that Petroziello's recourse was against the vendor. The lease further provided that USL and the vendor were unrelated. The equipment never performed as desired, and Petroziello stopped lease payments. In defense to USL's suit for payments due under the lease, Petroziello claimed that the lease's disclaimer of warranties was against public policy. *Held:* USL was entitled to lease payments. The court stated that the agreement was a commercial chattel lease, not a sale. As such, the public policy concerns of the UCC were inapplicable. The parties were free to waive all warranties, and the lease here unambiguously did so. The court stated that Petroziello was on notice that the warranties were waived when he signed the agreement and that his recourse was against the vendor not the lessor.

[Petroziello v. United States Leasing Corp., 338 SE2d 63 (Ga. Ct. App. 1985)]

Warranties of merchantability and fitness for purpose not available under financing lease. Nutt sought to lease a new computer system. It therefore contacted First Continental, from which it had previously leased equipment. Nutt specified to First Continental which equipment it wanted, and First Continental bought the equipment and leased it to Nutt. The lease provided for no warranties and explicitly denied a purchase option. When Nutt defaulted on its lease payments, it claimed as a defense to deficiency that the lease was the functional equivalent of a sale and that the warranties of merchantability and fitness for purpose were applicable and were breached by First Continental. *Held:* The warranties were inapplicable. In a three-party lease where the lessor is clearly a financing agent, the lessor has no liability under warranties as a seller. The court noted that warranties of merchantability applies to merchants— those dealing in goods of a kind. The warranty of fitness for purpose applies to those sellers that know the buyer's purpose for purchase and that the buyer is relying on the seller's skill or judgment. Continental was not a computer dealer nor did it hold itself out as having any computer expertise. Here, Nutt chose the equipment and First Continental simply served as the financing arm of the transaction.

[David Nutt & Assocs., PC v. First Continental Leasing Co., 599 So. 2d 576 (Miss. 1992)]

PART C.   DEFAULT AND TERMINATION

¶ 8.08 TERMINATION AND CANCELLATION

It is for the jury to determine whether ambiguous communication was intended as termination of lease.   Amplicon and Coachmen entered two computer leases. The leases provided that at the end of the lease term the agreement would automatically continue unless terminated in writing 120 days prior to the expiration date. As the expiration date approached, the parties tried to negotiate a new lease. Coachmen stated that it was thinking of terminating. Amplicon wrote to confirm this, but also wrote that it hoped that negotiations would continue. Coachmen then requested, in writing, an equipment-removal schedule. When the lease expired, Coachmen acquired new equipment from another source and Amplicon successfully sued for breach, claiming Coachmen did not give proper notification of termination. Coachmen appealed, claiming the issue of notification was not a jury issue. *Held:* There was no proper notification. The court stated that the question of whether there was a termination was properly put to the jury. It was ambiguous whether the phone call and written request for an equipment-removal schedule constituted notification of termination. The court felt that since there was no overt statement of termination, Coachmen could have been withholding such termination as a negotiation tool. Therefore, as a matter of law, the issue could not be decided. Extrinsic evidence as to the meanings of the communications were proper to determine whether there was a termination. This evidence was best considered by the jury.

[Amplicon Leasing v. Coachmen Indus., Inc., 900 F2d 468 (7th Cir. 1990)]

Risk of loss falls on the lessee when it is clearly specified in lease.   Allstar leased computer equipment from Baeder, a director of Allstar's predecessor. When Baeder left the board, he requested that the lease be terminated. Allstar continued to make lease payments for several months, then stopped payments and a few months later returned the equipment to Baeder. In the course of shipping the equipment, some equipment was lost. Baeder sued for the value of the lost equipment, stating that the lease placed the risk of loss on Allstar. Allstar claimed that it had terminated the lease and that Baeder agreed to pick up the equipment. *Held:* The risk of loss was on Allstar. The court found no evidence to support Allstar's claim that Baeder agreed to retrieve the equipment. Without such a showing, the lease clearly provided that the lessee, Allstar, was responsible for shipping the equipment back to Baeder. Since the lease clearly placed the burden on Allstar, it was responsible for the cost of the lost equipment.

[Allstar Video, Inc. v. Baeder, 730 P2d 796 (Wyo. 1986)]

¶ 8.09 BANKRUPTCY

Where lessee in bankruptcy has not missed any postpetition lease payments, it would be unreasonable to accelerate date on which lease was to be affirmed. Wheeling-Pittsburgh leased computer equipment that served as the informational hub of the corporation. The 42-month lease was assigned by the original lessor to Phoenix. Wheeling missed three lease payments and then filed a bankruptcy reorganization petition. After the petition, Wheeling missed no payments and had paid all taxes and insurance as required by the lease. Under the Bankruptcy Code, which allows for a creditor to request a reasonable acceleration of the affirmance of a contract, Phoenix sought to have Wheeling either affirm or reject the lease within a 90-day period. Phoenix claimed that because of a computer's rapid obsolescence, any delay in rejecting the contract would cost it money. *Held:* Phoenix's request to accelerate the date of the affirmance or rejection was denied. According to the court, the Bankruptcy Code provides that the debtor has until the date of confirmation of the reorganization plan to affirm or reject a lease. The court can accelerate this date on a request by a creditor if the date chosen by the creditor is reasonable. Here, the court found the request unreasonable. The court noted that Wheeling was up to date on all postpetition payments and that the prepetition deficiency was minor in comparison to the whole of the lease (3 missed payments out of 42 total payments). As to Phoenix's concerns about obsolescence, the court stated that this should have been a factor of the original lease and that Phoenix could not use the Bankruptcy Code to force a decision by Wheeling, especially where Phoenix was currently experiencing no harm.

[In re Wheeling-Pittsburgh Steel Corp., 54 BR 385 (Bankr. WD Penn. 1985)]

¶ 8.10 REMEDIES FOR LESSEE DEFAULT

Lessee may exercise its purchase option at any time before repossession sale where lease is found to be financing arrangement. HMO purchased computer equipment for Choicecare, which HMO leased to Choicecare. The lease provided that the purchase option price would be the unpaid lease payments, that Choicecare would maintain the equipment and bear the risk of loss, and that HMO disclaimed all warranties. Choicecare defaulted on the lease. HMO sought to repossess and collect damages, but Choicecare's receiver sought to exercise the purchase option. *Held:* Choicecare could exercise its purchase option. As a threshold matter, the court needed to determine whether the lease constituted a true lease or a financing arrangement. The court said that a lease is a financing arrangement if there is a purchase option for a nominal price; if the lessee acquires equity, bears risk, and pays taxes; if the lease has an acceleration clause; if the equipment was bought for the lessee; and if warranties are disclaimed. The court found all present except for a nominal purchase price. Although the price was not nominal, it was still below fair market value. Given the facts, the court found a financing arrangement and stated the lease was governed by UCC Article 9. Under UCC § 9-506, the debtor, Choicecare, had the right to redeem at any time before a foreclosure sale. Therefore, HMO could not prevent a purchase.

[HMO Sys. Inc. v. Choicecare Health Servs., Inc., 665 P2d 635 (Colo. Ct. App. 1983)]

All documents associated with lease can be read together to interpret lease to support conviction for failure to return leased property. Thorn leased computer equipment. The lease provided that at the end of the lease term, the equipment would be returned to the lessor at a time and place specified by the lessor. The equipment schedule provided that 53 days after delivery, the equipment would be ready to pick up by the lessor. Thorn acknowledged in writing receipt of the equipment, but at the end of the lease term the equipment was missing: Thorn had sold it. Thorn was convicted under a Missouri statute that criminalizes the failure to return leased property according to the written lease terms. Thorn appealed his conviction, claiming that the lease was not specific as to the return date and that the state could not sustain a conviction. *Held:* Conviction affirmed. The court noted that a lease does not have to be one document under the statute. Although neither the lease nor the equipment schedule alone was sufficient to support a conviction, the documents together provided a basis to support a conviction under the statute. The lease served as a written lease; the equipment schedule provided for place of delivery; and the schedule, along with Thorn's written acknowledgment of receipt, provided for the time of delivery. Since all the documents were in writing, the statutory requirements were met.

[State v. Thorn, 851 SW2d 601 (Mo. Ct. App. 1993)]

[1] Mitigation and Election of Remedies

Lessor has no duty to sell repossessed equipment where it has sufficient inventory to meet current demand. Lithonia leased equipment from Honeywell. After a time, both parties claimed that the other had breached the lease. After Honeywell repossessed the equipment, Honeywell disassembled it and put it in storage rather than selling or reletting it. In Honeywell's action for a deficiency, Lithonia claimed that Honeywell failed to mitigate damages and that any deficiency under the lease should be reduced by the value of the equipment. *Held:* Honeywell had no duty to mitigate. According to the court, there is a duty to mitigate if a supplier cannot fulfill orders from current inventory. Here, however, Honeywell had more supply than it did demand. Even if Honeywell had used individual components for other customers, it would have used the Lithonia equipment at the expense of Honeywell's own inventory. The court also noted that as the computer existed, it had no value; therefore, there was nothing to mitigate.

[Honeywell, Inc. v. Lithonia Lighting, Inc., 317 F. Supp. 406 (ND Ga. 1970)]

Lessor with security interest, which seeks to use courts to obtain judgment, does not lose remedy of self-help. Carroll Publishing leased computer hardware and software from Equity. Carroll stopped its lease payments, and Equity obtained a court order allowing it to repossess all leased materials. Carroll relinquished the hardware, but not the software. While still awaiting its trial for damages, Equity sued for contempt, alleging that the software should have been returned with the hardware. The trial court held that Equity voluntarily relinquished its interest in the software when it did not repossess it. Equity appealed. *Held:* Equity did not lose its security interest. According to the court, the lease was a secured transaction governed by UCC Article 9. The court noted that Article 9 remedies are cumulative rather than elective. When the creditor seeks to use judicial means to collect a debt, it is not foreclosed against using its security interest. Therefore, after Equity received its judgment, it could still proceed against the collateral. Although Equity first sought to satisfy its debt through a suit rather than repossession, this suit did not preclude a later repossession. Furthermore, Equity did not waive its rights to the software by not immediately repossessing as Equity sought to use the courts—through a contempt motion—rather than its remedy of self-help. The court did not see this use of judicial remedy as a waiver of the rights in collateral.

[Fleming v. Carroll Publishing Co., 621 A2d 829 (DC App. 1993)]

[2] Accelerated Rentals

Acceleration and liquidated damage clauses must represent reasonable forecast of actual damage. Bell Atlantic Tricon Leasing leased computer equipment to Pacific Contracting. The lease provided that if Pacific were in default, Tricon could declare due all rents payable under the lease. There were also provisions for unpaid taxes and a 20 percent charge on unpaid rent for fees associated with collection. Saas guaranteed the lease. When Pacific defaulted on its payment, Saas denied liability under the guarantee, contending that the acceleration and other clauses constituted a penalty. Tricon moved for summary judgment. *Held:* Summary judgment denied. Acceleration clauses will be upheld if they represent a reasonable forecast of compensation for harm caused by breach. However, if the clause represents a penalty, it will not be enforceable. Where two equal commercial parties bargain for a liquidated damage clause, it will have a presumption of validity. The court, however, refused to grant summary judgment, noting that the acceleration clause coupled with the damage clause may not have been a reasonable forecast of actual damages. Therefore, there was an issue for the trier of fact.

[Bell Atlantic Tricon Leasing Corp. v. Pacific Contracting Corp., 703 F. Supp. 302 (SDNY 1989)]

[3] Foreclosure and Other Sales

Reasonable notice of repossession sale is required before lessor may collect deficiency. Brace leased computer equipment from Chemlease. After three years, Brace stopped payments on the lease and Chemlease repossessed the equipment. On February 2, Chemlease sent a notice of sale to Brace and its guarantors stating that the equipment would be sold on or after February 12. Also on February 2, a purchaser picked up the repossessed equipment although the purchaser did not receive the bill of sale until February 13. Because the sale produced a deficiency, Chemlease sued, but Brace countered that it did not receive reasonable notice of the sale. *Held:* Brace did not receive reasonable notice. Under UCC § 9-504(3), a debtor is entitled to reasonable notice of sale. Here, the letters to Brace and its guarantors were mailed 10 days before the ostensible date of sale. The court stated that 10 days was not commercially unreasonable. However, the court had to consider whether February 2, the date of the pickup, or February 13, the date of the bill of sale, was actually the purchase date. Under UCC § 2-401(3), a seller becomes committed to selling goods on the shipment date if the seller commits to the contract by passing the goods to a carrier. Here, the goods were passed to the purchaser's carrier on February 2. Since only the posting of the notice of sale occurred on the same day, there was no reasonable notice.

[Chemlease Worldwide, Inc. v. Brace, Inc., 338 NW2d 428 (Minn. 1983)]

CHAPTER **9**

COMPUTER AND INFORMATION SERVICES CONTRACTS

PART A.   LAW OF SERVICES CONTRACTS

¶ 9.01 GENERAL CONSIDERATIONS

Nonexclusive requirements contract of mixed goods and services may fall within scope of UCC and its statute of frauds provisions.   Advent Systems engaged Unisys in a mixed goods and services agreement wherein Unisys would market and service Advent's software. Unisys breached the agreement, and Advent sued for breach of contract. The district court had held that although software was a good, the services aspect predominated; therefore, the UCC and consequently the statute of frauds did not apply. *Held:* The contract could not be segregated; the UCC applied; and the agreement was effectively a nonexclusive requirements contract that complied with the statute of frauds. The court remanded, in view of these findings, on the issue of enforceability.

[Advent Sys. Ltd. v. Unisys Corp., 925 F2d 670 (3d Cir. 1991)]

Agreement to license software is considered a sale of goods and falls under Article 2 of UCC.   EDS and Chubb Life America entered into an agreement for the license of computer software. EDS was to spend four years developing the system, then license the system to Chubb. When EDS did not live up to its obligations, Chubb sued for breach of contract and breach of express warranty. EDS moved for summary judgment, claiming the agreement was for services, not goods, and therefore did not come within the provisions of the UCC. *Held:* The summary judgment motion was denied. Article 2 of the UCC applied to the agreement because the essence of the contract was to license Chubb to use a computer software product, considered a "good" under the UCC.

[The Colonial Life Ins. Co. of Am. v. Electronic Data Sys. Corp., 817 F. Supp. 235 (DRI 1993)]

¶ 9.02 STANDARDS OF PERFORMANCE: CONTRACT PRODUCT

Information found in "how to use" book is intangible and not subject to product liability law.   Mushroom enthusiasts became severely ill after eating mushrooms identified as edible in a book on how to pick mushrooms and sued the publisher G.P. Putnam's Sons in tort. G.P. Putnam's Sons argued that information contained in a book is not a product for the purposes of strict liability under product liability law; such ideas are intangible, and product liability law is geared to the tangible world. The mushroom enthusiasts argued that the "how to use" book should be analogized to aeronautical charts, which some jurisdictions have considered "products." *Held:* The chart itself is indeed a physical product, while the "how to use" book is pure thought and expression. The court declined to expand product liability law to embrace the ideas and expression in a book; moreover, G. P. Putnam's Sons had no duty to investigate the accuracy of the contents of the book it published.

[Winter v. GP Putnam's Sons, 938 F2d 1033 (9th Cir. 1991)]

[1] Warranty of Result

Title searcher has no obligation to search under any other than exact name of debtor. Chemical Bank engaged TSI to conduct searches proper to a loan commitment. TSI submitted a UCC Form 11 to the Secretary of State identifying Boisclair as one of the debtors to be searched, and the Secretary of State conducted the actual search. Chemical brought suit against TSI, alleging that TSI failed to conduct the searches for liens against Boisclair properly, in that TSI had failed to reveal filings under "Bois Clair," to Chemical's detriment. Chemical argued that a searcher has an obligation to search under not only the exact name of the debtor, but also under various misspellings, and that TSI was negligent in failing to request the Secretary to search under possible misspellings. *Held:* TSI had no duty to hypothesize possible misspellings unless Chemical Bank proved that the method of searching for recorded liens was inappropriate. The court further stated that "in the absence of express language . . . courts are reluctant to construe contracts for professional services as implying a contract of guaranty or insurance of favorable results."

[Chemical Bank v. Title Servs., Inc., 708 F. Supp. 245 (D. Minn. 1989)]

Where court finds breach of express warranty, liability-limiting disclaimer is found to be valid part of warranty.   FDP, a hair design business, engaged Southwestern Bell Telephone in an advertising contract. Bell improperly published the yellow pages advertisement, and FDP claimed breach of contract and breach of express warranty under the Texas Deceptive Trade Practice–Consumer Protection Act (Tex. Bus. & Comm. Code Ann. §§ 17.41–17.63). Bell argued that there was no express warranty; and if indeed one was created, Bell's liability was limited by a disclaimer within the contract. *Held:* Bell's improper advertisement display was a defect in performance of the contract. Bell made and breached an express warranty; however, the liability limitation provision was part of the warranty, and FDP could not recover lost profits.

[Southwestern Bell Telephone Co. v. FDP Corp., 811 SW2d 572 (Tex. 1991)]

[2] Workmanlike and Reasonable Performance

Accountant may be held to reasonable professional standard of care when entrusted to obtain computer system for client.   In the presence of a long-standing relationship, DG entrusted its accountants, Ernst and Whinney, to assist it in obtaining a computer system, because it lacked computer expertise. Instead of Ernst and Whinney's promised "turnkey" system, DG received a system that was difficult to operate and failed to meet its needs. DG filed an action for negligence and breach of contract. Ernst and Whinney argued that it should be held to an ordinary rather than professional standard of care. *Held:* The American Institute of Certified Public Accountants Standards require that "due professional care" is to be exercised in providing management advisory services. Ernst and Whinney failed to exercise the great care necessary to carefully detail DG's computer needs and to properly develop specifications for the computer system.

[Diversified Graphics, Ltd. v. Groves, 868 F2d 293 (8th Cir. 1989)]

¶ 9.03 TORT OR CONTRACT CLAIM

Strict product liability claim cannot be based on malfunction of defective product purchased in commercial transaction where damages injure only a product, and only injury is economic.   Charterers of supertankers used turbine engines that were manufactured by Transamerica Delaval. The turbines on all the ships malfunctioned because of design and manufacturing defects. The charterers alleged tortious conduct based on a product liability theory. Transamerica claimed that tort claims were precluded since the defective turbines damaged only the product itself, and the charterers were restricted to no more than a warranty claim in contract. *Held:* No strict liability claim was found, because the charterers had failed to allege unreasonable danger or demonstrable injury. Recovery on a warranty theory would give the charterers their costs and lost profits, but Transamerica owed no duty under a product liability theory based on negligence to avoid causing purely economic loss.

[East River SS v. Transamerica Delaval, Inc., 476 US 858 (1986)]

Bank's absolute duty to pay beneficiary duty will not arise where terms of letter are not complied with strictly. Beyene agreed to sell two prefabricated houses to Sofan of the Yemen Arab Republic. Sofan attempted to finance the purchase by a letter of credit from The Yemen Bank for Reconstruction & Development (YBRD), which designated Irving Trust Company as the confirming bank. In the documents Irving received from the Yemen bank, Sofan's name had been misspelled as "Soran," and upon YBRD's failure to authorize payment because of the discrepancy, Irving refused to pay. *Held:* The misspelling of Sofan's name as "Soran" was a material discrepancy that entitled Irving to refuse to honor the letter of credit. The misspelling of the name could well have resulted in Sofan's nonreceipt of the goods and his justifiable refusal to reimburse Irving.

[Beyene v. Irving Trust Co., 762 F2d 4 (2d Cir. 1985)]

¶ 9.04 PAYMENT OBLIGATIONS

Where an efficiency expert did not produce contracted for results, it is guilty of material failure of consideration. Alexander Proudfoot Co., an efficiency expert, was engaged to supply a scheduling installation, a method designed to increase efficiency, for Sanitary Linen, a laundry service. However, no scheduling installation, as contemplated in the agreement, was ever devised or furnished to Sanitary. Sanitary sued under a theory of breach of express or implied warranty, in that the savings that Proudfoot promised did not occur. The lower court dismissed the claim but found that Sanitary was entitled to restitution of the money it had paid prior to Proudfoot's breach. Proudfoot claimed it was selling services, not results. *Held:* Proudfoot did not produce what it contracted to do. In Florida, the consideration fails if the services are not performed.

[Sanitary Linen Serv. Co. v. Alexander Proudfoot Co., 435 F2d 292 (5th Cir. 1970)]

Upon Lessee's breach of service agreement, computer maintenance company is entitled to recovery under theory of unjust enrichment. Foothills, Inc., an automobile dealership, entered into an equipment leasing agreement with BSL for a computer system that was to provide accounting for the dealership. Foothills also engaged Display Data Corporation to service the system. Foothills, along with its obligations, was sold to Foothills Automotive Plaza. After a dispute, Automotive Plaza disconnected the system, and subsequently BSL and Display sued Foothills and Automotive Plaza for breach of contract and unjust enrichment. Automotive Plaza argued that BSL was not entitled to recovery, because it had not mitigated its damages by repossessing and releasing the system. BSL asked the court to look to the waiver of mitigation requirement within the contract itself. *Held:* BSL had no duty to mitigate damages, as provided by the contract. Display, which had sought recovery as a third-party beneficiary under the agreement, was permitted to recover under an unjust enrichment theory.

[Business Sys. Leasing, Inc. v. Foothills Automotive Corp., 886 F2d 284 (10th Cir. 1989)]

¶ 9.05 DISCLAIMER AND INDEMNITY

If conclusory in nature, expert witness's affidavit on gross negligence issue will not preclude summary judgment on negligence claim in breach of service contract action.   Wang Laboratories sold and serviced a computer to Orthopedic & Sports Injury Clinic, and while servicing the computer lost medical and accounting data for a five-year period. Orthopedic sued for recklessness and gross negligence,seeking more than $1 million in damages. The district court granted summary judgment as to the tort claims, and limited Orthopedic's claims to only those damages allowed by the maintenance agreement. On appeal, Orthopedic maintained that its expert witness's affidavit presented sufficient evidence to defeat summary judgment. *Held:* The expert's affidavit did not sufficiently demonstrate a genuine issue of material fact, since it was wholly or almost wholly conclusory and not supported by facts. The lower court properly granted Wang's summary judgment motion on the gross negligence issue.

[Orthopedic & Sports Injury Clinic v. Wang Lab., Inc., 922 F2d 220 (5th Cir. 1991)]

¶ 9.06 WAIVER AND ESTOPPEL

Dissatisfied client does not waive right to seek damages for breach of contract when it uses service for 18 months after notifying provider of service of its dissatisfaction.   HCS agreed to develop and implement a billing system for Staten Island Hospital. Dissatisfied with the system, over a period of 18 months, the hospital sought, procured, and implemented a new system, and then abruptly suspended payments of its monthly management fees to HCS, whereupon HCS sued for breach of contract. The hospital counterclaimed for breach of warranty and sought to recover costs associated with the acquisition of its new system. HCS claimed in a summary judgment motion that by its continued payment of the monthly fee, while knowing of HCS's alleged breaches, the hospital waived its right to claim that HCS breached the contract. *Held:* This issue survived summary judgment. Staten Island Hospital did not intend to waive the defects in HCS's performance. Although the hospital's acceptance of services under the contract for 18 months after its notice of dissatisfaction could be viewed as conduct inconsistent with an intent to preserve claims for breach of agreement, other reasonable inferences could be drawn.

[Hospital Computer Sys. v. Staten Island Hosp., 788 F. Supp. 1351 (DNJ 1992)]

¶ 9.07 GOOD FAITH AND COOPERATION

Bank's postpetition super-priority claim will not be equitably subordinated because bank cut off credit to debtor in strict compliance with financing agreement in the absence of bad faith or inequitable conduct on part of bank. Debtor, a shoe retailer that had a banking relationship with First Bank of Whiting, continued its relationship with First Bank after filing Chapter 11 by entering into a financing agreement whereby First Bank was granted a super-priority lien on the debtor's assets for all postpetition loans. The postpetition loan agreement provided for cancellation of the line of credit on five day's notice. After providing some funding and honoring the debtor's letters of credit, First Bank gave notice that it would terminate financing. In its plan of reorganization, the debtor sought to equitably subordinate First Bank's postpetition claims, arguing that First Bank's refusal to make further loans caused the debtor to lose three of its upscale stores, reduced its chances of obtaining credit elsewhere, and caused it to lose credibility with its suppliers. The plan was confirmed over First Bank's objections and confirmation was affirmed by the district court. *Held:* Plan cannot be confirmed over First Bank's objection. First Bank complied with its contractual obligations under the loan agreement. The court will not adopt a rule requiring "good faith" to be something more than compliance with the terms of a contract.

[Kham's Nates Shoes No. 2, Inc. v. First Bank of Whiting, 908 F2d 1351 (7th Cir. 1990)]

¶ 9.08 INDEPENDENT CONTRACTOR OR EMPLOYEE

Sculptor's work under commission does not fall within scope of employment and "work for hire" doctrine of federal copyright law. CCNV commissioned artist Reid to produce a statue for display in Washington. CCNV offered suggestions and paid the full price. Then, both parties applied for a copyright on the sculpture. CCNV argued that it had "employed" Reid and the statue was a work made for hire as defined in the Copyright Act (17 USC §§ 101, 101(1), 101(2)). Reid claimed that he was an independent contractor. *Held:* The sculpture was not a "work for hire" within the federal copyright law. Reid had discretion and freedom beyond the scope of employment. However, if on remand the district court were to determine that the parties worked in such a manner that their contributions merged into inseparable or interdependent parts of a unitary whole, the two parties might be found to be co-owners of the copyright.

[Community for Creative Non-Violence v. Reid, 490 US 730 (1989)]

Third-party client's view is not dispositive in dispute over whether former employee was employee or independent contractor at time he developed product. MacLean formerly worked for Mercer-Meidinger-Hanson, and created a software system that Mercer integrated into one of its systems. MacLean sued Mercer for copyright infringement. A client, the New York Stock Exchange (NYSE), was confused whether MacLean was working for Mercer or not, and Mercer used this client's confusion to convince the district court to award it a directed verdict against MacLean. On appeal, Mercer argued that under a work for hire theory, Mercer and not MacLean held the copyright on the system; and, at any rate, by not informing the NYSE that he (MacLean) no longer was in Mercer's employ, MacLean had given Mercer a nonexclusive "implied license" to use the software system. *Held:* Whether MacLean was an employee or an independent contractor was a jury question; the judgment against MacLean was vacated and the case remanded. The court suggested that MacLean held the copyright and that no matter how the Mercer-MacLean relationship appeared to the NYSE, the two principals were clearly aware of their relationship, and MacLean, under the Copyright Act, was an independent contractor.

[MacLean Assocs. v. William M. Mercer-Meidinger-Hanson, Inc., 952 F2d 769 (3d Cir. 1991)]

PART B.   CONSULTING AND PROGRAMMING SERVICES

¶ 9.09 CONTRACT OBLIGATION: OUTCOME OR EFFORT

Article 2 of UCC does not apply to mixed contract whose primary purpose is provision of services, rather than sale of goods.   Kirkpatrick, an interior designer, entered into a written contract with Introspect. The contract required Kirkpatrick to create the interior design for an adolescent mental health care facility and to sell furnishings to Introspect to complete the design. Under the contract, the fee for Kirkpatrick's design services would be generated through markups on furnishings that she purchased and resold to Introspect for use in the facility. Introspect later advised Kirkpatrick that bids to provide the furnishings for the facility were being obtained from other sources. Kirkpatrick brought suit for damages, alleging, among other things, breach of contract. Introspect responded that Kirkpatrick's complaint failed to state an actionable claim for breach of contract because the contract failed to state a quantity term as required by the UCC's statute of frauds as found in New Mexico Stat. Ann. (NMSA) § 55-2-201(1) (Michie 1978). Introspect further argued that the contract, requiring the purchase and sale of furnishings, constituted a sale of goods under the NMSA and was governed by Article 2 of the UCC. *Held:* Because the primary purpose of the contract was for the provision of services, rather than for the sale of goods, Article 2 of the UCC did not apply, and Kirkpatrick's breach of contract claim was legally sufficient to survive Introspect's Rule 12(B)(6) motion. The contract was a mixed contract; Article 2 applies to mixed contracts only if the primary purpose of the contract is to sell goods rather than to provide services. Here, the contract's primary purpose was to provide interior design services, although the contract clearly contemplated that Kirkpatrick would purchase and resell goods to Introspect.

[Kirkpatrick v. Introspect Healthcare Corp., 845 P2d 800 (NM 1993)]

¶ 9.10 REASONABLE CARE, NEGLIGENCE, AND MALPRACTICE

Where statute of limitations may have tolled for contract and tort claims, claim of fraudulent indorsement may yet be viable. Honeywell manufactured computer equipment and sold it to Triangle. Thereafter, Triangle brought suit to recover damages for the alleged failure of performance of the system. The complaint alleged causes of action sounding in fraud, breach of contract, and negligence. All claims were dismissed as time barred by the lower court. *Held:* the lower court ruling was upheld for the contract and tort claims, but where the district court concluded that the fraud claims were simply restatements of the breach of contract claims, the circuit court found that Triangle was also alleging fraud prior to, and extraneous to, the contract, rather than merely fraudulent nonperformance of the contract itself. The complaint on the fraudulent indorsement claims was therefore timely, given the longer period of limitation for fraud claims.

[Triangle Underwriters, Inc. v. *H*oneywell, Inc., 604 F2d 737 (2d Cir. 1979)]

No claim of computer sales malpractice adheres where sales company acts in good faith in sales and implementation of system. NCR sold a computer system to CSI that failed to perform as promised. CSI claimed NCR breached both express warranties and the implied warranty of fitness, and sought to recover incidental and consequential damages. CSI also alleged fraudulent misrepresentation in the transaction, that NCR knew the misrepresentations were false with an intent to deceive, and that it was therefore entitled to punitive damages. NCR argued that it fully intended the system to be successful. *Held:* No tort liability was imposed; only compensatory damages were awarded. NCR neither abandoned the project nor were its actions deceptive; and while NCR's representations were overly optimistic, they were not fraudulent.

[Chatlos Sys. v. National Cash Register Corp., 479 F. Supp. 738 (DNJ 1979), aff'd in part 635 F2d 1801 (3d Cir. 1980)]

Claim of breach of ordinary duty of care and negligence in business setting is sufficient to preclude summary judgment where seller was negligent in advising purchaser of capabilities of computer system. Sperry sent a team of sales specialists to examine Invacare's needs as Invacare prepared to acquire a computer system. Invacare alleged that Sperry fraudulently induced it to purchase an inadequate system from Sperry. Sperry refused to cancel the purchase agreement or take back the system. Invacare sued, claiming precontract misrepresentation by Sperry, and alleging that Sperry had breached a duty of ordinary standard of care to which those in the computer sales industry are held. Sperry asserted that there were liability limitations within the contracts, and that it could not be held to an elevated standard of, effectively, professional malpractice. *Held:* Sperry's motion for summary judgment was denied. Sperry could not shield itself with the language of a contract when Invacare alleged that the contract itself was induced by fraud. Moreover, Invacare's claims alleged a breach of the ordinary standard of care recognized within the industry, simply negligence in a business setting.

[Invacare Corp. v. Sperry Corp., 612 F. Supp. 448 (ND Ohio 1984)]

In breach of contract action, computer service provider may be sued for fraud in the inducement, but not for professional malpractice. RKB engaged Ernst & Young to perform computer consulting services. Dissatisfied with its new system, which Ernst & Young had overseen, RKB sued for breach of contract as well as in tort, citing negligence, recklessness, and deliberate fraud. RKB argued a theory of professional malpractice against the service provider, as well as fraud in the inducement. *Held:* There is no cause of action for professional malpractice in the field of computer consulting, nor does a conventional business relationship create a fiduciary relationship in the absence of additional factors. However, a party fraudulently induced to enter into a contract may join a cause of action for fraud with one for breach of the same contract.

[RKB Enters., Inc. v. Ernst & Young, 582 NYS2d 814 (App. Div. Dept. 3d 1992)]

¶ 9.11 CONSULTANTS AND NEGLIGENT MISREPRESENTATION

[1] Consulting Sellers and Negligence

Consulting seller of computer system is liable for fraudulent and/or reckless claims made to induce sale. AccuSystems brought suit against Honeywell Information Systems, seeking damages for fraud, negligence, and breach of contract arising from Honeywell's sale of computer hardware and software to AccuSystems. After the sales and service agreements were made, AccuSystems became disaffected with the computer system, alleging that it did not perform up to the representations Honeywell made prior to the purchase agreement. AccuSystems argued that Honeywell assumed a duty of care in sales and service that it breached; Honeywell argued that it was not negligent in its dealings, but was supportive and responsive to AccuSystems's needs. *Held:* No negligence was found in the sale or service. The court did, however, find that representations made by Honeywell to AccuSystems prior to the agreement were known by Honeywell to be false, or were made recklessly, to induce AccuSystems to purchase, and that Honeywell was liable in damages limited to actual pecuniary loss.

[AccuSystems, Inc. v. *H*oneywell Sys., Inc., 580 F. Supp. 474 (SDNY 1984)]

¶ 9.12 COOPERATION IN DESIGN

Plaintiff's failure to supply specifications does not relieve defendant of other contractual obligations. Stone agreed to buy from Phoenix a computer system for its radio advertising business. The promised product consisted of a business system and a research system. When Stone did not supply required specifications for the research system, Phoenix, although it had received $168,000 of the $220,000 owed, failed to deliver either system. Stone sued for breach of contract. Phoenix counterclaimed, arguing that Stone had breached an implied covenant of good faith and fair dealing. *Held:* Both parties were found to have breached the sales agreement. Phoenix had not delivered the promised product, and Stone failed to provide sufficient information to enable the development of the research software. However, Stone's breach did not relieve Phoenix of its other, unperformed contractual obligations.

[HR Stone, Inc. v. Phoenix Business Sys., Inc., 660 F. Supp. 351 (SDNY 1987)]

¶ 9.13 COST AND SYSTEM CHANGES

Where service provider is unable to perform as promised because of technical inability, it is liable for damages in breach of contract action. Tymshare contracted to set up a computerized inventory control service for Napasco, a chemical products manufacturer and distributor. Napasco requested specific changes to the system Tymshare had implemented, and Tymshare did not respond efficiently. When Tymshare could not meet its obligations, Napasco sued for breach of contract. While Tymshare, in effect,could not do what it had promised to technically perform, at trial it argued that there had been no actual contract. *Held:* The agreement between the parties was binding, and Tymshare's breach was an active violation, defined under Louisiana law as "doing something inconsistent with the obligation it has proposed." However, the breach was not in bad faith; and therefore, Tymshare was liable only for such compensatory damages as may have been contemplated at the time of the contract.

[Napasco Int'l, Inc. v. Tymshare, Inc., 556 F. Supp. 654 (ED La. 1983)]

¶ 9.14 TIME OF COMPLETION

Buyer of computer system may not reject seller's delivery where seller was merely 16 days late if Seller has substantially performed.   DPT agreed to provide a computer system to Sherwood. The hardware portion of the order was delivered 16-days later than the specified delivery date, whereupon Sherwood returned the goods to DPT and refused to pay. DPT alleged that Sherwood breached the contract by refusing to accept delivery, and Sherwood moved for Rule 12(b)(6) dismissal for failure to state a claim. Sherwood relied on the perfect tender rule, which allows buyers to reject for any nonconformity with the contract, arguing that late delivery was a substantial nonconformance under the rule. *Held:* Noting the observation in White and Summers *Uniform Commercial Code* (3d ed.), that the perfect tender rule has been steadily eroded, the court denied Sherwood's Rule 12(b)(6) motion, and suggested that at trial the delay of 16 days should not be considered "substantial."

[DP Technology Corp. v. Sherwood Tool, Inc., 751 F. Supp. 1038 (D. Conn. 1990)]

In breach of contract suit, provision shortening the statute of limitations presents triable issue of fact that precludes summary judgment.   Angus sued Digital when Digital did not perform its task of converting Angus's software to operate on Digital's personal computers. Digital argued that Angus's suit was time barred by an agreed-on 18-month limitation provision within the contract. Angus argued that Digital verbally waived the limitation provision and that the usual, six-year statute of limitations on contract actions allowed its suit. *Held:* Whether or not the 18-month provision was part of the contract was a triable issue of fact that precluded summary judgment.

[Angus Medical Co. v. Digital Equip. Corp., 840 P2d 1024 (Ariz. App. Div. 1 1992)]

PART C. DATA-PROCESSING AND OUTSOURCING CONTRACTS

¶ 9.15 GENERAL CONSIDERATIONS

Contractual provision limiting liability to the amount paid by customer for computer services will be upheld in event of provider's breach.   Farris sought damages arising out of a breach of contract for data-processing services that were to be rendered by SC. The contract contained a provision that explicitly limited liability of the supplier, in the event of its breach, to the amount paid by the customer for the services. *Held:*   Under New York law, the court found such a contractual limitation valid and enforceable.

[Farris Eng'g Corp. v. Service Bureau Corp., 406 F2d 519 (3d Cir. 1969)]

Where bank ceases to use outside company for data processing, going in-house with its service requirements, service contract does not terminate and outside company is awarded contract price.   ADP and First National Bank of Cobb County agreed to a three-year data-processing services contract, wherein regardless of use, First National would pay monthly at least 80 percent of the cost of the average use during the prior six months. First National bought computers, taking much of its processing work in-house, and refused to pay ADP the agreed-on minimum monthly charge, whereupon ADP sued to collect the contract price. First National argued that when ADP cashed checks for smaller amounts than the minimum monthly charge, an accord and satisfaction had been reached. *Held:* No accord and satisfaction was found to have been reached, because there had been no meeting of the minds. The contract had not been terminated by First National's decision to take much of its processing work in-house; therefore, the 80 percent minimum charge was triggered, and ADP was allowed to recover the price agreed on for its services.

[ADP-Fin. Computer Servs., Inc. v. First Nat'l Bank, 703 F2d 1261 (11th Cir. 1983)]

¶ 9.16 MATERIAL BREACH AND PERFORMANCE

Computer service customer justified in terminating contract where provider fails to provide timely and adequate service.   RH terminated the service contract it held with Distronics, a data-processing service, claiming that Distronics had breached the agreement by chronic failure to furnish services promptly and accurately. Distronics argued that many of the claimed inadequacies of services were attributable to RH's own employees. *Held:* Distronics breached the contract by chronic failure to furnish services promptly and accurately. The breach was material and substantial, and RH was justified in terminating the contract.

[Distronics Corp. v. Roberts-Hamilton Co., 575 F. Supp 275 (D. Minn. 1983)]

¶ 9.17 MANAGING DISPUTES IN THE RELATIONSHIP

Provider of computer service may not unilaterally change terms of service provided by raising price of a service that falls within scope of service contract.   Applied agreed to process data for Empire. After 17 months, Applied sought to raise the price on what had been a monthly delivery to Empire of a policy master file. Empire refused to pay, "covered" the contract, and sued Applied to recover damages. Applied argued that it had the contractual right to suspend delivery of the master tapes, because their delivery was beyond the normal scope of service within the contract. *Held:* Applied breached the contract when it suspended delivery of the master tapes. The contract provision could not be construed to allow additional charges for the master file.

[Empire Mut. Ins. Co. v. Applied Sys. Dev. Corp., 505 NYS2d 607 (App. Div. 1989)]

¶ 9.18 RIGHTS IN THE DATA

List in telephone services directory does not meet federal requirements for copyright protection.   While compiling an areawide telephone directory, Feist approached 11 small telephone companies operating in northwest Kansas and offered to pay for the right to use their local white pages listings. Rural alone refused to license; Feist used Rural's list without consent, and Rural sued for copyright infringement. Feist argued that while directories as a whole may be copyrightable, the list of names is merely an unoriginal set of undistinguished facts, not accompanied by original expression. *Held:* The names, towns, and telephone numbers copied by Feist were not original to Rural and therefore were not protected by the copyright in Rural's combined white and yellow pages directory. Rural's white pages were merely basic subscriber information.

[Feist Publications v. Rural Tel. Serv. Co., 111 S. Ct. 1282 (1991)]

Mail-order house customer is required to post a bond before it can recover vital records from computer service that claims mechanic's lien on customer's materials.   LTD was a mail-order house whose business records were self-owned but used by its computer service provider, Beacon Data Processing Service Corp., which held an artisan's lien on them until paid-for services were performed. LTD sought to go in-house with its service needs and asked Beacon for the records, whereupon Beacon withheld the materials and billed LTD for unpaid services. LTD then sought and gained a temporary restraining order requiring Beacon to turn over the materials, but LTD was ordered to post a bond prior to receiving the materials, which the court could order paid to Beacon in the event LTD failed to obtain a preliminary injunction. *Held:* The preliminary injunction was denied and the amount of the bond, which in effect had ensured that neither party would be in an improved position before the status quo was changed by the turnover of the computer materials, was turned over to Beacon.

[LTD Commodities, Inc. v. Perederij, 699 F2d 404 (7th Cir. 1983)]

Where computer service provider maliciously retains records upon termination of relationship with customer, punitive damages may be awarded. Upon termination of its billing and collecting service to Magic Valley, PBS withheld vital billing and collection materials from its former customer. Magic Valley brought suit to obtain its records from PBS and, moreover, sought punitive damages against its former computer billing service. Magic Valley argued that not only did PBS breach its contract by retaining the billing information, it also did so maliciously. *Held:* PBS's purpose in retaining the information was to compel immediate payment of its contested, unenforceable claim of payment for service and also to harass and delay Magic Valley's transition to another billing service. Because PBS acted maliciously, and was in effect attempting to extort payment, Magic Valley was awarded punitive damages.

[Magic Valley Radiology Assocs. v. Professional Business Servs. Inc., 808 P2d 1303 (Idaho 1991)]

¶ 9.19 DAMAGES AND REMEDIES

In presence of monthly minimum provision within service contract, breaching customer may be liable only for this minimum payment projected over remaining term of contract. Community Medical Center purchased data-processing services from Informed Core, with contract language providing for a minimum monthly charge. After Community filed for bankruptcy, Informed claimed damages equal to a monthly billing average projected to the end of the contract term, less its own costs saved. Community claimed that the proper amount should be the monthly minimum stated in the contract. It also argued that the agreement was a contract for alternative performances. Informed argued that the allowance of its claim did no more than place it in the position it would have been had the contract been fulfilled. *Held:* The damages amount was only the minimum monthly charge projected over the remaining term of the contract. The parties had an alternative contract, and since

Informed had not within the contract retained a choice, the court was free to allow recovery only for the lesser alternative.

[In re Community Medical Ctr., 623 F2d 864 (3d Cir. 1980)]

Computer service company may be entitled to specific performance if value of contract's benefit is unique,as in the case of a credit bureau's data base. TUC entered into an agreement with CBC to share credit-reporting data with one another. Only two weeks after the execution of the agreement, a competitor of TUC, Associated Credit Services, acquired CBC. TUC was not given assurance as to the continued performance of CBC, so it claimed an anticipated repudiation by CBC and sought specific performance, because CBC's credit information was unique and impossible to value monetarily. *Held:* Given the uniqueness of the CBC's data base and the corresponding inadequacy of any remedy at law to compensate for its loss, an award of specific performance was appropriate.

[Trans Union Credit Info. Co. v. Associated Credit Servs., Inc., 805 F2d 188 (6th Cir. 1986)]

Where customer wrongfully repudiates service contract, provider may be entitled to prorated value of services performed. NTA, a consulting service, contracted with the Democratic National Committee to develop and maintain a voter data bank program. After 20 months, the Committee terminated the contract, claiming a failure of consideration, while in fact NTA had provided its services in good faith. *Held:* NTA fulfilled all its contractual obligations, and the Committee's termination constituted an unjustified repudiation of the contract. The proper measure of damages to NTA is the value of NTA's uncompensated services up to the date when the contract was improperly repudiated, determined by prorating the value of the entire contract and applying a monthly rate to months for which NTA had not been paid.

[NTA Nat'l, Inc. v. DNC Servs. Corp., 511 F. Supp, 210 (DDC 1981)]

Provider of backup computer services entitled to full contract price where subscriber improperly breaches service agreement. MMS engaged CDRS as a backup for its computer system. MMS paid CDRS a monthly subscription fee and, in the event of a computer system breakdown, agreed to pay additional service fees so that MMS was "insured" against computer system breakdown. MMS began using another company for its disaster insurance, and CDRS sued for breach of contract. MMS claimed that frustration of purpose and impossibility led to its breach, and therefore the contract was voidable. The basis for MMS's position was the fact that its new parent company provided the services for which CDRS had been contracted with MMS, thereby frustrating the contract's purpose. The potential of exchange of nonpublic information between the competitors if MMS kept CDRS as its backup formed the impossibility claim. *Held:* CDRS was awarded summary judgment, and full contract damages against MMS for its breach. The court found the contract theories of frustration of purpose and impossibility, in this case, not even sufficient to withstand summary judgment.

[Comdisco Disaster Recovery Servs., Inc. v. Money Management Sys., Inc., 789 F. Supp. 48 (D. Mass. 1992)]

PART D.   MAINTENANCE AND REPAIR CONTRACTS

¶ 9.20 GENERAL CONSIDERATIONS

State product liability act does not bar claims based on negligent repairs performed on a product after product is placed into stream of commerce. American National, claiming it was subrogated to the rights of Turbo Computer Corporation, a computer retail company, sued, among others, A. Secondino & Sons. Turbo had suffered extensive property and business damage as a result of flooding. American National alleged the damage was caused by a defective roof and various roofing products sold, supplied, designed, and installed by A. Secondino & Sons and by subsequent negligent service and repair to the roof. American National's claims were based on both common-law negligence and the Connecticut Products Liability Act (CPLA) (Conn. Gen. Stat. § 52-572n(a)). Secondino contended that the CPLA, which reaches all conduct affecting the safety of a product prior to entry into the stream of commerce, provided the exclusive remedy available to American National. *Held:* The common-law negligence claim was not barred by the CPLA. The CPLA was intended to cover all conduct affecting the safety of a product *prior* to its entry into the stream of commerce. A common-law negligence claim that involves the performance of services conducted *after* the installation and sale of the product is outside the purview of the statute.

[American Nat'l Fire Ins. Co. v. A. Secondino & Sons, 832 F. Supp. 40 (D. Conn. 1993)]

¶ 9.21 INFRINGEMENT ISSUES

Customer data base used by competitor to solicit new customers in computer software service business is considered misappropriated trade secret. MAI, a designer and manufacturer of computers and software, also serviced its products after sale. A competitor for the service business, Peak Computer, hired an MAI service manager, who brought to Peak technical servicing information as well as a computer data base. In its suit for copyright infringement and misappropriation of trade secrets, MAI claimed Peak was copying and using MAI software in violation of the Copyright Act and that the customer data base with which Peak was acquiring new service customers was a trade secret. Peak argued that its use of the software did not extend beyond diagnostic necessity and that the customer data base was neither a secret nor used improperly. *Held:* For purposes of copyright, Peak's loading of software into the RAM of a service customer's computers constitutes infringement, a "copy" under the Copyright Act. Also, the customer data base has potential economic value; competitors should have to expend their own resources in efforts to solicit customers already using the MAI computer system; moreover, the employee who brought these trade secrets to Peak was in breach of his confidentiality agreement with his former employer.

[MAI Sys. Corp. v. Peak Computer, Inc., 991 F2d 511 (9th Cir. 1993)]

Imitator liable for misappropriation of trade secrets where drawings are obtained for purpose of manufacturing new minicomputer.   One minicomputer manufacturer used diagrams containing the design of another manufacturer's novel model to create its own device. The innovator, Data General, brought suit against imitator Digital for misappropriation of trade secrets. Digital claimed the designs were public knowledge; Digital further argued that a patent on part of the device supported its public disclosure claim. Data General countered that the diagrams were available only to its customers for self-maintenance purposes and that there were sufficient precautions taken to ascribe confidential status. *Held:* Use of the diagrams for other than maintenance purpose was a pirating by Digital and therefore a misappropriation of trade secrets. Also, the granting of a patent on a part of the device was not a full public disclosure of Data General's total logic design of the minicomputer. Digital did not lawfully reverse engineer the product, but in fact designed and thereafter manufactured through reliance on the misappropriated and misused drawings. Defendant was enjoined from further use and measure of damages referred to jury consideration.

[Data Gen. Corp. v. Digital Computer Controls, Inc., 387 A2d 105 (Del. Ch. 1975)]

¶ 9.22 RESPONSE AND COMPLETION TIME

Buyer may not succeed on revocation claim where seller reasonably performs services promised.   Kearney sold a piece of automated industrial machinery to Fargo. Fargo complained of significant defects unremedied by Kearney and also of Kearney's inability to provide spare parts. Fargo withheld the last payment due, claiming breach of express warranty, and sought revocation of the contract. Kearney then sued for the balance due, disputing the nonperformance claims and revocation claim, in that such a sophisticated piece of machinery would require complicated service, which Kearney had reasonably provided, and given that Fargo had used the machine for five and one-half years, Fargo could not now make a revocation of acceptance claim. *Held:* One instance of delay had indeed caused loss to Fargo, but Fargo could not succeed on a UCC revocation claim. Kearney recovered the final payments with the service loss set off.

[Fargo Mach. & Tool Co. v. Kearney & Trecker Corp., 428 F. Supp. 364 (ED Mich. 1977)]

¶ 9.23 SCOPE OF COVERAGE

Plaintiff buyer of computer must show failure of performance was caused by defects in material or workmanship to demonstrate breach of very limited warranty given by seller. Burroughs sold a computer system to Bruffey, which, dissatisfied with the computer's performance, sought to rescind the contract. The sales contract include limited warranties of workmanship, but also a disclaimer of warranties except as specifically provided. It also provided that a remedy for breach of warranty was limited to correction of defects. *Held:* Bruffey could not revoke acceptance of the sales contract or recover damages. In light of the extremely limited, albeit acceptable under Michigan law, nature of the contractual warranty given by Burroughs, Bruffey had to show that the computer's problems were caused by defects in equipment and workmanship, which it could not do.

[Bruffey Contracting Co. v. Burroughs Corp., 522 F. Supp. 769 (D. Md. 1981)]

¶ 9.24 REMEDIES

Bank may rely on "timeshare" agreement to include customers within scope of its license agreement with computer service provider. State Street Bank and Trust Co. sought a preliminary injunction against the service provider of its banking computer software, CAI, which had brought suit for breach of contract and copyright infringement. CAI claimed that through the use of a "timeshare" plan with its customers, State Street was overstepping its license agreement. CAI sought to terminate maintenance support, which would leave State Street and its customers substantially, if not irreparably, harmed. *Held:* No copyright infringement was found, because no copies were being made. State Street's customers did not possess access codes, and their use of the software derived from State Street's license agreement, whose scope had not been exceeded.

[Computer Assocs. Int'l, Inc. v. State St. Bank & Trust Co., 789 F. Supp. 470 (D. Mass. 1992)]

CHAPTER 10

FRAUD AND COMPUTER-RELATED TORTS

PART A.   FRAUD: GENERAL ISSUES AND ELEMENTS

¶ 10.01 ELEMENTS AND RATIONALE

Clause creating time limitation on causes of action does not apply to fraud claim where language includes fraud neither specifically nor inferentially via reference to presigning events.   Financial Timing Publications, Inc., purchased a computerized printing system from Compugraphic. Three years later, Financial Timing sued Compugraphic for fraud in the inducement and sought rescission of the contract. The sales contract included a provision that stated that no action could be brought under the contract more than one year after the cause of action arose. Compugraphic thus asserted that Financial Timing's claim was time barred. Financial Timing responded that the limitations provision applied only to causes of action based on the contract, and not to a claim alleging fraud in the inducement and requesting rescission. *Held:* The limitations provision might not apply. To avoid the provision's effect, Financial Timing must show that (1) it complied with all the requirements for rescission and (2) the contractual language is neither sufficiently broad nor sufficiently specific to include fraud in the one-year period of limitations. The court remanded for further fact-finding as to the first requirement, but concluded that Financial Timing met the second requirement. The time-limiting provision lacked specificity, as it included no reference to fraud. It also lacked sufficient breadth because it only referred to the contract itself and not to events occurring before the signing. Provided that Financial Timing could demonstrate that it met all the requirements for rescission, the limitation provision would not apply.

[Financial Timing Publications, Inc. v. Compugraphic Corp., 893 F2d 936 (8th Cir. 1990)]

Software purchaser's breach of sales contract that included promises to recommend seller's product does not give rise to actions for fraud, constructive fraud, or tortious breach of contract.   North American Van Lines contracted with Comfax for development of accounting software. The contract provided that the parties would deal with each other in confidence and maintain the secrecy of all information disclosed to each other. North American agreed to allow Comfax to retain ownership of the software and to notify its agents of the availability of the Comfax software. While awaiting development, North American undertook to develop its own software. North American canceled the contract, allegedly for cause, then hired a Comfax programmer and completed its own product. Comfax requested compensatory and punitive damages for constructive and actual fraud, claiming that North American misrepresented its intentions when it signed the contract. Comfax also filed for tortious breach of contract. *Held:* Comfax's claims failed. The court declined to recognize the existence under Indiana law of the novel claim of tortious breach of contract. The court emphasized that allegations of actual fraud require misrepresentations of present or past fact. Promises, predictions, or statements of existing intent are not actionable in fraud. North American's misrepresentations regarding its intent to use and recommend Comfax software related to its future plans, not present facts. The court then defined constructive fraud as the breach of a legal or equitable duty that is fraudulent as a result of its tendency to deceive others, to violate a public or private trust, or to injure the public interest. The mere existence of a contractual obligation to exchange confidential material did not create the requisite fiduciary relationship needed to establish a basis for constructive fraud. Therefore, North American had no duty to Comfax outside the ordinary contractual obligation. The court in essence disposed of all noncontract claims. Finally, the court noted that punitive damages are generally not recoverable for breach of contract. To recover punitive damages, plaintiff must demonstrate that defendant's conduct involved malice, fraud, gross negligence, or oppressive conduct. The court concluded that on the claims before it Comfax had failed to make any such showing.

[Comfax Corp. v. North Am. Van Lines, Inc., 587 NE2d 118 (Ind. Ct. App. 1992)]

Plaintiffs must prove fraud by clear and convincing evidence, rather than by a preponderance of the evidence. Riley Hill purchased a computer system from Tandy in order to improve its accounting and bookkeeping functions. Riley Hill alleged, inter alia, that Tandy committed fraud by marketing the system knowing that it lacked safeguards to protect accounting files from potential corruption. The court instructed the jury that the law recognized a presumption against fraud, which plaintiffs must overcome by clear and convincing evidence. The court nevertheless also stated that the standard of proof remained proof by a preponderance of the evidence. The jury awarded Riley Hill both compensatory and punitive damages. On appeal, Tandy argued that the lower court's instruction to the jury as to the burden of proof in fraud cases impermissibly combined the "clear and convincing" and "preponderance of the evidence" standards. *Held:* Riley Hill must prove each element of fraud by clear and convincing evidence. "Clear and convincing" means that the truth of the facts asserted must be highly probable. The evidence must be free from confusion, fully intelligible, distinct, and must establish to the jury that defendant intended to deceive plaintiffs or did so with a reckless disregard for the truth. However, once plaintiffs prove the case in principle, they may prove the extent of damages by a mere preponderance of the evidence. To avoid confusing the jury, courts must not refer to these standards as creating "presumptions." The court remanded the case for reconsideration of the fraud issues.

[Riley Hill Gen. Contractor, Inc. v. Tandy Corp., 737 P2d 595 (Or. 1987)]

¶ 10.02 FRAUD AND CONTRACT BARRIERS

Parol evidence rule does not apply to a claim of fraud in the inducement despite valid integration clause. Centronics leased computer equipment to the El Conquistador Hotel. El Conquistador claimed that Centronics orally represented that if the computer failed to perform, El Conquistador would be under no obligation to pay. However, the agreement required the hotel to pay regardless of the operability of the equipment, and also included a valid integration clause. El Conquistador withheld a portion of the rent, alleging that the computers failed to operate for 319 days over four years. Centronics asserted that the contract terms controlled and sued El Conquistador for the rent withheld. The hotel claimed fraud in the inducement and sought rescission of the agreement. The trial court granted summary judgment to Centronics. *Held:* Summary judgment overruled. New York law rejects any strict application of the parol evidence rule when fraud is claimed. An oral representation that is fraudulent and that induces reliance may be a defense even though it contradicts a provision of a written contract. El Conquistador therefore could present its fraud defense. The merger clause also did not bar El Conquistador's claim. Only if the written contract included a specific disclaimer of the very representation later alleged to be the foundation for rescission would such proof be barred. Moreover, a general merger clause will not exclude proof of fraudulent misrepresentation.

[Centronics Fin. Corp. v. El Conquistador Hotel Corp., 573 F2d 779 (2d Cir. 1978)]

Experienced seller of computer business cannot claim fraud for buyer's parol promises not incorporated into final sales contract. Boggan owned 51 percent of Interprint, a supplier of computer equipment. DSNC negotiated with Boggan to purchase his interest in Interprint. In early discussions and contract drafts, DSNC included a setoff for "obsolete" inventory, which the drafts did not define. DSNC also asserted that it was backed in part by a prominent financier, that after the sale DSNC would provide Boggan with a management position, health insurance, a company car, and payments for both his and his employees' accrued vacation time. The final contract, which Boggan and counsel read, included a setoff from the purchase price for *all* inventory not sold or returned to vendors and omitted the other terms. Boggan argued that DSNC's statements were misrepresentations amounting to fraudulent inducement. *Held:* DSNC's statements did not constitute fraud. The court found that none of DSNC's statements amounted to misrepresentations of material fact. Negotiations and discussions leading up to a written contract cannot displace the contract's terms. The court noted that Boggan did not claim that he was duped into signing a final agreement that was in fact something else. Moreover, both Boggan, an experienced businessman, and his attorney reviewed the final contract. In the absence of evidence that the transaction was not at arm's length, the terms of the contract controlled. Any statements made outside the contract were therefore expressions of opinion or intent, not assertions of fact.

[Boggan v. Data Sys. Network Corp., 969 F2d 149 (5th Cir. 1992)]

Fraudulent promises to pay for services rendered and to provide future work do not provide continuity necessary for a pattern of racketeering activity under RICO. Infotronx contracted with a department store to create a software system. Although Infotronx knew it lacked funds to complete the project, it subcontracted with Uni*Quality for some of the work. As the work progressed, Infotronx made only partial payments to Uni*Quality, but repeatedly maintained that it would pay its debts in full, and promised to provide future work for Uni*Quality after the project was completed. In fact, Infotronx knew it was unable to pay either for past or future services, and only promised to pay in order to induce Uni*Quality to keep providing services. After the project was completed, Infotronx provided no further work. Uni*Quality alleged that Infotronx's actions constituted fraud, and therefore were predicate acts under RICO. Infotronx countered that the alleged acts failed to form the pattern RICO requires. *Held:* Uni*Quality's RICO claims failed. RICO requires a pattern of activity, defined in the statute as at least two racketeering acts. Two acts alone, however, are not enough under *HJ Inc. v. Northwestern Bell Telephone Co.*, 492 U.S. 229 (1989). Plaintiff must establish that the acts were related and continuous. Here, the court found continuity lacking. Continuity either arises through activity taking place over a long period of time or through an open-ended threat of repetition into the future. Uni*Quality charged only eight months of racketeering, and when the software project was completed, the fraud ended. The fact that the contract included no termination date did not provide continuity because the contract concerned only one specific project. Similarly, that Infotronx promised to provide future work also did not render the fraud open-ended.

[Uni*Quality, Inc. v. Infotronx, Inc., 974 F2d 918 (7th Cir. 1992)]

Parties to hardware contract that lacks arbitration clause must nevertheless arbitrate claim because it relates to subject matter of software contract that includes arbitration clause. ITG purchased computer hardware and software from CMI. The parties entered into two agreements: first, an oral hardware contract and second, six months later, a written software contract. The software contract included an arbitration clause that applied to any proceedings relating to the subject matter of that contract. CMI asserted that the hardware contract was merged into the software contract, and that the arbitration clause applied to any disputes arising under either transaction. ITG countered that the contracts were entirely separate and that therefore the arbitration clause applied only to the software contract and not to the hardware contract. *Held:* ITG must arbitrate claims arising under either contract. Whether the two contracts merged or remained separate did not matter because the claims arising under the hardware contract "related to" the software contract, and thus fell under its arbitration clause. Four factors supported including the hardware contract claims in the software contract's arbitration clause: (1) the two contracts involved the same overall computer system; (2) the software described in the software agreement was intended to be used on the hardware sold under the earlier agreement; (3)

the claims related to the system's inadequacy as a whole; and (4) federal policy favors arbitration.

[International Talent Group, Inc. v. Copyright Management, Inc., 629 F. Supp. 587 (SDNY 1986)]

In the absence of fraud, plaintiff cannot bring cause of action for negligent pre-contract misrepresentation where contract includes effective integration clause and warranty waiver.   Rio Grande purchased computer hardware from Data General. Before the sale, Data General represented to Rio Grande that the hardware would be able to perform specific functions. However, the sales contract contained an effective integration clause and an effective provision disclaiming all prior representations and all warranties, express or implied, not contained in the contract. Rio Grande brought suit for negligent misrepresentation. Data General asserted that the UCC's allowance of disclaimers of warranties, and the Code's general policy favoring freedom of contract, precluded such a cause of action on the basis of precontract representations. *Held:*   Rio Grande could not maintain its cause of action for negligent pre-contract misrepresentation. The contract included an effective integration clause and specifically provided, in boldface type, that no warranties except those specifically listed in the contract were granted. Rio Grande's claim would therefore allow it to circumvent the UCC in order to have the contract rewritten. Rio Grande did not allege fraud, nor any facts indicating that the two commercial entities did not enter into the transaction freely at arm's length. Both parties were therefore bound by the terms of their written agreement.

[Rio Grande Jewelers Supply, Inc. v. Data Gen. Corp., 101 NM 798, 689 P2d 1269 (1984)]

¶ 10.03 ENHANCED AND ACTUAL DAMAGES

RICO plaintiff may allege that defendant's predicate acts furthered only one illegal scheme, provided the acts were related to one another and posed a threat of continuing criminal activity.   H.J., Inc., was a customer of Northwestern Bell, whose rates were regulated by the Minnesota Public Utilities Commission (MPUC). H.J. alleged that Northwestern Bell bribed members of the MPUC, causing them to approve rates in excess of fair and reasonable amounts. H.J. alleged that these acts violated Minnesota statutory and common law, and constituted predicate acts under RICO. Northwestern Bell moved for dismissal of H.J.'s complaint, arguing that because all the alleged acts furthered a single scheme, the complaint failed RICO's requirement that the acts form a "pattern" of racketeering. *Held:* H.J.'s complaint was valid. A RICO plaintiff need not show that the predicates were committed in furtherance of multiple criminal schemes. From RICO's legislative history, the Court determined that "pattern" requires the showing of a relationship between the predicates and a threat of continuing activity. "Relationship" means criminal acts that have the same or similar purposes, results, participants, victims, or methods of commission, or otherwise are interrelated by distinguishing characteristics and are not isolated events. "Continuity" implies long-term, and refers either to a substantial period of repeated conduct or to past conduct that by its nature projects in to the future. RICO's language and history belie the assertion that a defendant's racketeering activities form a pattern only if they are characteristic of organized crime.

[HJ, Inc. v. Northwestern Bell Tel. Co., 492 US 229 (1989)]

RICO civil plaintiff need not allege a distinct racketeering injury or that defendant was convicted of the predicate acts. Sedima entered into a joint venture with Imrex to provide electronic components to a third firm. Sedima claimed that Imrex was overbilling it and cheating it out of a portion of the proceeds. Sedima filed for treble damages and attorney fees against Imrex and two of its officers under RICO, alleging RICO violations based on predicate acts involving mail and wire fraud. Imrex argued that RICO's language required Sedima to allege (1) that it suffered a distinct "racketeering injury" different from the injury caused by the predicate acts and (2) that Imrex had previously been convicted of the predicate acts. *Held:* To maintain its civil RICO action, Sedima need only show that Imrex committed the predicate acts, and that the acts injured Sedima. The Court found nothing in RICO's legislative history to support either of Imrex's proposed requirements. Sedima need allege neither a distinct "racketeering injury" nor that Imrex or any of its officers had been convicted of the predicate acts. The court emphasized that RICO requires only (1) conduct (2) of an enterprise (3) through a pattern (4) of racketeering activity, and nothing more.

[Sedima SPRL v. Imrex Co., 473 US 479 (1985)]

Repeated use and resale of the same stolen software does not constitute a pattern of racketeering under RICO. While working with HABCO on a joint software contract, MCS lent HABCO tapes that contained both contract and noncontract software. MCS alleged that HABCO copied the tapes and used the noncontract software to develop its own software products. In addition, MCS alleged that HABCO made unauthorized copies of the contract software, converted those copies for its own use on nondesignated equipment, and sold and licensed further copies to other purchasers. MCS brought civil claims against HABCO under the RICO. HABCO countered that MCS's allegations failed to establish a pattern of racketeering under RICO. *Held:* MCS's action failed. The court noted the establishment of a pattern under RICO requires plaintiff to allege at least two related predicate acts that occurred either over a long period in the past or with the threat of continuation into the future. Here, the court found that the allegations formed at most two predicate acts—alleged copying of contract programs, and alleged copying of the backup tapes. According to the court, HABCO's subsequent use of the allegedly stolen software could not be characterized as subsequent threats. Rather, these acts would go only to the issue of damages. Therefore, this case did not involve long-term criminal conduct that could, in common sense, be called a pattern of racketeering.

[Management Computer Servs. v. Hawkins, Ash, Bapties & Co., 883 F2d 48 (7th Cir. 1989)]

Manufacturer that only tested hand-built prototypes is liable for misrepresentation and punitive damages for claims that product had been tested extensively. Dancey was a distributor for Borg-Warner products. Borg-Warner announced a new kind of equipment, claiming that after extensive testing it proved the most efficient and adaptable model available, and solicited orders. Dancey ordered a large number. The equipment failed to work properly, and Dancey was deluged with complaints. In fact, Borg-Warner had only tested hand-built prototypes rather than production models. Dancey sought actual and punitive damages for fraudulent misrepresentation. Borg-Warner claimed that its statements as to testing were truthful, and that the remainder of the announcement was mere "puffing." The trial court issued a judgment for Borg-Warner. *Held:* Reversed and remanded. By alluding to testing while requesting orders, Borg-Warner implied that it had tested production models, rather than mere prototypes. At minimum, Borg-Warner made those statements without knowledge of their truth. Borg-Warner had a duty to obtain such knowledge prior to uttering the representation. As a distributor for Borg-Warner for over 20 years, Dancey reasonably relied on Borg-Warner's representations. Under Florida law, punitive damages may be granted for malice, moral turpitude, wantonness or outrageousness. Malice may be inferred from an entire want of care or attention to a duty, and thus Dancey could recover punitive damages.

[Dancey Co. v. Borg-Warner Corp., 799 F2d 717 (11th Cir. 1986)]

Action for punitive damages for negligent misrepresentation fails absent morally culpable acts and relationship with defendant distinct from contract. RKB Enterprises entered into a contract with Ernst & Young to perform computer consulting services in connection with RKB's procurement of a new data-processing system. E&Y recommended a proposal from System Software Associates, and agreed to oversee and assist System Software in the implementation of the new system. After experiencing cost increases and delay, RKB sued E&Y, inter alia, for negligent misrepresentation and breach of contract, and sought both compensatory and punitive damages. E&Y moved to dismiss the claim, and asserted that punitive damages were not available. *Held:* RKB's action failed. A claim for negligent misrepresentation requires a relationship distinct from and independent of the contract at issue.

RKB failed to provide evidence of such a relationship with E&Y. The allegations of negligence in the complaint thus merely parallelled the breach of contract claim. RKB had not alleged facts sufficient to demonstrate that E&Y's conduct rose to the level of high moral culpability that must be reached to support a claim for punitive damages. RKB did not seek to vindicate a public right or to deter morally culpable conduct. The court thus concluded that even were it to assume that E&Y did act in a wanton, willful, or malicious manner, the acts alleged would constitute private wrongs for which punitive damages may not be recovered.

[RKB Enters., Inc. v. Ernst & Young, 582 NYS2d 814, 182 AD2d 971 (1992)]

¶ 10.04 STANDARDS OF CARE OR CULPABILITY

Computer seller liable in fraud and negligence for recommending system inadequate for buyer's purposes.   Sperry had recommended that Invacare purchase a certain model of its system, which Sperry represented would fulfill Invacare's requirements. Invacare claimed that the equipment entirely failed to operate as promised, and that Sperry then suggested further purchases, which still did not render the system usable. Invacare alleged that (1) Sperry knew or should have known that its system was inadequate for Invacare's purposes; (2) Sperry knew that suitable equipment would have cost twice the system's original price; (3) Sperry recommended an inadequate model in order to make its price appear lower than that of competitors, so as to induce Invacare to make further purchases; and (4) Sperry assigned incompetent employees to evaluate Invacare's needs and make recommendations. Invacare alleged Sperry's conduct constituted fraud and negligence. Sperry asserted that (1) the contract's integration clause barred the fraud claim; (2) its statements as to suitability were mere promises of future performance; and (3) the negligence claim in fact constituted a nonactionable claim for computer malpractice. *Held:* Invacare presented valid claims. The integration provision does not apply to fraud. Sperry represented that the system could perform certain functions. The substance of Sperry's representations therefore went to the system's present capacity, not to its future performance, and supported an action for fraud. Negligence in a business setting is clearly actionable. The court extended to computer industry personnel the Restatement of Torts language requiring members of professions or trades to possess skill and knowledge normally possessed by members of that profession. The court noted that to disallow this action would hold the computer industry to a lower standard of care than that expected of machinists and plumbers. The court emphasized that it was holding computer personnel to an ordinary standard of care, not to a higher standard suitable for malpractice, and therefore refused to characterize the claim as one of computer malpractice.

[Invacare Corp. v. Sperry Corp., 612 F. Supp. 448 (ND Ohio 1984)]

Accountant's liability for negligent audit extends only to client and to those third parties specifically identified as intended beneficiaries.   Accounting firm Arthur Young issued a "clean" audit opinion on Osborne Computer's financial statements. Arthur Young represented in the opinion that it performed the audit in accordance with the generally accepted accounting principles and generally accepted accounting standards, and that the opinion fairly represented the company's financial position. Bily, an Osborne director, claimed that he relied on Arthur Young's evaluation in deciding to purchase Osborne stock. The company went bankrupt. Bily alleged numerous deficiencies in Arthur Young's methods, and filed actions for negligence and negligent representation. Arthur Young asserted that it owed no duty to Bily, a third-party investor. *Held:*   Bily's cause of action failed. Reviewing various theories for accountant liability to third parties, the court dismissed Bily's general negligence claim, excluding third parties from general negligence principles as applied to accountants. The court held that third-party investors could only recover under the narrow Restatement of Torts definition of negligent supplying of false information. The Restatement states that a party not a direct recipient of the information can only recover if the supplier transmitted the information for that party's benefit, in a specific transaction or type of transaction identified to the supplier. The court refused to adopt a broader rule, emphasizing that (1) a large pool of potential plaintiffs would result in liability far out of proportion with actual fault, especially since plaintiffs can easily fabricate their reliance on the controverted audits; (2) the generally more sophisticated class of plaintiffs in auditor liability cases reduces the need for state intervention on investors' behalf; and (3) the potential increased cost and decreased availability of auditor service should liability increase markedly. Bily, although an officer of Osborne, invested individually and therefore was neither Arthur Young's client nor a specifically intended beneficiary of the audit.

[Bily v. Arthur Young & Co., 3 Cal. 4th 370, 11 Cal. Rptr. 2d 51, 834 P2d 745 (1992)]

Sophisticated buyer dealing at arm's length and having equal opportunity to ascertain facts could not reasonably rely on seller's statements as to qualifications of third party.   Guernsey Petroleum Corporation purchased a computer system from Interactive Systems Corporation, including Data General hardware and Data General software that Interactive would customize. Guernsey was aware that Interactive did not have a good reputation. During negotiations, Data General stated that it would support Interactive if Interactive won the contract, and represented that Interactive was qualified to install and customize Data General software. The contract provided that time was of the essence, and Interactive guaranteed that the software would be ready and operating by a certain date. Guernsey claimed that performance was still incomplete 15 months after the contract's completion date, and sued Data General for fraud. Guernsey alleged that it relied on Data General's statements, which were false and misleading. *Held:*   Data General's statements were not obviously misleading, and did not justify reliance. As Data General had no reason to doubt Interactive's abilities, its statements were at most overly assertive assurances. Guernsey was a sophisticated company with equal knowledge and opportunity to ascertain the facts. The parties acted at arm's length. Only a business novice would have been mislead by Data General's statements. Guernsey presented no evidence that Data General was privy to the knowledge that Interactive did not intend to and could not perform satisfactorily.

[Guernsey Petroleum Corp. v. Data Gen. Corp., 183 Ga. App. 790, 369 SE2d 920 (1987)]

Exculpatory language in contract defeats defendant's action to sue for negligent representation. S&P and the Chicago Board Options Exchange entered into a licensing agreement whereby S&P was the official source for calculating and disseminating the closing value of certain indexes for the purpose of trading securities options. These index values formed the basis for the settlement value of options traded on the Options Exchange. S&P misreported the closing price for one of the stocks used in calculating its indexes, and Rosenstein alleged that the error caused his options to be settled at an artificially low value and sued for negligent representation. S&P asserted, inter alia, that it did not owe Rosenstein any obligation, that the indexes were merely saleable products, and that an exculpatory clause in its contract with the Options Exchange controlled. *Held:* Rosenstein's complaint failed. The court found that S&P did owe him a duty. Under Illinois law, plaintiffs can maintain negligent misrepresentation actions against parties in the business of supplying information for the guidance of others in their business transactions. Here, the court emphasized that the entire transaction was founded on information provided by the S&P. Traders on the Options Exchange were required to use S&P information. Although the information S&P provided was the product, it did not lose its character as information used to guide the economic destinies of others. However, the exculpatory language in the contract with the Options Exchange defeated Rosenstein's action. The court found that the clause's language applied to Rosenstein's situation, and refused to limit its effect. The court noted that public policy permitted exculpatory clauses provided the relationship between the parties did not militate against enforcement. Here, Rosenstein freely chose to voluntarily enter into the trading of options subject to the exculpatory clause.

[Rosenstein v. Standard & Poor's Corp., No. 1-91-3000, 1993 WESTLAW 176532 (Ill. App. Ct. May 26, 1993)]

Bank providing false information about debtor to another creditor is in the business of supplying information and is liable for negligent misrepresentation. Utility Coal Corporation was in default on a $300,000 loan from Norris City State Bank. DeVoe Brothers, Inc. sought to buy Utility. At the same time, DeVoe needed an emergency $25,000 loan and approached DuQuoin State Bank. DuQuoin granted the loan after Norris City's president promised that he would personally guarantee $10,000 of the loan, and would grant DuQuoin a mortgage on some property that he claimed DeVoe was buying from Utility. DeVoe defaulted on the loan. Because DeVoe did not own the mortgaged property, DuQuoin had no security to apply against the debt. DuQuoin sued Norris City, claiming negligent misrepresentation. Norris City claimed it was not in the business of supplying information and thus owed no duty to DuQuoin. *Held:* DuQuoin could recover. In Illinois, a plaintiff may bring an action for negligent misrepresentation against a defendant in the business of supplying information. The court found that Norris City was in the business of supplying information, emphasizing the degree to which DuQuoin relied on the false statements, and that time did not allow for DuQuoin to verify the information. Moreover, Norris City regularly supplied information to other banks. Here, it was in the business of trying to salvage its bad loan to Utility, and therefore supplied the information in order to guide the business decisions of DuQuoin.

[DuQuoin State Bank v. Norris City State Bank, 230 Ill. App. 3d 177, 595 NE2d 678 (1992)]

¶ 10.05 RELIANCE

Buyer who is more knowledgeable about computers than seller's representatives cannot reasonably rely on the representatives' statements or on seller's publicity brochures.   APL purchased a minicomputer from HP in order to program it for resale. HP represented in its brochures that its machine performed at a certain speed. HP's salesperson repeated these claims. APL's president and sole shareholder tested the machine before purchasing it, and was impressed. When installed, the machine proved much slower than the tests indicated. APL alleged fraud and misrepresentation. HP asserted that APL could not have relied on its statements because APL's president/sole shareholder was much more sophisticated about computing than HP's salesperson, and could not have been deceived by a brochure. *Held:* APL did not reasonably rely on HP's representation. APL's president was much too sophisticated to rely on HP's publicity blurbs. APL's president was also much more knowledgeable than HP's representatives, and thus could not have been deceived by them. Therefore, as a finding of fact, APL did not rely on HP's statements. That finding was fatal to APL's case.

[APLications, Inc. v. Hewlett-Packard Co., 672 F2d 1076 (2d Cir. 1982)]

Sophisticated purchaser that performs its own evaluation of software supplier cannot claim reliance on third-party hardware seller's representations regarding the software supplier.   Electro-Matic purchased computer hardware from Prime. Prime did not manufacture software for Electro-Matic's proposed uses, and referred Electro-

Matic to Creata Data, which manufactured software compatible with Prime hardware. According to Electro-Matic, Prime stated that Creata Data was reliable, that Prime had successfully worked with Creata Data in the past, that the software could perform the functions that Electro-Matic required, and that Prime would stand behind the computer system. After delays of almost one year, Electro-Matic discharged Creata Data and hired another party to complete the software installation. Electro-Matic then claimed that the completed system did not perform as Prime and Creata Data had promised and that Prime's statements constituted fraud. Prime alleged that Electro-Matic did not rely on Prime's statements because Electro-Matic had performed its own evaluations of Creata Data and the proposed system. *Held:* Electro-Matic's claims were dismissed. Electro-Matic pointed to no evidence that it acted in reliance on the statements. Moreover, Electro-Matic personnel, including their computer specialist and legal counsel, conducted an independent evaluation of Creata Data and the capabilities of the proposed system. The court noted that fraud does not arise when the means of knowledge are open to a plaintiff and the defendant does not interfere in their utilization. The court also emphasized that Electro-Matic was a sophisticated business entity that either was aware of the risks of contracting with Creata Data or had an opportunity to so apprise itself.

[Electro-Matic Prods., Inc. v. Prime Computers, Inc., 884 F2d 579 (6th Cir. 1989)]

Plaintiff who knows of alleged defect before purchase cannot recover in fraud, despite defendant's assurances that the product is suitable for plaintiff's purposes. Fruit Industries Research Foundation purchased a computer from NCR. Fruit Industries alleged that the NCR machine printed and read input too slowly, and had inadequate memory. Fruit Industries failed to allege any misrepresentation concerning the alleged defects, and knew of the slow print rate prior to purchase. Instead, Fruit Industries alleged that NCR committed fraudulent misrepresentation when NCR's salesperson assured Fruit Industries that the slow print rate had no practical significance, and that the machine was suitable, appropriate, and adequate for Fruit Industries's purposes. Fruit Industries asserted that it could recover because although it suspected a defect, NCR's assurances dissuaded it from investigating. *Held:* Fruit Industries' knowledge of the defect prevented it from recovering. The rule that a buyer who knows of a defect but declines to investigate upon the seller's reassurances applies only if the facts (1) were peculiarly within the seller's knowledge; (2) were unknown to the buyer; and (3) could not be ascertained by the buyer. Here, Fruit Industries already was aware of the slow print rate. Fruit Industries' representative was in as good a position as NCR, or better, to foresee the effect of the slow print rate on the operations of his own company. The court also emphasized that both parties were sophisticated and dealt at arm's length.

[Fruit Indus. Research Found. v. National Cash Register Co., 406 F2d 546 (9th Cir. 1969)]

Buyer that performs own feasibility study of seller's equipment prior to purchase cannot recover for negligent misrepresentation. FSLI purchased a microcomputer from Digital for modification and resale. FSLI claimed that Digital represented that the FSLI software would work on the model computer FSLI purchased. When the software failed to copy onto the Digital system, FSLI sued, claiming negligent misrepresentation. Digital alleged that FSLI conducted its own inquiry into the appropriateness of the Digital machine, and therefore could not have relied on any of Digital's statements. *Held:* FSLI could not recover for negligent misrepresentation. A plaintiff contending negligent misrepresentation must show that (1) the defendant owed a duty of care to the plaintiff; (2) the defendant negligently asserted a false statement; (3) the defendant knew the plaintiff would rely on the statement; (4) the plaintiff justifiably relied on the statement; and (5) the plaintiff suffered damages. The court found that FSLI did not reasonably rely on Digital's statements, emphasizing that FSLI performed its own feasibility study prior to purchasing the Digital system. That FSLI's review did not reveal the extent of the difficulty in using its software on the Digital system was the responsibility of FSLI, not Digital.

[Foundation Software Labs, Inc. v. Digital Equip. Corp., 807 F. Supp. 1195 (D. Md. 1992)]

Seller of computer components must reveal inadequacies to sophisticated buyer where seller holds itself out to be an expert and where seller knows of buyer's reliance on its representations. Strand purchased magnetic read/record heads from Librascope, a leading electronic component supplier, for incorporation into computers Strand was building. The computers failed to function properly, and Strand performed extensive tests over several months to determine the cause of the problem. During this period, Librascope assured Strand that the heads met all specifications and operated properly, and suggested that Strand's own circuitry or coatings may have been the source of his difficulties. After more than six months of tests, Strand determined that the Librascope heads caused electronic "noise" that interfered with functioning of the computer. Internal records revealed that at the same time that Librascope was assuring Strand of the heads' reliability, Librascope engineers knew that the heads' design was defective. Librascope subsequently ordered design changes, but did not inform Strand of the changes and refused to replace the original order with heads of the modified design. Strand alleged that he relied on Librascope's statements in deciding to purchase the heads, and that Librascope's failure to reveal the defect constituted fraud. *Held:* Librascope's failure to disclose the component's limitations constituted fraud. Although Strand was sophisticated about electronics, he justifiably relied on Librascope's superior knowledge and expertise because Librascope held itself out as an expert in the transaction. The court emphasized that Librascope knew of Strand's reliance, yet refused to disclose facts vital to Strand's needs, which Strand could only discover through months of testing. As a seller, Librascope was under obligation to make a complete disclosure because partial disclosure, in the form of its reassurances, was misleading. The court also noted that proper disclosure might have dissuaded Strand from entering into the transaction.

[Strand v. Librascope, 197 F. Supp. 743 (ED Mich. 1961)]

PART B.   FRAUD: TYPES OF MISREPRESENTATIONS

¶ 10.06 MISREPRESENTATION OF FACT

Where system is programmed by third party after sale, buyer cannot recover against seller for programming errors.   Oakleaf sold computers to retailer Reynolds. Leson Chevrolet purchased two Oakleaf systems from Reynolds and signed a service agreement under which Oakleaf would maintain, service, and program the systems. It bought a third system six months later. Leson sued Reynolds and Oakleaf for breach of contract and rescission, charging that the original machines failed to perform certain promised functions. *Held:* Leson's action failed. As to Reynolds, the court noted that Leson cited no specific instance of hardware malfunction, instead referring only to programming errors. Under the purchase agreement, Oakleaf, not Reynolds, was responsible for programming. Furthermore, evidence showed that Leson never requested the functions it alleged did not perform. Leson also bought a third unit more than six months after the alleged problems with the first two units developed. Together, these factors indicated that the system was not defective, and that any problems were the result of programming errors. The action against Reynolds failed. As to Oakleaf, the court found that programming errors occurred with some frequency, but not an unusually large number in the course of an automobile dealer's business. Leson lost no clients as a result. Thus, the charges as to the original machines failed.

[Leson Chevrolet Co. v. Oakleaf & Assocs., Inc., 796 F2d 76 (5th Cir. 1986)]

A duty of best efforts to sell and market a product could not be imposed on purchaser of the product when purchaser made substantial upfront royalty payments.   ParaData Computer Networks, Inc., sold to Telebit Corporation the communications products division of ParaData and exclusive rights to a computer networking product known as ACS. The parties entered into a formal contractual agreement. Telebit paid ParaData $1 million as a technology licensing fee and $1 million in prepaid royalties on Telebit's future sales of ACS products. Telebit also agreed to pay royalties to ParaData on ACS sales over the next four years according to an agreed formula. Dissatisfied with the efforts made by Telebit to sell ACS products, ParaData brought suit against Telebit, alleging that Telebit breached its contract by failing to aggressively market and sell ACS products. Specifically, ParaData argued that the court should imply a duty of best efforts on Telebit as an exclusive licensee to use best efforts to market and sell ACS products. ParaData also argued that Telebit's actions violated an implied covenant of good faith and fair dealing when Telebit failed to adequately support the sale and marketing of ACS products. *Held:* The court refused to imply a duty of best efforts on the part of Telebit; the court also refused to imply a covenant of good faith and fair dealing on the enforcement of the contract. Here, Para-Data received $1 million in upfront royalty payments in exchange for the exclusive rights to ACS products that it granted to Telebit. These prepaid royalty payments assured ParaData that it would receive something for its sale of the ACS products. The payments also gave Telebit an incentive to effectively market ACS in order to make up for the cost of acquiring the system. Since Telebit made a substantial upfront payment of royalties, the court found it unnecessary to imply a duty of best efforts. As to the action for breach of an implied covenant of good faith and fair dealing, the court noted that such an action would be recognized only where "a party to a contract makes the manner of its performance a matter of its own discretion." Whether a performance is a matter of a party's discretion depends on the nature of the agreement between the parties. Here, Telebit had no discretion in the performance of its duties under the terms of the contract. Specifically, Telebit had no express duties to market or sell ACS products under the contract. As discretion is the hallmark of the covenant, the court refused to imply a covenant of good faith and fair dealing on the enforcement of the contract.

[ParaData Computer Networks, Inc. v. Telebit Corp., 830 F. Supp. 1001 (ED Mich. 1993)]

[1] Duty to Disclose

Manufacturer's failure to disclose that it would soon discontinue purchaser's model of computer and misrepresentation of future availability of parts and peripherals constitutes fraud.   Schuster purchased peripherals from Philips in order to expand a Philips computer Schuster already owned. At the time of the sales, Philips knew that it would soon discontinue production of the model computer Schuster owned. Philips nevertheless represented to Schuster that parts and peripherals for his machine would continue to be available. In fact, Philips had no inventory of such parts or peripherals. Schuster claimed that the discontinuation of production of the computer, parts, and peripehrals rendered the equipment prematurely obsolete. Schuster alleged that by withholding information about the discontinuation of Schuster's model of computer, and by misrepresenting the future availability of appropriate parts and peripherals, Philips committed fraud under the common law and New Jersey's Consumer Fraud Act. *Held:* Schuster could recover. Philips knowingly withheld information regarding the cancellation and falsely represented the availability of parts. The court also noted that the peripherals Schuster bought did not meet Schuster's needs or Philips's representations. Cessation of production of Schuster's model meant that Schuster was unable to accomplish the objectives that originally motivated its purchases. Schuster relied on Philips's representations and suffered economic losses as a result, because the computer became prematurely obsolete.

[Hundred East Credit Corp. v. Eric Schuster Corp., 212 NJ Super. 350, 515 A2d 246 (1986)]

Seller's failure to inform buyer/dealer of word processors that seller had breached its contract with its third-party supplier constitutes fraud, where seller knows that dealer's customers need technical support that only supplier can provide. Ames was a dealer in Olivetti products, including an expensive, sophisticated word processing system that Olivetti did not manufacture, but purchased from a third-party supplier, NBI. Olivetti represented to Ames that Olivetti was purchasing the system under a five-year contract, under which NBI would provide Ames, and Ames's customers, with full software and hardware support. In fact, either Olivetti or NBI could terminate the contract after 14 months. Olivetti breached the contract after 13 months, but did not inform Ames or make any public announcement. Over an 18-month period following cancellation of the supply contract, Olivetti repeatedly denied rumors of the cancellation, instead asserting that relations with NBI were still good and that NBI would continue to provide technical support. Ames continued to purchase additional units, although continuing rumors of the contract's cancellation complicated sales efforts. Ames alleged that Olivetti's false statements constituted fraud, and that Ames had reasonably relied on those statements to its detriment. *Held:* Ames reasonably relied on Olivetti's false statements, which constituted intentional fraud. The court noted that Olivetti made its false statements intentionally, with the purpose of inducing Ames to continue to purchase the word processing system. Olivetti also knew that a long-term supply agreement was important in order to reassure buyers that they would receive continuing technical support. By keeping the contract's cancellation secret, Olivetti thus caused Ames to make purchases it otherwise would not have made.

[Olivetti Corp. v. Ames Business Sys., Inc., 81 NC App. 1, 344 SE2d 82 (1986), aff'd in part, 319 NC 534, 356 SE2d 578 (1987)]

[2] False Promises and Predictions

Seller of computer chips can recover in fraud for buyer's refusal to pay where evidence indicates buyer never intended to perform. Chip dealer Brian Bonar sold three orders of chips to component distributor Centon Electronics. Unable to resell some of the chips from the second order, Centon asked Bonar for permission to return some of the purchased chips. Bonar refused. Centon then placed a third order and immediately sent a check as payment, but two days later issued a stop payment order on the check. Centon conceded that it issued the check by mistake. Bonar alleged that the stop payment order amounted to fraud, arguing that Centon never intended to pay the full price for the third order of chips. Centon moved to dismiss. *Held:* Bonar could proceed. The court stated that under Alabama law, the only basis upon which one may recover for fraud predicated on promises of future action is when evidence indicates that at the time of the promise, the promisor had no intention of performing, and had the intent of deceiving. Failure to perform is not evidence of intent not to perform at the time of the agreement. Here, there was sufficient evidence to create a question of fact as to whether Centon ever intended to pay for the third order of chips.

[Centon Elecs., Inc. v. Bonar, 614 So. 2d 999 (Ala. 1993)]

Breach of software distributorship contract does not rise to level of fraud absent evidence that breaching party never intended to perform. BSW contracted with Cabnetware to distribute Cabnetware's software. The contract stated that the agreement would remain in effect so long as BSW sold a minimum number of programs. BSW was late in paying Cabnetware invoices, and customers began to complain about BSW's service. Although BSW always sold the required quota, Cabnetware canceled the distributorship. Cabnetware testified that it believed the distributorship to be terminable at will by either party. BSW sued in fraud for compensatory and punitive damages, alleging that Cabnetware's statements in the distributorship agreement were intentional or reckless misrepresentations. *Held:* BSW could not recover for fraud. The court found that the language in the agreement constituted a promise on the part of Cabnetware to refrain from terminating the agreement in the future. The only basis upon which one may recover for fraud predicated on promises of future action is when evidence indicates that at the time of the promise, the promisor had no intention of performing, and had the intent of deceiving. Failure to perform is not evidence of intent not to perform at the time of the agreement. The only indication of the parties' intent as to the duration of the agreement was in the agreement itself. Cabnetware's testimony that it believed the distributorship terminable at will did not indicate that at the time of the contract it had no intention of performing.

[Cabnetware, Inc. v. Birmingham Saw Works, Inc., 614 So. 2d 1034 (Ala. 1993)]

Plaintiff who sells interest in computer system in exchange for buyer's promise to develop it in the future cannot recover for fraudulent inducement to contract. CBW Financial Corp. conveyed all its interests in Time Machine Limited to Computer Consoles. In exchange, Computer Consoles agreed to pay CBW royalties, and to work with Time Machine in developing, manufacturing, and marketing a new computer. However, Computer Consoles retained sole discretion whether to produce the new system, and could thereby be relieved of any obligation to pay royalties.

One year after entering the agreement, Computer Consoles informed CBW that it had terminated development of the new system. CBW alleged that Computer Consoles was actually continuing to develop the system without paying CBW the promised royalties. CBW brought an action against Computer Consoles for fraudulent inducement to the contract, claiming Computer Consoles' promises to develop, manufacture, and market the new systems constituted misrepresentation. *Held:* The court dismissed CBW's complaint. Computer Consoles' promises were not inducements to contract, but were actually part of the express terms of the contract. An alleged failure to perform these promises is therefore a breach of the contract itself, and gives rise to an action on the contract, not to an action for inducement. Moreover, a cause of action for fraud in inducing a contact cannot be based solely on a failure to perform promises of future acts. The promises at issue concerned the future development, marketing, and manufacturing of a computer system.

[CBW Fin. Corp. v. Computer Consoles, Inc., 504 NYS2d 179 (App. Div. 1986)]

¶ 10.07 MISREPRESENTATIONS IN SYSTEMS CONTRACTING

Breach of express warranty may be found when a promise that a product has a certain quality is not fulfilled; moreover, an implied warranty of merchantability may be disclaimed if the agreement between the parties specifically mentions the word "merchantability" in a conspicuous manner. L.S. Heath & Sons brought this action against AT&T Information Systems, alleging, among other things, that AT&T breached implied and express warranties in connection with the sale of a computer network. In 1984, Heath decided that its current computer system was becoming outmoded and resolved to upgrade and enhance its computer and telecommunications capabilities. Heath established an executive committee to research the needs of the company and to solicit sales proposals from interested vendors. Honeywell, IBM, and AT&T were among the vendors submitting bids. In August 1984, AT&T presented its final recommendation and proposal to the executive committee. The recommendation provided for a phased implementation schedule whereby the network would be assembled in six phases. Heath agreed to the design, and a master agreement was signed by the parties in September and October 1984. By the end of 1987, after an abundance of trouble, the system was not working as Heath had anticipated. In response to Heath's suit, AT&T filed a motion for summary judgment on its counterclaims and on the claims raised by Heath. *Held:* AT&T's statement in the recommendation to Heath that AT&T's "completed integrated [sic] processing and voice/data communications network [will] satisfy all of your [Heath's] aforementioned objectives" could amount to an express warranty, and consequently, the district court's ruling in favor of AT&T on the breach of express warranty count was reversed. Moreover, the implied warranty of merchantability was disclaimed in the agreement executed by the parties and, therefore, the district court's ruling finding the disclaimer effective was affirmed. A statement can amount to a warranty even if unintended to be such by the seller "if it could fairly be understood . . . to constitute an affirmation or representation that the product possesses a certain quality or capacity relating to future performance." Evidence suggested that "complete integration" was not provided as promised and that the AT&T system did not have the ability to expand as promised in the recommendation. As to the breach of implied warranty claims, an implied warranty of merchantability may be disclaimed if the word "merchantability" is used in the written document and is "conspicuous," that is, a reasonable person against whom it is to operate ought to have noticed it. The writing in the master agreement specifically mentioned "merchantability" and the use of capital letters under the black-letter heading "WARRANTY EXCLUSIONS" made the writing conspicuous. Therefore, this provision of the master agreement amounted to a valid disclaimer of the implied warranties of merchantability and fitness for a particular purpose.

[LS Heath & Sons v. AT&T Information Sys., 9 F3d 561 (7th Cir. 1993)]

[1] New Systems and Disclosure

Distributor can recover from computer manufacturer for false statements that system would be capable of turnkey functions. Qantel, a computer manufacturer, entered into a written distributorship agreement with CSE. One year after agreeing to extend the distributorship, Qantel canceled it. CSE alleged that the Qantel system was to include both hardware and a particular software package. According to CSE, Qantel had represented that the software in question would be a "turnkey" system easily adapted for various uses. CSE alleged that although Qantel knew the software was not sufficiently sophisticated to qualify as a "turnkey" system, Qantel nevertheless made continual representations that the package merely had a few bugs and that a turnkey version would be available shortly. CSE brought claims including fraud. Qantel contended that CSE could not justifiably rely on the alleged misrepresentations concerning the software as it was aware of the problems when it renewed the agreement. *Held:* Qantel's conduct constituted fraud. The record contained more than sufficient evidence to support the finding that CSE neither knew, nor reasonably should have known, prior to its renewal of the distributorship agreement that Qantel's representations as to the state of development of Solutions was fraudulent. The court emphasized that Qantel made repeated reassurances that the software merely contained a few bugs that would soon be fixed. The court also found that Qantel was aware at all relevant times that a turnkey version of the software would require very substantial modifications before it could be called turnkey.

[Computer Sys. Eng'g, Inc. v. Qantel Corp., 740 F2d 59 (1st Cir. 1984)]

Seller's claim that equipment could perform a particular function, when it in fact did not yet have the stated capability, may constitute misrepresentation supporting fraud.   CRS, a group of physicians, wanted to purchase a computerized CAT-scan system that was capable of both head and full-body scanning. Syntex demonstrated one of its systems, claiming that it had been working as a full-body scanner, but that because of minor technical problems the body scanner part had been removed. CRS purchased a unit immediately after the demonstration. Syntex in fact did not develop a functional full-body scanner until two months after the demonstration and sale. It delivered a head scanner to CRS, but did not offer to deliver such a body scanner until two years later. CRS refused to accept the body scanner, and then revoked acceptance of the head scanner. It nevertheless retained the head scanner for another 22 months, for a total of almost 4 years' use. CRS asserted that Syntex's statements at the demonstration constituted misrepresentation supporting fraud. *Held:* Syntex's assertion that it had already successfully developed a full-body scanner, when it fact it would not produce such equipment for several months, may have constituted misrepresentation supporting fraud. The court remanded the claim for further determination. The court emphasized that a plaintiff must prove fraud by clear and convincing evidence, and suggested that CRS's retention of the head scanner might be inconsistent with fraud. Similarly, the fact that CRS was comprised of physicians familiar with CAT-scan technology might undermine their claim.

[Computerized Radiological Servs. v. Syntex, 786 F2d 72 (2d Cir. 1986)]

Seller's knowledge of defects shown by internal warnings and use of demonstrator model specially modified to avoid known defects constitutes fraud.   Glovatorium purchased a computer system from NCR. At the time of sale, NCR stated that the system would be able to perform four accounting functions Glovatorium specifically requested. None of the functions were operational upon delivery. Two functions could never be installed, and two failed to work properly even after several months' delay. Glovatorium also claimed that the system was too slow. It alleged that NCR sold the system knowing of these defects. NCR demonstrated the system to potential customers using a specially-designed model that performed much more quickly and effectively than ordinary production models. A former NCR manager testified he had informed NCR headquarters about the system problems. Other evidence indicated that the system was not designed to perform functions Glovatorium requested, and should not be modified. NCR sold Glovatorium a modified system. *Held:* NCR's behavior constituted fraud. It was reasonable to infer NCR's knowledge of the defects in light of the manager's testimony. Also, the use of a specially designed model constituted a cover-up, and indicated that the highest levels of NCR were aware of the system's deficiencies. Furthermore, under California law, fraud is properly inferred from the immediate failure to perform a promise. NCR promised that the system would be delivered capable of performing the accounting functions. The failure of the accounting functions to operate thus contravened NCR's promises and constituted fraud. That NCR sold Glovatorium a modified system, in violation of its own conclusions that the system should not be modified, also supported the conclusion of fraud.

[Glovatorium, Inc. v. NCR Corp., 684 F2d 658 (9th Cir. 1982)]

[2] Obsolete and Discontinued Systems

Buyer can recover for fraud from seller who knowingly contracts to sell product that had been canceled and would not be manufactured.   Eisenberg contracted with Tandy to purchase computer equipment. Tandy knew at the time of contract that the equipment to be sold had been canceled and would not be manufactured. Eisenberg alleged that Tandy's conduct constituted fraud. Eisenberg asserted that Tandy intended to capture Eisenberg in order to sell him a substitute product, and prevent him from buying an equivalent product from a competitor. *Held:*   Eisenberg could recover. The court found that Eisenberg had been deceived, and that Tandy's actions froze Eisenberg in the market as a captive customer. Tandy in effect persuaded Eisenberg to purchase its preferred substitute, rather than reenter the market to purchase an alternative product with the same capacity and quality from another supplier. These actions constituted fraud under Florida statute. The court noted that the contract's exculpatory clause did not apply to an action for fraud, as against Florida public policy.

[Tandy Corp. v. Eisenberg, 488 So. 2d 927 (Fla. Dist. Ct. App. 1986)]

[3] Suitability for Intended Use

Novice buyer can recover in fraud against seller that claims its system will be most suitable for buyer's needs, that promises free services but fails to deliver, and that fails to disclose its manager's misgivings as to system's suitability. Dunn Appraisal sought to update its computer system and consulted with Honeywell. Honeywell's salesman recommended a system that would require conversion of the programs Dunn used on its existing equipment. The salesmen represented that Honeywell's system was the most suitable for Dunn's purposes, that it could be installed quickly, that Honeywell would convert the programs at little effort and without charge, and made a variety of statements about the system's capabilities. A Honeywell manager cautioned the salesmen against selling Dunn the equipment, because conversion of Dunn's programs would be too difficult. Nevertheless, Honeywell sold Dunn the system. Although the contract limited the number of programs to be converted, the sales agents represented that Honeywell would convert all Dunn's programs. After months of delay and conversion problems, including Honeywell's refusal to convert more than specified in the contract, Dunn canceled the contract. Dunn sued Honeywell, claiming that Honeywell's promises were fraudulent and that it should have disclosed the manager's misgivings about the sale. Honeywell asserted that its statements were opinions on which Dunn could not rely. *Held:* Honeywell's behavior constituted fraudulent misrepresentation. Because it concerned the inherent, existing capabilities of the product, the statement that the system was the best suited for Dunn's purposes was a statement of a present fact rather than an opinion about the future. The salesmen's failure to disclose the manager's misgivings, or to modify their recommendations in light of those misgivings, supported Dunn's allegations of willful disregard for the truth. The statement that Honeywell would convert all the programs, although a representation concerning a future event, was fraudulent because Honeywell did not intend to convert all the programs. The court emphasized that Dunn had little knowledge of computers, and that Dunn's agents were personal friends with Honeywell's salesmen and trusted them to keep Dunn's best interests at heart.

[Dunn Appraisal Co. v. Honeywell Information Sys., Inc., 687 F2d 877, 882 (6th Cir. 1982)]

Unsophisticated purchaser of computer equipment may recover in fraud for seller's factual misstatements, even in absence of intent. Clements Auto Company purchased data processing services from SBC. SBC told Clements that the proposed data processing system would be an effective and efficient tool for inventory control. SBC also stated that (1) the only way for Clements to obtain an inventory system such as that used by a certain car dealer was by automating; (2) the system included controls adequate to prevent all but minimal errors; (3) certain equipment would be suitable for Clements's needs, and could be used by normal clerical personnel; and (4) weekly sales management reports would allow management by exception. After more than three years of attempting to use the system, Clements charged that the input method was too slow, and the reports too error-prone and voluminous to be of use in purchasing inventory. Clements therefore alleged that SBC's precontract statements were actionable misrepresentations. SBC asserted (1) that Clements failed to show any intent, and therefore the contract's warranty disclaimer applied to SBC's statements and (2) SBC's statements either were mere opinions and predictions rather than assertions of fact, or were so patently unbelievable as to merit no reasonable reliance. SBC also claimed that in the absence of intent, a contract clause limiting liability to the amount of the contract should limit any damages award. *Held:* SBC was liable for fraud. Under Minnesota law, the element of scienter, intent to deceive, or recklessness is not necessary to prove fraud. Therefore, a general disclaimer-of-warranty clause was ineffective to negate reliance or innocent misrepresentations. The court found that SBC's general statement that its system would be an effective and efficient tool for inventory control was a factual statement of the inherent capabilities of a particular product. The court emphasized that SBC was an expert in data processing, and that Clements, with its limited knowledge of computers, could reasonably rely on SBC's statements. Furthermore, SBC's specific assertions indicated that the statements, considered as a whole, were factual and not mere predictions. These statements were erroneous and solely within SBC's field of expertise. Thus, SBC committed fraud by making factual misrepresentations upon which Clements relied. Finally, the court noted that public policy generally precluded application of clauses limiting liability in cases of fraud. Because Minnesota did not require intent to prove fraud, the clause limiting liability would not apply, regardless of the absence of intent.

[Clements Auto Co. v. Service Bureau Corp., 444 F2d 169 (8th Cir. 1971)]

Buyer can recover for misrepresentation only for value of defective components, where components do not affect utility of system as a whole and buyer fails to show that seller did not intend to perform general promises as to system's performance.   Iten purchased computer equipment from Burroughs. Several components failed to operate properly. Iten asserted that several Burroughs representations were false, including statements that Burroughs' system would satisfy Iten's needs, and that the system would perform properly. Burroughs countered that the statements only concerned future actions, or were not material to the system as a whole. *Held:* Iten could recover only for the components themselves. The court held that Burroughs knew or should have known that the representations that the functions would operate were false. However, the representations were not material to the purchase of the total system. Iten's evidence failed to establish as false Burroughs' representation that its system would accomplish the objectives, needs, and requirements of Iten. The court emphasized that there was no evidence that Burroughs did not intend to perform the future representations at the time they were made. As to the materiality of the defects, the court found that the functions affected were not central to Iten's decision to purchase the system and did not seriously affect Iten's use thereof.

[Iten Leasing Co. v. Burroughs Corp., 684 F2d 573 (8th Cir. 1982)]

[4] Time and Cost Savings

Where computer system produces more information than novice buyer could gain otherwise, buyer cannot recover in fraud despite system's mechanical problems.   Badger Bearing purchased a computer system from Burroughs. Burroughs stated that the system would have the capacity to meet Badger's existing and future needs, and made various representations as to specific functions. Burroughs also generally claimed that the system would allow more work in less time, and that it would provide more meaningful management information than ever before possible. Once installed, the system experienced frequent mechanical problems. Badger removed the system after an independent analyst concluded that it was not performing several of the promised functions and that Burroughs' claims as to more work in less time and more meaningful information were therefore incorrect. Badger filed suit, claiming that Burroughs' statements constituted fraud and misrepresentation. *Held:* Badger's allegations failed to support either misrepresentation or fraud. The purchaser's preexisting system provided virtually no management information, whereas despite the mechanical breakdowns, the Burroughs system did provide considerable information. Moreover, some of the system's functions did allow Badger to complete more work in less time. Therefore, Burroughs' general claims were truthful and would not support Badger's cause of action. As to the specific functions, Badger failed to show that it relied on any particular Burroughs representation. Promises of future performance are not actionable in fraud unless at the time of the statement the speaker intended not to perform. Therefore, in the absence of evidence of intent not to perform, Burroughs' claim that the system would fill Badger's future needs failed because it was a promise of future performance.

[Badger Bearing Co. v. Burroughs, 444 F. Supp. 919 (ED Wis. 1977), aff'd mem. 588 F2d 838 (7th Cir. 1978)]

¶ 10.08 TESTING AND PERFORMANCE

Where seller made knowing or reckless false statements, time-limit clause does not apply to sophisticated buyer's claim for fraud in the inducement, but buyer cannot recover for negligent misrepresentation in absence of trust relationship.
AccuSystems purchased a computer system from Honeywell for modification and resale. Honeywell represented (1) that its system would perform certain functions and (2) that it had been extensively tested, and worked well. In fact, Honeywell did not perform any testing until one year after AccuSystems bought the system. Accusystems asserted that the system failed to perform as promised, and therefore alleged that Honeywell's conduct constituted negligent misrepresentation and fraud in the inducement to the contract. Honeywell claimed that AccuSystems, as a computer company, could not reasonably rely on Honeywell's statements, and that AccuSystems failed to allege the kind of trust relationship necessary for negligent misrepresentation. Honeywell also asserted that contractual provisions time-limiting any cause of action barred AccuSystems' claim. *Held:* AccuSystems could recover for fraud only. New York courts do not recognize a cause of action for negligent misrepresentation in the absence of a special relationship of trust or confidence between the parties. Plaintiffs in fraud must show that defendant made the statement knowing it to be false, or made it recklessly without knowing its truth or falsity. Honeywell knew that the system had not been tested when it represented both that the system had been tested successfully and that it could perform certain functions. Honeywell's statements therefore constituted fraud in the inducement, whether analyzed under the knowing or recklessness test. Although AccuSystems was familiar with computers, its reliance on

Honeywell as to Honeywell's own system was reasonable. Fraud in the inducement negates provisions of a written contract at the behest of an injured plaintiff. Therefore, the time-limiting clause did not apply.

[AccuSystems, Inc. v. Honeywell Information Sys., 580 F. Supp. 474 (SDNY 1984)]

¶ 10.09 SECURITIES LAW

Investor cannot recover under Securities Act for inaccurate statements where issuer indicated that accuracy of statements was under review or future events were unpredictable. Wielgos invested in Commonwealth Edison, which had several nuclear power plants under development. The prospectus included estimates of completion date, but stated that the completion and operation of the new plants was subject to regulatory approvals that could be subject to delay. The prospectus also stated that the estimates themselves were from the prior year and were under review. After Wielgos invested, the Atomic Safety and Licensing Board denied Commonwealth Edison's application for the operating license for one of the plants. The Board had never outright denied an operating license before, and its decision was later reversed. In the meantime, the stock plummeted. Wielgos brought actions for damages under Section 11 of the Securities Act of 1933, alleging that Commonwealth Edison (1) underestimated the reactors' completion costs and (2) failed to reveal that the license application was before the Board. *Held:* Commonwealth Edison was granted summary judgment. Each year, Commonwealth Edison updated the estimates of completion date for the plants under construction. Although the statements incorporated into the prospectus were factually erroneous, the court found that they were not fraudulent. Applying one of the safe-harbor rules under Rule 175, the court reasoned that forward-looking statements need only have a reasonable basis to remove the statement from the realm of fraud. Here, the rising costs of building nuclear power plants made the estimates almost inevitably inaccurate. Moreover, firms need not reveal its data, assumptions, or methods. Although the data were stale by the date of the prospectus, Commonwealth Edison did reveal that the estimates were under review, and it was well known that nuclear plants tended to be delayed. As to the Board, the court noted that information is only material when there is a substantial likelihood that a reasonable shareholder would consider it important. Materiality, the court stated, depended both on magnitude and probability. Here, the Board had never before denied an operating license. That possibility was so improbable as to render the information immaterial.

[Wielgos v. Commonwealth Edison, 892 F2d 509 (7th Cir. 1989)]

Stockholder may recover under Rule 10b-5 for corporation's overly optimistic statements regarding troubled new product. Stockholder Hanon alleged that computer printer manufacturer Dataproducts made false and misleading statements to shareholders concerning the viability of a new product line, violating Rule 10b-5 under the Securities Exchange Act of 1934. Dataproducts issued a press release promoting the market's "strong interest" in and "high acclaim" for Dataproducts' new line of printers. In the months before and after the release, high-level Dataproducts memoranda admitted that the printers could not be built reliably, suffered from ink-durability and cold start problems, and had a poor field reputation. Dataproducts argued, inter alia, that the problems were not significant enough to mandate disclosure and that companies should not be required to denigrate their own products. *Held:* Hanon could proceed with this action. The court found that a reasonable jury could conclude that Dataproducts publicly released optimistic statements about the new line at a time when it knew the printer suffered serious technical problems and could not be built reliably. The reported problems undermined the product's essential function, and the court noted that there is a difference between knowing that any product-in-development may run into snags and knowing that a product has already developed problems so significant as to require months of delay. Accordingly, a jury could conclude that the statements had a misleading effect on the price of Dataproducts stock. Finally, the court held that Rule 10b-5's mandated disclosure might require a company to denigrate its products in order to make its statements not misleading.

[Hanon v. Dataproducts Corp., 976 F2d 497 (9th Cir. 1992)]

Shareholders may recover for fraud under the securities acts where management intentionally deceived, manipulated, or defrauded them. Plaintiff shareholders brought six claims for relief under the Securities Act of 1933 and the Securities Exchange Act of 1934 against STC, a computer equipment manufacturer that filed for bankruptcy. Plaintiffs alleged that STC officers and directors recklessly concealed and misrepresented STC's financial status and the development of its products through statements of unfounded optimism and failure to reveal their competitors' advantages in the market. STC asserted that its actions were simple mismanagement, and moved to dismiss. *Held:* STC's motion to dismiss denied. In a securities fraud action, plaintiff must allege acts indicating management's intent to deceive, manipulate, or defraud, rather than mere negligence on the part of management. Plaintiffs cannot allege fraud-by-hindsight, in which shareholders claim that the prior communications of a company in trouble had omitted negative information, which would have revealed the root causes of the company's current problems. However, deliberate management decisions to cover up facts likely to depress the market in the company's stock may constitute a violation of the securities acts. Plaintiffs' allegations that STC recklessly concealed and deliberately manipulated information would, if proven, meet this standard, and therefore dismissal was inappropriate.

[In re Storage Technology Corp. Sec. Litig., 630 F. Supp. 1072 (D. Colo. 1986)]

PART C.   NEGLIGENCE AND PRODUCT LIABILITY

¶ 10.10 NEGLIGENCE, MALPRACTICE, AND CONTRACTS

Computer consultants held to professional rather than ordinary standard of care.   DG hired consulting firm Ernst & Whinney to assist it in obtaining a computer system that was easy to use and fit DG's needs. DG knew little about computers, but maintained that it had a long-standing, trusting relationship with Ernst & Whinney. The computer system Ernst & Whinney recommended failed to meet DG's requirements and proved difficult to use. DG asserted claims of negligence and breach of fiduciary duty. Ernst & Whinney argued that an ordinary, rather than a professional, standard of care applied to the transaction. *Held:* A professional standard of care applies, under which Ernst & Whinney was negligent. Professional persons and those engaged in any work or trade requiring special skill must possess a minimum of special knowledge and ability as well as exercise reasonable care. The court noted that Ernst & Whinney subscribed to an established set of standards covering management advisory services. These standards formed a clear basis for determining the proper standard of care for those providing computer consulting services. Furthermore, the court found it implicit in the agreement that DG anticipated Ernst & Whinney possessed superior knowledge, and relied heavily on Ernst & Whinney's professed expertise. The court emphasized the complexity of the system DG sought to buy, and DG's concomitant need for competent advice in choosing between alternatives.

[Diversified Graphics, Ltd. v. Groves, 868 F2d 293 (8th Cir. 1989)]

Investor cannot recover under Exchange Act for fraud on the market where widely available information counterbalances issuer's misstatements.   Schneider invested in Apple Computer at a time when Apple was developing two new products, a computer and disk drive. Both products were unsuccessful. Schneider alleged that the market inflated Apple's share price on the basis of several optimistic statements Apple insiders made, including statements that the disk drive ensured greater data integrity and had been tested and verified, and that the computer would sell briskly. Schneider alleged that Apple's unqualified optimism was false and misleading under Section 10(b) of the Securities Exchange Act of 1934 and Rule 10b-5, and constituted "fraud on the market." Apple countered that press reports questioning the viability of both programs were adequate to make their statements not misleading. *Held:* Schneider could proceed only with his complaint as to the disk drives. Generally, when a plaintiff alleges actual reliance on a particular statement, it does not matter that the market is aware of the facts necessary to make the statements not misleading. In a fraud on the market case, however, the defendant's failure to disclose material information may be excused where that information has been made credibly available to the market by other sources. This standard requires more than brief mention in a few poorly-circulated journals, and envisions that the nondisclosed information be transmitted to the public with a degree of intensity and credibility sufficient to effectively counterbalance any misleading impression created by the insiders' one-sided representations. In this case, the same popular business magazine that included several of Apple's optimistic statements also included considerable analysis of Apple's risks. These statements sufficiently counterbalanced any misleading Apple representations, and Schneider's claim failed. In contrast, the market was unaware of the problems with the disk drive. Internal Apple memoranda indicated it knew the drive was unreliable when it issued its misstatements. Schneider thus had a triable cause of action as to the drives.

[In re Apple Computer Sec. Litig., 886 F2d 1109 (9th Cir. 1989)]

[1] Negligent Contract Performance

Plaintiff cannot recover under either negligence or strict products-liability for a product's injuring itself. Transamerica Delaval manufactured and installed turbines into four transport ships. A component of the turbines was defective, causing further damage to the turbines. The ships' operators brought actions against Delaval in admiralty jurisdiction, alleging that Delaval was strictly liable for the design defects. Plaintiffs did not allege that the damage caused any harm to other property or to persons. *Held:* Plaintiffs could not recover in products liability. The Court noted that products liability grew out of a public policy judgment that people need more protection from dangerous products than is afforded under warranty law. The paradigmatic product-liability action is therefore one where a product reasonably certain to place life and limb in peril causes injury to person or to other property. Here, the components damaged only the turbines themselves, endangering neither persons nor other property. The Court reasoned that allowing consumers to recover in tort when one part of an integrated package injures another would dissolve the distinction between contract and tort law. Manufacturers would be subject to unlimited tort liability for what in essence is a contractual claim: that the product has not met the customer's expectations for product value. Plaintiff could therefore recover in contract for product value and for lost opportunities.

[East River SS Corp. v. Transamerica Delaval, Inc., 476 US 858 (1986)]

Unlicensed practice of engineering and failure to produce computer components on time support misrepresentation and contract claims, but do not support negligence per se, gross negligence, or fraud. A division of TI contracted with Teletron, a manufacturer of computerized thermostat systems, to produce custom microprocessors. TI did not reveal that this would be only the third or fourth project it had ever worked on for an outside customer, or that none of its "engineers" was licensed as required by Texas law. Teletron claimed that TI failed to produce the microprocessor on time, causing the collapse of Teletron's business. Teletron thus alleged that TI's unlicensed, unlawful practice of engineering constituted negligence per se, and also sued for breach of warranty, misrepresentation, fraud, and gross negligence. *Held:* Teletron could not recover. Credible evidence indicated that TI tried to work around situations that it did not control, including poor assembly of the units, manufacturing errors, and improper handling. TI's evidence tended also to show that it worked to solve a "complicated engineering puzzle" while Teletron refused to accept advice from TI that might have eliminated some of the units' problems. Although the court agreed that TI's knowing practice of engineering without a license supported findings of misrepresentation and breach of warranty, it nevertheless held that TI's misconduct did not constitute negligence per se, gross negligence, or fraud.

[Teletron Energy Management Inc. v. Texas Instruments, Inc., 838 SW2d 305 (Tex. Ct. App. 1992)]

[2] Reasonable Care Malpractice

Builder of custom computer system must perform with skill and diligence ordinarily possessed by well-informed members of that trade. L.H. Smith Oil Corp. contracted with DPS for development of a custom computer system. Smith claimed that DPS represented that it had the necessary expertise and training to design the system. In fact, according to Smith, DPS knew that it lacked the necessary skills, should have known that Smith was dependent on DPS, and should have foreseen that Smith would incur losses if DPS did not perform. Smith alleged that DPS breached its duty as a service provider to have the reasonable skill and ability to do the job for which it contracted. DPS asserted that the software it sold was a "good" under the UCC, and that standards for service providers did not apply to the transaction. *Held:* The software was a service, and DPS breached its duties as a service provider. The court noted that Smith bargained for DPS's skills in developing a system appropriate for Smith's needs. The court found that this relationship bore greater resemblance to a client seeking a lawyer than to a customer purchasing goods. The tangible end product in the form of disks or tape merely provided a means for transmitting the skill and knowledge of the programmer. Thus, the duties of service providers applied as much to computer personnel as to other professions or trades. Those who hold themselves out to the world as possessing skill and qualifications impliedly represent that they possess the skill and will exhibit the diligence ordinarily possessed by well informed members of the trade or profession. DPS failed to perform to this standard.

[Data Processing Servs. Inc. v. LH Smith Oil Corp., 492 NE2d 314 (Ind. Ct. App. 1986)]

¶ 10.11 THIRD-PARTY PRODUCT LIABILITY

Manufacturer of component of computerized energy management system is not liable for injuries caused when system failed to permit laboratory exhaust fan to operate during off hours. Sparacino, a teacher, was injured by chlorine gas while engaged in an experiment during off hours in his school laboratory. The gas accumulated in the laboratory because the school's computerized energy management system (EMS) did not permit the laboratory's exhaust fan to operate during off hours. Sparacino sued Andover, manufacturer of the EMS's microprocessor system, claiming that Andover was strictly liable because the EMS was inherently dangerous, defective, and unreasonably unsafe in design and manufacture. Andover argued that its product was safe, that it could not be responsible for a system of which it only manufactured a component, and that it could not have reasonably anticipated Sparacino's injury. *Held:* Andover was not liable. A product is unreasonably dangerous where it fails to perform in the manner reasonably expected in light of its nature and intended function. Manufacturers need not anticipate how components not themselves dangerous or defective can become potentially dangerous dependent upon their integration into a unit designed, assembled, installed, and sold by another. Andover's product performed precisely in the manner in which it was programmed to perform. There was no evidence that the EMS malfunctioned or was inherently dangerous. In order to find that the manufacturer should have known of the danger inherent in the product, it must be objectively reasonable to expect the use of the product to be injured in the manner in which the plaintiff was injured. It is not enough that the injury was merely conceivable. It was not objectively reasonable to expect that a chemistry experiment would be taking place in the school during off hours. Andover was not responsible for wiring or installing the EMS such that it would disable the exhaust fan, and thus could not be held responsible for Sparacino's injuries.

[Sparacino v. Andover Controls Corp., 592 NE2d 431 (Ill. App. Ct. 1992)]

[1] Software

Plaintiff exposed to toxic dust while loading pellets cannot recover from pellet manufacturer for implied warranty where plaintiff does not allege pellets were unreasonably dangerous and plaintiff's employer exercised direct supervision. Vito La Rossa was an employee of Witco Chemical. Witco contracted with Scientific Design to design and build a new plant, which included a reactor that employed a pellet-form catalyst. The pellets generated toxic dust when La Rossa loaded them into the reactor. After breathing the dust, La Rossa developed cancer, from which he died. La Rossa's widow filed suit for breach of implied warranty, arguing that Scientific Design impliedly warranted that it would insure the safety of all those who might be affected by the pellets. She did not allege that the pellets themselves were unreasonably dangerous, instead focusing on their installation. *Held:* Plaintiff could not recover. The court concluded that because plaintiff did not argue that the pellets were unreasonably dangerous, the case concerned professional services rather than a product. Examining the origins of strict liability, the court declined to extend the theory to providers of services. The court emphasized that a purchaser of a service can only expect reasonable care and competence, and thus is not justified in expecting infallibility. Moreover, plaintiff was only one of a small group of workers, rather than a member of the broad consuming public. Therefore, no implied warranty ran from Scientific Design to plaintiff's decedent. Plaintiff instead could recover from Witco, which exercised direct supervision over the decedent and therefore was a more appropriate insurer against harm to him.

[La Rossa v. Scientific Design Co., 402 F2d 937 (3d Cir. 1968)]

Publisher of defectively designed aeronautical chart is liable for injuries caused through pilot's reliance.   Jeppesen published instrument approach charts to aid pilots in making instrument approaches to airports. Aetna contended that the chart for the Las Vegas airport was defective, and caused a crash. The parties agreed that the actual information in the chart, which Jeppesen culled from government reports, was accurate, but that the chart's composition was defective. Most charts consisted of two tables depicting different perspectives, but drawn to approximately the same scale. In the Las Vegas chart the scales differed substantially. Aetna alleged that the crew, assuming the scales were identical, misread the charts and crashed. *Held:* Jeppeson's chart was defective and Aetna could recover. The court treated the chart as a tool. Jeppesen invited reliance on the graphic depiction of information that otherwise was in the public domain. The chart's usefulness stemmed from the fact that it could be instantly understandable. The conflict between the scales of the two tables so diminished the chart's utility as to render it unreasonably dangerous and a defective product. Aetna could therefore recover for injuries caused by use of a product with a defective design.

[Aetna Casualty & Sur. v. Jeppeson & Co., 642 F2d 339 (9th Cir. 1981)]

A book, unlike computer software or nautical charts, is never a product for products liability purposes.   Winter, a mushroom enthusiast, purchased *The Encyclopedia of Mushrooms*, published by G.P. Putnam's Sons. Winter became critically ill after eating mushrooms that he had collected in reliance on the book's description of safe mushrooms. Winter sued Putnam on a products liability theory. Putnam asserted that the claims in the book were not a product for products liability purposes. Winter sought an exception for books providing instructions as to physical activity, and analogized to aeronautical charts, which are defined as products. *Held:* Winter's claim failed. Products liability law imposes strict liability as a means for redistributing risk from purchaser to manufacturer. However, policies favoring freedom of expression militate against subjecting publishers to the threat of liability without fault. Products liability law therefore does not extend to books. The court refused to attempt to distinguish between ideas and actions. Unlike the book in question, an aeronautical chart is itself a tool, like a compass, whereas a book might instruct a reader as to how to use a chart or tool. The court also noted that computer software that fails to yield the result for which it was designed might be a product for liability law purposes.

[Winter v. GP Putnam's Sons, 938 F2d 1033 (9th Cir. 1991)]

CHAPTER 11

INTERNATIONAL TECHNOLOGY EXPORT AND IMPORT [RESERVED]

PART III

INFORMATION AGE
ISSUES

CHAPTER 12

COMPUTER CRIME

PART A.   COMPUTER CRIME IN GENERAL

¶ 12.01 SEARCH AND SEIZURE ISSUES

Plaintiff must show that warrantless search of data on legitimately seized hard disks violated objectively reasonable expectation of privacy in its contents. UNISYS suspected that Lyons, a former employee, had stolen a computer and components. The FBI, pursuant to search warrant, confiscated UNISYS computer in Lyons's home. Sometime after seizure of the equipment and without obtaining a further search warrant, a UNISYS technician inspected the contents of hard disks and found several valuable proprietary programs. Lyons claimed that discovery of software violated the Fourth Amendment. *Held:* Because Lyons made no attempt to show any rightful claim to the hard disks seized, his claim failed. The issue here is whether Lyons had an objectively reasonable expectation of privacy in the contents of the hard drive. Because Fourth Amendment rights are personal, Lyons had the burden of proving that he had an actual, subjective expectation of privacy in the property searched, and that society would recognize that expectation as objectively reasonable. Expectations of privacy, however, derive in part from the right to exclude others from the property in question. Therefore, lawful possession is an important factor in determining legitimate privacy expectations.

[United States v. Lyons, 992 F2d 1029 (10th Cir. 1993)]

In seizing computer documents and electronic communications federal agents must comply with privacy and communication statutes.   The Secret Service (SS) obtained an overbroad search warrant and confiscated hundreds of computer files and print material of a games publisher, Steve Jackson Games, that also ran a public bulletin board service (BBS). The search violated the federal Privacy Protection Act that forbids search and seizure of any work product of persons reasonably believed to be preparing material for public dissemination in any public medium. The SS also retained the materials for an unreasonable period, and refused Jackson's reasonable request for immediate return of the materials or permission to copy the materials. The SS read Jackson's private and public E-mail, and deleted information contained in the files without consent. The SS further violated federal law relating to interception of stored wire, oral, and electronic communication. The BBS was a "remote computing service," and therefore agents could obtain the warrant only by disclosing to magistrate the relevance of the information to a "legitimate law enforcement inquiry." The SS's actions eliminated all safeguards and failed to give Jackson notice as to basis of search warrant and Jackson's right to quash or modify the order, or eliminate or reduce any burden connected with it, including permission to make backup copies of the information seized. *Held:* The SS did not demonstrate "good faith" reliance on the court order or search warrant. In attempting to prevent Jackson from destroying evidence, the SS clearly exceeded its authority. Government officials must conduct reasonable preliminary investigations and comply with all federal statutes, no matter how difficult this makes prosecution.

[Steve Jackson Games, Inc. v. United States Secret Serv., 816 F. Supp. 432 (WD Tex. 1993)]

Police may use scientific analysis to extract information from validly seized computer without additional search warrant. Copenhefer, a convicted murderer, claimed that although the police had a valid warrant to confiscate his computer and search the files on the hard drive, they needed an additional warrant to search files that were deleted, but recoverable, from the hard drive. *Held:* Deletion or destruction of files does not create a new and different legal or constitutional right to privacy requiring an additional warrant prior to a search. The attempt to destroy evidence does not create a legally protected expectation of privacy. Copenhefer's hope of secrecy did not prohibit the state from using scientific analysis to extract information from validly seized physical evidence.

[Commonwealth v. Copenhefer, 587 A2d 1353 (Pa. 1991)]

Line trap that traces hacker's activity but does not record content or other elements of telephone transmission does not infringe hacker's privacy rights. For several hours during the course of 3 days, Riley, a computer hacker, had his computer dial Telco's access number every 40 seconds and transmit random six-digit numbers in order to steal long-distance access codes. A Telco employee observed this activity and had a "line trap" placed on equipment to trace the source of activity. After tracing the activity to Riley, a search was conducted on the basis of a defective search warrant, and stolen material was confiscated. Riley admitted intent to steal telephone access codes. Riley appealed his conviction, contending his conduct did not constitute "computer trespass" and that evidence was obtained in violation of the Fourth Amendment. *Held:* The "line trap" did not violate state privacy laws since, unlike "pen registers," its only use was to trace the telephone number of the caller, and no other information, public or private. Further, Telco was authorized by state law to use such devices in its operations. Although evidence seized through use of a defective search warrant was fruit of the poisonous tree and therefore inadmissible, the record did not indicate that Riley's confession was also tainted. Therefore, because his confession was corroborated by independent evidence from Telco employees' observance of hacking activity and tracing of activity to Riley's home, his conviction as to computer trespass was upheld. Finally, the record clearly indicated that Telco's long-distance switch is a computer through which long-distance calls are processed. Riley's dialing activity clearly constituted computer trespass—intentionally gaining unauthorized access to a computer system.

[State v. Riley, 846 P2d 1365 (Wash. 1993)]

PART B. FINANCIAL CRIMES

¶ 12.02 TRADITIONAL THEFT AND FRAUD

In crimes involving manipulation of bank data, computer records are properly admitted into evidence as business record exceptions to hearsay.   Hutson appealed her conviction of embezzlement, claiming that introduction of computer records into evidence was improper since the reports were mere accumulations of hearsay and not "business records exceptions" permitted under the Federal Rules of Evidence (FRE). *Held:* Computer records are admissible if the requirements of Section 803(6) of the FRE are met. Because the records from which the computer records were made were themselves business records, there was no accumulation of evidence. The rules of evidence do not require that the witness laying the foundation be the person who "entered the data into the computer" or that the records be prepared by the business having custody of them. While the dates of the printouts of the records were seven months after the transactions in question, it was sufficient for the requirement of Section 803(6)—that the records be "made at or near the time of the business transaction"—that each printout also showed the date that the transaction transpired. Finally, the records were not untrustworthy because they did not account for all the missing funds. Since access to the computer was restricted, evidence of Hutson's illegal manipulations was properly admitted.

[United States v. Hutson, 821 F2d 1015 (5th Cir. 1987)]

Electronic transmission of money is equivalent to sending a check or issuing a draft.   Without any authorization from the board of directors, Warner, the owner of the controlling interest in an S&L, personally ordered six margin calls between August and October to be honored; a total of $12.2 million was transferred by wire to ESM, a small broker-dealer. A state jury found Warner guilty pursuant to a statute that forbids unauthorized transfers by a "draft . . . or other written instrument." A state appeals court reversed, but the Ohio Supreme Court (OSC) reinstated the conviction. Warner brought a habeas corpus proceeding, and consequently appealed the district court's adverse decision, claiming the statute was void for vagueness, and did not cover "wire transfers." *Held:* Warner's argument was unacceptable; clearly, the legislature intended to criminalize unauthorized transfers of assets regardless of form. To be unconstitutionally void for vagueness, a statute precise on its face must have been unforeseeably and retroactively expanded by judicial construction. The authors of the statute evidently assumed that transfers would take place by means of written instruments. However, it was not unforeseeable that the OSC would rule that the authors' assumption was not a requirement of the statute. A literal reading of the statute would defeat the legislative purpose, especially in regulating an industry where electronic transfers are commonplace.

[Warner v. Zent, 997 F2d 116 (6th Cir. 1993)]

Using computers to effect unwarranted transfers and attempting to withdraw the wrongfully credited funds constitute bank larceny by false pretenses. Registe opened a bank account for $100 and the next day someone "transferred" $14,000 to it by computer manipulation, although the bank received no funds to justify the deposit. Registe tried to cash a check for $9,980, but when told the bank could only give $5,000 in cash, he cashed it for that amount, although the account really contained only $100. Registe was indicted for entering the bank with intent to commit larceny by false pretenses, in violation of 18 USC § 2113(a). Registe claimed that this computer manipulation did not fall under the statute. *Held:* Computer manipulation constituted a crime under the federal statute. The essence of this crime is entering a bank for the purpose of committing larceny by false pretenses. First, larceny by false pretenses is indeed punishable under federal law, and is proscribed in this statute's definition section (18 USC § 2113(b)). Second, in prohibiting entering a bank to commit "any larceny" in Section 2113(a), Congress intended to include both common-law larceny and larceny as statutorily defined in Section 2113(b).

[United States v. Registe, 766 F2d 408 (9th Cir. 1985)]

¶ 12.03 COMPUTER FINANCIAL FRAUD

Computer fraud sentences may be enhanced by taking into account intended (versus actual) loss associated with conspiracy. Defendants obtained bank codes and conspired to produce and use counterfeit ATM cards to steal millions of dollars from Bank of America (BA). Before they could act, they were arrested and pled guilty to violating 18 USC § 1029. They appealed the enhancement of their sentences, claiming the court miscalculated the probable loss. They also contended that expenses claimed by BA, for which they were required to make restitution, were too indirect to be recoverable under the Victim and Witness Protection Act (VWPA). *Held:* The district judge was free to base his calculations on either the "probable or intended loss," and not required to consider the "probable loss" that would have resulted from the intended plan. The U.S. Sentencing Commission *Guidelines Manual* notes clearly state that "if a probable or intended loss that the defendant was attempting to inflict can be determined," that figure should be used if it is larger than the actual loss. Further, the guidelines mandate only calculation of the intended loss, and not a consideration as to whether such intentions were realistic. Finally, the sentencing guidelines permit restitution only for losses directly resulting from the defendants' offense. Under this standard, BA's expenses incurred in connection with reprogramming the stolen ATM account information, notifying customers of the theft, and answering customer inquiries were recoverable.

[United States v. Koenig, 952 F2d 267 (9th Cir. 1991)]

To constitute computer fraud, use of computer must serve as a primary element of scheme, and not as a mere incident to the fraud.   Jemison, an employee of the Department of Social Services (DSS), conspired with her sister and brother-in-law to create two fictitious welfare recipients. As caseworker for these "recipients," Jemison submitted documentation containing fraudulent information to her supervisor, who, in turn, gave the paperwork to a computer operator, who fed the information into the DSS computer system. Files were opened and welfare checks worth more than $60,000 were issued during a six-year period. A jury convicted Jemison of computer fraud. *Held:* Computer fraud did not occur, because the computer played only an incidental role in processing DSS paperwork, to "cause access to be made" requires more than merely supplying information that finds its way into a computer system in the normal course of business. The statute requires a showing that a person, with intent to defraud "gain[s] access to or cause[s] access to be made to a computer, computer system, or computer network." "Access" here means to approach, communicate with, store data in, retrieve data from, or otherwise use computer resources. To constitute computer fraud, the computer must serve as the device by which the fraud is perpetrated and defendant must participate in accessing or causing access to be made to the computer.

[People v. Jemison, 466 NW2d 378 (Mich. App. 1991)]

Restitution award in computer fraud may take into consideration value of property lost and costs incurred by victim in investigating and prosecuting the crime. Lindsly admitted knowingly and fraudulently gaining access and using part of PNB's computer system. He agreed to reimburse PNB for pecuniary damages in the amount of $1,000, the expense of his fraudulent long-distance phone calls. However, he argued, PNB's pecuniary damages should not include the significantly greater $35,000 in expenses that PNB incurred in investigating his criminal activity, which were "incidental to" the activity itself. *Held:* The investigative expenses qualified as pecuniary damages under state law, which authorizes restitution when a person's criminal activity results in pecuniary damages. Lindsly damaged the system by taking valid passwords that needed to be replaced. Further, the investigation of his break-in required the diversion of substantial resources of PNB; the consumption of those resources was a damage directly attributable to Lindsly's criminal activities.

[State v. Lindsly, 808 P2d 727 (Or. App. 1991)]

Statute prohibiting deletion of data applies to nonphysical deletion of data through programming alterations.   Burleson was convicted of harmful access to a computer for tampering with his former employer's computer, causing it to be unable to generate payroll checks and also triggering its temporary shutdown. Burleson appealed, claiming the statute was vague, overbroad, and not designed to give fair notice as to the conduct prohibited. *Held:* Even if the statute is vague to the extent it applies to someone who negligently alters data without consent, the indictment, as applied to Burleson's case, was specific enough to give him notice that the conduct alleged was criminal. To show that the statute is unconstitutionally vague, Burleson had to show that it both fails to give fair notice to the general populace of the activities criminalized and is vague as applied to his specific conduct. An indictment for a crime involving computer technology is not required to be hypertechnical. It is sufficient if it uses such language as to give the accused notice of the offense charged. Thus, the indictment was not deficient because it failed to reference or describe every file deleted and to make the semantic distinction between physical and "logical" deletions of data. Although that distinction may be significant to a programmer, it is a distinction without a difference for the purposes of this statute. By his actions, Burleson effectively deleted the files by making them inaccessible for processing of the payroll files.

[Burleson v. State, 802 SW2d 429 (Tex. Ct. App. 1991)]

Crimes involving false signatures may be subject to harsher penalties than those that do not.   Gomez charged and signed for items on a stolen credit card. The state charged him, under the Utah Code, Section 76-6-506.1 (01), with a second-degree felony for credit card fraud. Gomez persuaded the judge that the charge should be reduced to either a third-degree felony or a class A misdemeanor, pursuant to Section 76-6-506.2 (02) of the Code, which he claimed was identical to the former one. After the case was dismissed because the state refused to amend the complaint to a reduced charge, the state appealed. *Held:* The exact same conduct may not be subject to two different penalties depending on which of two statutory sections a prosecutor arbitrarily chooses to charge. Here, the sections do differ because 01 requires a "signing" of a sales slip, while 02 does not; further, 02 requires proof of the value of the fraudulently purchased items, while 01 does not. The legislature has determined to punish more severely instances of fraudulently signing a card or sales slip. While it is difficult to fathom the reason for distinguishing between signed and unsigned credit card transactions, especially when most sales probably involve a "signing," such a distinction is neither irrational nor arbitrary.

[State v. Gomez, 722 P2d 747 (Utah 1986)]

PART C.   INFORMATION AND SOFTWARE THEFT CRIMES

¶ 12.04 TRADE SECRET THEFT

Secret information constitutes form of property protected under due process and other relevant laws.   Monsanto submitted health, safety, and environmental data on its pesticides to the EPA, pursuant to federal law (FIFRA). As amended in 1978, FIFRA permitted disclosure of this data and a mandatory licensing arrangement that would allow competitors to use one another's data, after a 10-year period of exclusive use. Monsanto considered such information valuable trade secrets and objected to these provisions as constituting a "taking" of its property in violation of the Fifth Amendment. *Held:* To the extent that Monsanto had an interest in its health, safety, and environmental data cognizable as a trade-secret property right under state law, that property right is protected by the Constitution. Property interests are not created by the Constitution, but find their origins and boundaries from independent sources such as state law. Missouri law recognizes property rights in trade secrets as defined in the Restatement of Torts. Because of the intangible nature of a trade secret, the extent of the property right therein is defined by the extent to which the owner of the secret protects its interest from disclosure to others. Monsanto clearly protected its data from disclosure. Intangible property rights protected by state law are protected by the taking clause. However, the EPA's actions, under the amended statute, constituted government regulation and not a taking. A close reading of the amended statute reveals that Monsanto gave up its claim to exclusivity by registering its products, since it knew that the information would become public after the 10-year period. Under the prior statute, from 1972 to 1978, Monsanto did have a claim against the EPA under the takings clause. However, since the governmental takings were for public use, Monsanto had to seek its remedy under the Tucker Act.

[Ruckelshaus v. Monsanto Co., 467 US 986 (1984)]

¶ 12.05 THEFT OF COMPUTER PROGRAMS

[1] State Theft Laws

In some jurisdictions, computer theft is prosecuted under criminal intellectual property laws. Tanner, a former employee of FPB, opened his own radio beeper service, APS, and hired Geiger, FPB's bookkeeper, to keep his books. On two occasions, Geiger and Tanner entered FPB's offices after hours, during which time copies of FPB's copyrighted accounting software programs and manuals were pirated. Tanner, who was acquitted of burglary, appealed his conviction of an offense against intellectual property since, he claimed, it was Geiger who copied the programs. *Held:* Tanner's conviction affirmed. In Louisiana, computer theft is prosecuted under criminal intellectual property laws. To support a conviction under such a law, the state must prove that Tanner intentionally destroyed, inserted, modified, disclosed, used, copied, took, or accessed, without consent, intellectual property. Intellectual property consists of "data, computer programs, computer software, trade secrets, copyrighted materials, and confidential or proprietary information, in any form or medium, when such is stored in, produced by, or intended for use or storage with or in a computer, computer system, or a computer network." Evidence submitted by the state was sufficient to prove an offense against intellectual property.

[State v. Tanner, 534 So. 2d 535 (La. Ct. App. 1988)]

State statute does not cover descriptions of software programs under development. O'Connor executed a contract with MST for development of a computer software program. In exchange for the specifications for the computer program, O'Connor gave MST an uncollectible check for $25,350. O'Connor was subsequently convicted of obtaining computer software from MST by false pretenses. *Held:* Clearly, the set of documents, i.e., the specifications, that O'Connor obtained did not constitute a computer program within the statute, since it was not something that could be executed by a computer, causing the computer to perform a computer operation. The Virginia Code defines "computer software" as a "set of computer programs, procedures, and associated documentation concerned with computer data or with the operation of a computer, computer program or computer network." The Code further defines "computer program" as an "ordered set of data representing coded instructions or statements that, when executed by a computer, causes the computer to perform one or more computer operations." The statute covers only existing operable computer programs, not descriptions of programs whose development is proposed.

[O'Connor v. Commonwealth, 430 SE2d 567 (Va. Ct. App. 1993)]

[2] Federal Copyright Laws

To support felony conviction for willful infringement of copyright, government must prove sufficient number of wrongful sales. Cross ran a video store from which he rented and sold unauthorized copies of videocassettes. After being warned by the FBI to cease infringing activities, Cross resumed the illegal operations. A jury convicted Cross on, inter alia, a charge of felony criminal infringement of copyright. *Held:* The government did not introduce enough evidence to support a conviction on the felony criminal infringement charge. While it introduced 11 allegedly infringing "second-generation" videocassettes, the government failed to show that 5 of the tapes were rented during the relevant 180-day period. The rental of six infringing videocassettes during the 180-day period charged in the indictment constituted a misdemeanor under 18 USC § 2319(b)(3).

[United States v. Cross, 816 F2d 297 (7th Cir. 1987)]

Criminal actions based on claims of copyright infringement require proof that various exceptions (e.g., valid first sale) to improper copying do not apply.   Goss was convicted for infringing copyright by distributing pirated copies of video games. The government attempted to prove Goss's guilt by showing that he sold counterfeit circuit boards. However, the protected material of the copyrighted audiovisual works here was fixed in the board's memory chips, also known as ROMs; the government failed to produce any evidence of illegally distributed copies of ROM chips. The government's evidence was analogous to proving illegal distribution of phonograph records by showing that defendant sold a record player that had been made without authorization. Further, Goss alleged that he was lawful owner of these ROMs and that under the "first sale doctrine" he was entitled to sell them without the copyright owner's authorization. *Held:* Goss's conviction reversed. The court held that the chips rather than the boards were the relevant copies and that there was inadequate evidence to show that these were illegal, given the fact that Goss owned the chips through a valid first sale. "[Selling] such legally obtained [chips] would not infringe the copyright . . . regardless of whether [they] were attached to a counterfeit board." Selling legally obtained ROMs does not infringe copyright even if they are attached to counterfeit circuit boards.

[United States v. Goss, 803 F2d 638 (11th Cir. 1986)]

Copying and distributing copies of computer programs can trigger criminal sanctions for willful infringement under federal copyright law.   O'Reilly sold counterfeit copies of video games to undercover FBI agents. O'Reilly appealed his convictions on the ground that the government failed to prove the material was copyrighted and that the government's expert witness did not compare the entire play of the counterfeit boards with that of the copyrighted games. *Held:* The expert testimony, the jury's own observations, and other incriminating statements by O'Reilly were sufficient to establish copyright infringement beyond a reasonable doubt. By introducing copyright registration for the three games at issue as "audio-visual works," the government presented clear proof that the video images were copyrighted. That other aspects of the game were protected by copyright or patent law does not vitiate the government's proof. Second, it was unnecessary for the expert witness to compare the entire games, since infringement may be found where substantial portions of the copyrighted work are taken. The jury, itself, viewed portions of the copyrighted game side by side the counterfeit copies.

[United States v. O'Reilly, 794 F2d 613 (11th Cir. 1986)]

PART D.   ACCESS AND USE CRIMES

¶ 12.06 UNAUTHORIZED ACCESS

[1] Access and Trespass

Trespass statutes may not apply to unauthorized access to computers, since trespass statutes entail physical entry.   ACTL sued Jack Farrell Implement Co. to collect payments for computer hardware leased from ACTL. Farrell counterclaimed that ADP, a computer software developer, had committed trespass by unlawfully entering its computer system and by appropriating and destroying its accounting and inventory records when it deactivated its computer via modem. *Held:* The trespass statute did not apply to computers. Minnesota's trespass law provides damages for trespass only with respect to property "produced by and grown upon the land." The statute does not apply to home furnishings, toys, clothing, or computerized data.

[American Computer Trust Leasing v. Jack Farrell Implement Co., 763 F. Supp. 1473 (D. Minn. 1991)]

Proscribing unauthorized access to computers creates crime analogous to trespassing.   Olson, a police officer at the University of Washington (UW), was convicted of computer trespass for accessing the UW computer to get information on various UW co-eds. *Held:* The evidence indicated that Olson was authorized to access the computer system. Computer trespass is analogous to criminal trespass: It criminalizes entry into the computer system without authorization, not unauthorized use of the information obtained. While Olson's personal use of this data after access exceeded the scope of his authority and violated departmental policy, it did not constitute computer trespass, since computer access was not conditioned on the uses made of the data.

[State v. Olson, 735 P2d 1362 (Wash. App. 1987)]

[2] Intent to Access

In some computer fraud statutes, defendant need not know computer was being accessed.   Azar moved to quash his indictment for computer fraud because the charging statute was unconstitutionally vague. The statute provided that "computer fraud is the accessing or causing to be accessed of any computer, computer system, computer network, or any part thereof with the intent to: (1) [d]efraud; or (2) [o]btain money, property, or services by means of false or fraudulent conduct, practices, or representations, or through the alteration, deletion, or insertion of programs or data." The term "access" is defined as "to program, to execute programs on, to communicate with, store data in, retrieve data from, or otherwise make use of any resources, including data or programs, of a computer, computer system, or computer network." *Held:* The definition of "access" is not unconstitutionally vague, either in itself or in the statute. In regard to "access," the state need only prove that Azar accessed a computer or caused it to be accessed; whether he "knowingly" accessed a computer is irrelevant under this statute. Finally, Clause 2 of the computer fraud statute is unconstitutionally vague, since it fails to indicate whether the acts of altering data or a program to obtain money are required to be with fraudulent intent; however, since this phrase can be severed, the rest of the statute remains constitutional.

[State v. Azar, 539 So. 2d 1222 (La. 1989)]

¶ 12.07 UNAUTHORIZED COMPUTER USE

Computer crime statutes may apply to unauthorized use of telephone voice mailboxes.   Gerulis infiltrated two separate voice mailbox (VMB) systems; changed VMB passwords, which prevented authorized users from gaining access; and left messages for her fellow infiltrators with lists of stolen credit and calling card numbers on the VMBs. Gerulis appealed her conviction on charges of unlawful use of a computer, since she used the telephone, not a computer. *Held:* Gerulis clearly "accessed" a computer. She altered VMB passwords by transmitting instructions to them, thereby gaining entrance into both computer systems. The Pennsylvania statute defines "computer" as "an electronic, magnetic, optical, hydraulic, organic or other high speed data processing device or system which performs logic, arithmetic or memory functions and includes all input, output, processing, storage, software or communication facilities which are connected or related to the device in a system or network." Further, under the statute, a VMB is a "computer, computer system, computer network, computer software, computer program or data base or any part thereof." Gerulis used the VMBs to store and retrieve data. Thus, contrary to Gerulis's assertion, the instrumentality at issue was a telephone linked to a sophisticated computerized communications system.

[Commonwealth v. Gerulis, 616 A2d 686 (Pa. Super. Ct. 1992)]

PART E.   FEDERAL LAW

¶ 12.08 GENERAL FEDERAL CRIMES

[1] Theft of Government Property

Federal theft statute covers theft of "intangible" government information.   Girard, a former agent of the Drug Enforcement Agency (DEA), sold DEA records that he had obtained from the DEA's computerized files to a third party. Girard appealed his conviction of theft of government property, since 18 USC § 641 only covers tangible property or documents, not intangible information; he also argued that the statute was unconstitutionally vague and overbroad. *Held:* Here, the statute's plainly legitimate sweep in regulating conduct is not so overbroad that any overbreadth that may exist cannot be cured on a case-by-case basis. The statute forbids the unauthorized sale of "any record . . . or thing of value" of the United States with the knowledge that it was embezzled, stolen, or converted. Section 641 covers theft of any "thing of value" that belongs to the United States regardless of whether that "thing" is tangible or intangible, such as information theft from government files. The statute is more than a statutory codification of the common law of larceny, since the requisite element of the offense is not theft but rather unauthorized sale or conversion. The evidence showed conversion of DEA's computerized records. Finally, the statute is not vague, since the conduct it proscribes may be delimited and clarified by the DEA's own rules and regulations forbidding such disclosures. Further, the overbreadth doctrine, which concerns exercise of First Amendment rights, is not properly invoked.

[United States v. Girard, 601 F2d 69 (2d Cir.), cert. denied, 444 US 871 (1979)]

Federal theft statute is not void for vagueness.   McAusland obtained inside information on competitors' bids and proposals for DOD contracts and confidential information regarding how the bids and proposals were evaluated by DOD officials. He appealed his conviction of violating 18 USC § 641 for knowingly converting "without authority" a "thing of value" of the United States. Relying on *United States v. Girard* (601 F2d 69 (2d Cir.), cert. denied, 444 US 871 (1979)), he claimed that the phrase "without authority" was devoid of meaning and must derive its meaning from other, more particular prohibitions against disclosure established by statute or administrative rule. He contended that because published federal acquisition regulations (FARs) did not clearly prohibit disclosure of information, the statute as applied was unconstitutionally vague. *Held:* The absence of published FARs proscribing disclosure does not make the statute vague as applied. While the existence of a federal regulation proscribing disclosure prevents the statute from being vague as applied, the latter is not the exclusive method for preventing vagueness. Lack of authority can be shown through McAusland's knowledge of the government's long-standing practice of keeping such information confidential. The government produced considerable evidence to demonstrate McAusland's knowledge of regulations prohibiting disclosure of information in proposals; further, McAusland's conduct also indicated knowledge that disclosure was without authority.

[United States v. McAusland, 979 F2d 970 (4th Cir. 1992)]

Federal conversion statute covers theft of computer time and storage capacity from government computer.   An indictment alleged that Sampson gained unauthorized access to NASA computers, which he used to carry out his personal business. He was charged with conversion of government property in violation of 18 USC § 641. Sampson moved to dismiss the indictment on the grounds that "computer time and computer storage capacity" are "philosophical concepts" and not property within the meaning of the statute. *Held:* A computer is unquestionably property; thus, the unauthorized use of government computer time and space constitutes "unauthorized use of property" or conversion. The uses of a computer and the product of such uses appear to be a "thing of value" within the meaning of Section 641, enough to form the basis of a legally sufficient indictment. Consumption of computer time and use of its capacities seem to be inseparable from the physical identity of a computer.

[United States v. Sampson, 6 CLRS 879 (ND Cal. 1978)]

[2] Interstate Stolen Goods

Federal statute prohibiting transportation of stolen goods does not cover shipment of infringing copies of copyrighted works.   Dowling and his cohorts made bootleg copies of Elvis Presley sound recordings. They appealed their conviction under 18 USC § 2314 for transporting stolen goods through interstate commerce, claiming the goods were neither stolen, converted, nor taken by fraud. *Held:* Congress did not intend this statute to cover copyright infringement. Criminal statutes must be construed strictly. The language of the statute applies to transporting "goods, wares or merchandise" that have been "stolen, converted or taken by fraud." The language of the statute clearly assumes the physical identity between the items unlawfully obtained and thereafter transported. Here, defendants produced the physical copies themselves; they did not assume physical control over the copyright. Additionally, the legislative history of the statute taken in conjunction with Congress's constitutional authority to regulate copyright indicate the implausibility of the contention that Congress took such a circuitous route to combat copyright infringement. This statute was originally introduced to combat auto theft. The government's rationale would justify harsh criminal penalties for any infringement of copyright involving interstate transportation, a factor not otherwise relevant to copyright law. If the intangible ideas protected by copyright were effectively made tangible by their embodiment upon the infringing tapes, this rationale would apply in other areas of intellectual property law, such as patents. Congress, however, has evidenced no intention to expand the statute's coverage.

[United States v. Dowling, 473 US 207 (1985)]

Federal theft statute does not cover interstate transport of stolen intangible information. An FBI search of Brown's apartment revealed notebooks and a hard disk containing portions of source code owned by his former employer (TSL) in Georgia that had been transported to him in New Mexico. The government, relying on *United States v. Riggs,* 739 F. Supp. 414 (ND Ill. 1990), appealed dismissal of charges under 18 USC § 2314 for transportation of stolen goods worth more than $5,000. *Held:* The computer program is intangible intellectual property. Under the Supreme Court's decision in *United States v. Dowling,* 473 US 207 (1985), Section 2314 applies only to physical "goods, wares or merchandise." *Riggs* was wrongly decided. The element of physical "goods, wares or merchandise" is critical in Section 2314: Purely intellectual property does not fall within this category, and therefore Section 2314 is inapplicable. The government's argument fails because the government cannot prove that Brown stole the notebooks nor the physical drive on which the source code was contained; it only alleges that the latter contained the stolen source code. Absent evidence of physical theft or transportation of physical property belonging to TSL, there was no proof of a crime.

[United States v. Brown, 925 F2d 1301 (10th Cir. 1991)]

Federal theft statute covers interstate transport of stolen intangible information. Riggs and Neidorf schemed to steal Bell South's proprietary text file on emergency telephone service (E911). Riggs stored the file on his computer bulletin board service (BBS) in Illinois for Neidorf, who downloaded it in Missouri and subsequently published it in his hacker newsletter. The pair challenged their indictment, inter alia, under 18 USC § 2314 for interstate transport of stolen property, because (1) the plain language of the statute does not cover transferring "electronic impulses" across state lines since they are not "goods, wares or merchandise"; (2) the "thing" actually transferred never assumed a tangible form; and (3) the things allegedly transferred were not the type of property capable of being "stolen, converted or taken by fraud." *Held:* Merely because the information crossed state lines via computer-generated electronic impulse does not defeat a charge under Section 2314. Superficial, semantic distinctions cannot be allowed to blur what actually transpired: Transport of the E911 file, not of electronic impulses, from a computer in Illinois to one in Missouri. The E911 file is clearly a "good, ware or merchandise" within the meaning of Section 2314. Further, it is of little moment whether the file transported was affixed to a floppy disk, printed out on computer paper, or stored in a computer, since, in each case the information is in a transferrable, accessible, even salable form. Second, reading a tangibility requirement into the definition of goods would unduly restrict Section 2314 in this modern technological age. Here, there is no need to reach the tangibility issue, since the accessibility of the information in readable form from a particular storage place (here, a computer terminal) makes the information tangible. Finally, unlike *United States v. Dowling,* supra, this case involves stealing confidential proprietary business information, not copyrights. Owners have a clear property interest in such information, which is also protected under Section 2314.

[United States v. Riggs, 739 F. Supp. 414 (ND Ill. 1990)]

[3] Electronic Funds Transfer Crimes

Federal credit card statute covers fraudulent use of valid unassigned account numbers.   Taylor obtained and used "valid, but as yet unassigned" credit card account numbers by illegally accessing and manipulating the American Express computer system. He challenged his conviction for violating 18 USC § 1029(a)(2), which prohibits fraudulent use of "unauthorized access devices," on the grounds that the credit cards used did not access account numbers that had been assigned to any person, and therefore were not "access devices" within the meaning of the statute. *Held:* The cards in question are clearly "unauthorized access devices" within the meaning of Section 1029 since their use clearly constituted the access devices by which Taylor perpetrated fraudulent transactions. The statute defines "access device" as "any card, plate, code, account number, or other means of account access that can be used, alone or in conjunction with another access device, to obtain money, goods, services, or any other thing of value, or that can be used to initiate a transfer of funds." Further, it defines an "unauthorized access device" as an access device that is "lost, stolen, expired, revoked, canceled, or obtained with intent to defraud." Taylor's argument that the cards could not be "unauthorized access devices" because no assigned accounts existed and the accounts were "valid" slices the language of Section 1029 too thinly. The phrase "account number or other means of account access" expressly covers the transactions he made.

[United States v. Taylor, 945 F2d 1050 (8th Cir. 1991)]

¶ 12.09 FEDERAL COMPUTER CRIMES

Computer Act may be violated by person who unintentionally damages computer system.   Morris, a graduate student wishing to demonstrate the inadequate security protection on the information superhighway, transmitted a "worm" program—a computer "virus" that travels from one computer to another but does not attach itself to the operating system of the computer it infects—into the INTERNET system that connects university, governmental, and military computers across the country. Morris miscalculated the effects of this worm, so despite his intention not to harm the system, it inflicted considerable damage to computer systems across the country. Morris was convicted of violating the Computer Act (18 USC § 1030(a)(5)(A)), which punishes anyone who "intentionally accesses a federal interest computer without authorization, and by means of one or more instances of such conduct alters, damages, or destroys information . . . or prevents authorized use of any such computer or information, and thereby (A) causes loss. . . ." He appealed, claiming he was an authorized INTERNET user and that he lacked the requisite mens rea to cause damage or to prevent authorized use of federal interest computers. *Held:* Morris's assertion that he was an authorized INTERNET user with privileges to send mail and communicate with other computers whose conduct at most "exceeded authorized access" is erroneous. While the line between exceeding authorized access and unauthorized access may be difficult to draw, Morris's conduct here falls well within the area of unauthorized access. Rather than using his access privileges in their intended function, he used them to find holes in the INTERNET that permitted him a special and unauthorized access route into other computers. Morris's privileges to access some federal interest computers did not insulate him from liability for gaining unauthorized access, through his worm, to other federal interest computers. The statute is ambiguous, since the word "intentionally" may modify both verbal phrases; however, the wording, structure, and purpose of the section, examined in comparison with its predecessor provision indicate that the "intentionally" standard applies only to the "accesses" phrase of Section 1030(a)(5)(A), and not to the "damages" phrase.

[United States v. Morris, 928 F2d 504 (2d Cir. 1991)]

¶ 12.10 COMMUNICATIONS SYSTEM ABUSE

[1] Mail and Wire Fraud

Wire and fraud statutes apply where interstate transmission is an essential element of fraudulent scheme.   Paladino and Giovengo, two TWA customer service agents in Pittsburgh, conspired to pocket cash payments made by customers for one-way plane tickets. The scheme involved requesting the ticket by sending passenger information from a computer terminal to TWA computers in Missouri, by wire signals via special interstate telephones circuits leased by TWA from AT&T. TWA in turn sent signals authorizing the originating terminal to print corresponding tickets. The scheme worked in such a way that the agents retrieved the tickets from the unknowing passengers when boarding, and then sent them back to TWA's main office marked as void. Paladino appealed his conviction on charges of wire fraud, in violation of 18 USC § 1343, claiming that the statute only covered FCC-regulated wire transmissions and that they did not use interstate wire "for the purpose of executing" a fraudulent scheme. *Held:* Use of interstate wires was essential to this fraudulent scheme; since, without access to interstate transmissions, the agents would have had no tickets to sell to TWA customers, and their plan to defraud could never have succeeded. The language of Section 1343 requires that use of interstate wires be essential rather than convenient to the fraudulent scheme. Finally, nothing in the language of Section 1343, which applies to anyone who commits fraud "by means of wire . . . in interstate or foreign commerce," suggests that its scope is limited to fraud committed by use of interstate wires subject to FCC regulation.

[United States v. Giovengo, 637 F2d 941 (3d Cir. 1980)]

Wire and fraud statutes may apply to misappropriation of computer software via modem across state lines.   Seidlitz, a computer expert, quit his job, and started his own computer firm. However, he continued, without authorization, to use his own computers in Maryland and Virginia to dial into and download WYLBUR software from the computer system the former employer had set up for the Federal Energy Administration in Maryland. He was convicted on charges of transmitting telephone calls in interstate commerce as part of a scheme to defraud his former employer of property consisting of information from the computer system in violation of 18 USC § 1843. Seidlitz appealed, claiming that he did not act with fraudulent intent and, further, that the WYLBUR software was not a trade secret, and therefore not "property" within the meaning of the wire fraud statute. *Held:* Although the government did not show that Seidlitz used the data retrieved in his own business or to sell to others, there was ample circumstantial evidence to support a finding that he acted with fraudulent intent in acquiring it. In essence, he complained that the jury did not credit his explanation of his actions. Furthermore, there was sufficient evidence from which the jury could conclude that the software in question was "property" under the statute. Even though similar software systems were available at facilities other than that of his former employer, the employer had invested millions of dollars in developing and modifying its software system and had taken affirmative steps to prevent outsiders from obtaining this information so that it could maintain its competitive edge. The WYLBUR software was hardly in the public domain.

[United States v. Seidlitz, 589 F2d 152 (4th Cir. 1978)]

Wire and fraud statutes do not apply where interstate transmission is not pertinent to fraudulent scheme.   Computer Sciences Corporation moved to dismiss an indictment charging them, inter alia, with wire fraud for fraudulently billing services, in violation of 18 USC § 1343. *Held:* Since none of the false representations are alleged to have been communicated over interstate wires, Section 1343 is inapplicable. The gravamen of the present indictment is not wire fraud, but rather that Computer Sciences knowingly presented false, fictitious, or fraudulent claims for services. The prosecutors' theory would permit charges of wire fraud any time false claims were submitted, which would be absurd. There is no allegation that the computer service was in any way deficient or fraudulent.

[United States v. Computer Sciences Corp., 511 F. Supp. 1125 (ED Va. 1981)]

[2] Electronic Privacy Law

Both wiretap and communications law apply to sale of cloned cable transmission descramblers. Harrell was convicted of modifying and selling descrambler modules for decrypting satellite transmissions in violation of the Wiretap Act (18 USC § 2512(1)(b); 47 USC § 605(e)(4)). Harrell appealed, claiming the modifications were slight and therefore "were not primarily useful for the purpose of surreptitious interception" of wire communications. He also claimed that the latter statute was vague and only prohibits commercial cable transmissions as opposed to individual television signals. *Held:* Harrell's conduct is clearly prohibited by Section 2512; the modified modules are primarily designed for electronic eavesdropping proscribed by Section 2512(1)(b). The purpose of such modifications is to allow individuals to view unpaid-for cable signals, without thereby incurring the duty to pay for them. People who pay approximately $300 for modified descramblers will, presumably, not restrict their viewing primarily to programming they could have viewed prior to the modifications. Finally, Section 605(e)(4) is not vague, and the term "cable" is not limited to commercial use. In fact, the statute prohibits the surreptitious interception of any encrypted satellite signal intended for private or commercial use.

[United States v. Harrell, 983 F2d 36 (5th Cir. 1993)]

Both wiretap and communications law apply to sale of cloned cable transmission descramblers. FBI agents raided claimant's (OMVC) premises, seizing clone scramblers that illegally intercepted encrypted signals of premium pay channels such as HBO and ESPN. The district court dismissed the government's forfeiture action, holding that the statutory language, legislative history, and case law of the Electronic Communications Privacy Act (ECPA) did not bring satellite descramblers within the scope of 18 USC §§ 2511 and 2512. The government appealed. *Held:* The lower court erred, since the statutory language, legislative history, and case law indicate that the ECPA prohibits modification of descramblers to allow unauthorized viewing of scrambled satellite television. OMVC erred in claiming that an earlier statute concerning unauthorized interception of communications transmitted by means of new technologies (47 USC § 605) is the only applicable statute in this action; for, where two statutes have similar but ambiguous language, they must operate independently of each other. As neither statute specifically excludes modification of descramblers from its application, OMVC is subject to prosecution under each statute. Thus, the descramblers in question are subject to forfeiture.

[United States v. One Macom Video Cipher II, 985 F2d 258 (6th Cir. 1993)]

Wiretap Act applies to manufacture and sale of cable satellite transmission descramblers.   Davis was convicted of manufacturing and selling an electronic device primarily useful for the surreptitious interception and decryption of electronic communications, in violation of the Wiretap Act (18 USC §§ 2511 and 2512). He appealed, claiming that Section 2511(1)(a) did not apply to interception of commercial satellite programming; and, that Section 2512(1)(b) applied only to devices "primarily useful for the purpose of the surreptitious interception of wire, oral, or electronic communications," since his device was primarily useful for nonsurreptitious and legitimate purposes. *Held:*   The language of the Wiretap Act is broad enough to include programming transmitted by satellites. The exclusion of specific types of unencrypted and unscrambled satellite transmissions from the reach of various subsections of Section 2511 establishes that satellite transmissions are contemplated by the Wiretap Act. Finally, the crucial test under Section 2512 is whether the design of the device renders it primarily useful for surreptitious listening, not whether it is susceptible to innocent, nonsurreptitious uses. The modifications that Davis performed on the computer chips of the satellite descramblers made it all but impossible to use these devices in any legitimate fashion. Individuals possessing such modified descramblers were perforce required to use them surreptitiously to prevent the cable companies from learning of Davis's tampering.

[United States v. Davis, 978 F2d 415 (8th Cir. 1992) (en banc)]

Both wiretap and communications law apply to sale of cloned cable transmission descramblers.   Splawn manufactured and sold cloned computer chips enabling customers to receive premium cable channel broadcasts without paying the required subscription fee. Splawn appealed his conviction of violating the Wiretap Act (18 USC § 2512(1)(b)), claiming that Congress did not intend the Wiretap Act to encompass his conduct. Conceding that his conduct was specifically prohibited under the Communications Act of 1934 (47 USC § 605(a)), for the manufacture, sale, or distribution of equipment intended to be used in receiving communication by wire or radio outside authorized channels of reception, Splawn argued that the government was not free to prosecute under the less specific felony statute. *Held:*   The Wiretap Act encompasses Splawn's conduct. Section 2512(1)(b) punishes anyone who "intentionally . . . manufactures, assembles, possesses, or sells any electronic, mechanical, or other device, knowing or having reason to know that the design of such device renders it primarily useful for the purpose of the surreptitious interception of wire, oral or electronic communications, and that such device or any component thereof has been or will be . . . transported in interstate or foreign commerce." It is indisputable that satellite communications, which contain sound and images carried via radio waves, constitute electronic communications and that the cloned devices intercept them. The central issue is whether the clones are designed primarily for the purpose of surreptitious interception of communication. Legitimate satellite descramblers have unique electronic addresses contained in their computer chips. In cloning a computer chip from a legitimate descrambler and placing it in another descrambler, Splawn altered the design of the descrambler making it nonunique. While descramblers may be necessary to receive satellite transmissions for which no authorization is necessary, the sole purpose of Splawn's modifications was to permit the surreptitious interception of satellite television transmissions. Since Splawn's devices were designed to make them primarily useful for surreptitious interception of electronic communications, they are clearly prohibited by the language of Section 2512(1)(b). Finally, where a defendant's conduct is prohibited by two statutes, the government is free to prosecute under either as long as it does not discriminate against any class of defendants.

[United States v. Splawn, 982 F2d 414 (10th Cir. 1992)]

PART F.   SPECIAL CRIME ISSUES

¶ 12.11 HACKING

Innocent parties may bear loss caused by hackers.   Jiffy Lube set up a telephone system that included a remote-access feature, by which an off-premises caller could dial a secret 800 number (provided by MCI), access Jiffy's private branch exchange (PBX), and obtain a local dial tone. After getting a dial tone, the caller would enter a special code that would allow the caller to make long-distance calls, international and domestic, on a long-distance line provided by AT&T. Sometime thereafter, Jiffy contended a computer hacker broke through Jiffy's security system; that same hacker apparently published Jiffy's 800 number along with the access code for other hackers. By the time Jiffy found out and put a stop to it, AT&T had sent it a bill for more than $50,000 in fraudulent calls. Jiffy refused to pay, claiming that the calls did not "originate" at its PBX but rather at the hacker's computer. *Held:* Just as if a criminal trespasser had broken into Jiffy's offices and made those calls, Jiffy bore the liability for the calls. FCC tariffs clearly state that calls originate at a customer's number when calls, authorized or not, are made from the customer's telephone system. In trying to shift responsibility to AT&T, Jiffy ignored that but for its creation of a telephone system with a remote-access feature, the disputed calls could not have been made. It was hardly just or reasonable to require AT&T to absorb the costs associated with such unauthorized calls. Jiffy argued that AT&T had greater knowledge of hacker fraud problems and greater ability and power to detect, combat, and prevent them; however, such arguments are better put to the FCC, the federal agency having expertise in the communications arena and best able to weigh such policy considerations.

[American Tel. & Tel. v. Jiffy Lube Int'l, Inc., 813 F. Supp. 1164 (D. Md. 1993)]

¶ 12.12 VIRUSES

Intentional insertion of virus within computer program may warrant award of punitive damages.   An insurance company hired Lewis, a computer consultant, to modify its accident claim software to make it compatible with its new computer. Six months later, the new computer system shut down at claim number 56789. The insurance company contended that Lewis intentionally placed a hidden conditional command in the program instructing it to stop when it reached claim number 56789. The program was in executable form, and could be modified only by using its source code. When asked to fix the problem, Lewis stated that he had destroyed the source code and that it would have to be recreated. Another consultant discovered the conditional command and rectified the problem. The insurance company sued Lewis for breach of contract and requested punitive damages. *Held:* Although punitive damages are not awarded for breach of contract claims unless they would deter morally culpable conduct, here Lewis's malicious, intentional act in causing the computer to crash justified the imposition of such damages.

[Werner, Zaroff, Slotnick, Stern & Askenazy v. Lewis, 588 NYS2d 960 (County Ct. 1992)]

CHAPTER **13**

COMPUTER ERROR AND USE LIABILITY

¶ 13.01 DERIVATIVE OR PRIMARY OBLIGATIONS

Lender's claim that it failed to comply with consumer credit Regulation Z is rejected where lender chose format to conform with that of national computer system with which it was affiliated. Allen and her ex-husband borrowed money from defendant lender. Allen brought action, alleging, among other things, that defendant had not made the required disclosures to her in a "meaningful sequence" as required by Regulation Z of the Truth-in-Lending Act. The court noted that Regulation Z involves at least two requirements. First, those disclosures that are logically related must be grouped together. Second, the terms in the groupings must be arranged in a logically sequential order emphasizing the most important terms. The court held that Beneficial's disclosure statements failed to meet both of these requirements under Regulation Z. Beneficial argued that its form was designed so that it could be used in the national computer system to which it was affiliated. *Held:* The court found that creditor's convenience was no justification for a departure from a meaningful sequence on a disclosure statement under Regulation Z. Here, the court noted, "when dealing with computers, we must always bear in mind that they are designed to serve humans, not the reverse." As such, the court found that Beneficial's failure to follow the requirements relating to Regulation Z's meaningful sequence produced a form that was unnecessarily confusing.

[Allen v. Beneficial Fin. Co. of Gary, Inc., 531 F2d 797 (7th Cir. 1976)]

Data entry error that incorrectly indicates extension on a payment date does not authorize such an extension nor does it operate to discharge co-obligor. Moses appealed from a judgment for Midway Bank & Trust Company in an action seeking judgment on two promissory notes. Among other things, Moses asserted on appeal that the trial court should have found that the bank's de facto extension of the promissory notes discharged him from liability. In this case, Midway and a joint obligor on the notes entered into an unauthorized extension agreement on the notes; Moses asserted that this discharged his obligations under the notes. Here, a bank employee mistakenly assumed that the time for payment on the notes had been extended and entered this information into the bank's computer. Under Iowa law, a valid agreement between the payee and the maker of a note to extend time for payment discharges any co-maker who has not consented to the extension. *Held:* The bank employee's mistake did not validly extend the time to pay on the two promissory notes. As such, there was no valid agreement extending the time to pay and Moses was not released from his obligations under the notes.

[Midway Bank & Trust Co. v. Moses, 375 NW2d 292 (Iowa Ct. App. 1985)]

Computer-generated invoices stating that defendant's account has been accelerated and his credit and advertising privileges have been rescinded do not intervene and supersede any misrepresentation by plaintiff telephone company. Southwestern Bell Media, Inc., sued Lyles for balances allegedly due for advertising purchased by Lyles in the 1986 and 1987 yellow pages. Lyles counterclaimed, alleging breach of contract and violation of the Deceptive Trade Practices Act (DTPA) because Southwestern Bell applied money intended for new advertising to Lyles's outstanding balance, misrepresented the application of the money, and excluded him from advertising in the 1988 yellow pages. The trial court awarded damages to both parties and offset awards that resulted in payment by Southwestern Bell of more than $78,000. Southwestern Bell appealed and raised eight points of error by the trial court—claiming, in part, that there was no nexus between its alleged misrepresentations and Lyles's damages (i.e., Southwestern Bell's misrepresentations did not produce or contribute to Lyles's damages). *Held:* The decision of the trial court was affirmed on the grounds that contradictory information was given to Lyles simultaneously with the computer-generated invoices; thus, the invoices did not supersede misrepresentations by Southwestern Bell that were the basis of violation of the DTPA. Evidence showed that at the same time Lyles was receiving invoices, Southwestern Bell's representatives had given Lyles verbal assurances during a meeting that they were there to keep Lyles's account from being accelerated and that any computer-generated invoices received in the future should be disregarded.

[Southwestern Bell Media, Inc. v. Lyles, 825 SW2d 488 (Tex. Ct. App. 1992)]

¶ 13.02 COMPUTER ERROR AND NEGLIGENCE DEFINED

Airline reservation computer system that fails to detect alterations to airline tickets does not create affirmative liability on part of airline. Swiss Air brought suit to recover $2,056, the difference between the purchase price of two Swiss Air tickets and the value of the air travel provided by Swiss Air on account of alteration of those two tickets. Here, Benn's son and a friend tendered altered tickets for flights from New York to Geneva, Switzerland. Swiss Air did not discover that the tickets had been altered until after the air travel was completed. *Held:* Benn was liable in quasi-contract for the difference between the purchase price and the value of the tickets. The court noted, however, that, "I do not recognize Swiss Air's reliance on its computer system as a legally cognizable defense. Had Swiss Air been properly equipped with a more sophisticated computer system, it could have promptly discovered the irregularity of the Benn's ticket." The appellate court reversed the trial court's holding, noting that Benn's actions did not indicate an innocent purchase. Furthermore, the appellate court noted that it did not accept the trial court's observation that Swiss Air failed to maintain an adequate computer system. In this case, the court noted that the record did not show that the procedures and equipment used by Swiss Air deviated from accepted practice in the airline industry.

[Swiss Air Transp. Co., Ltd. v. Benn, 494 NYS2d 781 (NY App. Div. 1985)]

PART A.   DUTY OF REASONABLE CARE AND INQUIRY IN RECORD KEEPING

¶ 13.03 GENERAL ISSUES AND THEMES

Under South Carolina law, cardiac pacemaker that allegedly malfunctioned because of defective computer-link monitoring system is not basis for liability because product was unavoidably unsafe.   Brooks, who had a history of heart trouble, was fitted with a pacemaker manufactured by Medtronic. On that very day, Brooks suffered 15 episodes of ventricular fibrillations, which ended when the pacemaker was disconnected. A second pacemaker was installed without incident. Brooks filed this suit alleging negligence, strict liability, and breach of warranty. *Held:* The court of appeals affirmed the district court's judgment in favor of the manufacturer. Under South Carolina's strict products liability law, certain products are deemed to be "unavoidably unsafe." The court noted that these products, "particularly ethical drugs and medical devices, often cause unwanted side effects despite the fact that they have been carefully designed and properly manufactured." As such, these products are not defective or unreasonably dangerous if they are marketed with proper directions for their use or include adequate warnings of their potential side effects. Here, Medtronic had no duty to warn Brooks directly; instead, Medtronic had a duty to warn the prescribing physician.

[Brooks v. Medtronic, Inc., 750 F2d 1227 (4th Cir. 1984)]

Party who fails to pay required delay rental lease payments possibly partly because of faulty computer records is not liable where contract expressly disclaims liability stemming from mistakes or oversights.   Huggs, Inc., assigned mineral leases to an assignee. The assignee failed to make required payments under the leases. Another company succeeded the assignee and failed to discover that rent payments had not been made. Huggs brought this suit against the successor to the assignee.

The pertinent contractual documents contained clauses shielding the successor from "loss of a lease or interest therein through mistake or oversight if any delay rental or shut-in gas royalty payment is not paid or is erroneously paid." The trial court found that the leases were not properly set up in the assignee's records, and thus were never entered into the successor's computer system when the two corporations merged. *Held:* The court of appeals held that the terms of the contract shielded the successor company from liability. Here, the court of appeals accepted the trial court's reasoning that there is no better example of oversight than the situation where an operator overlooks a lease and makes the mistake of failing to put the lease on its delay rental records.

[Huggs, Inc. v. LPC Energy, Inc., 889 F2d 649 (5th Cir. 1989)]

¶ 13.04 HUMAN VERIFICATION

Bank acting as transfer agent for mutual fund shareholder is not liable for disregarding instructions written on memorandum portion of check because it was following its normal operations, the basis for the relationship between the parties. Woods was a shareholder of a mutual stock fund. The bank was the shareholder servicing and transfer agent for the mutual fund; as such, it handled investments coming into and out of the fund. Woods deposited $21,000 with the bank with a notation directing it to deposit the money in a certain reserve account. Instead, the bank deposited the money into the fund—and not the reserve account. Woods subsequently lost money in the mutual fund. Thereafter, Woods sued the bank and the mutual fund based on theories of negligence and conversion. *Held:* The court of appeals held that the bank had no duty to read the inscription on the check. To do so, the court reasoned, would be commercially unreasonable in light of the volume of checks that the bank had to process. Here, the bank's mutual fund operation made approximately 45,000 payments per week. In this instance, the bank had assumed no obligation to be bound by written instructions on the checks; rather, its duty was merely to process the checks in the ordinary course of business.

[Woods v. Bank of NY, 806 F2d 368 (2d Cir. 1986)]

Under certain situations, human intervention and review of the underlying data used in computer systems are basic requirements of reasonable computer system. A decedent's husband opened an account with Merrill Lynch. When the decedent's husband died, a Merrill Lynch account executive oversaw and handled the account. Subsequently, during a 31-month period, the decedent's account was churned by the account executive in the form of between 106 and 141 unauthorized trades. The decedent's executor brought suit against the stockbroker for alleged violation of Section 10(b) of the Securities Exchange Act of 1934, common-law fraud, and breach of fiduciary duty. The trial court awarded the executor $100,000 in compensatory damages and $2 million in punitive damages. The stockbroker appealed. *Held:* The trial court's punitive damages award was upheld. The court of appeals reasoned that officers of the broker may have ratified the unauthorized trades by failing to investigate the account's unusual activity.

[Davis v. Merrill Lynch, Pierce, Fenner & Smith, 906 F2d 1206 (8th Cir. 1990)]

¶ 13.05 INTERNAL FRAUD DETECTION

Depositary bank bears loss with respect to $150,000 forged check where its own negligence substantially contributed to loss. A third party to this action opened a personal checking account with Sun Bank/Miami, NA. Subsequently, that third party deposited forged checks into that account and wrote checks against those forged checks. The payor banks in this transaction questioned the authenticity of the checks deposited in the third party's checking account with Sun Bank, which resulted in the Federal Reserve sending a "wire notice" to Sun Bank, the purpose of which was to provide notice of dishonor to depositary banks. The wire notice of dishonor contained several errors. Sun Bank failed to find the transaction that was dishonored, which resulted in that bank paying out $150,000 in funds based on a fraudulent check. Sun Bank sued the other banks in this transaction for those funds. *Held:* The court concluded that Sun Bank was in the best position to prevent the loss and that its negligence substantially contributed to the loss. Here, the court noted that upon receipt of the wire notice, Sun Bank's employee was required to locate the customer's account and put a manual hold against the dishonored check. Sun Bank's employee did not conduct a search that could have been done on its computer system that would have located the relevant account and check. Furthermore, Sun Bank's employee did not (1) ask the Federal Reserve for more information when she could not locate the check or (2) even notify her supervisor, in breach of bank policy. Accordingly, the court held that Sun Bank could not recover anything because, among other things, it had the last clear chance to avoid the loss.

[Sun Bank/Miami, NA v. First Nat'l Bank of Md., 698 F. Supp. 1298 (D. Md. 1989)]

¶ 13.06 INCORRECT DATA AND COMMON-ERROR TOLERANCE

Bank assumed risk that it would not be able to stop payment of check despite limiting language on its stop-order form. Staff was a corporation that maintained a checking account with Midlantic National Bank. Staff executed a stop-payment order for $4,117.72 instead of the correct amount of $4,117.12; in all other respects, the stop order was correct. A statement at the bottom of the stop order provided that all information on the stop order had to be correct, including the exact amount of the check to the penny or the stop order would be void. As a result of Staff's incorrect information, the check was paid out. Thereafter, Staff brought action for wrongful payment on the check. The bank made a motion for summary judgment. *Held:* The bank's motion for summary judgment was denied. The bank chose a system that searched for stopped checks by amount alone. By choosing such a system, the bank assumed the risk that it would not be able to stop payment on the check despite the customer's accurate description of the account number, payee's name, number and date of the check, and a de minimis error as to the check amount. The court noted that the bank should not be able to relieve itself of this risk unless it called attention to its computerized system and its necessity for the exact check amount.

[Staff Serv. Assocs., Inc. v. Midlantic Nat'l Bank, 504 A2d 148 (NJ Super. 1985)]

¶ 13.07 ENCODING AND DATA ENTRY ERRORS

Depositary bank is liable to payor bank for excess funds paid out by payor bank where depositary bank incorrectly encodes check. Currently, the method of processing checks in the United States is the Magnetic Ink Character Recognition (MICR). Under this system, magnetic characters identify the bank on which the check is drawn, account number of the maker, and amount of the check. After magnetic encoding, checks work their way through the bank clearing system without further human intervention. Here, the depositary bank incorrectly encoded a $100,000 check for the amount of $10,000. The check, in its lessened amount, was paid by the payor bank. At no time relevant hereto did the customer's account at the payor bank have sufficient funds to pay the $100,000. The depositary bank brought an action against the payor bank for the remainder, $90,000, of the funds. *Held:* The payor bank was not liable to the depositary bank. Under Section 4-213(1) of the UCC, the "amount of the item" due and owing was held by the court to be the face amount of the check or the encoded amount, whichever was less. As such, here the encoding bank (e.g., the depositary bank) was estopped from claiming more than the encoded amount of the check.

[First Nat'l Bank of Boston v. Fidelity Bank, 724 F. Supp. 1168 (ED Pa. 1989)]

System operator of gas pipeline is liable in negligence for losses stemming from misdelivery of gas because of computer system mistake and failure to design a system adequate to capture the mistake. Shell Pipeline Corporation, an oil pipeline operator, brought this action seeking appeal from a judgment awarding Coastal States Trading damages in the amount of $1,762,350. Coastal was in the oil trading business. Because of a mistake by Shell, a Coastal transaction was entered in Shell's computer system as being with the company's sister corporation (Basin) instead of the transacting corporation (Basin Refining). When Coastal sought its money from the company that it had actually transacted with (Basin Refining), that company had filed for bankruptcy. As such, Coastal was unable to recover monies owed on the contract. Because of Shell's error, oil was delivered to the wrong party (i.e., the sister company instead of the transacting company). *Held:* The pipeline operator had a legally enforceable duty to the oil trader that was breached when there was a misdelivery of the crude oil. Here, the appeals court adopted the trial court's finding that Shell was negligent both in misdelivering the oil and in designing a system susceptible to error.

[Shell Pipeline v. Coastal States Trading, 788 SW2d 837 (Tex. App.—Houston (1st Dist.) 1990)]

¶ 13.08 AWARENESS OF SYSTEM INADEQUACIES

Bonded warehouse status of company is suspended for one year where inadequacies of computer monitoring system for release of bonded merchandise produced data that failed to distinguish and identify whether particular merchandise was in-bond. Holt filed this action to contest the final determination by the regional commissioner of the U.S. Customs Service suspending company's bonded warehouse status for one year. The notice of suspension stated that Holt released certain bonded materials without prior payment of duties and proper customs authorization. Additionally, certain bonded and nonbonded merchandise was intermingled, which prevented reconciliation of inventory. In 1982, Customs amended its procedures, thereby requiring bonded warehouses to maintain documentation as to in-bond movement to the warehouse. *Held:* Holt's bonded warehouse suspended status was proper. Here, Holt prematurely released merchandise because the in-bond status of those items was not recorded in its computer system. Thus, Holt claimed that its personnel did not know that the materials it released were in-bond. The court noted that Holt clearly did not have an adequate control system over the release of bonded merchandise because these problems were not detected for a two-year period.

[Holt Hauling v. US Customs Serv., 650 F. Supp. 1013 (Ct. Int'l Trade 1986)]

Consignment seller of horses is negligent in publishing health and other information relating to horses where data came from an unreliable computer information source. Plaintiffs, doing business as Chancellor Farm in New York state, obtained a thoroughbred brood mare at a breeding stock sale. Subsequently, plaintiffs became aware that the mare had a defect that made her unsuitable for breeding purposes. Despite this, plaintiffs offered the mare for sale on a consignment basis, and offered incomplete information to the consignment seller. The sales catalog of the consignment seller listed the mare as being in a better condition than she actually was. Appellee, Cloverfield Farm, Inc., bought the mare for $85,000, a price exceeding the mare's true value in light of her breeding history. *Held:* The consignment seller had a fiduciary duty to the purchaser and the Commonwealth to use ordinary care to ensure that its catalog was as accurate and comprehensive as possible. Here, the consignment seller knew that the relevant computer service, the Jockey Club of America's computer system, was insufficient because of this system's reputation for delinquent entry of data into the network. As such, the consignment seller was on notice that its sales catalog was incomplete and it had a duty to report such inaccuracies or correct those errors itself. However, the consignment seller was not liable to the buyer of the mare merely because no claim was ever asserted against this party.

[Chernick v. Fasig-Tipton Ky., Inc., 703 SW2d 885 (Ky. Ct. App. 1986)]

¶ 13.09 WRONGFUL NONUSE OF A COMPUTER

Government's failure to repair or replace a sporadically malfunctioning weather-reporting buoy is not adequate basis for action under FTCA. A government weather buoy malfunctioned, causing it to cease transmission to the National Weather Service (NWS). The government knew of the buoy's malfunction and attempted to repair or replace the buoy; however, those attempts failed. Subsequently, the government ceased attempts to repair or replace the buoy. Decedents, prior to engaging in lobster fishing, listened to the NWS's marine weather predictions. Based on those predictions, the decedents embarked on their fishing trip. Unfortunately, the weather was much more severe than the NWS predicted. The personal representatives of decedents' estates brought suit alleging negligence against the United States for failing to maintain the weather buoy. *Held:* The government was not liable for the death of the fishermen who died in the storm despite the government's failure to repair or replace the occasionally malfunctioning weather buoy. The court noted that under the Federal Tort Claims Act (FTCA), government liability can be rejected if the government undertaking was "discretionary." Here, the court noted that a weather forecast is a "classic example" of a prediction of indeterminate reliability. As such, it refused to establish a duty of judicially reviewable due care and refused to hold the government liable for the fishermen's deaths.

[Brown v. United States, 790 F2d 199 (1st Cir. 1986)]

Lack of sophisticated system of computerized data that might have enabled insurer to expect claim does not satisfy notice of claim. Three lawyers had formerly represented Vernon Savings & Loan Association while partners at the law firm of Jenkens & Gilchrist. They later moved to Baker & McKenzie, where they received an identical letter from the FDIC, captioned "Notice of Claims," telling them the FDIC intended to seek recovery from them of the losses that Vernon had sustained as a result of misconduct by Jenkens & Gilchrist. At the time the partners received the letter, National Union of Pittsburgh held the professional responsibility policy on Baker & McKenzie; the policy was in its first year. National Union did not receive written notice of the FDIC's claim until the second policy period. During the first policy period, however, an attorney employed by National Union received a copy of Baker & McKenzie's application for insurance, a copy of the FDIC's "Notice of Claims" letter to the three lawyers, and copies of several other notices of claim against Jenkens & Gilchrist and its former partners, including the three lawyers, arising out of the collapse of Vernon. *Held:* National Union was not liable for the claim brought by the FDIC against the three lawyers because the claim was first made during the first policy year but was not reported until the second policy period. The "Notice of Claims" letter, received during the first policy period, placed Baker & McKenzie on notice of an impending claim. The fact that National Union's lawyer had, during the first policy period, documents from which National Union could infer that a claim would eventually be made under the Baker & McKenzie policy was irrelevant. Notice of a claim was not satisfied by demonstrating that a sophisticated system of computerized data and retrieval might have enabled National Union, through collation of documents from different sources, to form an informed judgment that it was likely someday to receive a claim from Baker & McKenzie. Insureds must comply with notice requirements as stated in the policies.

[National Union Fire Ins. Co. v. Baker & McKenzie, 997 F2d 305 (7th Cir. 1993)]

Negligence claim against United States is proper where marine accident allegedly occurred because of Coast Guard's manual charting of sunken wreckage, admittedly an inferior method to computerized procedures. Plaintiffs-Appellees' vessel struck an underwater object that was allegedly the remains of an unlighted navigational buoy maintained by the U.S. Coast Guard. Apparently, the navigational buoy might have been knocked down and/or partially destroyed. The Coast Guard set up a temporary, unlighted radar reflecting buoy on the missing buoy's estimated chart position. Importantly, the Coast Guard personnel who estimated the lost buoy's chart position used only a three-arm protractor method to estimate the missing buoy's location. The Coast Guard manual relevant to such procedures states that the protractor method is to be used only as a "last resort." The preferred methodology is to employ a computer analysis because of its greater accuracy. Under the Public Vessels Act, Congress permits parties injured by public vessels to sue the United States in admiralty; thus, this Act waives the United States's sovereign immunity in this area. Furthermore, the Eleventh Circuit has held that there is an exception to this waiver of sovereign immunity, in certain instances, for "discretionary acts" of governmental personnel. *Held:* The discretionary function exception to the government's waiver of sovereign immunity did not apply to the Coast Guard's decision to use the three-arm protractor method. Here, the court noted that in the Coast Guard manual, the protractor method was the method of "last resort." As such, this decision was an operational decision and, accordingly, fell outside the scope of the discretionary function exception. The court remanded the negligence issue.

[US Fire Ins. Co. v. United States, 806 F2d 1529 (11th Cir. 1986)]

Bank that accepts various stolen investment securities is subject to true owner's claims where owner has filed notice of the stolen status of the securities with a readily accessible computerized verification system. A bank brought an action to recover bond and stock certificates that it accepted as collateral for a series of loans. The securities at issue in the case at bar were stolen from their rightful owner. Accordingly, the bank sought to prove that it was a bona fide purchaser of those securities. Among other things, the bank did not check with the Securities Information Center (SIC) to see if the securities were stolen. *Held:* The bank was not a bona fide purchaser of the securities because it failed to observe commercially reasonable practices. The court noted that to establish bona fide purchaser status, an individual or institution that regularly deals in securities needs to be able to show that it observed reasonable commercial practices with respect to that security. In many instances, this requirement will in effect impose a duty of inquiry with the SIC because this is what a reasonable commercial dealer would have done. The court found that the burden of checking with the SIC via a telephone call was light; nevertheless, the court declined to find that the SIC inquiry would be required in every case. For example, a dealer would not necessarily have to check with the SIC where it receives a security from a well-known customer in his name.

[First Nat'l Bank of Cicero v. United States, 653 F. Supp. 1312 (ND Ill. 1987)]

Mechanical measuring system used by gasoline station owner is reasonable where such system resulted in spillage of no more than one cup of gasoline three times per week. Landowners brought an action against Ware Oil, owner of a gas station, alleging that contaminants released or deposited by it seeped through the ground to the basement area of the landowners' nearby residence. Among other things, the landowners complained of Ware's system for measuring how much gasoline was in the tanks. Ware used a manual system that resulted in no more than a cupful of gasoline being spilled approximately three times a week. The landowners' complaint herein related to Ware not using a computerized system for its measuring purposes. *Held:* The court found that Ware was not negligent in using a manual system instead of a computerized measuring system. Here, the court noted that "this amount of spillage was obviously so small as to be insignificant."

[Malone v. Ware Oil Co., 534 NE2d 1003 (Ill. App. 4th Dist. 1989)]

Attorney unable to find a case dealing with statute of limitations in bail-jumping case does not breach any obligation to act carefully where that case is misindexed even though it could be found using a computerized data base. An individual was charged with bail jumping in the second degree. At issue herein was whether bail jumping is a continuing offense for statute of limitations purposes. The appellate division, first department definitively ruled on this issue as reported in a case. *Held:* The court found that, among other things, counsel's failure to find this case was understandable since the most commonly used and most expedient research tools were not helpful in this instance. Here, the court noted, the editors at West Publishing indexed the relevant case law as solely a "habitual offender" case.

[People v. Barnes, 499 NYS2d 343 (S. Ct. NY County 1986)]

¶ 13.10 NARROWING OF OBLIGATIONS UNDER CONTRACT LAW

Delay of more than six weeks in distributing a benefits check because of a data entry error may constitute negligence, but is not willful misconduct. Johnson was receiving weekly workmen's compensation payments as a result of an injury he sustained on the job. Continental Insurance terminated Johnson's benefits and Johnson filed suit. As a result of that suit, Johnson's benefits were to have been reinstated. However, because of a data entry error, Johnson's benefits were not properly reinstated. When Continental discovered its error after seven weeks, it made a retroactive payment in full for the missed weekly benefits. Under Louisiana law, benefit recipients can accelerate installments of benefits where there has been a "willful refusal" of payments. *Held:* The insurer's nonpayment of Johnson's benefits for six weeks did not constitute willful refusal to pay benefits. Here, the insurer made prompt payment of the benefits once the delinquency was brought to its attention. Thus, Johnson's request to have his workmen's compensation benefits accelerated was denied.

[Johnson v. Continental Ins. Cos., 410 So. 2d 1058 (La. 1982)]

Unilateral mistake on the part of insurance company to pay claim is not a proper reason to decline payment. Beneficiaries of a life insurance contract brought an action against the insurance company and insurance broker for bad faith in refusing to pay an insurance claim. At trial, the court found for the beneficiaries. The defendant insurance company appealed. Premiums that were unpaid by the decedent insured were to have been paid by an automatic loan to pay premiums (APL) pursuant to the insurance policy. However, the defendant insurer incorrectly coded the decedent's policy as not having this provision. *Held:* The defendant insurer's unilateral error in not correctly encoding the decedent's insurance policy did not shield it from liability. In this case, defendant insurer intentionally encoded the decedent's insurance policy as not having an APL despite the decedent's request for defendant to do so.

[Mutual Life Ins. v. Estate of Wesson, 517 So. 2d 521 (Miss. 1987)]

¶ 13.11 ENHANCED DAMAGES

Computer data entry error is defense to claim for fraud in connection with sales of mortgage investments based on inaccurate data.   In this case, the seller, First Guaranty Mortgage Corporation, a wholly owned subsidiary of the Resolution Trust Corporation as receiver for the bank, promoted a mortgage servicing offering through a broker. The broker's offering contained an error: The fees a buyer could expect to receive from servicing the mortgages was described as "net"; in fact, those fees were gross figures. The buyer discovered this after buying the mortgages. The buyer brought suit, alleging, among other things, willful deception. *Held:* The court granted summary judgment on this claim. Here, the inaccuracies occurred because of an error in data entry, and the misinformation was corrected and disclosed immediately after it was discovered. As such, the defendants made an error, but did not engage in willful fraud.

[Real Estate Fin. v. Resolution Trust Corp., 950 F2d 1540 (11th Cir. 1992)]

Computer programming error that results in understatement of company's discounted future net cash flows is deemed a violation of duty of disclosure by majority shareholder.   A majority shareholder, as a result of a tender offer, increased ownership interest in minority shareholder's outstanding stock to 94.6 percent and then initiated a short-form merger. Under the terms of the short-form merger, shareholders would receive an extra $2 per share if the right to seek an appraisal was waived. In connection with the short-form merger, the majority shareholder distributed several documents to the minority shareholders. Because of a computer error, these documents underestimated discounted future net cash flows and stated a decline instead of an actual increase in the value of the shares. Minority shareholders sued, alleging that disclosure violations constituted a breach of the majority shareholder's fiduciary "duty of candor." On appeal, the Supreme Court of Delaware upheld the lower court's decision in favor of the minority shareholders. *Held:* The majority shareholder violated its duty of disclosure of all material facts relevant to the minority shareholders' decision to accept the short-form merger or seek an appraisal. A majority shareholder bears the burden of showing complete disclosure of all material facts relevant to a minority shareholder's decision. The majority shareholder, playing a significant role in preparing and distributing the disclosure materials, was responsible for errors that were material and misleading.

[Shell Petroleum, Inc. v. Smith, 606 A2d 112 (Del. 1992)]

¶ 13.12 COMPUTER MODELS

Statutory requirements are met where Forest Service computer system considers alternative proposed by environmental group indirectly and not in the form of a full-blown alternative analysis as per an environmental impact statement. This litigation involved an area comprising 858,000 roadless acres situated within 47 different roadless zones of the Idaho Panhandle Forest. A coalition of six conservationist/environmental organizations challenged the National Forest Service's decision to recommend against wilderness designation for 43 of the 47 roadless areas, claiming violation of the National Forest Management Act and the National Environmental Policy Act. The district court granted summary judgment for the defendants at the trial level. Under federal law, for purposes of evaluating the adequacy of an Environmental Impact Statement (EIS), courts employ a "rule of reason" test to determine if the EIS contains a reasonably thorough discussion of significant aspects of probable economic consequences. Furthermore, the existence of a viable, but unexamined, alternative renders the EIS inadequate. In this case, the coalition had submitted an alternative plan that included both higher wilderness acreage and the required timber yield. The Forest Service rejected the environmental group's plan because the Forest Service's computer program had been set up to generate only alternatives that met certain criteria. *Held:* The Ninth Circuit found for the Forest Service. The court accepted the Forest Service's explanation that its computer program was designed to reject alternatives that involved unacceptable environmental damage to already developed areas. As a result, the court held that the Forest Service did consider the coalition's plan; however, not in the form of a full-blown EIS alternative analysis. The court found that the Forest Service had met federal statutory requirements.

[Idaho Conservation League v. Mumma, 956 F2d 1508 (9th Cir. 1992)]

Investment manager of charitable foundation is not liable for negligent design and implementation of investment program where he developed and relied on computer model system to manage decisions and target companies for possible investment. This action concerned the administration of two charitable foundations valued at approximately $100 million at the time of suit. A former trustee brought this action against an individual who was, among other things, investment manager of the trusts. The investment manager, who had no training in portfolio management, was involved in the development, design, and implementation of a computer model system to manage the trusts' portfolios. The trusts suffered losses and the plaintiff brought suit, alleging negligence on the part of the investment manager. *Held:* The investment manager discharged his duties in good faith with the degree of diligence, skill, and care that an ordinarily prudent person would apply in an investment context. The court noted that, while different investment models existed, no alternatives were so fully and widely accepted as to set the standard against which reasonable care could be measured. In concluding that the investment manager was not negligent, the court stated: "It was prudent to design a mechanical system, based on a recognized theory of investment, which routinized the identification of investment targets reflecting the goal of buying strength. It would have been a bad decision and imprudent to have a system based on [some other financial theory], if that system had to be operated by [the investment manager], because of his lack of formal training."

[Johnson v. Johnson, 515 A2d 255 (NJ Super Ch. 1986)]

PART B.   CONTRACT AND CREDIT PERFORMANCE

¶ 13.13 WRONGFUL DEBT ENFORCEMENT

Punitive damages are justified where creditor wrongfully repossesses car despite being shown canceled checks not entered into creditor's data base and where creditor seeks to limit its liability by having appellee sign release in exchange for his car.   Appellee bought a Ford motor car in 1963. The unpaid part of the purchase price was subject to a security agreement that was assigned by the dealer to Ford Motor Credit Company. Although the appellee was current in his payments, employees of Ford's collection office visited him and told him that he was delinquent. The appellee showed those Ford employees his canceled checks, which clearly established that he was current in his payments. Two months later, essentially the same incident reoccurred and again the appellee proved that he was current in his payments. Subsequently, Ford repossessed the appellee's car. The appellee then went to Ford's offices where the office manager of the collections department offered to return the appellee's car if he executed a liability release form. The appellee sued Ford for wrongful repossession of his car. At trial, the jury entered a judgment for the appellee for $2,000 in compensatory damages and $5,000 in punitive damages. Ford appealed. Ford argued that this whole incident occurred because of a computer mistake. *Held:* The appellate court affirmed the trial court's judgment. The court noted that "trust in the infallibility of a computer is hardly a defense, when the opportunity to avoid the error is as apparent and repeated as was here presented." Here, punitive damages were justified where the creditor sought to limit its liability by seeking a release in exchange for the appellee's car.

[Ford Motor Credit Co. v. Swarens, 447 SW2d 53 (Ky. Ct. App. 1969)]

Repossession of car despite creditor's promise to defer action, based on inaccurate data in two different computer systems and apparent loss of a money order, justifies use of punitive damages.   Price, a debtor, brought an action against Ford Motor Credit Company for wrongful conversion of his automobile. Ford made two errors that had the cumulative effect of showing that Price was delinquent in his account by two months. The first error involved Ford's agent forwarding funds to an account other than that of Price. The second error involved a mistake in the summary of payments for collection of payments; essentially, a payment was not entered into Ford's data base. Additionally, Price sent a payment to Ford in the form of a money order that Ford allegedly never received. At various times, Ford agents knew of Price's payment status because his wife had shown a Ford employee receipts for money orders. Despite Ford's knowledge, it ordered Price's car repossessed. Furthermore, Ford's employee spoke with Price's wife and reassured her that the car would not be repossessed until Price could verify that the money orders had been received. Ford's employee, however, did not rescind the order to repossess the car. The car was subsequently repossessed. The lower court rendered a judgment for Price and awarded him $600 in actual damages and $25,000 in punitive damages. Ford appealed. *Held:* The trial court's decision was affirmed. Here, the court noted that Ford's good faith must be measured against the broken promise not to repossess the car. From the evidence adduced at trial, the jury could have found that in light of Ford's promise and failure to notify the repossession agent to delay action, it knew or should have known that the repossession was wrongful, or at the very least, that it acted with reckless disregard of Price's rights.

[Price v. Ford Motor Credit Co., 530 SW2d 249 (Mo. Ct. App. 1975)]

¶ 13.14 WAIVER AND ESTOPPEL BY COMPUTER

Genuine issue of material fact exists with respect to claims for breach of implied covenant of good faith and fair dealing and negligent infliction of serious emotional distress precluding summary judgment where insurer sent plaintiff two years of incorrect insurance billings.   Mutual Benefit Life Insurance Company insured Johnson for major medical coverage. After the policy was issued, Johnson was treated for cancer, which illness would have made her uninsurable were she to have sought insurance from another insurance carrier. For two years, Mutual Benefit made billing mistakes with respect to Johnson's coverage—including mistakenly canceling her coverage at one point. Johnson brought action, inter alia, for breach of the implied covenant of good faith and fair dealing and negligent infliction of serious emotional distress. The trial court granted Mutual Benefit summary judgment. Johnson appealed. *Held:* The trial court's granting of summary judgment was reversed and remanded. The court of appeals noted that the implied covenant of good faith and fair dealing requires that neither party to a contract "will injure the right of the other to receive the benefits of the agreement." Here, the court stated that peace of mind is one of the benefits that one seeks by obtaining insurance. Thus, Mutual Benefit's incorrect billing for two years arguably deprived Johnson of one of her benefits of the agreement. The court found that a genuine issue of material fact existed as to whether Mutual Benefit acted unreasonably or arbitrarily in dealing with Johnson's justifiable contractual expectations. The court of appeals also reversed the district court's grant of summary judgment with respect to Johnson's claim for negligent infliction of serious emotional distress. Here, the court reasoned that there was sufficient indicia of genuineness of Johnson's mental distress, including that she was uninsurable because of her history of cancer; she received two incorrect termination notices; she was confronted with billing errors for two years; and she was required to seek psychiatric aid.

[Johnson v. Mutual Benefit Life Ins. Co., 847 F2d 600 (9th Cir. 1988)]

Notice or knowledge is properly imputed to insurance company based on notice to insurance agent and claims adjuster resulting in waiver of expiration issue.
An automobile insurance company brought this action for declaratory judgment of nonliability on a policy of automobile insurance that it issued to Bockhorst. Bockhorst had an insurance policy with the insurance company that Bockhorst allowed to lapse. Thereafter, Bockhorst was involved in an automotive accident that resulted in the death of a pedestrian. Later on the day of the accident, Bockhorst mailed a check to renew his automotive insurance. The insurance company agent told Bockhorst that he was unsure if Bockhorst's insurance would be reinstated. The agent immediately mailed Bockhorst's check to the company regional office; however, the agent did not include information relating that the accident occurred before he received Bockhorst's payment. Similar coverage concerns were raised by the company's claims adjuster. While the claims division was conducting its investigation, Bockhorst's check was processed by the insurance company and a notice was issued reinstating Bockhorst's insurance. The trial court held that by issuing the policy retroactively despite being informed of all the facts by Bockhorst, the insurance company intentionally waived its right not to renew the insurance policy. *Held:* The trial court's judgment was affirmed. The court of appeals noted that there was no fraud or collusion in the case at bar—Bockhorst was forthright in his admission of the facts. Thus, the insurance company was aware of the critical facts when it executed the contract and accepted the premium. The court noted that the company's local agent, as well as several other officers and employees, were aware of the facts concerning the accident. The fact that the company's policy servicing division did not have knowledge of the accident until after Bockhorst's premium payment was placed in the computer was not controlling, since "one hand of the company must be charged with what the other hand knows and does."

[State Farm Mut. Auto. Ins. Co. v. Bockhorst, 453 F2d 533 (10th Cir. 1972)]

Computer-generated insurance premium estopps insurance company from rescinding insurance contract. Decedent insured purchased automobile insurance from State Farm insurance company. As part of the application process, the decedent misrepresented his past driving record, including that he had an intoxication conviction on his record. On January 9, 1985, through no fault of his own, the decedent was killed while driving one of the insured vehicles. As part of its underwriting investigation, State Farm discovered on January 11, 1985, that the decedent had misrepresented his driving record. On January 23, Lowry received a notice directing her to pay the second portion of the premium—which she did. Thereafter, State Farm's claim committee reviewed the matter and advised Lowry that the decedent's insurance contract was void from its inception because of the decedent's "material misrepresentations." Lowry brought action to recover death benefits pursuant to the automobile insurance issued by State Farm to her deceased husband. State Farm moved for summary judgment, arguing that the insurance contract had been rescinded ab initio because the insured had misrepresented his driving record. The district court granted State Farm's motion for summary judgment. Lowry appealed from that determination. *Held:* The issue of whether State Farm waived its right to unilaterally rescind the policy because of its delay in communicating its rescission or by accepting the premium payment after it learned of the decedent's driving record could not be determined as a matter of law. The court rejected State Farm's argument that computer-generated premium notices could never constitute waiver. In fact, the court noted that, "The fact that an entity chooses to generate its documents by electronic rather than human means provides no basis for automatic absolution of its errors, be they errors of omission or commission." State Farm is as responsible for the product of its machines as it is for the product of its people. Accordingly, the court found that summary judgment was inappropriate in this instance and the case was reversed and remanded.

[Lowry v. State Farm Mut. Auto. Ins. Co., 421 NW2d 775 (Neb. 1988)]

City does not waive right to additional utility charges where inaccurate data processing undercharged users of power. Bud Moore, Inc., occupied certain business premises in Lincoln, Nebraska beginning in January 1977. As part of Bud Moore's business, it installed refrigeration units that ran on electricity. The existing meter was a four-digit meter, capable of registering electrical consumption up to 9,999 kilowatt hours. Monthly bills were sent based on meter readings; those bills ranged in amount from $25 to $256. A five-digit meter was installed and the City of Lincoln found out that Bud Moore had been underbilled by 10,000 kilowatt hours for each month from February through December. Apparently, the city miscalculated Bud Moore's bills because the city's accounting system failed to take into account that the four-digit meters turned over repeatedly during the month. Bud Moore was billed an additional $3,053.07, which it refused to pay. This action ensued. The trial court found for the city; this decision was affirmed on appeal. Bud Moore appealed to the Supreme Court of Nebraska. *Held:* Under Nebraska law, a party may recover for furnishing goods and services delivered where a mistake is inadvertent and unilateral. Here, the facts clearly showed that the city furnished a precise amount of electricity to Bud Moore, that it made a mistake in calculating the dollar amount due from Bud Moore, that such mistake was innocently and inadvertently made, and that the mistake caused the city financial injury and resulted in profit to Bud Moore. The lower courts' opinions were affirmed.

[City of Lincoln v. Bud Moore, Inc., 315 NW2d 590 (Neb. 1982)]

PART C. NOTICE REQUIREMENTS AND SYSTEM ADEQUACY

¶ 13.15 PROOF OF NOTICE

Affidavit of supervisor of mailing operation establishes a prima facie showing that notice was sent to third parties. In 1974, Georgia enacted its no-fault insurance statute that, among other things, made available to insurance policyholders optional personal injury protection coverage up to at least $50,000. Insurers were required to mail notice of these options to their existing policyholders. Insureds who were not mailed proper notice were entitled to the full amount of the optional coverage. Here, Lane was injured in an automobile accident. Lane and his father submitted affidavits that they did not receive the mailing from Allstate Insurance Company offering the optional personal injury protection coverage. Allstate produced an affidavit from one of its employees asserting that he supervised a mass mailing in which all of Allstate's insureds were sent a package notifying them of the optional coverage. *Held:* The affidavit of Allstate's employee stating that he supervised a mass mailing in which all insureds were sent a package notifying them of the new optional personal injury protection coverage was sufficient to establish that the insurer complied with Georgia law. The court of appeals relied on a decision of the Supreme Court of Georgia that considered an affidavit by Allstate's same employee identical to the one submitted in the case at bar and held that there it constituted "evidence of proper mailing of an adequate document." The Supreme Court of Georgia noted that actual receipt of the notice was not required. Here, the court noted that despite any shortcomings of mass mailings, Lane failed to overcome the obstacle presented by the Georgia Supreme Court decision.

[Lane v. Allstate Ins. Co., 746 F2d 1444 (11th Cir. 1984)]

¶ 13.16 FILING SYSTEM ERROR

Minor misspelling of tenant's name does not invalidate lien, even though standard governmental computer search method would not find lien. A debtor's name was misspelled on an agricultural lien as Cipriano Esparsa, instead of debtor's actual name—Cipriano Esparza. One issue before the court was whether the lien should be given effect despite the misspelling of the debtor's name. *Held:* The lien was valid despite the misspelling of the debtor's name. The relevant Washington state filing statute provides that "The statement shall be in writing . . . and shall contain in substance the following information: . . . (b) The name and address of the debtor." Here, the court emphasized that the modifying term "in substance" must be given effect. To the court, this modifying phrase meant that something less than absolute precision was required in spelling. Thus, the court analyzed this issue by determining whether "Esparsa" was in substance sufficiently similar to "Esparza" to impart notice to one searching for the correct spelling, "Esparza." The court referred to UCC Article 9 standards for perfecting a lien. Under Article 9, a lien is perfected if a "reasonably diligent searcher would be likely to discover a financing statement indexed under the incorrect name." Most courts have been willing to tolerate incorrect names and incorrect indexings as effective when the inaccuracies were not "seriously misleading." Importantly, the reasonable search standard set forth by the court required more than the typical governmental search that only brought up exact name matches.

[In re Esparza, 821 P2d 1216 (Wash. 1992)]

PART D.   GOVERNMENT COMPUTER USE AND ERROR LIABILITY

¶ 13.17 CRIMINAL JUSTICE

Federal detainer issued against defendant under prosecution for state charges is not equivalent to arrest for purposes of the time provisions of Speedy Trial Act.   Copley was arrested on charges pursuant to Ohio state law. Later, the U.S. Marshal's office filed a detainer with the state sheriff's office requesting that at the end of the state proceedings, Copley be released to the custody of the U.S. Marshal. State charges were dropped against Copley but a computer error caused Copley to stay in county jail for 70 extra days. Copley then sought to have his federal indictment dismissed pursuant to the federal Speedy Trial Act, which requires an indictment to be charged within 30 days of an arrest. Copley argued that the detainer functioned as a federal arrest after state charges were dropped and thus the indictment was untimely. *Held:* The federal detainer did not serve to significantly restrain Copley's liberty for purposes of responding to a federal charge. Here, the state was not holding Copley for the purposes of responding to federal charges. Instead, the state was erroneously holding Copley because of a computer error. Thus, the court held that the detainer was not the functional equivalent of a federal arrest for Speedy Trial Act purposes.

[United States v. Copley, 774 F2d 728, 6th Cir. 1985)]

Proper test for affiant who obtained search warrant based on incorrect information contained in computer data base is whether affiant acted in good faith or reckless disregard for the truth.   A search warrant was issued for the residence of a movant based in part on the affidavit of an IRS agent. This agent, as part of his affidavit, alleged that the movant had failed to file an income tax return for the tax year 1983. Here, the movant's tax return was important since, if not filed, it would mean the movant allegedly failed to report taxable income from the sale of illegal drugs. In fact, the movant had filed a tax return; however, the IRS agent was not informed of this because of a computer processing delay. Here, the IRS agent was told that the movant could have filed his return and that this information could possibly not be reflected in a search of the computer records. *Held:* The IRS agent did not act with reckless disregard for the truth. The court found that the movant did not meet his burden of proof, which required him to prove the state of mind of the agent with respect to his conclusion in his affidavit that the movant did not file a tax return.

[United States v. Residence Located at 218 3d St., 805 F2d 256 (7th Cir. 1986)]

Sheriff's failure to correct county jail system's lack of internal procedures for keeping track of whether inmates had been arraigned or had attended other court appearances constitutes government policy and violates inmates' liberty interest in speedy pretrial procedures.   Oviatt was incarcerated for 114 days before being arraigned. As such, he spent those 114 days in jail without an arraignment, bail hearing, or trial. The jail system had no internal procedures for keeping track of whether inmates had received an arraignment or attended any other scheduled court appearance. Rather, the jail system relied on inmates, attorneys, and others to bring missed arraignments to the proper official's attention. For whatever reason, no one brought Oviatt's missed arraignment to the proper official's attention. Oviatt brought suit against the county sheriff and the county of Multnomah, Oregon, alleging violations of 42 USC § 1983 and Oregon's common law of false imprisonment. The jury at the district court level awarded Oviatt a verdict of $65,000, and the court awarded him $45,385.65 for attorney fees under 42 USC § 1988. The defendants appealed and Oviatt cross-appealed. *Held:* The county's jail system violated Oviatt's constitutional liberty interest in freedom from incarceration without speedy pretrial procedures. The court noted that the county jail system had no procedures for keeping track of clerical errors with respect to arraignments; instead, the jail system relied on protestation by the inmate, his family, or his attorney. Furthermore, the court noted that the jail system had various manual and computerized procedures for locating missed arraignments that it could have implemented.

[Oviatt By & Through Waugh v. Pearce, 954 F2d 1470 (9th Cir. 1992)]

Computer problem that caused registration check to take longer than usual does not turn an admittedly legal initial detention into unlawful arrest.   Officers saw Rutherford enter a residence where police suspected illegal drugs were kept. Rutherford entered that residence empty-handed and left with a bag. Later, police stopped Rutherford, arrested him on a traffic violation, and subsequently searched his vehicle and found illegal drugs. Rutherford argued, among other things, that the lawful investigatory detention ripened into a de facto arrest without probable cause because of its duration. *Held:* The detention, although some 25 to 30 minutes, did not constitute a de facto arrest where a computer glitch caused a registration check to take more time than usual. The court noted that there is no strict time limitation on Terry-type stops.

[United States v. Rutherford, 824 F2d 831 (10th Cir. 1987)]

Reliance on computerized stolen vehicle report that may or may not have been inaccurate does not preclude officer's finding of probable cause to arrest defendant.   The defendant was convicted of possession with intent to distribute cocaine. On appeal, the defendant asserted that the officer had relied on inaccurate computer information and, for this reason, conviction should be reversed. The defendant was arrested while driving a vehicle belonging to Walker. Walker had previously reported the vehicle stolen, and this information was entered into the law enforcement agency's computer. Although the officer attempted to verify an earlier version of the computerized stolen vehicle report before stopping the vehicle, the dispatcher told the officer that the computer was temporarily down and that he should rely on an earlier computer printout that stated the vehicle was stolen. Although Walker allegedly would have testified that the vehicle was reported to have been recovered prior to the defendant's arrest, the computer did not reflect this information at the time of arrest. *Held:* Conviction affirmed. A time delay of three days to update the computer to accurately reflect that the vehicle had been recovered did not preclude a finding of probable cause in arresting the defendant. There is no requirement that law enforcement agencies must instantly update their computerized information. The Fourth Amendment only requires a standard of reasonableness, not certainty, in finding probable cause for arrest. Some delay in correcting or updating computer records is expected and is, therefore, reasonable.

[In re REG, 602 A2d 146 (DC App. 1992)]

Seven-day delay in removal of outdated arrest warrant from police computer records is unreasonable and makes subsequent detention and/or arrest by officer illegal. An officer, noting that nothing appeared suspicious, approached a parked car and asked the occupants for identification. A computer check indicated that an outstanding warrant existed for one of the occupants. A search incident to the arrest resulted in discovery of cocaine. The outstanding warrant, on which the arrest and search were based, was later found to have been satisfied, but not removed from the computer. The defendant filed a motion to suppress evidence seized incident to his allegedly legal arrest. The appellate court reversed and remanded the defendant's motion. Certiorari was granted to the defendant/petitioner. *Held:* Reliance on computer information indicating an outstanding arrest warrant is not sufficient information or evidence to establish probable cause for arrest. Probable cause depends on the accuracy of the outstanding warrant information in the computer. Keeping computerized information accurate and current is the responsibility of the sheriff's department. To allow inaccurate, outdated information to remain in the computer puts citizens at risk of detainment or arrest without sufficient legal basis. Here, but for the petitioner's arrest, there would have been no probable cause to search the car, since according to all evidence, the petitioner and his companion did nothing criminal in the officer's presence. Such an arrest was a violation of the petitioner's Fourth Amendment right against illegal search and seizure. Thus, the search incident to his arrest and the arrest were illegal, and the fruits of the search should be suppressed.

[Ott v. State, 600 A2d 111 (Md. 1992)]

¶ 13.18 RIGHTS ADMINISTRATION

Computerized administration system, without manual backup or replacement systems, is sufficient in class action alleging funds mismanagement in child support enforcement program where the system appeared to be adequate to court. Class representatives in a class action suit challenged the manner in which Pennsylvania officials administer the child support enforcement program established under the Social Security Act. The district court held for the representatives. The representatives appealed from the limited relief ordered by the lower court, and officials of Pennsylvania's Department of Welfare, cross-appealed. One issue before the court of appeals was whether, where allegations of mismanagement of funds was proved, the district court properly rejected the class representative's backup paper reassignment system as part of a remedy that was designed to prevent reoccurrence of the violations. *Held:* The court of appeals upheld the district court's decision that the computerized system was adequate. Here, the court concluded that the rejection of the class representatives' backup paper reassignment system was within the permissible range of district court discretion in fashioning a remedy; if such an order was not complied with, the proper remedy would be a contempt proceeding.

[Bennett v. Whit, 865 F2d 1395 (3d Cir. 1989)]

Illinois's computerized Medicaid system, which among other things determined user eligibility, must include notice and opportunity to appeal before benefits are discontinued.   A class of people whose continued use of Medicaid had been restricted or terminated filed suit against the Illinois Department of Public Aid. The Department had set standards for determining which Medicaid recipients had overused medical services and implemented a system for forcing compliance with its standards. The Department maintained a computerized records-keeping system that identified, on a quarterly basis, Medicaid eligibility based on a formula applying an analysis of averages and standard deviations applicable to the relevant Medicaid population as a whole. Recipients who exceeded a maximum usage rate for a given period became ineligible for further benefits or were restricted in their rights to benefits on an automatic, computerized basis. *Held:* The automated procedure was acceptable as a starting point for identifying recipients who might be abusing the Medicaid system; however, the lack of a notice and opportunity to appeal violated due process. Here, the court noted that remedying the problems required minimal cost and effort. First, the court noted that due process could be, in part, satisfied by enclosing the computer printout that identified the problem treatments with the notice forms already used. Second, the Department could give recipients additional time to appeal.

[Tripp v. Coler, 640 F. Supp. 848 (ND Ill. 1986)]

¶ 13.19 ORDINARY AGENCY REVIEW

EPA's use of computerized atmospheric model to establish air pollution emissions standards is arbitrary and capricious in absence of site-specific validation studies.   Various states and coal companies filed a petition seeking a review of air pollution emission limitations established by the EPA for plants adjacent to Lake Erie. In this case, the Sixth Circuit earlier held that the EPA's use of CRSTER, a computerized atmospheric model, was arbitrary and capricious in the absence of site-specific validation studies. The court ordered the parties to propose a program that would validate the CRSTER model; interim emissions standards were then set. This action involved the parties' responses to the Sixth Circuit's earlier decision. The EPA urged the court to defer to the EPA's decisions regarding scientific and computer models. *Held:* The court affirmed its earlier decision. Here, the court noted that the legislative history of the 1977 Clean Air Act indicates that the courts are to conduct a "searching review" of the basis of EPA modeling and test procedures like the one at issue. Thus, the parties should have chosen a site in order to validate the model.

[State of Ohio v. US EPA, 798 F2d 880 (6th Cir. 1986)]

District Court grants summary judgment for IRS in wrongful disclosure of tax return information case where that disclosure to third party occurred because of computer error without negligence on the part of IRS. Christensen, among other things, sought compensatory and punitive damages for eight allegedly unauthorized disclosures of tax return information. These alleged unauthorized disclosures included Notices of Levy on various entities, including Christensen's bank and Christensen husband's employer. Section 7431 of the IRC establishes a cause of action if an officer or employee of the United States knowingly or negligently makes a disclosure of a tax return or tax return information in violation of Section 6103 of the IRC. *Held:* Summary judgment was granted for the government. With respect to seven of the disclosures, Christensen did not prove that the IRS breached any confidentiality provisions under the IRC, specifically Section 6103. For the Notice of Levy to the husband's employer, Christensen did not prove that the United States knowingly disclosed such information, because the disclosure was the result of a computer error. Furthermore, the disclosure was not negligent, because to hold the IRS liable for a computer error would hold it to a higher standard than anticipated by Congress. The court noted that to expect the massive internal revenue system to be free of computer errors was not "reasonable."

[Christensen v. United States, 733 F. Supp. 844 (DNJ 1990)]

CHAPTER 14

ELECTRONIC TRANSACTION ENVIRONMENTS

PART A.　ELECTRONIC FUNDS TRANSFERS

¶ 14.01　THE INTERSTATE BANKING STRUCTURE

National bank's use of shared ATM, which it does not rent or own, does not constitute branch banking under National Bank Act.　Wegmans grocery stores installed ATMs and entered into an agreement with Marine Midland Bank that allowed the bank's customers to use the machines. The state bankers association argued that the ATMs were "branch" banks operating in violation of the National Bank Act. The district court agreed, and permanently enjoined Marine from using Wegmans. On appeal, Marine argued that the ATMs, which were owned and operated by a supermarket and shared by innumerable other financial institutions (by way of network systems), was not a "branch" under the National Bank Act (12 USC § 36(f)). *Held:* A national bank's use of a shared ATM, which it does not own or rent, does not constitute branch banking under Sections 36(c) and 36(f) of the Act. The court encouraged Congress to update the 1927 National Bank Act in view of current computer technology.

[Independent Bankers Ass'n v. Marine Midland Bank, 757 F2d 453 (2d Cir. 1985)]

Computer banking terminals considered branch banks within National Bank Act.　The Comptroller of the Currency appealed a ruling by the district court that CBCTs were "branches" within the National Bank Act (12 USC § 36(f)). A Minnesota state banking association had argued that the CBCTs were branches and were therefore subject to Section 36(f) as to establishment, operation, and capital requirements that were regulated by state law. The banking association also argued that since the CBCTs were places where "deposits are received, checks paid or money lent," they reached the status of "branch." *Held:* CBCTs were found to be branches and subject to state regulations as provided by Section 36(f). Each of the bank functions could be interpreted broadly enough to satisfy the meaning of the language of Section 36(f).

[Independent Bankers Ass'n of Am. v. Smith, 534 F2d 912 (DC Cir. 1976)]

[1]　Interstate Branching Restrictions

State statutes providing for bank acquisitions on regional basis are consistent with Douglas Amendment and not discriminatory against out-of-region bank holding companies.　Several New England bank holding companies applied to the Federal

Reserve Board for approval to acquire banks in New England states other than the ones in which they were principally located. Competitors opposed the acquisitions as not being authorized by the Douglas Amendment to the Bank Holding Company Act; and, moreover, if such acquisitions were authorized by the Douglas Amendment, the state statutes in question were discriminatory against non–New England bank holding companies. The Bank Holding Company Act regulates the acquisition of state and national banks by bank holding companies, and the Douglas Amendment to that Act prohibits a bank holding company or bank located in one state to acquire a bank in another state. Connecticut and Massachusetts had enacted statutes that selectively authorized interstate bank acquisition on a regional basis. *Held:* The Connecticut and Massachusetts statutes fell within the intention of the Douglas Amendment. Also, the Court found no discrimination against non–New England out-of-state bank holding companies.

[Northeast Bancorp v. Board of Governors of the Fed. Reserve Sys., 472 US 159 (1985)]

Where state law prohibits branch banking, competitive equality policy forecloses Comptroller of the Currency from modifying that standard in favor of national bank. A national bank in Florida provided an armored car pickup service for deposits one mile from its main office. Florida prohibited branch banking at the time, and under the McFadden Act a national bank could establish branches only under the same terms as state law authorized a state bank to do so. The Supreme Court had to determine whether this "mobile drive-in" facility, serviced daily by an armored car, was, in effect, "branch banking" prohibited by Florida law and contrary to the policy of "competitive equality" between national and state banks. *Held:* The mobile drive-in service was indeed a branch bank under the National Bank Act (12 USC § 36(f)) and, therefore, following the policy of competitive equality, the national bank was in violation of state law.

[First Nat'l Bank in Plant City v. Dickinson, 396 US 122 (1969)]

National bank may establish branches in accordance with requirements and conditions applicable to state banks by state law. Under Utah law, banks could open branches only if they took over an established bank. The Comptroller of the Currency issued certificates for several national banks in Utah to open branches, in violation of this state law. The Comptroller argued that Utah's established bank-takeover restriction did not apply to national banks, and, moreover, the federal law superseded state law only as to "whether" and "where" branches may be located and not the "method" by which branches may be created. *Held:* National banks may establish branches only as provided by state law to state banks. Congress, the court held, intended to place national and state banks on a basis of "competitive equality" insofar as branch banking was concerned.

[First Nat'l Bank of Logan v. Walker Bank & Trust, 385 US 252 (1966)]

National banks granted privilege to branch statewide.   State banks in Mississippi were not allowed by state statute to branch statewide. The Comptroller of the Currency approved a national bank's application to open a branch bank, and the state banking commission obtained an injunction from the district court. In its appeal, the Comptroller equated the functions of state banks with state savings associations. By state law, banks were not allowed to branch outside the county, whereas savings associations were allowed to branch statewide. The Comptroller argued that savings associations were, in effect, banks by function and, therefore, if they were allowed by statute to branch statewide, a national bank should be allowed to branch statewide as well. *Held:* The savings associations were engaged in banking business within the meaning of the National Bank Act, 12 USC § 36(h), and the statutory freedom granted them to branch statewide should be extended to national banks as well.

[Department of Banking & Consumer Fin. v. Clarke, 809 F2d 266 (5th Cir. 1987)]

Computer terminal banking is considered branch banking under National Bank Act.   The Illinois State Commission of Banking sought declaratory and injunctive relief with respect to whether banks' CBCTs were branch banks under the National Bank Act (12 USC § 36(f)). The district court had held they were, except for the withdrawing of cash by the use of cash cards and payments made on installment loans, permissible functions for CBCTs and not to be considered "branch banking." *Held:* The CBCTs were branch banks and the banks were permanently enjoined from using the system. Moreover, the withdrawal of funds by use of cash cards, which the district court had found not to be a banking function, was also "banking," in that (1) these cards functioned essentially as check cashing, and (2) the cards served the same purpose as a check.

[Illinois ex rel. Lignoul v. Continental Ill., 536 F2d 176 (7th Cir. 1976)]

In Missouri, electronic banking terminals are branch banks in violation of federal and state law.   Missouri law allowed each bank to have only three separate locations. First National Bank of St. Louis opened two electronic banking terminals (CBCTs) separate and apart from its three bank locations. The Missouri Commission of Finance sued for alleged violation of the branch banking law. *Held:* Under the definition of "branch banking" provided by the National Bank Act, 12 USC § 36(f), these CBCTs constituted branch banks in violation of federal and state laws.

[Missouri ex rel. Kostman v. First Nat'l Bank, 538 F2d 219 (8th Cir. 1976)]

In Colorado, electronic banking terminal is branch bank as described in National Bank Act, and therefore prohibited by Colorado law.   Colorado law prohibits branch banking. The First National Bank of Fort Collins opened a CBCT two miles from its main bank building, and the state banking board sought a declaratory judgment on the issue of whether the withdrawal of money and transfer of funds from savings to checking accounts by the use of the CBCT constituted branch banking. *Held:* The banking functions of this CBCT fell within the definition of "branch banking" provided by the National Bank Act (12 USC § 36(f)); therefore, the national bank in this case must conform with the state law, which precludes branch banking.

[Colorado State Banking Board v. First Nat'l Bank of Fort Collins, 540 F2d 497 (10th Cir. 1976)]

[2] Unauthorized Banking Services

When bank installs computer banking terminal in retail store, store is not engaged in illegal or unauthorized branch banking business. The State of Nebraska brought an action against a supermarket chain for opening computer banking terminals within its stores. The state alleged that by receiving deposits and paying withdrawals, the stores were carrying on the business of banking in violation of state banking laws and guidelines. The American Community Stores Corp. argued that the computer terminal was analogous to communications equipment in that it simply transmitted information to the central computer of First Federal, the bank that had installed them. *Held:* The store was simply the operational intermediary between the depositor and First Federal, and such an operation did not constitute illegal banking by the store nor the carrying on of unauthorized branch banking business.

[Nebraska ex rel. Meyer v. American Community Stores Corp., 228 NW2d 299 (Neb. 1975)]

¶ 14.02 ANTITRUST CONSIDERATIONS

As with mergers, joint ventures are subject to Clayton Act criteria in determining lessening of competition or creating a monopoly. The chemical companies, Pennsalt and Olin, jointly formed Penn-Olin to produce sodium chlorate for a burgeoning southeastern market. The government sought to dissolve the joint venture for violating federal antitrust laws. The companies argued that Section 7 of the Clayton Act (15 USC § 12 et seq.), prohibiting joint ventures that effectively lessen competition or create a monopoly, did not apply to their progeny, a newly formed company, but only to acquired companies presently engaged in commerce. *Held:* The companies' Section 7 argument was rejected because the formation of a joint venture would substantially lessen, if not foreclose, actual or potential competition between the companies. Moreover, the same considerations apply to joint ventures as to mergers, and Section 7 of the Clayton Act, which addresses threats of mergers and acquisition that the Sherman Anti-Trust Act (15 USC § 1 et seq.) does not reach, provides the criteria used in determining the probability of the lessening of competition. The Court remanded, with instruction to apply the Section 7 factors.

[United States v. Penn-Olin Chem. Co., 378 US 158 (1964)]

[1] Market Effects and Reduced Competition

New York Stock Exchange exceeds scope of self-regulatory power in boycotting two broker-dealers.   Two nonmember broker-dealers in securities had their temporarily approved direct wire telephone connection to the New York Stock Exchange (NYSE) abruptly discontinued by the NYSE. The broker-dealers brought suit, claiming that the denial of their applications without notice and hearing reached beyond the NYSE's privilege of self-regulation, since it was in effect a group boycott, and constituted a violation of Section 1 of the Sherman Anti-Trust Act. *Held:* The protection of the Securities Exchange Act afforded no justification for anticompetitive, collective action taken without accorded fair procedures. The NYSE plainly exceeded the scope of its authority under the Act to engage in self-regulation.

[Silver v. New York Stock Exch., 373 US 341 (1963)]

Scheme to monopolize news-gathering service distribution, benefitting members to the exclusion of others, violates federal antitrust laws.   The Associated Press (AP) set up a system of by-laws that prohibited AP members from selling news to nonmembers, and that granted each member powers to block its nonmember competitors from membership. The United States charged a violation of the Sherman Anti-Trust Act in that the AP's acts constituted a combination and conspiracy in restraint of trade and commerce in news and also an attempt to monopolize that trade. The lower court granted the government summary judgment. *Held:* The AP's by-laws hindered and restrained the sale of interstate news to nonmembers who competed with members. The Sherman Act prohibits independent businesses from becoming "associates" in a common plan that will reduce competitors' opportunity to buy or sell the things for which the group competes. Application of the Sherman Act was appropriate and services a First Amendment freedom of the press abridgment argument.

[Associated Press v. United States, 326 US 1 (1945)]

Association formed to unify railroad terminal service violates federal antitrust laws by maintaining too much control over access to city crucial to interstate commerce.   The railroad companies of St. Louis combined and created a unitary system of terminal service, the Terminal Railroad Association, to obtain every feasible means of railroad access in to St. Louis. The association argued that the unification of facilities was an aid to interstate commerce and not an unreasonable restraint. *Held:* Monopolization of commerce by the terminal association, constituted an illegal restraint of interstate traffic. The terminal association, by using the physical locality, succeeded in obtaining total control of the terminal facilities and terminal traffic.

[United States v. St. Louis Terminal, 224 US 383 (1912)]

[2] Ancillary Restraint: Joint Action

Company's conspiracy with other distributors to set prices and failure to renew distributor's contract under its terms violates Sherman Act. Spray-Rite Service Corp. was a successful, authorized distributor of Monsanto herbicides when Monsanto terminated the distributorship, citing poor sales practices. Spray-Rite brought an antitrust action, alleging that Monsanto and some of the other distributors conspired to fix the resale prices of Monsanto herbicides and that Monsanto encouraged a boycott against Spray-Rite. *Held:* The Court found sufficient evidence of a "conscious commitment to a common scheme designed to achieve an unlawful objective" and found Monsanto and its distributors parties to an agreement or conspiracy to maintain set resale prices and terminate price cutters such as Spray-Rite. Moreover, Spray-Rite's termination was also part of this unlawful agreement, and therefore Monsanto violated Section 1 of the Sherman Act.

[Monsanto Co. v. Spray-Rite Serv. Corp., 465 US 752 (1984)]

Governing association's effort to limit televised college football games violates antitrust law. In the face of a National Collegiate Athletic Association (NCAA) plan limiting the television coverage of member football games, a group of football-playing universities, the College Football Association, negotiated its own contract with NBC. Facing NCAA discipline for its actions, the Football Association sued under the Sherman Anti-Trust Act, claiming restraint of competition. The NCAA argued that its plan of limiting broadcasts was procompetitive, a cooperative joint venture that assisted in marketing broadcast rights and protected live attendance. *Held:* The Court found no justification for the NCAA's restrictions. Under the rule of reason, the NCAA plan's anticompetitive limitation and its claims of procompetitive justification were in violation of antitrust laws.

[NCAA v. Board of Regents of Univ. of Okla., 468 US 85 (1984)]

Credit card system's by-law restricting banks from dual major credit card issuance must be analyzed under rule of reason standard. BankAmericard, a major credit card system, prohibited its card-issuing banks from issuing cards of a rival system. Worthen Bank won a summary judgment, where the court found such a restrictive by-law to be a per se violation of Section 1 of the Sherman Anti-Trust Act. The bankcard system appealed, arguing that under a rule of reason standard that critically analyzed the competitive effects and possible justification of the restrictive by-law, the case should be tried on its merits. *Held:* The summary judgment was reversed and the case remanded with direction to implement the rule-of-reason standard.

[Worthen Bank & Trust v. National BankAmericard, 485 F2d 119 (8th Cir. 1973)]

Credit card system's interchange rate has procompetitive effect. Visa U.S.A. fixed its interchange rate so that member banks in its system could readily do business with each other. NaBanco, a processing agent for various banks, was in effect an "outsider," and could not compete with this low interchange fee. NaBanco claimed price fixing and unlawful restraint of trade. NaBanco argued that the Issuer's Reimbursement Fee (IRF) restricts competition between proprietary Visa members (card issuers) and merchant signing members. Visa argued that the IRF had a net procompetitive effect. *Held:* The court balanced the procompetitive and anticompetitive purposes and effects and decided that the restraint did not substantially impede competition. The IRF maintains stability in the system and acts as an internal control mechanism that helps members create a product they could not produce singly.

[National Bancard Corp. (NaBanco) v. Visa USA, Inc., 779 F2d 592 (11th Cir. 1986)]

Regional ATM system's aggressive effort to increase market share does not violate federal antitrust laws. The TREASURER, Inc., and PNB MAC systems were regional ATM networks. PNB planned a merger agreement with another bank, which TREASURER claimed would give PNB monopoly power in the regional ATM market. TREASURER asserted violations of the Sherman Anti-Trust and Clayton Acts, and applied for a temporary restraining order and preliminary injunction. *Held:* TREASURER did not demonstrate any antitrust injury; it was free to compete with MAC for the merging banks' system members. Rather than a monopolistic intent on the part of MAC, the court found "an obviously successful, comprehensive marketing strategy," and dismissed the case.

[The TREASURER, Inc. v. Philadelphia Nat'l Bank, 682 F. Supp. 269 (DNJ 1988)]

[3] Essential Facilities and Access

Rule-of-reason standard should be applied in antitrust cases that involve restrictions on retailer's freedom to dispose of purchased products. GTE Sylvania sought to limit retail franchises and control its TV sales locations. A retailer, Continental, claimed those restrictions violated the Sherman Anti-Trust Act. *Held:* When anticompetitive effects are shown to result from particular vertical restrictions, they can be adequately policed under the rule of reason; and under this standard, GTE was not in violation of antitrust law. The Court used this case to overrule *United States v. Arnold Schwinn & Co.*, 338 US 365 (1967), which held that the buying and selling of Schwinn bicycles through territorial and customer restrictions was per se illegal. Under the rule of reason, the fact finder must weigh all the circumstances of a case in deciding whether a restrictive practice should be prohibited as imposing an unreasonable restraint on competition. Per se rules are appropriate only when they relate to conduct that is manifestly anticompetitive. The Court returned to the rule-of-reason standard that governed vertical restrictions prior to *Schwinn.*

[Continental TV, Inc. v. GTE Sylvania, 433 US 36 (1977)]

Nevada statute permitting state banks to charge fee to ATM network users does not violate Commerce Clause of U.S. Constitution. A Nevada bank sought to charge a separate transaction fee to ATM users as provided by Nevada statute. The purpose of the statute was to enable deployment of more ATM machines and therefore provide better service to tourists. Plus System, Inc. claimed that the statute violated the Commerce Clause. Plus argued that the statute directly regulates and discriminates in favor of Nevada and against interstate commerce, in itself the kind of activity not suited to diverse regulation by the states. *Held:* The statute furthers legitimate state interests and, on balance, does not impose an excessive burden on interstate commerce. Nor does it constitute direct regulation of interstate commerce or discrimination against interstate commerce.

[Valley Bank of Nevada v. Plus Sys., Inc., 914 F2d 1186 (9th Cir. 1990)]

¶ 14.03 ELECTRONIC FUNDS TRANSFER ACT

Transfers of funds initiated by telephone conversation are not covered under EFTA. The amount of $4,900 was transferred from Kashanchi's savings account following a telephone conversation between a bank employee and someone other than Kashanchi. When the bank refused to recredit the account, Kashanchi sued under the EFTA (15 USC § 1693). *Held:* The withdrawal of funds was not covered by the

EFTA. Congress intended to exclude from EFTA's coverage any transfer of funds initiated by a telephone conversation between any natural person and an officer or employee of a financial institution, which was not made pursuant to a prearranged plan and under which periodic and recurring transfers were not contemplated.

[Kashanchi v. Texas Commerce Medical Bank, NA, 703 F2d 936 (5th Cir. 1983)]

¶ 14.04 LIABILITY FOR FRAUDULENT USE

EFTA does not entitle ATM card user to funds after reporting ATM cards as stolen and then perpetrating fraud on the bank. Goldblatt's son used Goldblatt's ATM cards to withdraw money after Goldblatt had reported the cards stolen. Goldblatt failed to identify photos of his son as the person engaging in unauthorized ATM transactions. He then signed an affidavit stating that the withdrawals were not made with his permission and that he would assist in the criminal prosecution of the unauthorized user. He was then granted access to his funds, and withdrew $900. When the bank realized that it was Goldblatt's son who had used the cards, it seized the remainder of Goldblatt's account. On appeal from his conviction for bank fraud and bank larceny, Goldblatt argued that under the EFTA (15 USC § 1693) he was entitled to the money in his account, that at the time of his $900 withdrawal he was the owner of the funds, and that he was entitled to them unless it could be shown that his son's withdrawals had been authorized by him. *Held:* Goldblatt waived his rights under the EFTA when he lied after failing to identify his son in the photo shown to him by bank employees.

[United States v. Goldblatt, 813 F2d 619 (3d Cir. 1987)]

PART B.   CHECKS AND FUNDS TRANSFER LAW

¶ 14.05 GENERAL LEGAL ISSUES OF
FUNDS TRANSFERS

Bank may have duty to mutual fund shareholders to scrutinize directions on memorandum portion of incoming check. A shareholder of a mutual fund stock mailed a check for $21,000 to the Bank of New York with a note to apply it to a new investment. In a brief annotation on the check, he wrote the name of the newly desired investment as well. The bank applied the money to the old fund, which lost most of the $21,000, lost the directing note, and refused to reimburse the shareholder, who then sued for conversion and negligence. The bank argued that it had no duty to read and act on the memorandum portion of the check. *Held:* Although generally a bank owes no duty to its clients to scrutinize directions placed on the memorandum portion of an incoming check, it might have such a duty where it assumes such an obligation by its own procedures for processing checks. The trial court's judgment in favor of the shareholder was reversed and the case remanded.

[Woods v. Bank of NY, 806 F2d 368 (2d Cir. 1986)]

¶ 14.06 FINAL PAYMENT AND DATA PROCESSING

Upon receipt of check in processing center, payor bank must pay, return, or dishonor check before midnight of following banking day pursuant to UCC. Barry drew 10 checks payable to Chrysler Credit Corporation in the sum of $53,337.75. They were received at the payor bank's main branch and processing center, and two days later were dishonored as drawn on uncollected funds. Chrysler sued to recover the money, arguing that under the Pennsylvania UCC (13 Pa. Cons. Stat. Ann. § 4302(1)), a payor bank must pay, return, or dishonor a check before midnight of the next banking day, or be liable for the amount of the worthless check. *Held:* Chrysler was entitled to the amount of the dishonored checks. The midnight deadline of Section 4302 is to be measured from the time checks are presented to a payor bank's computer processing center.

[Chrysler Credit Corp. v. First Nat'l Bank & Trust Co. of Wash., 746 F2d 200 (3d Cir. 1984)]

¶ 14.07 EFFECT ON STOP ORDERS

Amounts in excess of $100,000 mistakenly paid by FDIC to holders of cashier's checks drawn against insolvent bank must be restored to FDIC under National Bank Act. Just prior to its insolvency, a bank wrote three cashier's checks for substantially more than the $100,000 limit that the FDIC guaranties. The amounts were mistakenly paid by the FDIC computer, which had been programmed to reject any items in excess of $100,000. Upon discovery, the FDIC brought an action to recover the amounts above the insured limit. The defendants argued that they were good-faith holders in due course, entitled to the application of the "final payment" rule (UCC § 3-418). The FDIC maintained that the defendants were now creditors of an insolvent national bank, and as such their rights and liabilities became fixed by the National Bank Act, 12 USC § 191, which has precedent over the UCC. *Held:* Insured deposits, including outstanding cashier's checks and any amount inadvertently paid over the $100,000 limit, constitute unjust enrichment to which the FDIC is entitled in restitution.

[FDIC v. McKnight, 769 F2d 658 (10th Cir. 1985)]

PART C.   FUNDS TRANSFERS UNDER ARTICLE 4A

¶ 14.08 CREATION OF RIGHTS AND OBLIGATIONS

Banks are liable to suspected drug traffickers where electronic transmission of funds to banks in Europe and South America are suspended by government order. New York banks cooperating with the government stopped the electronic transmission of suspected drug money to banks in Europe and South America. Claimants to the funds sued for loss of use of the funds, and the Banks moved to dismiss. *Held:* The court dismissed the complaints, holding simply that those assisting the government are not liable to those claiming ownership to already forfeited funds. The claimants had no cause of action against the banks, either under forfeiture proceedings or under a variety of other claims, i.e., the right to privacy, conversion, or negligence. Claimants failed to state a claim under any federal or state theory.

[Manufacturers Int'l, LTDA v. Manufacturers Hanover Trust Co., 792 F. Supp. 180 (EDNY 1992)]

¶ 14.09 MISTAKE AND RESTITUTION

In New York, mistaken electronic transfer of funds is governed by "discharge for value" rule. Security Pacific Bank mistakenly wired nearly $2 million on behalf of Spedley Securities to the account of Bank of Worms. Security Pacific asked for its return under the "mistake of fact" doctrine, which states that if the receiver has not changed position to its detriment it must return the money. Bank of Worms, however, as a creditor of Spedley, argued that it should retain the errant transfer under the "discharge for value" rule, which states that a creditor of another who receives benefit from a third party in discharge of the debt or lien is under no duty to make restitution. *Held:* As a creditor of Spedley, Bank of Worms was a beneficiary entitled to the funds under the "discharge for value" rule. Under the provisions of New York's UCC Article 4A, electronic payments are the same as cash, irrevocable except to the extent provided by the article. Moreover, the discharge-for-value rule may appropriately be applied to electronic transfers.

[Bank of Worms v. Bankamerican Int'l, 77 NY2d 362, 570 NE2d 189 (1991)]

PART D.   ELECTRONIC DATA INTERCHANGE

¶ 14.10 ENFORCEABILITY: STATUTE OF FRAUDS

Convincing foundation testimony is sufficient to establish authenticity of faxed document.   In an effort to lease office space, Hagan altered a bank statement (to show favorable balances) and faxed it to a corporate real estate firm. The firm faxed a copy to the bank for verification, and subsequently Hagan was charged with fraud. Hagan attempted to discredit the authenticity of the faxed documents in the face of substantial evidence against his assertions of lack of proof. *Held:* Sufficient evidence was found to establish authenticity. The court relied primarily on properly established foundation testimony regarding fax transmissions. The sources of information and method and time of preparation indicated trustworthiness and justified admission.

[People v. Hagan, 583 NE2d 494 (Ill. 1991)]

¶ 14.11 TERMS AND CONDITIONS IN ELECTRONIC CONTRACTING

Seller's "box-top" license is not part of computer products sales agreement, and seller's disclaimers are unenforceable under UCC.   TSL sold computer products to Step-Saver Data Systems. Upon complaints from its customers regarding TSL's system, Step-Saver sued TSL for breach of warranties. TSL disclaimed all warranties by the use of a "box-top" license. Step-Saver argued that this box-top license was not intended by the contracting parties to be the complete and final expression of the terms of their agreements; and that, on the contrary, it was an alternative to the parties' contract under Section 2-207 of the UCC. *Held:* Step-Saver was not bound by the terms of the box-top license, which did not constitute a conditional acceptance under Section 2-207(1) of the UCC. Moreover, under Section 2-207(2)(b), the disclaimer of warranty of the box-top license did not become a part of the parties' agreement.

[Step-Saver Data Sys., Inc. v. Wyse Technology, 939 F2d 91 (3d Cir. 1991)]

Secretary of Interior has discretion to reject oil and gas lease bid that does not contain holographic signature.   Gilmore appealed a rejection of his oil and gas lease offer by the Bureau of Land Management, which refused the offer because it did not contain a holographic signature as required by the bureau's regulations. *Held:* It was within the bureau's discretion not to depart from its regulations in this case.

The court's own decision was "compelled by the narrow scope of the court's review of agency decisions."

[Gilmore v. Lujan, 947 F2d 1407 (9th Cir. 1991)]

¶ 14.12 USE OF ELECTRONIC DATA INTERCHANGE IN COMMERCIAL SETTINGS

Failure to implement franchisor's computer network is sufficient cause to terminate franchise where new network is found to be both essential and reasonable requirement.   International Harvestor sought to terminate its truck franchise agreement with Groseth International because Groseth refused to comply with Harvestor's requirements for a computerized communications system, the network. The issue was whether there was good cause to terminate the franchise under the essential and reasonable provisions of South Dakota law. *Held:* Groseth's failure to implement the network was good cause for Harvestor's termination of the franchise in view of the "essential and reasonable" provisions of the applicable South Dakota statute. A franchisor seeking to terminate a franchise must show that it has good cause for termination. Implementation of the network was a necessary step in the effort to reorganize Harvestor.

[In re Groseth Int'l, Inc., 442 NW2d 229 (SD 1989)]

¶ 14.13 SERVICES PROVIDER OBLIGATIONS

Oil pipeline service provider is 50 percent negligent when its computerized trading system mistakenly sends product to wrong party.   Shell Pipeline had developed a computerized trading system to handle the increase in oil trading in the product that flowed through its "common stream" pipeline. Because of a confusion in similar names on stationery, 93,000 barrels of oil were misdelivered by Shell's computerized trading system. The oil trader that sold the oil, Coastal, was then unable to recover its money when the beneficiary of the mistake filed for bankruptcy. Coastal sued Shell for negligence. *Held:* Shell was 50 percent negligent as the service provider; Coastal and its trading partners were 50 percent negligent. Coastal's loss was $2,824,700, and it was awarded $1,412,350.

[Shell Pipeline v. Coastal States Trading, 788 SW2d 837 (Tex. Ct. App. 1990)]

CHAPTER **15**

INFORMATION PRODUCTS: ELECTRONIC PUBLISHING

PART A.   GENERAL ISSUES

¶ 15.01 INFORMATION PRODUCTS

Statute that is not narrowly tailored to serve a significant government interest is facially unconstitutional and violates First Amendment right to free expression. C&P of Virginia provided local wireline telephone exchange and exchange access service in portions of Virginia, including the city of Alexandria, and is a common carrier subject to the Cable Communications Policy Act of 1984, 47 USC §§ 533(b)(1) and 533(b)(2), which prohibits telephone companies from providing video programming. After C&P failed to obtain a cable franchise from Alexandria, it sued the United States, challenging Section 533(b) as violative of the First Amendment of the U.S. Constitution, both facially and as applied to its proposed provision of video programming in the city of Alexandria. *Held:* Section 533(b) is facially unconstitutional as a violation of plaintiff's First Amendment right to free expression. The statute is content-neutral, and must be subjected to the intermediate level of scrutiny applicable to both "time, place, and manner restrictions" and to incidental burdens on speech. A statute will pass the intermediate level of scrutiny if, in addition to being content-neutral, it (1) is narrowly tailored to serve a significant government interest and (2) leaves open ample alternative channels for communication. As to the second element, C&P was by no means "silenced" by the operation of Section 533(b). C&P remained unfettered in its ability to communicate by any means other than video programming. As to the first element, the government contended that Section 533(b) served two separate but related government interests: promoting competition in the video programming market and preserving diversity in the ownership of communications media. The court determined that Section 533(b) did not, in a direct fashion, promote competition in the video programming market; the statute actually served as a bar to entry into video transport services and the video programming market. The court also found that the statute was not narrowly tailored to serve the government's interest in preserving diversity in the ownership of communications media. Section 533(b) regulates anticompetitive behavior in the video programming market, and no evidence suggested that the standard methods of regulation would be ineffective to control anticompetitive activities by the telephone companies in the video programming market. Effective alternatives exist that would allow telephone companies to enter the cable television market, yet prevent the evils Section 533(b) targeted. As such, Section 533(b) was not "narrowly tailored to serve a significant government interest," but instead, the statute burdened substantially more speech than was necessary to further the government's legitimate interests.

[Chesapeake & Potomac Tel. Co. v. United States, 830 F. Supp. 909 (ED Va. 1993)]

State law banning automated telemarketing devices for commercial solicitations is unconstitutional under Oregon constitution. Moser operated a business that used automatic dialing and announcing devices to solicit customers. He brought action seeking declaratory judgment that an Oregon statute, Or. Rev. Stat. § 759.290, forbidding the use of such devices "to solicit the purchase of any realty, goods or services" but excepting application of the law to charitable and political organizations, was unconstitutional under both the state and federal constitutions. *Held:* Audio recordings constitute speech. Therefore, the statute violates the Oregon constitution because it impermissibly restricts speech with respect to content (commercial), manner (automatic dialing), and classification (charitable and political entities versus all others). The state constitution protects communication in whatever form it takes, whether it is person-to-person, via telephone, computer, etc. Although some content-based restrictions are permissible if wholly confined within some well-established historical exception, no exception was applicable here. Finally, a statute may be constitutional if its focus, as written, is on an identifiable, actual harmful effect or serious and imminent harm that may be proscribed, rather than on the communication itself. The instant statute does not meet this test. It is broader than the comparable federal statute, 47 USC § 227, which restricts its focus to solicitation of *residences* as opposed to businesses.

[Moser v. Frohnmayer, 845 P2d 1284 (Or. 1993)]

¶ 15.02 ANTITRUST, TYING, AND ESSENTIAL DATA SERVICES

[1] Essential Facility Access

Obtaining market dominance through superior product or superior marketing does not violate antitrust restrictions. ASC owned three skiing ranges in Aspen in competition with one range owned by AHS. After a period or more than 10 years during which the two competitors (and a third, which was later bought out by ASC) cooperated in selling "six-day 4-area tickets" (4AT) that allowed skiers to use both companies' ranges and paid each company according to its share of skiers, ASC tried to freeze AHS out by selling its own multi-area pass and refusing to sell further 4ATs in cooperation with AHS unless AHS accepted an unacceptable, low flat-fee percentage on all 4AT sales, irrespective of skier use. After a jury found that ASC violated Section 2 of the Sherman Act, ASC appealed, arguing that there cannot be a requirement of cooperation between competitors. *Held:* ASC's predatory conduct violated antitrust laws, and ASC had no valid business reason not to deal with AHS. ASC did not merely reject a novel offer to participate in a competitive venture proposed by a competitor, but to change the character of the pattern of ticket distribution that had originated in a competitive market and that had persisted for several years. The judge properly instructed the jury to determine the distinction between practices that tend to exclude or restrict competition on the one hand, and the success of a business that reflects only a superior product, a well-run business, or luck, on the other. There is no general duty to engage in a joint marketing program with a competitor, since a businessman has the right to select his customers and associates. However, this right is not unqualified.

[Aspen Skiing Co. v. Aspen Highlands Skiing Co., 472 US 585 (1985)]

Refusal to grant access to essential facility violates Section 2 of Sherman Act.
MCI sued AT&T, inter alia, for violating Section 2 of the Sherman Anti-Trust Act by denying it access to an essential facility, that is, use of AT&T's intercity telephone services, including point-to-point private lines, foreign exchange lines, and common control switching arrangements. AT&T appealed a jury verdict in favor of MCI. *Held:* AT&T violated Section 2 of the Sherman Act by refusing to connect MCI to its network, a facility that could not be duplicated feasibly. This refusal eliminated competition, rather than merely impeding it. AT&T could have feasibly provided these services. The record revealed no legitimate business or technical reason for AT&T's denial of the requested interconnections. AT&T had the power to eliminate competition in a downstream market, exercised this power, and thereby monopolized the market. Thus, there was sufficient evidence to satisfy the four elements of liability under the essential facilities doctrine: (1) control of the essential facility by a monopolist, (2) a competitor's inability practically or reasonably to duplicate the essential facility, (3) the denial of the use of the facility to a competitor, and (4) the feasibility of providing the facility.

[MCI Communications v. American Tel. & Tel., 708 F2d 1081 (7th Cir.), cert. denied, 464 US 891 (1983)]

Firm only violates "essential facilities" doctrine if it eliminates downstream competition. Alaska Airlines brought suit against defendants, United Airlines and American Airlines, claiming that the airlines had *individually* violated Section 2 of the Sherman Anti-Trust Act in operating their proprietary computerized reservation systems (CRSs). Alaska claimed that the airlines denied reasonable access to their CRSs (by extracting substantial booking fees for their use), which they alleged to be "essential facilities" and that they used their dominance in the CRS market to gain competitive advantage in the downstream air transportation market. *Held:* There was no violation of Section 2, since the airlines never refused Alaska access to their CRSs. The "essential facilities" doctrine imposes liability when one firm, which controls an essential facility, denies a second firm reasonable access to a product or service that the second firm must obtain to compete with the first; it does not impose liabilty in cases such as this where the airlines' respective CRSs did not give them power to *eliminate* competition in the downstream air transportation market. The airlines' CRSs constituted less than 14 percent of their relevant market, and therefore their ability to abuse downstream competitors by manipulating their CRSs was severely limited. That the airlines profited from their CRSs at their rivals' expense is not actionable under Section 2. Market restraints precluded the airlines from raising fees to exclusionary levels, since they would destroy their own CRSs rather than their competition. Finally, because there was no violation of Section 2 under the above theory, Alaska's claim that the airlines "leveraged" their monopolistic advantage in CRSs to gain advantage in other downstream markets was also untenable.

[Alaska Airlines, Inc. v. United Airlines, 948 F2d 536 (9th Cir. 1991)]

Although a data base may constitute an essential resource, its owner does not violate antitrust law in refusing to make such data available to potential competitor on commercial terms. FPI owned a data base in its white and yellow pages telephone directories, and refused to grant RTS a commercial license for the white pages. RTS went ahead and used FPI's white pages. When FPI sued for copyright infringement (which suit RTS won in a Supreme Court decision, *Feist Publications, Inc. v. Rural Telephone Service Co.*, 111 S. Ct. 1282 (1991)), RTS counterclaimed that FPI's refusal to grant it a license was an act designed to maintain its monopoly position and was anticompetitive in effect. RTS appealed the lower court's decision that it violated Section 2 of the Sherman Anti-Trust Act. *Held:* There was no violation of Section 2 since FPI failed to prove that RTS's refusal to deal had anticompetitive effects. To prove a violation of Section 2, the plaintiff must show first, that the monopolist's conduct had anticompetitive effects and second, that it had an illicit motivation for its action (i.e., that it was not done for legitimate business reasons). Intent to stifle competition, absent anticompetitive effect, is insufficient to establish a Section 2 violation. FPI could not identify anyone who refused to purchase advertising in their yellow pages because of the incompleteness of their listings. Indeed, during the period in question, FPI gained a 20 percent share of the relevant market.

[Rural Tel. Serv. Co. v. Feist Publications, Inc., 957 F2d 765 (10th Cir. 1992)]

[2] Tying and Leveraging

Realty board requiring realtors to acquire associate membership to qualify for access to computerized multiple listing service does not constitute antitrust "tying" arrangement. WRE, a real estate firm, sued GLBR, a trade organization of realtors, claiming that GLBR's conditioning access to its multiple listing service (MLS) of real estate on membership in the GLBR constituted an impermissible tying arrangement, a per se violation of the Sherman Anti-Trust Act. The MLS system gave the exclusive right to sell listed houses to GLBR members under a negotiated fee-splitting arrangement that effectively precluded nonmembers from attempting to broker sales of those homes. WRE appealed a directed verdict in favor of GLBR. *Held:* It is doubtful whether this situation constituted a tying of separate products, since GLBR is not a "seller" of sale listings but a trade organization. While membership does have its privileges—access to the MLS—it also brings with it certain responsibilities (e.g., to adhere to constitution and by-laws of national association). To show an illegal tying arrangement, WRE had to prove (1) a tie existing between two separate products where purchase of one is conditioned on purchase of the other, (2) that the seller had sufficient market power to compel acceptance of the tying arrangement, and (3) that the tie affected a "not insubstantial" amount of interstate commerce in the tied product's market. WRE failed to prove the first element. It also failed to prove the existence of a market in membership in real estate boards, let alone that a substantial volume of commerce in such memberships was foreclosed by the tie-in, or that the tie-in had any anticompetitive effects.

[Wells Real Estate, Inc. v. Greater Lowell Bd. of Realtors, 850 F2d 803 (1st Cir. 1988)]

Single firm may be liable for "monopoly leveraging" even in absence of threat that the leveraged market will be monopolized. Kodak had a monopoly in the film and camera markets. Berkey sued, contending that Kodak had leveraged its dominant position in these areas to gain an advantage in the photofinishing equipment and services markets. The record indicated that Kodak was never close to gaining and did not attempt to monopolize either of these markets. *Held:* Kodak violated Section 2 of the Sherman Anti-Trust Act by using its monopoly power in one market to gain a competitive advantage in another, even though it did not attempt to monopolize the second market. Monopolies are tolerated only insofar as necessary to preserve competitive incentives and to be fair to the firm that has attained its position innocently. There is no reason to tolerate them, however, where power is wielded to the detriment of competition in either the controlled or any other market. That competition in the leveraged market may not be destroyed but merely distorted does not make it more palatable. Social and economic policy dictates against allowing such extension of monopoly power.

[Berkey Photo, Inc. v. Eastman Kodak Co., 603 F2d 263 (2d Cir. 1979)]

Forcing buyers to use computerized ticketing system to lease unique facility constitutes antitrust tying.   TXP sued OPC for violating Section 1 of the Sherman Anti-Trust Act by conditioning (1) the lease of seats at the Omni, the largest local arena, on (2) the use of SEATS, an affiliated computerized ticket-selling agency under common ownership and management, to sell tickets. OPC appealed the lower court's finding in favor of TXP. *Held:* The tying arrangement challenged here was particularly destructive to competition since it made it unlikely that any prospective competitor would risk investing the amount of money required to develop a competing computerized system in light of the virtual impossibility of ever getting any Omni business because of the tying arrangement. The principal evil of tie-ins is that they foreclose competition *on the merits* in the tied market by forcing buyers to purchase one product in the package, the tied product, by virtue of the seller's control or dominance over the other product in the package, the tying product. OPC had sufficient market power to force acceptance of the tie-in because Omni is a unique facility because of its size and configuration. Further, this tie-in arrangement clearly affected the tied market, since TXP's $10,000 in lost profits was a "not insubstantial amount of interstate commerce."

[Tic-X-Press, Inc. v. Omni Promotions Co., 815 F2d 1407 (11th Cir. 1987)]

¶ 15.03 CONTRACTS AND ESSENTIAL SERVICES

Specific performance may be available where defendants breach agreement to share unique data base information.   TUC, a national data-processing and credit-reporting service, entered into an agreement with CBC, a credit bureau controlling 95 percent of the market in the Cincinnati area, to provide one another with unrestricted access to computer files of credit information at set prices. Because of this agreement, TUC postponed a plan to develop its own files of credit information in competition with CBC in the Cincinnati area. Shortly after the agreement was executed, ACS, a national competitor of TUC, bought all outstanding CBC shares. TUC sued, requesting specific performance of the agreement. CBC opposed, claiming that TUC had breached the contract. *Held:* TUC did not breach the agreement and CBC must perform under it. An award of specific performance was appropriate here given the unique value of CBC's data base to TUC and the corresponding inadequacy of any remedy at law to compensate TUC for the loss of it. Here, the damages to TUC as a result of (1) its loss of access to CBC's current and past credit information in light of CBC's monopolistic position in the Cincinnati market and (2) TUC's consequent loss of goodwill and increased reputation that it would have otherwise enjoyed under the agreement were difficult to calculate.

[Trans Union Credit Info. Co. v. Associated Credit Servs., Inc., 805 F2d 188 (6th Cir. 1986)]

Remote-access license is subject to termination at will.   TL and FS entered into a terminal operating agreement (TOA) whereby TL "licensed and authorized" FS as a TL outlet to use TL terminals to sell tickets to various entertainment events through TL's computerized ticketing system. TL provided FS with all necessary equipment to sell tickets. Prior to termination of the contract, TL's successor in interest turned off FS's Ticketron equipment. FS sued for breach of contract. *Held:* The TOA is a licensing agreement, not a contract, and therefore TL had the right to revoke the license at any time. A license under Illinois law entitles a party to use property subject to the management and control of another party; it is revocable at any time unless revocation would operate as a fraud upon the licensee. There was ample evidence that the TOA was a license: TL retained ownership of all the equipment and supplies; TL was responsible for all repair and maintenance, and the costs of all utilities other than electrical utilities; TL retained the right to add or delete attractions at any time and to change prices, dates of performances, and seating arrangements; TL never guaranteed FS a certain number of available tickets. While parties may contract to change the nature of their license, there was no evidence that the TOA granted FS an irrevocable license, nor that revocation operated as a fraud against FS since FS was not required to make any investments of material or capital under the TOA.

[Ticketron Ltd. Partnership v. Flip Side, Inc., No. 92 C 0911, 1993 WL 214164 (ND Ill. June 17, 1993)]

Contract terms or applicable regulatory arrangements determine responsibility of customer for paying for services delivered by vendor.   JL set up a telephone system that included a remote-access feature, by which an off-premises caller could dial a secret 800 number (provided by MCI), access JL's private branch exchange (PBX), and obtain a local dial tone and make long-distance calls on a long-distance line provided by AT&T. Computer hackers broke through JL's security system and made more than $50,000 in calls before JL found out what happened and put a stop to it. JL refused to pay for the fraudulent calls, claiming that the calls did not "originate" at its PBX but rather at the hackers' computers. It further argued that AT&T should be held liable because it had greater knowledge of hacker fraud problems and greater ability and power to detect, combat, and prevent them. AT&T argued that FCC tariff Section 2.4.1.A makes the customer responsible for calls "[o]riginated at the Customer's number(s)." *Held:* JL was liable for the calls. The issue here was whether the calls "originated" at the hackers' telephones or at JL's. Case law interpreting Section 2.4.1.A of the FCC tariff regulations clearly indicates that calls "originate" at a customer's number when calls, authorized or not, are made from the customer's telephone system. In trying to shift responsibility to AT&T, JL ignored the fact that but for its creation of a telephone system with a remote-access feature, the disputed calls could not have been made. It is hardly just or reasonable to require AT&T to absorb the costs associated with such unauthorized calls. JL's other arguments as to AT&T's expertise in this area were better addressed to the FCC, the federal agency that has expertise in the communications area and that is best able to weigh such policy considerations.

[American Tel. & Tel. v. Jiffy Lube Int'l, Inc., 813 F. Supp. 1164 (D. Md. 1993)]

Limitation of consequential damages clause precludes city from recovering damages where clause was not "unconscionable." AT&T sought to recover unpaid long-distance charges from the city of New York. The city impleaded Northern Telecom, Inc., as a third-party defendant, alleging that Northern Telecom, as the seller of the city's phone equipment, was liable for the long-distance charges in dispute. The city purchased a private branch exchange (PBX) from Northern Telecom for three of the city's Human Resource Administration (HRA) offices. After manipulation by an HRA technician, the PBX simulated a remote-access feature, enabling unauthorized off-premises callers to place long-distance calls through the HRA's PBX. When AT&T, the long-distance provider, demanded payment for the long-distance calls, the city refused, claiming that the calls did not originate at the HRA's telephone number. After AT&T brought suit to recover sums due, the city brought a third-party action against Northern Telecom, as seller and installer of the PBX system, alleging, among other things, a breach-of-contract action, and seeking to hold Northern Telecom liable for the money owed to AT&T for the long-distance calls that resulted from the remote-access fraud at HRA. Northern Telecom moved for summary judgment, arguing that the city could not recover consequential damages for any alleged breach of the contract's express warranties since the contract expressly excluded liability for such damages. *Held:* Summary judgment in Northern Telecom's favor was appropriate. The city could not recover consequential damages resulting from the unauthorized long-distance calls because it could not defeat the limitation of consequential damages clause contained in the contract. Under this clause, "the Seller and City shall not be liable for incidental or consequential damages of any nature whatsoever for any default under or breach of this Contract." Such a provision is valid unless it is unconscionable. A determination of unconscionability generally requires a showing that the contract was both procedurally and substantively unconscionable when made— that is, some showing of an absence of meaningful choice on the part of one of the parties together with contract terms that are unreasonably favorable to the other party. With respect to the procedural element of unconscionability, the court must engage in "an examination of the contract formation process and the alleged lack of meaningful choice." With respect to substantive unconscionability, "[t]his question entails an analysis of the substance of the bargain to determine whether the terms were unreasonably favorable to the party against whom unconscionability is urged." The city's assertion that the consequential damages clause is unconscionable was completely without merit. With respect to procedural unconscionability, the contract at issue was not the type of contract entered into by an unwary consumer, but rather was a complex and painstakingly negotiated commercial agreement between two highly competent parties resulting from a competitive bidding process. With respect to substantive unconscionability, the terms contained in the contract were not unreasonably favorable to Northern Telecom. The limitation of consequential damages clause precluded the city from asserting a claim for breach of contract seeking recovery for the long-distance charges resulting from Northern Telecom's alleged breach.

[American Tel. & Tel. v. New York City Human Resources Admin., 833 F. Supp. 962 (SDNY 1993)]

Data base licensor may enforce minimum-use provision in license-lease agreement. HT, a travel service, assumed three contracts with UAL regarding licensed use of UAL's computer reservation system. The contracts contained a minimum usage requirement and liquidated damages clause. When HT decided to use a competitor's system and failed to meet its minimum-use requirements (one half of the average use during the first six months of the contract), UAL sued for and was granted summary judgment against HT for breach of contract. HT appealed, inter alia, on the grounds that the contracts were unenforceable because their minimum-use provisions violated Department of Transportation (DOT) regulations and that a liquidated damages clause was void as an unenforceable penalty. *Held:* The minimum-use provisions of the contracts did not violate DOT regulations, since they created a benchmark for use that was wholly in control of HT's predecessor in the contract. Indeed, the DOT has admitted that its current amended regulations, including the prior 14 CFR § 255.6(b) that a vendor shall not "directly or indirectly prohibit a subscriber from obtaining or using any other system," are inadequate to prevent minimum-use clauses. Finally, the damages clause is enforceable since at the *time of contracting* it constituted a reasonable forecast of just compensation for harm caused by the breach, and not an unenforceable penalty. UAL's damages from lost bookings and variable fees were incapable of precise estimation at the time of contracting, and the liquidated damages clause based on average use prior to the breach was a reasonable formula for forecasting damages caused by the breach.

[United Air Lines, Inc. v. Hewins Travel Consultants, Inc., 622 A2d 1163 (Me. 1993)]

PART B.   REGULATION OF ELECTRONIC SERVICES

¶ 15.04 ENHANCED AND ESSENTIAL SERVICES

FCC lacks authority to regulate data-processing activities that merely use communications systems.   The FCC promulgated rules, 47 CFR § 64.702 (Supp. 1972), relating to rendition of computer data-processing services by communications common carriers (CCCs) that essentially prescribed the conditions under which CCCs could offer data-processing services to others. Because of the danger that the CCCs' statutory duty to provide adequate and reasonable services could be adversely affected by their also providing data-processing services, the FCC required CCCs to set up separate corporate entities with separate names to provide the latter services and forbidding the CCCs to purchase, lease, or otherwise obtain data services from their separate corporations. GTE and other telephone companies participating in the data-processing field challenged these regulations as being beyond the FCC's authority and an abuse of discretion. *Held:* The CCCs should be allowed to use their own separate corporate entities with their own names for data processing. The FCC lacks authority to regulate data-processing activities that merely use communications systems. The FCC is apparently concerned with the telephone companies' monopolistic, albeit legal, leverage being applied to the data-processing market. Since the FCC itself created the separate corporate entities, it cannot forbid the parents from using the progeny by claiming the latter were created as a device to avoid regulation. Further, the FCC is charged by Congress with regulation of communications, not data processing, over which the FCC has never asserted jurisdiction; its attempt to regulate the data-processing subsidiaries is ultra vires. Similarly, the regulation barring use of the parent carrier's name or symbol is also void as an ultra vires act.

[GTE Serv. Corp. v. FCC, 474 F2d 724 (2d Cir. 1973)]

FCC orders, which do not implement any significant, unexplained departure from prior policy concerning access arrangement, do not violate Administrative Procedure Act. MCI Corporation and the state of California petitioned for review of four FCC orders approving access arrangements, known as Open Network Architecture (ONA), to the telephone transmission network. MCI and numerous supporting intervenors (collectively referred to as MCI) were all competitors of the Bell Operating Companies (BOCs) in providing "enhanced services" to telephone customers based on rapidly expanding computer technology. MCI claimed that the orders did not provide sufficient protection from the BOCs' possible discrimination against competitors in the face of impending elimination of the structural separation of the BOCs' basic telephone services from their own enhanced telecommunications services. MCI further contended that the FCC, by approving these orders, violated the APA both by departing without adequate explanation from prior policy and by refusing to consider evidence of the inadequacy of ONA, as adopted to prevent discrimination. The FCC defended the orders on the ground that there had been no unexplained substantive departure from previously approved ONA concepts that were always viewed as evolutionary. *Held:* The orders did not in and of themselves violate the APA because the FCC has not implemented any significant, unexplained departure from prior ONA policy. In the FCC's third computer inquiry, *Computer III*, the FCC adopted general standards for ONA that the BOCs needed to satisfy as a precondition for lifting structural separation and that, when met, would eliminate the need for Comparably Efficient Interconnection (CEI) plans. The plans actually submitted pursuant to *Computer III*, however, did not meet those standards. The FCC recognized in the orders that the technology in *Computer III* that it thought would soon permit open access and serve as a prerequisite to structural separation was not available, yet it approved the plans. This action constituted a change in policy; however, the FCC explained that the change was necessary because existing technology was insufficient to implement complete ONA. Thus, although the FCC substantially approved the plans' implementation, it did not approve the ONA technology embodied in these plans as sufficient to constitute the prerequisite to the fundamental unbundling of services as described in *Computer III*. The BOCs were still required to file CEI plans for each enhanced service and to comply with other reporting requirements intended to prevent discrimination by the BOCs. Furthermore, although the orders advanced the view that structural separation could be lifted before the implementation of a fully realized ONA, the orders did not lift structural separation, and thus did not need to fully explain the conditions under which separation can be lifted.

[California v. FCC, 4 F3d 1505 (9th Cir. 1993)]

FCC orders do not violate Federal Communication Act by establishing federal tariffs for services that were technically compatible with interstate use. MCI Corporation and the state of California petitioned for review of four FCC orders approving access arrangements, known as Open Network Architecture (ONA), to the telephone transmission network. In the California petitions, the state and Public Utilities Commission, supported by the intervenors, sought review of those aspects of the orders that required federal tariffing of certain services the Bell Operating Companies (BOCs) offered to the enhanced service providers. The FCC ordered federal tariffs of services that were technically compatible with interstate use. California contended that the federal tariff provision violated Section 2(B)(1) of the Federal Communication Act (FCA), 47 USC § 152(B)(1)(2), because the FCC lacks jurisdiction to regulate services that are used only in connection with intrastate service, regardless of whether such series are technically compatible with interstate use. *Held:* The orders did not in and of themselves violate the APA because the FCC has not implemented any significant, unexplained departure from prior ONA policy. The orders under review in the California petitions established a federal tariff for potential interstate services and did not regulate intrastate communications. The FCC was not attempting to preempt the states from regulating intrastate services. The ONA orders established a dual federal and state tariffing structure for basic service elements (BSEs), and the states retained authority to set rates for those BSEs that were used for intrastate service. The system complied with the FCA, which is designed to establish a dual regulatory scheme.

[California v. FCC, 4 F3d 1505 (9th Cir. 1993)]

FCC's nonstructural approach to regulating BOCs is arbitrary and capricious.
Plaintiffs challenged the FCC's rulemaking in *Computer III* that (1) ceased requiring
divested Bell Operating Companies (BOCs) to maintain corporate separation between regulated (basic) common carrier communications services and unregulated (enhanced) data-processing services over computer networks and (2) ordered the preemption
of any state regulation of enhanced services offered by carriers. The FCC argued that
divestiture and increased competition in the enhanced services market diminished the
value of structural separation as a safeguard against monopoly abuse, and that the costs
of separation outweighed the benefits. *Held:* There was insufficient evidence on the
record to justify the FCC's conclusion that changed circumstances reduced the danger that the BOCs would subsidize their competitive activities in the enhanced market with monopoly revenues improperly derived from the regulated one. The FCC has
failed to justify its new position that accounting controls may be effectively substituted
for the prior structural separation requirements to diminish the risk of undetected
cost-shifting by the BOCs. Competition in the unregulated enhanced services market
does nothing to diminish the BOCs' monopoly power in the basic services market,
which few ordinary users have the ability to bypass, nor its ability to shift costs to
their regulated services without detection in ratemaking proceedings. Finally, the FCC's
attempt to preempt state law violates the broad language of 47 USC § 152(b)(1) that
grants the states regulatory authority over enhanced services delivered by common carriers "in connection with intrastate communications" services.

[California v. FCC, 905 F2d 1217 (9th Cir. 1990)]

¶ 15.05 AT&T DIVESTITURE: INFORMATION SERVICES

Removal of ban against BOC entry into information services market is proper.
After the circuit court's decision in *United States v. Western Electric*, 900 F2d 283
(DC Cir. 1990), the district court grudgingly followed the Department of Justice (DOJ)
recommendation to alter the consent decree to permit BOCs to enter the information
services market. While asserting that none of the DOJ contentions was supported
by "credible evidence," the court deferred to its conclusions. *Held:* The lower
court properly deferred to the DOJ's determination to modify the consent decree and
remove the ban against BOC entry into the information services market since that
determination was "reasonable under the circumstances." There was sufficient evidence on the record to support the DOJ's contentions that (1) there was no substantial risk that removal of the ban would lessen competition; (2) regulation would minimize
anticompetitive risks; and (3) removal of the ban would benefit consumers by en-
hancing competition. Competition from large non-BOCs and existing information
networks serve to neutralize a BOC's local monopoly and prevent it from discrimi-

nating with respect to prices or service. Moreover, local interconnection costs represent a minor element in the total costs of providing information services. Thus, the record indicates that BOCs would be unable to use their local monopoly power to discriminate effectively against competitors. Finally, advances in efficacy of monopoly regulation combined with the distinct possibility of increased competition benefiting consumers all support the reasonableness of the DOJ's recommendation.

[United States v. Western Elec., 993 F2d 1572 (DC Cir. 1993)]

Proper test to determine restriction of BOCs' entry into information services is to determine if entry would promote the public interest.   As part of its review of the consent decree divesting AT&T, the district court lifted restrictions against BOC participation in nontelecommunication businesses, while leaving intact interexchange and manufacturing restrictions. Although all parties agreed to a removal of the ban against BOC entry into the information services market, the court, applying the test of Section VIII(C) of the consent decree that there be "no substantial possibility" that the BOCs could use their monopoly power to impede competition, partially modified but did not remove those restrictions. *Held:* The proper test with respect to the *uncontested* motion concerning entry into the information services market is that specified in Section VII of the consent decree: to determine whether modification of the decree is within the *zone of settlements* consonant with the "public interest" *today*; the test is not to determine the solution that would "best serve society" but only to confirm a settlement within the "*reaches* of the public interest." Because the "public interest" test takes its meaning from antitrust laws, the appropriate question is whether the proposed modification would be certain to lessen competition in the relevant market. Since application of the "public interest" test might have resulted in different findings with respect to anticompetitive risk under *present* market conditions and the conflicting nature of the record with respect to competitors' ability to bypass BOC local-exchange networks, the issue was remanded to the lower court for application of the proper test. In all other respects the lower court's decision was affirmed.

[United States v. Western Elec., 900 F2d 283 (DC Cir. 1990)]

NYNEX service bureau is "information service" and not permissible activity of leasing customer premises equipment.   As part of the consent decree divesting AT&T, regional carriers were precluded from providing "directly or through any affiliated enterprise . . . information services." NYNEX was charged with criminal contempt for violating the decree by acquiring Telco, which operated with MCI an "MCI service bureau" providing MCI employees remote access to Telco's MicroVax computers and software and designing long-distance networks for MCI customers. NYNEX maintained that the MCI service bureau was not an information service, but merely the lease of customer premises equipment (CPE) plus software. *Held:* Telco's MCI service bureau is an information service, in violation of the consent decree since it offered "a capacity for generating, acquiring, storing, transforming, processing, retrieving, utilizing [and] making available information which may be conveyed via telecommunications." NYNEX's characterization of the MCI service bureau as a lease of CPE plus software is incorrect. That MCI never had physical or constructive control of the MicroVax computers is inconsistent with NYNEX's claim that this was a CPE lease. NYNEX's willful conduct in violating the consent decree justified a citation for criminal contempt.

[United States v. NYNEX Corp., 814 F. Supp. 133 (DDC 1993)]

PART C.   PROPERTY RIGHTS

¶ 15.06 INFORMATION AS PROPERTY

Information is a "thing of value" under federal theft-of-property laws.   McAusland obtained inside information on competitors' bids and proposals for DOD contracts and confidential information regarding how the bids and proposals were being evaluated by DOD officials. He appealed his conviction of violating 18 USC § 641 for knowingly converting without authority a "thing of value" of the United States. *Held:* Information such as that involved in this case is a "thing of value" under Section 641.

[United States v. McAusland, 979 F2d 970 (4th Cir. 1992)]

Insured's misplacement of judicial petition against owner does not constitute property damage for comprehensive general liability policy.   SH claimed that when FS took possession of its property in a foreclosure sale, it failed to forward a petition concerning a lawsuit brought against SH by Campbell. SH failed to defend, and default judgment of $500,000 was entered against it. ZI refused to defend FS, claiming that loss of notice of the lawsuit by Campbell did not constitute "property damage" for purposes of the insurance policy's comprehensive general liability (CGL). *Held:* Mishandling of a legal document leading to entry of a default judgment does not constitute "property damages" for CGL insurance purposes. The citation and petition had no intrinsic value beyond notifying SH that legal action had commenced against it. The substantive resulting loss consisted of loss of notice, not property. *Dissent:* Loss of a document may constitute property damage if the information contained therein had some identifiable value to its owner or intended recipient, even though such information had no market value. Here, although the petition and citation were of little value to nonparties to the lawsuit, they were of considerable value to the party being sued.

[Snug Harbor, Ltd. v. Zurich Ins., 968 F2d 538 (5th Cir. 1992)]

¶ 15.07 COPY RIGHT

Copyright does not protect facts or diagrams that lack sufficient originality.   AI claimed that Palmer had misappropriated its copyrighted diagrams depicting human personality. *Held:*   There can be no copyright infringement of the diagrams since they present facts, not creative expressions of ideas. Since AI consistently claimed that the diagrams present scientific discoveries concerning "ego fixations," verifiable facts of human nature, as opposed to inventions, it was estopped from asserting that they are not factual in order to better serve its position in litigation. AI was able to establish that descriptive elements of the system such as the labels affixed to the diagrams were protected expression. However, Palmer's use of the latter elements constituted fair use; hence, there was no infringement at all.

[Arica Inst., Inc. v. Palmer, 970 F2d 1067 (2d Cir. 1992)]

Computer program testing reading skills has expressive content subject to copyright protection.   NESS appealed imposition of a preliminary injunction for infringing Autoskill's copyrighted reading skills computer program complaining, inter alia, that the lower court erred by granting copyright protection to unprotectible ideas, procedures, processes, and methods. *Held:*   The manner in which Autoskill used ideas and communicated them to students and teachers in the context of a reading program amounted to protected expression. Copyright protection extends to original expressions of organization, structure, and sequence contained in a computer program. The lower court correctly excluded higher level abstractions such as the division of learning disabilities into three subtypes and "a reading program designed to diagnose, remediate and teach reading skills" using a computer as unprotected ideas in the public domain.

[Autoskill, Inc. v. National Educ. Support Sys., Inc., 994 F2d 1476 (10th Cir. 1993)]

Overbroad injunction enjoining infringement may be overturned.   VMS sold copies of a registered copyrighted CNN program, and its records indicated receipts of $300,000 in sales of CNN transmission programming. CNN obtained an injunction enjoining VMS from "copying or selling" any of CNN's programming. VMS appealed, claiming the injunction was overbroad since it covered far more activity than infringement of CNN's copyrights. VMS also monitored CNN broadcasts on behalf of copyright owners of certain commercials and news releases and the injunction would have forced them to cease this activity, which involved taping all CNN broadcasts. *Held:* The lower court erred, the order was reversed, and the case was remanded. It was error to grant such a broad injunctive remedy for unregistered claims of copyright and for putative copyrights in works not yet in existence. Such broad relief endangers free speech, since individuals have the right to reproduce a copyrighted work for a "fair use." Also, it is inconsistent with copyright law, since it would allow copyright claimants to avoid registering *existing* works, a requirement that ensures public access to works granted a copyright monopoly and that has been held to be a prerequisite to invoking a federal remedy to infringement (17 USC § 411(a)). The injunction would also protect *future* works that may or may not meet the requirements for copyrightability; indeed, future works are by definition not subject to copyright, since they are not fixed in a tangible medium as required by 17 USC § 102. While certain CNN segments consisting of preexisting collected materials of a factual nature may be copyrightable as compilations because of the manner of their selection, coordination, and arrangement, others, such as facts or news reported in obvious ways, may not have sufficient originality in content or compilation to warrant protection.

[Cable News Network, Inc. v. Video Monitoring Servs. of Am., 940 F2d 1471 (11th Cir. 1991), vacated, 749 F2d 378 (11th Cir. 1991)]

Street address portion of taxi driver guide is protected by copyright. NMG sued HMC, inter alia, for copyright infringement of its taxi driver guide. NMG alleged that HMC copied the numbers and sequences of many street and address listings representing NMG's creative and original work, including certain "obscure and erroneous listings" that did not affect the accuracy of NMG's guide but that were inserted to detect copying by others. HMC maintained that it copied facts or information that was presented as factual. It further asserted that NMG was estopped from claiming copyright in "false facts." *Held:* NMG's combination of cross streets with assigned numbers represented a creative selection, adaptation, and arrangement of facts. By copying this combination, HMC infringed NMG's copyright. NMG used sufficient creativity in implementing a plan to locate addresses along major streets to qualify that section for copyright protection. It is true that copyright protection should not be granted to "false" facts interlarded among actual facts since such a rule would prevent disseminating information. Nevertheless, while false facts themselves are not copyrightable, taking them as actual facts, their order, selection, and presentation, as in the instant case, may be copyrighted.

[Nester's Map & Guide Corp. v. Hagstrom Map & Guide Corp., 796 F. Supp. 729 (EDNY 1992)]

[1] Text and Video in Electronic Form

Purchaser of work by independent contractor does not automatically obtain copyright in work.   CCNV hired Reid to make a sculpture based on an idea supplied by CCNV. CCNV paid Reid for the materials used, while Reid agreed to donate his services. There was no written contract or agreement as to copyright. After a dispute, Reid filed for copyright. CCNV filed a competing copyright registration, claiming it was "work made for hire" under 17 USC § 101. *Held:* Reid was an independent contractor and his contribution was not work for hire; therefore, absent a written agreement specifying that Reid's contribution was work for hire, copyright in the work belongs to Reid, the author of the work. CCNV may, however, be a joint author of the work if CCNV and Reid prepared the work with the intention that their contributions be merged into a unitary whole (17 USC § 101).

[Community for Creative Non-Violence v. Reid, 490 US 730 (1989)]

Plaintiff held as having valid copyright under fair use doctrine.   LANS sued AVRS, a video news clipping service, for copying and selling segments of LANS's copyright registered video tapes of a train wreck and an airplane crash. AVRS averred that the tapes were not original works of authorship and that it made fair use of them. *Held:* LANS had a valid copyright in the two videotapes in question. The record clearly indicated that preparation of both tapes required sufficient intellectual and creative input as to entitle them to copyright protection. Further, the "fair use" doctrine does not protect AVRS from liability for infringing LANS's copyrights. A consideration of the four factors mandated by 17 USC § 107 weighs heavily against AVRS's claim. While one factor, the nature of the works as newsworthy events, weighs in AVRS's favor, the other factors—that AVRS made commercial use of the most valuable part of LANS's material and that this would have an adverse impact on LANS's potential market—weigh heavily against a finding of fair use.

[Los Angeles News Servs., Inc. v. Tullo, 973 F2d 791 (9th Cir. 1992)]

[2] Factual Data and Effort

Copyright protection does not cover facts that do not meet the copyright originality standard.   RTS sued Feist, a publisher of telephone directories, claiming Feist infringed its copyright by copying names, towns, and telephone numbers from RTS's telephone book. *Held:* There was no infringement since the elements claimed by RTS were not copyrightable. While compilations of preexisting factual material may be copyrighted if their arrangement and selection display a minimal amount of originality or creativity, such was not the case here, an alphabetical arrangement of RTS's subscribers that was devoid of even the slightest trace of creativity. A factual compilation is copyrightable if it features an original selection or arrangement of facts;

but, the copyright is limited to the particular selection or arrangement, not to the facts themselves. While the amount of originality necessary to trigger copyright eligibility is extremely low, it is not satisfied by mere effort in compiling facts. Copyright rewards originality, not sweat of the brow.

[Feist Publications, Inc. v. Rural Tel. Serv. Co., 111 S. Ct. 1282 (1991)]

Originality in context of copyright merely requires the existence of intellectual production, thought, and conception. Sarony sued BGL for violating his copyright by making and selling thousands of copies of his photograph of Oscar Wilde. BGL argued that the photograph in question, qua photograph, was merely a mechanical reproduction of the physical features of an object and that it did not involve any originality or novelty sufficient to merit copyright protection. *Held:* The photograph in question in its arrangement of the subject and selection of lighting and shade qualified for copyright protection as an original work of art. Copyright protection is limited to original intellectual conceptions of the author, who, when accusing another of infringement, must prove the existence of originality of intellectual production, thought, and conception. Here, the photograph was clearly the product of Sarony's intellectual invention, of which Sarony was the author.

[Burrow-Giles Lithographic Co. v. Sarony, 111 US 53, 60 (1884)]

Copyright may preempt application of misappropriation doctrine where there is no independent basis for cause of action other than copying of another work product. FII sued MIS for copyright infringement and misappropriation, claiming MIS copied its financial bond cards. *Held:* No copyright existed in cards that collected five, limited items of information about individual issues of public bonds since there was insufficient proof of "independent creation" to render the cards copyrightable. FII's pendent state claim of misappropriation was preempted since it was equivalent to the exclusive rights granted by the Copyright Act. There is no exception to the general rule of preemption in the misappropriation area that punishes "any form of commercial immorality." If the work is unprotected by federal law because of lack of originality, its use is neither unfair nor unjustified. This decision does not reach the issue as to whether wholesale misappropriation of a data base would be actionable, since the material in question was obtained through conventional channels.

[Financial Info., Inc. v. Moody's Investors Serv., Inc., 808 F2d 204 (2d Cir. 1986)]

Copyright does protect maps with superimposed data on land ownership where the maps' "idea" can be expressed in a variety of ways. MDI copied real estate ownership maps made by Mason based on U.S. survey maps. Mason sued for copyright infringement, and summary judgment was granted to MDI on the grounds that the maps were not copyrightable under the idea/expression merger doctrine (as expressed in *Kern River Gas Transmission Co. v. Coastal Corp.*, 899 F2d 1458 (5th Cir. 1990)). Mason appealed. *Held:* It was error to apply the merger doctrine to this case, since Mason's maps were copyright protected. The merger doctrine must focus on whether the idea is capable of various modes of expression. The record indicates that there were numerous ways to express these maps. Mason's maps exhibited his individual choices as to selection of sources as well as his skill and judgment in depicting information. The idea of these maps was to bring together available information on boundaries, landmarks, and ownership and to choose an effective way to represent selected locations pictorially. Mason's creative efforts separated that idea and its final expression; therefore, his maps were entitled to protection from competitors, who remain free to express that idea in other ways.

[Mason v. Montgomery Data, Inc., 967 F2d 135 (5th Cir. 1992)]

Copyright does not cover lines on map marking proposed location of gas pipeline. As part of a proposal to build a gas pipeline, KRGT submitted copies of U.S. survey maps with lines added to depict the proposed pipeline route. WC, a rival, copied portions of the maps and submitted them in furtherance of its own application to build a pipeline in the same corridor. KRGT brought suit for copyright infringement. *Held:* The idea of the location of the pipeline and its expression embodied in the maps in question are inseparable and not subject to protection. The doctrine of "merger" holds that when the expression of an idea is inseparable from the idea itself, the expression and the idea merge. In such circumstances, copying the expression is not barred since copyright does not confer a monopoly on ideas.

[Kern River Gas Transmission Co. v. Coastal Corp., 899 F2d 1458 (5th Cir. 1990)]

[3] Organization and Selection

Racing statistics compilation does not merit copyright protection. VLE sued BRA for copyright infringement for BRA's publishing photocopies of VLE's race track betting statistics sheet in its own betting sheet. VLE appealed an award of summary judgment on behalf of BRA. *Held:* VLE's chart failed to meet the minimum standards of originality required for copyright protection. As a compilation of preexisting facts, a chart would only merit protection if it features original selection, coordination, or arrangement of those facts. Here, the arrangement of the factual data was purely functional and the format of the charts was conventional; further, there was no selectivity in what VLE's charts reported nor creativity in how they reported it. Since the charts did not merit protection, BRA's use of them could not constitute infringement.

[Victor Lalli Enters., Inc. v. Big Red Apple, Inc., 936 F2d 671 (2d Cir. 1991)]

Particular selection of statistics from myriad of information combinations is subject to protection. Kregos sued the AP, inter alia, for infringing his copyrighted baseball pitching form, which contained nine categories of statistical information and which Kregos distributed to various newspapers. Kregos appealed the granting of summary judgment in favor of the AP. *Held:* The validity of Kregos' copyright in a compilation of statistics cannot be rejected as a matter of law for lack of the requisite originality or creativity. In selecting the nine items for his pitching form out of the universe of available data, Kregos displayed originality; indeed, the record does not reflect any prior form identical to his nor one from which his varies in only a trivial degree. The observation that most of the statistics in Kregos's form had been established in previously existing forms is largely irrelevant to the issue of whether Kregos's selection displays sufficient creativity to warrant a copyright. Should Kregos prevail at trial, copyright protection will only be afforded him with respect to the protectable features of his form.

[Kregos v. Associated Press, 937 F2d 700 (2d Cir. 1991)]

Compilation of five signs with wording on front and back does not merit copyright protection. ST, a sign manufacturer, obtained a copyright certificate on a set of five double-sided signs as a compilation. It sued K mart, inter alia, for infringing its trademark by selling similar signs manufactured by HK, a competitor. ST appealed an award of summary judgment to K mart on the issue of copyright. *Held:* ST's signs do not merit protection under copyright law as a compilation. ST failed to arrange and select preexisting material in such a way as to form an independent work. The five signs in question may be displayed in retail stores together, but they are sold separately to both retailers and the public. To merit protection, the whole of a compilation must be greater than the sum of its parts. Here, even in the absence of any sign from the set, the others would remain just as marketable. The independent work here was the individual unprotected sign, not the set.

[Sem-Torq, Inc. v. K mart Corp., 936 F2d 851 (6th Cir. 1991)]

Similarities in design cover and other features of catalog do not result in copyright infringement of sales catalog as a compilation. SS, a seller of office supplies, sued NC, inter alia, for infringement for copying its copyrighted catalog. *Held:* There was no infringement of the catalog as a compilation; that is, the arrangement of materials to make a catalog. While there were some similarities with respect to the design of the cover and other features of the catalog, there were not so many—given the inevitably standardized format of a mail-order office supply catalog—so as to constitute infringement. Nevertheless, NC may have infringed specific copyrighted materials within the catalog without infringing the compilation.

[Schiller & Schmidt, Inc. v. Nordisco Corp., 969 F2d 410 (7th Cir. 1992)]

Car manual containing information about parts and systems needed to conform to emission standards is copyrightable compilation. Sinai sued BAR for infringing his Corvette emission manual by publishing a chart on Corvette models emission controls. Both the manual and chart contained information on how to revamp Corvettes to comply with California emission control laws. *Held:* There was no infringement here since copyright of factual compilations as stated by the Supreme Court in *Feist Publications, Inc. v. Rural Telephone Service Co.*, 111 S. Ct. 1282 (1991), only protects the particular selection or arrangement, not the facts themselves. Here, there was little selectivity involved, since the universe of information on how to make Corvettes meet California emission laws is necessarily a small one. Further, Sinai's arrangement of the information did not merit copyright protection as a compilation since arrangement of information in the form of a columnar grid is not original enough to meet even the extremely low threshold articulated in *Feist.*

[Sinai v. California Bureau of Automotive Repair, 25 USPQ2d 1809 (ND Cal. 1993)]

Civil action for unauthorized access to computer may be based on criminal law. STI, a title insurance company, sued LNT for scheming to defraud it of revenues by failing to report all its uses of STI's computer, in violation of an access agreement signed by both parties. STI also charged LNT with violating a since-repealed state criminal statute prohibiting unauthorized access and use of a computer. LNT moved to dismiss the latter charge pursuant to Federal Rule of Civil Procedure 12(b)(6). *Held:* LNT's motion is unfounded. The complaint alleged that LNT and its employees knowingly gained access or obtained use of the computer system without consent. The statute in question prohibited "knowingly gaining access to a computer system without consent of the owner" as well as knowingly doing so as part of a plan to "obtain money, property or services." STI should be given the opportunity to prove a set of facts surrounding its claim to show that LNT somehow gained access to its computer. Finally, it should be noted that since the acts in question occurred while the criminal law was effective, and since Illinois law has a savings clause that allows bringing such an action before repeal of the law becomes effective, STI should be allowed to pursue this claim despite the statute's subsequent repeal.

[Safeco Title Ins. Co. v. Liberty Nat'l Title Ins. Co., 1989 WL 11079 (ND Ill. Feb. 9, 1989)]

Grid is not copyrightable if there is no creative expression, distinct from the idea, in the arrangement of elements of implementation of the idea in "garden-variety" grid. CFA accused Polaroid of infringing its copyrighted grid chart showing the relationship between "decision making styles" and "problem solving steps." *Held:* None of the elements of CFA's chart contributed to the copyrightability of the chart in a way relevant to claims in this particular litigation. CFA's use of a grid was not copyrightable because there was no creative expression, distinct from the idea, in the arrangement of elements of an implementation of the idea in a "garden-variety" grid. The elements of the CFA chart were not copyrightable since they too fell under the merger doctrine. First, the choice to use the seven decision-making styles was not a creative expression distinct from the idea. Also, there was a merger of the idea of exploring a problem-solving method and the expression of that idea because there are only a limited number of methods of problem solving and because the expression involved was that of selecting a particular method to explore. Finally, even if there were a wholesale copying of CFA's chart, Polaroid was not liable under the "fair use" doctrine. Polaroid obtained copies of the chart from CFA at a lecture. Polaroid did not sell or show the chart to outsiders. There was no evidence that any limited infringement had any effect on the potential market for or value of the CFA chart, which CFA itself does not even sell.

[Coates-Freeman Assocs., Inc. v. Polaroid Corp., 792 F. Supp. 879 (D. Mass. 1992)]

Report formats must be relatively unique and valuable to achieve protection on theory of misappropriation.   HJC sued Johnston and other former employees for plagiarizing its customer financial report form, thereby committing the tort of misappropriation. *Held:* This is a case of permissible imitation, not misappropriation. The defendants did not appropriate any unique, artistic, or creative work in copying the design of HJC's client reports. The essence of a financial report is the data, not the format of presentation. The record indicates that the defendants used their own efforts, money, and resources to produce their own data.

[Hamilton, Johnston & Co. v. Johnston, 607 A2d 1044 (NJ 1992)]

¶ 15.08 ACCESS RIGHT

[1] Protected Locations

Physical trespass differs from unauthorized access.   Olson, a police officer at the University of Washington (UW), was convicted of computer trespass for accessing the UW computer to get information on various UW co-eds. *Held:* The evidence showed only unauthorized access of computer data, not criminal trespass. Historically, trespass is an intrusion or invasion into tangible property that interfered with the right of exclusive possession. Computer trespass is analogous to criminal trespass: It criminalizes the entry into the computer system without authorization, not the unauthorized use of the information obtained. Olson was authorized to access the computer system, and because computer access was not conditioned on the uses made of the data once the system was entered, he is not guilty of computer trespass.

[State v. Olson, 735 P2d 1362 (Wash. App. Ct. 1987)]

[2] Copyright and Remote Data Base Access

Retransmission of television signals without inclusion of teletext falls outside passive carrier copyright exemption.   WGN, an independent television superstation, used UV, a satellite common carrier, to transmit its signals to its various affiliates. WGN's transmission feed of its nine o'clock news included an encoded teletext that made available special signals to subscribers with suitable decoder devices. WGN sued UV to enjoin, as a copyright infringement, its refusal to retransmit its teletext along with the nine o'clock news. *Held:* WGN is entitled to an injunction since WGN's newscast copyright covers the teletext as well as because it is intended to be seen by the same viewers watching the nine o'clock news, during the same interval of time in which that news is broadcast, and as an integral part of the news program. The copyright exists in the programming, not in the method of transmission. If WGN used teletext not intended to be viewed in conjunction with its news broadcast, such text would not be protected under the news broadcast's copyright. UV is not exempted from carrying the teletext signal under 17 USC § 111, which exempts passive intermediary transmitters of television signals from copyright liability, for UV was not a passive transmitter since it substituted its own teletext for WGN's feed.

[WGN v. United Video, Inc., 693 F2d 622 (7th Cir. 1982)]

Trespass statutes may not apply to unauthorized access to computers since they entail physical entry.   JFI countersued ADP, inter alia, for wrongfully deactivating its computer software, in violation of RICO, 18 USC § 641, and gaining unlawful access of its system to misappropriate wire communications in violation of 18 USC § 2511. Held: ADP had a legal right to deactivate JFI's software pursuant to the software license agreement that stated that ADP's software licenses could be canceled upon the client's default. Exercise of rights under a software license agreement to deactivate the software does not violate the RICO statute. Further, ADP's access to JFI's computer system was authorized under the contract. JFI acknowledged that it was aware that ADP could access its computer, and since it allowed it, it cannot now claim that it was unlawful.

[American Computer Trust Leasing v. Jack Farrell Implement Co., 763 F. Supp. 1473 (D. Minn. 1991)]

[3] Control of Access Devices

Wiretap Act applies to manufacture and sale of cable satellite transmission descramblers.   Davis was convicted of manufacturing and selling a cable satellite descrambler in violation of 18 USC §§ 2511 and 2512. He appealed, claiming that Section 2511(1)(a) did not apply to interception of *commercial* satellite programming, and that Section 2512(1)(b) only applied to devices "primarily useful for the purpose of the surreptitious interception of wire, oral, or electronic communications," since his device was primarily useful for nonsurreptitious and legitimate purposes. *Held:* The manufacture and sale of a satellite descramble device violated the Wiretap Act since its language is broad enough to include programming transmitted by satellites. The exclusion of specific types of unencrypted and unscrambled satellite transmissions from the reach of various subsections of Section 2511 establishes that satellite transmissions are contemplated by the Act. Finally, the crucial test under Section 2512 is whether the design of the device renders it *primarily* useful for surreptitious listening, not whether it is susceptible to innocent nonsurreptitious uses. The modifications that Davis performed on the computer chips of the satellite descramblers made it impossible to use these devices in any legitimate fashion, because people possessing such modified descramblers would have to use them surreptitiously to prevent the cable companies from learning of Davis's tampering.

[United States v. Davis, 978 F2d 415 (8th Cir. 1992) (en banc)]

Federal law prohibiting unauthorized access devices applies to unassigned credit cards used to obtain merchandise fraudulently. Taylor obtained and used "valid, but as yet unassigned" credit card account numbers by illegally accessing and manipulating the American Express computer system. He challenged his conviction for violating 18 USC § 1029(a)(2), which prohibits fraudulent use of "unauthorized access devices," on the grounds that the credit cards used did not access account numbers that had been assigned to any person and therefore were not "access devices" within the meaning of the statute. *Held:* The statute defines "access device" as "any card, plate, code, account number, or other means of account access that can be used, alone or in conjunction with another access device, to obtain money, goods, services, or any other thing of value, or that can be used to initiate a transfer of funds." Further, it defines an "unauthorized access device" as an access device that is "lost, stolen, expired, revoked, canceled, or obtained with intent to defraud." The cards in question were clearly "unauthorized access devices" within the meaning of Section 1029 since their use clearly constituted the access devices by which Taylor perpetrated fraudulent transactions. Taylor's argument that the cards could not be "unauthorized access devices" because no assigned accounts existed and the accounts were "valid" slices the language of Section 1029 too thinly. The phrase "account number or other means of account access" expressly covers the transactions he made.

[United States v. Taylor, 945 F2d 1050 (8th Cir. 1991)]

Both wiretap and communications law apply to sale of cloned cable transmission descramblers. Splawn manufactured and sold cloned computer chips enabling customers to receive premium cable channel broadcasts without paying the required subscription fee. Splawn appealed his conviction for violating the Wiretap Act, 18 USC § 2512(1)(b). *Held:* Although descramblers may be necessary to receive satellite transmissions for which no authorization is necessary, the sole purpose of Splawn's modifications was to permit the surreptitious interception of satellite television transmissions. Since Splawn's devices were designed to make them primarily useful for the surreptitious interception of electronic communications, they are clearly prohibited by the language of Section 2512(1)(b), which punishes anyone who "intentionally . . . manufactures, assembles, possesses, or sells any electronic, mechanical, or other device, knowing or having reason to know that the design of such device renders it primarily useful for the purpose of the *surreptitious* interception of wire, oral or electronic communications, and that such device or any component thereof has been or will be . . . transported in interstate or foreign commerce." It is indisputable that satellite communications, which contain sound and images carried via radio waves, constitute electronic communications under Section 2510(12), and that the cloned devices intercept them. Legitimate satellite descramblers have unique electronic addresses contained in their computer chips. In cloning a computer chip from a legitimate descrambler and placing it in another descrambler, Splawn altered the design of the descrambler, making it nonunique and capable of surreptitious interception of transmissions, thereby violating the Wiretap Act.

[United States v. Splawn, 982 F2d 414 (10th Cir. 1992)]

Enforcement of copyright by terminating plaintiff's permission to resell downloaded reports is valid. CS illegally obtained a CD-Rom copy of T&T's state trademark data base (STD). CS sued T&T for violation of Section 2 of the Sherman Anti-Trust Act and to enjoin T&T to allow CS to use its data base, while T&T countersued CS for copyright infringement of its STD. *Held:* T&T permissibly enforced its copyright by terminating CS's permission to resell downloaded reports from the STD, since those reports contained verbatim copies of T&T's STD enhancements. T&T has a valid copyright in its STD that extends to its internally generated information and to its particular enhancements to the items collected in its STD, but not to the items themselves. T&T was under no obligation to extend its special permission to CS to use downloaded materials; CS had signed a license agreement that specifically prohibited resale of information without explicit written permission from T&T. T&T's enforcement of its copyright does not violate antitrust laws since it does not prevent CS or any other competitor from creating its own STD and thereby entering the relevant submarket; rather, its enforcement reflects a valid marketing strategy that would differentiate T&T's STD, a cheaper preliminary trademark on-line search tool, from T&T's costlier full search reports based on T&T's more comprehensive internal data base. T&T was entitled to protect its products in this manner because of its long-term development and assemblage of trademark information.

[Corsearch, Inc. v. Thomson & Thomson, 792 F. Supp. 305 (SDNY 1992)]

¶ 15.09 DATA BASE INFRINGEMENTS

[1] Downloading and Using Contents

Copyright on selection or arrangement does not indirectly protect otherwise unprotected factual data. KP, a publisher of a white and yellow pages Chinese business directory with more than 9,000 listings sorted into one of more than 260 categories, sued CTPE for copyright infringement for publishing an allegedly derivative directory with approximately 2,000 listings divided among 28 different categories. Approximately 75 percent of the listings in the latter directory were listed in the KP directory. CTPE appealed judgment in favor of KP. *Held:* Although KP has a valid copyright in its telephone directory as a compilation, since it exhibits originality in its selection and classification of businesses, CTPE did not infringe it since the elements it took are not protected by copyright. To prove infringement of compilations, a plaintiff must show substantial similarity between those elements, and only those elements, that provide copyrightability to the allegedly infringed compilation. Thus, the key question here was whether the organizing principle guiding selection of businesses for the two publications is substantially similar. As a matter of law, there was no substantial similarity between the two directories since there was a difference in the number and type of classification between the two directories that reflected differing principles of selectivity and arrangement. Placing listings within categories is a mechanical task that does not merit copyright protection. Also, deliberate copying of 1,500 out of 9,000 listings where no listings were primarily copied from any one classified section does not constitute infringement, especially considering the inevitability of overlap in such a narrowly conceived directory.

[Key Publications, Inc. v. Chinatown Today Publishing Enters., Inc., 945 F2d 509 (2d Cir. 1991)]

Copyright infringement claim cannot be maintained when plaintiff fails to establish that original elements of selection, coordination, or arrangement had been copied. Bellsouth Advertising & Publishing Corporation, publisher of a classified business directory, brought an action against Donnelley Information Publishing, Inc., and others for copyright and trademark infringement and unfair competition. The district court found, and Donnelley admitted, that Bellsouth owned a valid compilation copyright in its classified directory. Donnelley stipulated that, in preparing its data base and sales lead sheet, it obtained from each listing in the Bellsouth directory the telephone number, name, address, kind of business, and unit of advertising for the listed subscriber. From the process by which Donnelley prepared its competitive yellow pages directory, the district court identified three acts of copying. Based on these acts of copying, the court granted Bellsouth's motion for summary judgment on its copyright infringement claim. *Held:* By copying the name, address, telephone number, business type, and unit of advertisement purchased for each listing in the Bellsouth directory, Donnelley copied no original element of selection, coordination, or arrangement; accordingly, Donnelley was entitled to summary judgment on Bellsouth's claim of copyright infringement. To establish a claim of copyright infringement, Bellsouth had to prove ownership of a valid expressive act. Here, Bellsouth's arrangement and coordination were "entirely typical" for a business directory and lacked the requisite originality required for copyright protection. The court further noted that because there is only one way to construct a useful business directory, the arrangement had "merged" with the idea of a business directory, and thus was uncopyrightable. Finally, the court noted that given that the copyright protection of a factual compilation is "thin," a competitor's taking the bulk of factual material from a preexisting compilation without infringement of the author's copyright is not surprising. Copyright ensures authors the right to their original expression, but encourages others to build freely on the ideas and information conveyed by a work.

[Bellsouth Advertising & Publishing Corp. v. Donnelley Info. Publishing, 999 F2d 1436 (11th Cir. 1993)]

No infringement of copyright occurred in publication of baseball pitcher statistics. On remand from the circuit court, *Kregos v. Associated Press*, 937 F2d 700 (2d Cir. 1991), the district court was asked to determine whether the AP's 1986 baseball form infringed on Kregos's copyrighted form in that it used five out of 10 statistical categories used by Kregos. Since Kregos's form is only protected as a compilation, the question here was does 50 percent similarity equate to substantial similarity? *Held:* No reasonable person could conclude that the 1986 AP form that included five different statistical categories out of the 10 used by Kregos could be substantially similar to Kregos's form. The focus, of course, was on whether there was substantial similarity between the copyrightable elements of Kregos's form and the allegedly infringing form. Here, there was no substantial similarity between the one category that Kregos apparently invented, "a pitcher's record against the opponent at that specific ball-park," and the AP's more inclusive category, a pitcher's performance against that opponent. In making such fine distinctions, courts must balance the rights of authors with the rights of others to create outside the area protected against infringement. The differences between the two forms here involved the very elements that made Kregos's form copyrightable. Thus, Kregos won a Pyrrhic victory in the circuit court, for the very creativity that allows him to claim copyright shields the defendant from an infringement claim.

[Kregos v. Associated Press, 795 F. Supp. 1325 (SDNY 1992)]

[2] Computerizing and Copying Structure

Arrangement of land ownership data as reflected in plat map is copyrightable. RMP, a publisher of copyrighted land ownership plat maps, sued DSC, another map publisher, for copyright infringement. DSC admitted using RMP's maps as templates for performing its own research as to land ownership in the locations in question, but challenged the copyrightability of RMP's maps, especially since DSC was industrious and made numerous changes in the RMP maps. *Held:* DSC infringed RMP's maps, which were copyrightable as an arrangement and presentation of landownership information, a translation from dusty books of legal jargon to a picture. It was precisely this contribution that DSC borrowed. That DSC was industrious or that DSC had the right to check its research against RMP's did not give it the right to start using RMP's copyrighted work. Everyone must do the same basic work, the same industrious collection. Whether that work takes a second or a year has no weight in copyrighting a compilation; what matters is that there has been an improvement, however small. The smaller the contribution, the fewer the rights afforded by copyright.

[Rockford Map Publishers v. Direct Serv. Co. of Colo., Inc., 768 F2d 145 (7th Cir. 1985)]

Pagination of case reports that reflects arrangement and selection of author is protected by copyright. WPC sued to enjoin MDC from introducing "star pagination" (SP) keyed to WPC's case reports into MDC's LEXIS data base and thereby infringing WPC's copyright in its books' arrangement of cases that is reflected and expressed in its pagination. Users of SP would be able to "jump" to citations from WPC's reporter system without needing to physically refer to the books themselves. *Held:* WPC's case arrangements, an important part of which is internal page citations, are original works of authorship entitled to copyright protection. The crux of this decision was not that page numbers are per se copyrightable; rather, it was that the copyright on these books as a whole was infringed by the unauthorized appropriation of these particular numbers. WPC's arrangement, which is reflected in its pagination, is copyrightable since it is the result of WPC's considerable labor, talent, and judgment. Otherwise, a LEXIS user could use SP to scroll through WPC's books without ever using them; infringement, however uneconomical, is still infringement.

[West Publishing Co. v. Mead Data Cent., Inc., 799 F2d 1219 (8th Cir. 1986)]

Organizational categories employed in yellow pages telephone directory constitute copyrightable arrangement of data. BAP provided DIP with a list of all its relevant yellow pages business subscribers. Thereafter, DIP hired a subcontractor to key a copy of BAP's yellow pages into a computer data base, and used that data base to make "sales lead sheets" for selling advertisements in DIP's own directory. BAP sued DIP for copyright infringement and was granted summary judgment. *Held:* Summary judgment was appropriate here since BAP had a valid copyright in its yellow pages, as a compilation. DIP infringed this copyright by substantially appropriating the selection, coordination, or arrangement that comprised the format of BAP's directory. First, infringement occurred when the work was keyed into the computer, thereby fixing the copy in a material object. Second, although DIP's subcontractor keyed the information into the computer using various codes that DIP "authored," this in effect distilled BAP's compilation down to its basic elements; DIP retained the tools required to reconstitute the compilation. Thus, DIP's encoded compilation appropriated the selection, coordination, and arrangement of BAP's original directory. Finally, for this reason, DIP's lead sheets also infringed. Even though they were arranged differently than BAP's yellow pages and served a different purpose, they too were generated from the infringing data base, and thus substantially appropriated protected elements of the original. Also probative of DIP's infringement was the fact that it had all the information contained in BAP's yellow pages pursuant to the licensing agreement. It was interest in the *format* that caused it to make a data base version of the directory.

[Bellsouth Advertising & Publishing Corp. v. Donnelley Info. Publishing, Inc., 933 F2d 952 (11th Cir. 1991)]

Genuine issue of fact exists as to whether publisher who combined related categories of yellow pages into more general ones infringed original. BAP, a publisher of yellow pages phone directories, sued ABL, a publisher of business directories, for copyright infringement. ABL requested summary judgment on the issue. *Held:* Summary judgment was inappropriate since a genuine issue of fact existed as to whether or not ABL's actions in keying yellow pages information into its data bases substantially appropriated the constituent elements of the original format. Unlike *Bellsouth Advertising & Publishing Corp. v. Donnelley Information Publishing, Inc.*, 933 F2d 952 (11th Cir. 1991), ABL did not recreate BAP's specific headings, since it often combined information found under several related headings under the most general heading. Thus, ABL did not have the ability to recreate BAP's yellow pages in its structure and organization.

[Bellsouth Advertising & Publishing Corp. v. American Business Lists, Inc., 1992 WL 338392, 1993 Copy. L. Dec. ¶ 27,017 (ND Ga. 1992)]

Preliminary injunction is not appropriate where borrowed data is in public domain. NADA, a used-car price guide publisher, sued CCC for copying nearly all the information from NADA's copyrighted monthly price guide books into CCC's own computer data base, which it resells to its clients. Prior to this action, NADA rebuffed CCC's request for a license to use the price guide information. NADA requested a preliminary injunction to prevent further infringement of its copyright. CCC argued that since several states require by law the use of NADA numbers in vehicle valuations, the prices are in the public domain and cannot be copyrighted. *Held:* CCC's argument that the prices are in the public domain reduced NADA's likelihood of success on the merits, especially in those states that mandate the use of NADA numbers. CCC properly argued that since due process requires that the public must have free access to the laws by which they are bound, NADA could not enforce a copyright over the numbers that have been incorporated by reference into the statutes. Therefore, since a balancing of the hardships favored CCC and since NADA's chances were weak, especially in the statutory states, a preliminary injunction was inappropriate.

[NADA Servs. Corp. v. CCC Info. Servs. Inc., 1991 WL 287961 (ND Ill. 1991)]

[3] Copying Selections

Copyright may exist in data base because of creative choices exercised in selecting data for inclusion. Eckes sued CPU for infringing its copyrighted publication on baseball card prices (Guide), a listing of some 18,000 baseball cards, by publishing CPU's own monthly update guide (MUG) to 5,000 cards that the Guide had identified as premium cards. Eckes appealed the lower court's ruling that while the Guide was copyrightable, it was not infringed by CPU since there was no substantial similarity between the two works. *Held:* Eckes's exercise of selection, creativity, and judgment in determining that 5,000 out of 18,000 cards were premium merits copyright protection; further, CPU infringed by copying that selection. There was substantial similarity between the two works, especially given that the two lists of premium cards were substantially the same. Inasmuch as Eckes testified that there was considerable debate within the company and among dealers as to which cards were premium, a necessarily subjective determination, it is impossible to suppose that CPU's list came about without wholesale copying. Further, the existence of numerous errors in common constituted further evidence of piracy. Finally, the most egregious example of copying was that the first issue of the MUG contained the Guide's base prices as list prices, thus leading to the false impression that the MUG was an authorized update of the Guide.

[Eckes v. Card Prices Update, 736 F2d 859 (2d Cir. 1984)]

[4] Fair Use and Private Copying

Where pitching forms of two different companies are not substantially similar, one company's copyright infringement claim cannot be maintained. George L. Kregos, d/b/a American Sports Wire, was a compiler of baseball statistics. Kregos brought an action against a newspaper syndicate, the Associated Press (AP), and others for, among other things, copyright infringement for use of his pitching form, which was created by computer software he had developed. *Held:* Because the Kregos and AP forms were not substantially similar, the AP could not be held liable for copyright infringement. To make out a copyright infringement claim, Kregos had to establish that the defendants copied his form. Since direct evidence of copying is rarely obtainable, copying is generally established by showing (1) that the defendant had access to the copyrighted work and (2) the substantial similarity of protectable material in the two works. Because Kregos's form had been published in newspapers since 1983, the defendants clearly had access to them. Moreover, in 1983, Kregos had sent the AP a copy of his form, hoping for syndication, and the AP admitted to using his form as a model for its virtually identical 1984 form. As to the second prong of the test, Kregos had to prove that the forms did not differ by more than a "trivial degree." The AP form differed from Kregos's form by far more than a "trivial degree"; four of the AP's 10 statistics were different from those calculated on the Kregos form. In addition, much of the similarity between the AP and Kregos forms was necessitated because there were a limited number of statistics generally considered outcome-productive by those familiar with baseball. As the forms were not substantially similar, the AP could not be held liable for copyright infringement.

[Kregos v. Associated Press, 3 F3d 656 (2d Cir. 1993)]

Verbatim copying of several questions from standardized test does not constitute fair use. ETS was granted an injunction that enjoined PR, an organization preparing students to take tests, from using test questions used in ETS's copyrighted examinations. PR appealed, claiming, inter alia, that it had made "fair use," since it used ETS's questions as part of its teaching instruction offered. *Held:* PR's courses did not qualify as teaching within the meaning of 17 USC § 107, but even if it were found that they did, ETS would still likely succeed on the issue of fair use. PR's use of the questions was highly commercial. Further, considering the unique nature of secure tests, any use of the questions was destructive of ETS's copyrights. Indeed, given that nature, replication of even a few test questions is not necessarily insubstantial use. Finally, by publishing ETS's test, PR adversely affected ETS's market by making the standardized test materials worthless.

[Educational Testing Serv. v. Katzman, 793 F2d 533 (3d Cir. 1986)]

Fair use doctrine may permit indexing of copyrighted work by outsider without permission of holders of copyrights to original. NYT sued to enjoin RDT from making a personal name index (PNI) to NYT's annual copyrighted newspaper indexes without its permission, thereby infringing its copyright. *Held:* A consideration of the fair use doctrine shows that an injunction should not be granted since NYT would not likely succeed on the merits. RDT's work did not appropriate copyrightable aspects of NYT's indexes (which, as compilations, have limited copyright protection); though entirely based on the NYT indexes, RDT's index was not another version of NYT's work, but a work with a different function and form. More important, RDT's work was addressed to a different market than NYT's work, and it did not impinge on the commercial value of NYT's work. RDT's index only referred to NYT indexes, not to the NYT newspapers themselves. Thus, anyone using RDT's index must consult a copy of the NYT indexes to get the full benefit. Had RDT's index directly correlated data to the newspapers themselves, instead of copying names from NYT's indexes, NYT would have had a strong claim to copyright infringement.

[New York Times v. Roxbury Data Interface, Inc., 434 F. Supp. 217 (DNJ 1977)]

Contractual rights are primary means for creating and enforcing restrictions on access to electronic data bases. TS, an electronic data base provider, sought to preliminarily enjoin Caro, a software provider, from distributing software that allowed TS subscribers to violate copyright laws and the Telecommunications Act, as well as tortiously interfere in their contracts with TS. *Held:* TS should be awarded a preliminary injunction. Use of the software would cause subscribers to violate the standard contract, which states "[t]he equipment may not be moved, modified or interfaced with any other equipment without [TS's] prior written consent." Since, in order to serve the software, the TS terminal and data lines must be moved and altered, use of the software would likely interfere with the contractual relations between TS and its subscribers. Caro could also be contributorily or vicariously liable for copyright infringement since the software has no "substantial noninfringing" uses. Caro's assertion of fair use because only small portions of the entire data base could be copied at any time was misleading, since copying a few pages may be substantial in light of the structure and typical use of the data base. Finally, Caro may have violated the Telecommunications Act, 47 USC § 605, which forbids aiding the authorized interception or publication of any interstate communication by wire or radio not intended for the general public. Here, it was uncontested that the software program intercepted TS transmissions, allowing subscribers to download information in violation of their contracts. Further, courts interpreting Section 605 have held that the act of viewing a transmission that the viewer was not authorized to receive constitutes a publication. Thus, unauthorized, downloading constitutes a publication within the meaning of the statute.

[Telerate Sys., Inc. v. Caro, 689 F. Supp. 221 (SDNY 1988)]

Fair use doctrine protects copying and distribution of stock list to limited audience where plaintiff is not likely to succeed on merits. DJ, publisher of a stock list index, sued to enjoin the Board of Trade of Chicago (BTCC) from using its copyrighted material, the "Dow Average" (DA), in connection with offerings of futures contracts, thereby violating DJ's copyright. The BTCC had made more than 2,000 copies of DJ's list of component stocks in the DA as part of a rulebook that the BTCC distributed to its membership and staff. *Held:* An injunction was not in order since DJ was not likely to win on the merits in view of the fair use doctrine. Since copyright protection for compilations of factual material cannot be reconciled with general principles of copyright law, authors of compilations must be held to grant broader licenses for subsequent use than persons whose work is truly creative. Because of the nature of DJ's index lists, where no component stock has any independent value except as a component of that particular index, if there is to be *any* fair use of the lists, that use must entail literal reproduction of that list. Thus, here, there existed a departure from the general rule that exact copies cannot constitute fair use. Finally, given the insubstantiality of the portion copied in respect to the copyrighted work as a whole, as well as DJ's failure to demonstrate any prejudice with respect to potential sales or decrease in value of DJ's publications as a result of copying, the balance of factors clearly weighed in favor of a finding of fair use.

[Dow Jones Co. v. Board of Trade of Chicago, 546 F. Supp. 113, 217 USPQ 901 (SDNY 1982)]

Copying entire book into computer data base constitutes fair use where use of computerized form is same use intended for book. NADA, a used-car price guide publisher, sued BDV for copying nearly all the information from NADA's copyrighted yearly price guide books into BDV's own computer data base (VDF); individual jurisdictions in Virginia would submit forms concerning car registration to BDV, which in turn would generate tax assessment values from its VDF on behalf of each jurisdiction. BDV claimed that it made fair use of the information. *Held:* BDV did not infringe, since it used the information in NADA's guides for the purpose for which they were intended, namely, to assess values of various cars. It did not sell the VDF tape to its customers; rather, it used the tapes to provide a service of assessing vehicles. Even if such use did constitute infringement, it would be permissible under the fair use doctrine. The single most important factor to consider in determining fair use is market effect. Thus, although BDV's use was commercial, and it admittedly copied a substantial portion of NADA's guide, its use was fair, since it has not and will not impair the market for NADA guides.

[NADA Serv. Corp. v. Business Data of Va., 651 F. Supp. 44 (ED Va. 1986)]

PART D.   PRODUCT LIABILITY

¶ 15.10 GENERAL PRODUCT ISSUES

[1] Contractual Relationships

Contractual relationship creates liabilities based on relationship itself. In 1988, TRC hired BRS to convert its trademark file cards into a computer data base and corresponding search and retrieval system. TRC sued for breach of contract because BRS delivered an operational system in January 1992 although it was required to deliver a fully operational system no later than January 1990. TRC also sued for lost profits from its prospective sale of CD-ROM versions of the data base. *Held:* BRS breached the contract since it failed to perform in a timely manner, even though it knew that "time was of the essence." However, an award of lost profits for lost CD-ROM sales must be denied since it is too speculative. New York law requires that recovery of lost profits as damages for breach of contract must be capable of proof with reasonable certainty. Inasmuch as this was a new product whose future is subject to many uncertain variables, and TRC could offer neither its own experience nor that of a competitor in support of its lost profits projections, under New York law, this record was insufficient to justify an award of lost profits. Also, TRC's claim for lost profits failed for the independent reason that liabilty for such damages was not fairly contemplated by the parties at the time of contracting as required under New York law.

[Trademark Research Corp. v. Maxwell Online, Inc., 995 F2d 326 (2d Cir. 1993)]

Information provider can contractually eliminate tort liability for breach of duty to provide correct data. AR, an investor, sued S&P for negligent misrepresentation for S&P's incorporation of an erroneous closing price of a particular stock in its stock lists, thereby establishing the sale price for AR's option contracts. *Held:* Although S&P breached its duty to AR, the exculpatory clause in the license agreement between S&P and the Chicago Board Options Exchange (CBOE), whereby S&P expressly disclaimed its liability as an information provider for inaccuracies, was enforceable against AR because the license agreement was incorporated into the rules of the CBOE, which regulated all AR's transactions. S&P did owe AR a duty to provide accurate information, since all transactions were founded on information provided by S&P. S&P had a special position as publisher of stock market indexes, S&P knew that AR and others relied on S&P representations, and AR was a member of a limited class foreseeable to S&P. Nevertheless, the exculpatory clause in the license agreement excused S&P's breach. Illinois courts enforce such clauses where it is clear from the contract that the parties intended to shift the risk of loss, unless such a shift was contrary to settled public policy or because of a disparity in bargaining power between them. Even where a semi-public nature is found to permeate the transaction between the parties, exculpatory clauses will be recognized; since no offsetting policy rationale existed here, AR bore the risk of loss.

[Rosenstein v. Standard & Poor's Corp., No. 1-91-3000, 1993 WL 176532 (Ill. Ct. App. May 26, 1993)]

Information agreements require exercise of reasonable and workmanlike care in delivering services and resulting information. DeLanney sued SBT for negligently failing to perform its contract to publish a yellow pages advertisement. SBT appealed the jury's award of lost profits for its negligence. *Held:* SBT's failure to publish the advertisement was not a tort. Accompanying every contract there is a common-law duty to perform with care, skill, reasonable expedience, and faithfulness the thing agreed to be done, and a negligent failure to observe any of these conditions is a tort, as well as a breach of the contract. SBT did not fail to observe these conditions. While it is sometimes difficult to distinguish causes of action sounding in tort and contract, where the only damage or loss, as in the instant case, is to the subject matter of the contact, the action is ordinarily on the contract. Here, SBT's conduct in failing to publish the advertisement only gave rise to liability because it breached the parties' agreement.

[Southwestern Bell Tel. v. DeLanney, 809 SW2d 493 (Tex. 1991)]

¶ 15.11 MISINFORMATION AND LIBEL

Publication regarding public figure that incorrectly attributes comments to that individual is not actionable except upon proof of malice, even if misquote is intentional.   Malcolm, a writer for *New Yorker Magazine*, wrote an article about Masson, a psychoanalyst. Masson sued *New Yorker*, claiming that the article libeled him by misquoting him and fabricating quotations. He appealed an award of summary judgment to *New Yorker. Held:* Since Masson is a public figure, he cannot recover unless he proves that *New Yorker* published the defamatory statement with actual malice. Even deliberate alteration of the words uttered by Masson is not equivalent to publishing with knowledge of falsity, unless the alteration results in a material change in the meaning conveyed by the statement. That quotation marks are used to attribute words not in fact spoken bears on the issue of malice, but it is not dispositive. Thus, if the alterations here gave a different meaning to the statements, bearing on their defamatory character, the device of quotation marks might be critical in finding the words actionable.

[Masson v. New Yorker Magazine, Inc., 111 S. Ct. 2419 (1991)]

Constitution does not create absolute immunity for published statements couched as expressions of opinion.   LJC's newspaper published an article about Milkovich that implied that Milkovich committed perjury. Milkovich sued for defamation, and appealed a ruling that the article was constitutionally protected opinion. *Held:* The connotation that Milkovich committed perjury is sufficiently factual to be susceptible of being proved true or false. Thus, LJC could not avoid libel laws by claiming that the First Amendment protects statements of "opinion." Neither the Constitution nor case law has created a wholesale defamation exemption for any statement styled as "opinion" as opposed to "fact." A person who couches his statement, "I think Jones is a liar," can cause just as much harm as the one who says, "Jones is a liar." Existing constitutional doctrine adequately secures freedom of speech without the creation of an artificial dichotomy between "opinion" and "fact."

[Milkovich v. Lorain Journal Co., 110 S. Ct. 2695 (1990)]

Publication of incorrect information about public figures and public issues is insulated from civil liability, absent finding of malice or intent to mislead.   Sullivan, an elected official, sued NYT, alleging that it published an advertisement containing statements about him that were libelous per se. *Held:* In the absence of a showing of malice, an award of damages for libel was inappropriate. The First and Fourteenth Amendments require a federal rule that a public official may not recover damages for a defamatory falsehood relating to his official conduct unless he proves that the statement was made with "actual malice"—that is, with knowledge that it was false or with reckless disregard of whether it was false or not. This privilege prevents the threat of damage suits from inhibiting vigorous debate about public questions and insulating public officials from criticism. Even commercial speech, as the advertisement here, enjoys such protection if the allegedly libelous statement would be otherwise constitutionally protected.

[New York Times Co. v. Sullivan, 376 US 254 (1964)]

[1] Inaccurate Business Information

Constitutional restrictions on liability standards do not apply to information service's erroneous report that company had filed for bankruptcy.   D&B, a credit service, sent reports to five subscribers that GB had filed a voluntary petition for bankruptcy. The report was false and grossly misrepresented GB's assets and liabilities. Although D&B later issued a corrective notice, GB was dissatisfied and brought suit for defamation. D&B appealed an adverse verdict awarding presumed and punitive damages, claiming that GB did not prove that D&B acted with "actual malice." *Held:* Since this was a credit report concerning no public issue, but was solely in the individual interest of the speaker and its specific business audience, there was no need for GB to show actual malice in order to prevail. That First Amendment requirement only applies to speech involving matters of public concern. Moreover, since the credit report was made available to only five subscribers who were restricted under their licensing agreement from disseminating it further, it could not be said that the report involved any strong interest in the free flow of commercial information, especially when that information was wholly false and clearly damaging to the victim's business reputation.

[Dun & Bradstreet v. Greenmoss Builders, Inc., 472 US 749 (1985)]

Publisher is liable for negligent inclusion of bank among those that would have no capital within a year.   VI, a publisher of information concerning financial institutions based on data submitted to federal regulatory agencies, erroneously included BRB among a list of commercial banks that could reach zero equity within a year. BRB sued VI for libel. *Held:* BRB only had to show that VI was liable under a negligence theory, not that it acted with malice. Although VI's speech did concern a matter of legitimate public concern, BRB was not a "general public figure," someone with widespread or pervasive power and influence in community affairs. Nor was BRB a "limited-purpose public figure" with respect to the particular issue raised in VI's report: corporate financial health. A plaintiff should not be considered a limited-purpose public figure absent the existence of a predefamation public controversy directly involving the plaintiff. A business enterprise does not lose the protection afforded by the traditional law of defamation simply by virtue of its being subject to pervasive governmental regulation. Since BRB was not a public figure, the negligence standard should have been applied to VI's actions. The evidence—that VI used an unreliable method in estimating and predicting BRB's financial viability and that it failed to conduct any inquiry or investigation, in the face of illogical and unreasonable data concerning BRB that would have revealed the mistake—was sufficient to sustain a finding that VI was negligent.

[Blue Ridge Bank v. Veribanc, Inc., 866 F2d 681 (4th Cir. 1989)]

Existence of inaccuracies in information product does not necessarily establish liability of information providers.   During a two-year period, D&B, a credit service, sent reports to more than 300 subscribers that grossly understated the size of SC's business. During that period, SC's gross sales suffered a serious decline and there were rumors concerning its financial difficulties. SC won a jury award against D&B for defamation. D&B appealed. *Held:* SC did not meet its burden of proving that D&B was liable since it did not provide evidence that anyone who read the report found it to have the defamatory meaning inferred by SC; therefore, the case was remanded. SC did not argue that the reports were per se libelous; rather, it claimed a correlation between the decline of its business and the inaccurate reports. To establish liability under Colorado law, which follows the Restatement (Second) of Torts § 613, SC had to prove not only the defamatory character of the communication, but also the recipient's understanding of its defamatory meaning. The only evidence it presented—the chronological correlation between the business's decline and the erroneous report—was insufficient to establish proof of defamation. Finally, credit reports are conditionally privileged under Colorado law. To be actionable, D&B must have abused its privilege to make certain mistakes in the issuance of credit reports by conduct amounting to reckless disregard.

[Sunward Corp. v. Dun & Bradstreet, Inc., 811 F2d 511 (10th Cir. 1987)]

[2] Publishers and Distributors

Libraries and distributors of information are exempted from liability for libel, slander, or similar misconduct. CompuServe (CIS) contracted with CCI to make available a journalism forum (JF) to its online subscribers. Cubby brought suit against CIS, claiming that Rumorville USA (RUSA), a publication available on CIS's JF, had libeled it. CIS moved for summary judgment. *Held:* Since CIS, as a news distributor, did not know or have reason to know of the allegedly defamatory RUSA statements, it could not be held liable for them; therefore, an award of summary judgment on behalf of CIS was granted. A computerized data base is functionally equivalent to the more traditional news vendor. CIS should therefore be held to the same standard of liability that is applied to public libraries, bookstores or newsstands, and other vendors and distributors of information, and should be excused from liability for defamatory publications where it had no prior knowledge or reason to know of the defamation. To hold it to a higher standard would unduly burden the free flow of information.

[Cubby, Inc. v. CompuServe, Inc., 776 F. Supp. 135 (SDNY 1991)]

News service is not liable to readers for negligent false statements. Daniel, a securities investor, subscribed to DJC's online news retrieval system. After making a bad investment based on misleading information from a news report in DJC's data base, he brought suit against DJC for negligent publication of false and misleading statements. DJC moved for summary judgment. *Held:* Because there was no special relationship between Daniel and DJC, summary judgment was awarded to DJC. A news service is not liable to its readers for negligent false statements, absent the existence of a special relationship between the parties. Here, Daniel was one of 200,000 subscribers to the data base. The special relationship required to allow an action for negligent misstatements must be greater than that between the ordinary buyer and seller. The relationship between subscribers to DJC's online news service is functionally identical to that of a purchaser of a newspaper. New technology here does not make requisite a new legal rule merely because of its novelty. News services are instruments for the free flow of all forms of information and are protected by the First Amendment's guaranty of freedom of the press. This online news service was entitled to the same protection as more established means of news distribution.

[Daniel v. Dow Jones & Co., 137 Misc. 2d 94, 520 NYS2d 334 (Civ. Ct. 1987)]

¶ 15.12 MISINFORMATION CAUSING PERSONAL INJURY

Publisher has no duty to investigate accuracy of information of its publications and is not accountable under product liability theory. Winter and his friend purchased *The Encyclopedia of Mushrooms*, a publication distributed but not edited by GPP, to help them collect and eat wild mushrooms. Using the book as their guide, they collected and cooked deadly mushrooms, and became so ill that they both required liver transplants. They brought suit against GPP, inter alia, for liability based on product liability. *Held:* GPP was not liable for the mushroom enthusiasts' injuries under theories of strict liability or negligence. Strict liability standards apply to tangible items, not to ideas and expressions in a book. To apply such standards to a book would seriously inhibit freedom of thought and expression. While several courts have applied product liability law to books containing detailed aeronautical charts, such an application is inappropriate here because an aeronautical chart is analogous to a compass, while *The Encyclopedia of Mushrooms* is analogous to a book on "how to use" a compass or aeronautical chart. The chart is like a physical "product," while the how-to-use book is pure thought and expression. Further, negligence theories are also inappropriate, since no publisher is under a duty to act as a guarantor of the accuracy of an author's statements of fact. GPP never assumed that burden, and was under no duty to investigate the accuracy of the books it publishes. First Amendment considerations prevent extension of negligence liability to the ideas and expressions contained in a book.

[Winter v. GP Putnam's Sons, 938 F2d 1033 (9th Cir. 1991)]

There is no cause of action for publication of advertisement or article that causes harm when applied to fact setting. Miller, a minor, read a supplement on shooting sports published in *Boy's Life* magazine, and consequently died while playing with a rifle. His mother, Way, sued the Boy Scouts of America (BSA) as publishers of the magazine for "negligent publication." She appealed an award of summary judgment in favor of the BSA. *Held:* Since the record does not support the conclusion that the child's experimentation with the rifle was a reasonably foreseeable consequence of the publication, an award of summary judgment was appropriate. Under the common law, negligence consists in breach of a legal duty owed by one person to another and damages resulting from that breach. Foreseeability provides the touchstone in determining whether circumstances give rise to a duty. A risk-utility analysis of the publication shows that the information in the supplement promoted safe and responsible use of firearms. Because of the risk of improper use of firearms by children, this publication is of considerable social utility. Finally, it is inappropriate to apply strict tort liability on these facts. Product liability law applies to dangerous tangible things. Words, ideas, thoughts, and information conveyed by the magazine and supplement, here, were not *products* within the meaning of the Restatement (Second) of Torts.

[Way v. Boy Scouts of Am., 856 SW2d 230 (Tex. Ct. App. 1993)]

¶ 15.13 MISINFORMATION CAUSING ECONOMIC LOSS

Auditor owes no general duty of care to public at large for accuracy of its audits. Bily and other plaintiffs invested in Osborne Computers (OCC) based on two unqualifiedly favorable reports issued by AYC auditors. When OCC filed for bankruptcy seven months later, Bily sued AYC, inter alia, for professional negligence. AYC appealed a jury verdict in favor of Bily. *Held:* Because an auditor owes no general duty of care regarding the conduct of an audit to persons other than the client, the verdict should be instated in favor of AYC. Increasing auditors' liability for error would simply serve to reduce the availability of audit services to fledgling industries. It is doubtful whether the auditor is the most efficient absorber of the losses stemming from inaccurate financial information in a relationship between auditor, client, and third party, where the third party is a sophisticated investor. However, an auditor may be held liable for negligent misrepresentations in an audit report to those persons who act in reliance on those misrepresentations in a transaction the auditor intended to influence. Further, an auditor may be held liable to reasonably foreseeable third persons for intentional fraud in the preparation and dissemination of an audit report.

[Bily v. Arthur Young Co., 3 Cal. 4th 370, 11 Cal. Rptr. 2d 51, 834 P2d 745 (1992)]

CHAPTER **16**

PRIVACY, DISCLOSURE, AND ACCESS TO INFORMATION

PART D. PRIVATE DATA

¶ 16.01 PRIVACY RIGHTS DEFINED

U.S. Supreme Court holds that disclosure of individual's FBI rap sheet would be unwarranted invasion of privacy under the federal FOIA.   The FBI compiles and maintains criminal identification records or "rap sheets" on millions of people based on information provided to it by local, state, and federal law enforcement agencies. These rap sheets contain descriptive information as well as a history of arrests, charges, convictions, and incarcerations. Plaintiffs-respondents, a CBS news correspondent and the Reporters Committee for Freedom of the Press, sought an individual's rap sheet from the FBI pursuant to the FOIA. This request was denied. Subsequently, plaintiffs-respondents filed suit in district court seeking the rap sheet for Charles Medico because it contained "matters of public record." The district court granted summary judgment for the U.S. Department of Justice. The court of appeals reversed and the suit was brought before the Supreme Court on certiorari. *Held:* Disclosure of the contents of an individual's FBI rap sheet to a third party was not allowed; the court of appeals' decision was reversed. The Supreme Court reasoned that such a disclosure "could reasonably be expected to constitute an unwarranted invasion of personal privacy" within the meaning of the FOIA, and thus such disclosure was prohibited by the FOIA. The Court relied on the law enforcement exemption to the FOIA, 5 USCA § 552(b)(7)(C), which excludes records or information compiled for law enforcement purposes, "but only to the extent that the production of such [materials] . . . could reasonably be expected to constitute an unwarranted invasion of personal privacy." The Court rejected the respondents' argument that because the events summarized in the rap sheet had been previously disclosed to the public, the individual's interest in avoiding disclosure of these events was practically nonexistent. The Court thus noted the difference between scattered disclosure of bits of information contained in a rap sheet and disclosure of the rap sheet as a whole.

[Department of Justice v. Reporters Comm., 109 S. Ct. 1468 (1989)]

Patient's constitutional right to privacy does not bar disclosure of her mental health records where state's interest in securing information outweighed her privacy interests.   After receiving formal written complaints that a psychiatrist (Dr. K) and his former patient (Patient A) were having a romantic relationship, and that the psychiatrist was depressed and abusing alcohol, the State Board of Physician Quality Assurance initiated an investigation and subpoenaed Dr. K's records relating to Patient A's treatment. On appeal, Dr. K and Patient A argued that Patient A's constitutional right to privacy barred the disclosure of her mental health records to the Board. *Held:* Although Patient A had a constitutional right to privacy in Dr. K's records of her psychiatric treatment, this right was outweighed by the interest of the state in securing the information contained therein. The right to privacy is protected by the federal constitution; medical records clearly fall within this constitutionally protected sphere. However, this right is not absolute. The individual privacy interest in the patient's medical records must be balanced against the legitimate interests of the state in securing the information contained therein. Factors to consider include the type of record requested, the information it contains, the potential for harm in subsequent nonconsensual disclosure, the injury in disclosure to the relationship for which the record was generated, the adequacy of safeguards to prevent unauthorized disclosure, the government's need for access, and whether there is an express statutory mandate, articulate public policy, or other public interest militating toward access. Here, after weighing all these factors, the court concluded that the state's interest outweighed Patient A's privacy right. The court noted that to give a patient, in effect, a veto over the Board's power to regulate licensed physicians would be to eviscerate the Board's ability to protect the larger public interest. Furthermore, the court noted that a decision in favor of Patient A would allow those physicians who are unscrupulous and in a position to exert influence over their patients to stop a preliminary investigation by the Board.

[Dr. K v. State Bd. of Physician Quality Assurance, 632 A2d 453 (Md. Ct. App. 1993)].

Statute restricting use of automatic dialing-announcing devices is not unconstitutional, as it narrowly regulates the facets of use that are most likely susceptible to violating privacy. The trial court issued a temporary injunction enjoining Hall d/b/a "721 Associates" and "Associated Marketing" from using automatic dialing-announcing devices (ADADs) in contravention of Minnesota Statutes 325e.26–325e.31 (ADAD statute). Hall, claiming that the ADAD statute was unconstitutional on the ground that it violated the First Amendment and Minnesota Constitution Article 1, § 3, sought, among other things, a declaration that the ADAD statute was unconstitutional. *Held:* The ADAD statute did not unconstitutionally offend commercial speech protection. The regulatory scope of the ADAD statute was limited to commercial speech. Commercial speech is given a limited measure of protection, commensurate with its subordinate position in the scale of First Amendment values, allowing modes of regulation that might be impermissible in the realm of noncommercial expression. In assessing the constitutionality of commercial speech regulation, a court must first determine if the commercial speech concerns lawful activity and is not misleading. Next, a court must examine whether the asserted government interest is substantial. If both inquiries yield positive answers, the court must determine whether the regulation directly advances the governmental interest asserted, and whether it is not more extensive than is necessary to that interest. The regulation must be narrowly tailored to achieve its purpose. As the trial court had not determined whether Hall's prerecorded messages were true or false, the court assumed that the messages were neither false nor misleading. It concluded that the state had a substantial interest in protection of privacy in the home and that the statute directly advanced this interest. Finally, the court noted that the ADAD statute was "narrowly tailored to achieve the desired objective." The ADAD statute did not restrict commercial solicitation by a live operator, nor did it prohibit commercial solicitation by ADADs. Absent advance consent, the ADAD statue required that the ADAD operator introduce the tape-recorded message by a live operator, that the live operator make certain disclosures, and that the live operator call at a decent hour. The statute does not impose a blanket proscription on computer-generated commercial telephone solicitation, but rather narrowly regulates the facets of ADAD use that are most susceptible to violating privacy. As such, the statute is carefully calculated to advance the state's substantial interest in protecting privacy.

[Minnesota v. Casino Marketing Group, 491 NW2d 882 (Minn. 1992)]

PART A.   DATA COMMUNICATIONS

¶ 16.02 COMPUTER AND COMMUNICATIONS PRIVACY

Cordless telephone conversations are not protected by statutes prohibiting interception of wire, oral, and electronic communications without judicial approval. Smith's cordless telephone calls were intercepted by his next door neighbor via a Bearcat scanner. That neighbor tape recorded some of Smith's calls, which led to his arrest and conviction on five counts arising out of drug trafficking activities. Smith appealed, arguing, among other things, that the interception of his conversations violated both Title III of the Omnibus Crime and Control Streets Act of 1986 (Title III) and the Fourth Amendment. *Held:* The court of appeals affirmed Smith's convictions. The court noted that the argument that Title III applies to cordless telephone communications had been uniformly rejected by every court that had considered the issue. Title III prohibits the nonconsenual interception of "wire," "oral," and "electronic" communication without prior judicial approval. Here, Title III's exclusionary rule was not invoked because cordless telephone conversations are, inter alia, expressly excluded by that title. The court also found that Smith failed to show that his Fourth Amendment rights were infringed in this case.

[United States v. Smith, 978 F2d 171 (5th Cir. 1992)]

¶ 16.03 INTERCEPTED DATA COMMUNICATIONS

Supreme Court holds that information about numbers called and number of calls made from a telephone is not subject to Fourth Amendment protection. The telephone company installed a pen register at its central offices to record the numbers dialed from a robbery suspect's home. Here, the suspect was suspected of placing calls to the robbery victim's home. The police did not get a warrant or court order prior to having the pen register installed. Based on information obtained via the pen register, the police obtained a search warrant to search the suspect-petitioner's residence. The petitioner was ultimately indicted in the criminal court of Baltimore for robbery. He sought to suppress "all fruits derived from the pen register" on the ground that the police did not have a warrant for its use. *Held:* The Supreme Court held that the installation and use of a pen register was not a "search" pursuant to the Fourth Amendment; accordingly, no warrant was required prior to its use. The Court reasoned that the application of the Fourth Amendment depends on whether the person seeking to invoke its protection can claim that a "legitimate expectation of privacy" has been breached by the government. In its analysis, the Court noted that this standard has two parts. First, whether the individual has exhibited an actual (subjective) expectation of privacy. Second, whether the individual's expectation, viewed objectively, is "justifiable" under the circumstances. Here, the Court noted that telephone users do not normally have an expectation of privacy in the numbers that they dial since, among other things, the telephone company has the facilities for recording such information. Next, when the petitioner "exposed" such information to the phone company, he assumed the risk that the company would reveal that information to the police.

[Smith v. Maryland, 99 S. Ct. 2577 (1979)]

Electronic funds transfers, which took the form of bank credits at intermediary banks, are seizable properties under civil forfeiture statutes. Two groups of claimants, the "Atlantico Claimants" and the "Barranquilla Claimants," appealed from a final judgment and other rulings of the district court following a jury verdict that forfeited to the government more than $10 million pursuant to 18 USC § 981 and 21 USC § 881, the civil forfeiture statutes. The government seized these funds, which were proceeds of narcotics trafficking, as they passed through the U.S. banking system as electronic funds transfers (EFT), for ultimate deposit in the Columbian bank accounts of the claimants. The claimants raised numerous arguments on appeal, including the argument that EFTs were not seizable properties for the purposes of the civil forfeiture statutes because they were merely electronic communications. They further argued that an EFT is not a direct transfer of funds, but rather a series of contractual obligations to pay. Finally, the claimants argued that only after a transmission is complete and the communication is accepted and received by the beneficiary does it become a seizable res. The funds at issue were seized at intermediary banks after the first transaction had concluded and before the second had begun. *Held:* The EFTs, even though they took the form of bank credits at the intermediary banks, were clearly seizable properties under the forfeiture statutes. Section 881(a)(6) of Title 21 provides for the seizure of "moneys, negotiable instruments, securities, or other things of value . . . all proceeds traceable" to narcotics transactions. Similarly, 18 USC § 981(a)(1)(A) provides for the seizure of "any property, real or personal, involved in a transaction or attempted transaction . . . or any property traceable to such property." Moving these "traceable proceeds" from bank to bank did not insulate the proceeds from forfeiture.

[United States v. Daccarett, 6 F3d 37 (2d Cir. 1993)]

No expectation of privacy exists in telephone numbers displayed on digital pager properly seized by government officials pursuant to warrant because owner of pager had no control over telephone numbers transmitted into it and sender had no control over who was at receiving end. Drug Enforcement Agency (DEA) agents executed a search warrant of a residence in Detroit, Michigan. There, the agents seized, among other things, a RAM communications pager, which was seized in the "on" position. The agents monitored and recorded 40 incoming calls to the pager. One of the numbers appearing on the pager was chosen at random and a DEA agent called that number. During that phone conversation, the DEA agent and appellant arranged a cocaine drug sale; the appellant was subsequently arrested. The appellant moved to suppress evidence of his phone number and all subsequent phone conversations with DEA agents based on his Fourth Amendment rights. *Held:* The appellant's motion to suppress was denied. The court of appeals noted that the Fourth Amendment protects a person's legitimate expectation of privacy from invasion by government action. This analysis involves a two-pronged inquiry: first, whether the individual, by his conduct, has exhibited a subjective expectation of privacy; and second, whether that expectation is one that society accepts as reasonable. Here, the court noted that the appellant had no expectation of privacy in information he voluntarily turned over to third parties. In this situation, the court noted that a person who sends a message to a pager runs the risk that the message will be received by whomever is in possession of the pager. As such, the court declined to protect the appellant's misplaced trust that the message would actually reach the intended recipient.

[United States v. Maryland, 917 F2d 955 (6th Cir. 1990)]

Under California state constitution, court finds protected right of privacy in unlisted telephone number, name, and address; search of this information without a warrant is unreasonable. On December 5, 1980, a confidential informant contacted the police and claimed she had some information about illegal offtrack betting. The police had the informant call the contact, "Lucille," and attempt to place a bet. Acting without a warrant, the police checked the telephone number of Lucille and received the name and address of the subscriber, whose real name was Margaret McGee. The police then obtained two warrants relating to McGee. The first search warrant sought all billing information and an activity printout for a six-month period. The second warrant, obtained a week later, authorized a search of McGee's house and car. In the affidavit for the second warrant, McGee's name and address were obtained from the telephone company. The respondents moved to suppress the evidence seized during the search of McGee's home. They contended, inter alia, that the police unlawfully obtained McGee's name and address from the telephone company without a warrant because that number was unlisted. *Held:* The co-defendant had a reasonable, constitutionally protected expectation of privacy in her unlisted name, address, and telephone number. Obtaining that information from the phone company without a search warrant was unreasonable and violated California's constitution. All physical evidence obtained via the second, tainted warrant was therefore suppressed.

[People v. Chapman, 679 P2d 62 (Cal. 1984)]

Pennsylvania court finds telephone caller-identification services violate state's wiretapping statute and, when operated without a blocking mechanism, also violate state constitution privacy rights. The Pennsylvania Public Utility Commission approved the use of a customer service reintroduced by Bell of Pennsylvania—Caller*ID. This matter came before the court on a petition for review of that decision. This service would permit callers to identify, by telephone number, callers. This service was to be offered with limited blocking. Here, one blocking option would permit customers to block transmission of their phone numbers prior to placing a call. *Held:* The use of this caller-identification service, with or without the blocking service, violated Pennsylvania's Wiretapping and Electronic Surveillance Control Act and the Commission's authorization of the identification service without the blocking mechanism violated privacy rights protected by the state constitution. Under Pennsylvania law, no person may install or use "a trap or trace device" without first obtaining a court order. Here, the court held that Caller*ID clearly violated Pennsylvania's Wiretapping and Electronic Surveillance Control Act as a trap and trace device. Next, when operated without a blocking mechanism, telephone customers would have less control over the distribution of their telephone numbers and, thus, Caller*ID violated privacy rights under Pennsylvania's constitution.

[Barasch v. Public Util. Comm'n, 576 A2d 79 (Pa. Commw. 1990)]

¶ 16.04 RECORDING DATA: PEN REGISTERS AND CALLER IDENTIFICATION SYSTEMS

Defendant has no legitimate expectation of privacy in message transmitted into paging receiver. Pursuant to a lawful search for narcotics, DEA agents recovered, among other things, a communications pager belonging to one of two men who were arrested. The pager was an electronic digital display-type capable of receiving and storing messages from a touch-tone telephone; pressing a button would display stored numbers. One of the stored numbers was chosen at random and called by the agents. Meriwether spoke to the agent and arranged to purchase cocaine from him; when Meriwether arrived to make the purchase, the agents arrested him. Meriwether sought to suppress evidence of his phone number and all subsequent phone conversations with the agents, claiming that his Fourth Amendment rights were violated when the agent seized his phone number from the pager, because seizure of the phone number was not within the scope of the warrant. Furthermore, Meriwether claimed that he had a reasonable expectation of privacy in the transmitted phone number that was protected under the Fourth Amendment. *Held:* The agent's seizure of Meriwether's phone number from the pager was authorized by the warrant, and Meriwether had no subjective expectation of privacy in a message transmitted into a paging receiver. The warrant specifically authorized the agents to search for and seize "telephone numbers of customers, suppliers, couriers." A warrant authorizing seizure of phone numbers is specific enough to empower the executing officer to seize the numbers in whatever form they may appear. When considering whether a person has a legitimate expectation of privacy protected by the Fourth Amendment, courts must consider first, whether the individual, by his conduct, has exhibited a subjective expectation of privacy, and second, whether that expectation is one that society accepts as reasonable. A person has no legitimate expectation of privacy in information he voluntarily turns over to third parties. Here, when Meriwether sent his message to the pager, he ran the risk that either the owner or someone in possession of the pager would disclose the contents of his message. Meriwether's Fourth Amendment rights were not violated.

[United States v. Meriwether, 917 F2d 955 (6th Cir. 1990)]

Information obtained from pen register placed on telephone line can be used as evidence despite court order authorizing its installation not complying with statutory requirements. Thompson, along with 29 other individuals, was indicted on various drug-related and money-laundering charges. As part of its investigation, the government made extensive use of, among other things, pen registers to monitor the contacts made among the various conspirators. Thompson moved to suppress the information stemming from the pen registers on the ground that, absent the information from one of the pen registers, the affidavit supporting a Title III wiretap application would not have provided sufficient probable cause. The district court denied Thompson's motion. Thompson appealed on this suppression issue. *Held:* Information obtained from a pen register can be used as evidence at a criminal trial even if the court order authorizing installation does not comply with statutory requirements. Here, the court of appeals found that the affidavit in support of the application for installation of the pen registers was faulty. However, the court noted that the use of a pen register does not constitute a search for purposes of the Fourth Amendment and does not warrant invocation of the exclusionary rule. Thus, despite the application's flaw, the court allowed the use of the evidence obtained from the pen registers.

[United States v. Thompson, 936 F2d 1249 (11th Cir. 1991)]

Warrant is not required where defendant's pager is searched incident to his lawful arrest. Chan was arrested and charged in a two-count indictment alleging violation of 21 USC §§ 2 and 846. Approximately two minutes after Chan's actual arrest, the DEA agent seized an electronic pager in Chan's possession. The agent subsequently searched the pager by activating its memory and retrieving certain telephone numbers that were stored in it. Two numbers that incriminated Chan in a prior heroin deal were found in the pager. No heroin was found on Chan and no warrant had been obtained to seize and activate the pager. Chan argued that the activation of the pager was a search requiring a warrant because the pager was in a container in which he had a reasonable expectation of privacy and that the retrieval of numbers constituted a search that was not justified as a warrantless search incident to an arrest or as a warrantless search involving exigent circumstances. *Held:* Even though Chan had a reasonable expectation of privacy in the contents of the pager's memory, the activation of the memory following Chan's arrest was a valid search incident to arrest. In determining whether an individual's Fourth Amendment rights have been violated, the relevant inquiry is two-fold: (1) whether the individual has exhibited a subjective expectation of privacy and (2) whether the expectation is one that society recognizes as "reasonable." Here, Chan presumably maintained a subjective expectation that an item kept on his person would be free from government invasion; moreover, as the possessor of a pager has control over the electronically stored information, an expectation of privacy in the contents of the pager's memory is reasonable. Nevertheless, Chan's protected privacy interest in the contents of the pager's memory was irrelevant because the pager was searched incident to his arrest. When making a lawful arrest, police may conduct a warrantless search of the area within the arrestee's immediate control; that is, the area from within which he might gain possession of a weapon or destructible evidence. Such a search must be conducted at about the same time as the arrest and not be remote in time or place from the arrest. An officer may also search the contents of a container found on or near the arrestee in a search incident to arrest. Here, the pager was the product of a search of Chan's person, an area within his immediate control. Additionally, the retrieval of the numbers from the pager's memory was not remote in time or place from the arrest; the search occurred approximately two minutes after the arrest. A separate warrant was not required prior to a search of the pager's memory. Chan's expectation of privacy was destroyed as the result of a valid search incident to the arrest.

[United States v. Chan, 830 F. Supp. 531 (ND Cal. 1993)]

Telephone company's proposed caller identification system violates Pennsylvania's "trap and trace" prohibition in state's Wiretap Act.   On January 18, 1989, Bell Telephone Company of Pennsylvania proposed adding various new services, including the optional service known as Caller*ID. Caller*ID allows a telephone subscriber to identify and record the telephone number from which a call is being made, including private and unlisted numbers. Caller*ID, as proposed by Bell, did not allow the caller the option to refuse to divulge his or her number. A number of parties filed complaints against the inception of Caller*ID. On March 31, 1989, the Pennsylvania Public Utility Commission (PUC) suspended the Caller*ID application for investigation and the matter was assigned to an Administrative Law Judge (ALJ) for hearings and a recommended decision. The ALJ's recommended decision found that Caller*ID was not in the public interest unless it was provided with a free "per-call" blocking option with which callers could block transmission of their telephone numbers if they so chose. The PUC decided to reject the ALJ's recommended decision. On petitions for review of the PUC's order, the commonwealth court found, inter alia, that Caller*ID as proposed would violate Pennsylvania's "trap and trace" provisions of the Wiretap Act. Bell appealed. *Held:* Pennsylvania's Supreme Court affirmed the lower court's opinion that Caller*ID violates the Wiretap Act. Under Pennsylvania law, a trap and trace device is defined as: "A device which captures the incoming electronic or other impulses which identify the originating number of an instrument or device from which a wire or electronic communication was transmitted." By definition and by agreement of the parties, the Caller*ID terminal "captures the incoming electronic or other impulses which identify the originating number" of the telephone from which the call was transmitted. Thus, the court found that Caller*ID violated Pennslyvania's Wiretap Act.

[Barasch v. Bell Tel. Co., 605 A2d 1198 (Pa. 1992)]

Caller identification system is sustained because, among other things, public benefits of system outweigh privacy rights in disclosure of telephone numbers. This case involved "Caller Id", an optional service offered by Southern Bell that reveals the numbers of incoming telephone calls and may be programmed to store a list of numbers that have attempted to connect with a subscriber's telephone number. On December 6, 1989, Southern Bell applied for permission to offer Caller Id from the South Carolina Public Service Commission (PSC). The appellant, the Consumer Advocate for the state of South Carolina, moved to intervene and was made a party. The appellant sought a continuance to see if Caller Id would violate South Carolina's "trap and trace" statute, Section 17-29-20, unless all callers could block the display of their numbers. The PSC approved Southern Bell's application and the appellant filed an action for rehearing and reconsideration. Section 17-29-20 provides that a person may install a trap and trace device if it is used to protect the user from abuse or unlawful use of telephone service. *Held:* The PSC's decision to allow Caller Id was sustained. The court noted that South Carolina's statute only requires the consent of the user in order to use a trap and trace device. Additionally, the court held that the PSC's authorization was not tantamount to state action sufficient to trigger the state statutory or constitutional barriers. Here, the court noted that the PSC's actions were merely that of a quasi-judicial/executive entity. Finally, the court reasoned that the caller's right to privacy was outweighed by the public benefits of the system.

[Southern Bell Tel. & Tel. Co. v. Hamm, 409 SE2d 775 (SC 1991)]

Procurement of telephone records, including those linking defendant's name to his unlisted phone number, do not constitute illegal search under Fourth Amendment. Saldana was convicted of possession of cocaine with intent to deliver. Saldana appealed, contending, among other things, that certain records concerning telephone calls made to and from his unlisted telephone number at his residence were seized, or otherwise intercepted, in violation of Wyoming Constitution arts. 1, 4 and Wyoming Statutes §§ 7-3-601–7-3-610. Saldana further argued that because of the violation of the constitution and statutes, the telephone company records should not have been admitted as evidence at his trial. *Held:* The telephone records were lawfully obtained and were admissible into evidence. The constitutional guaranty against government intrusion into an individual's legitimate expectation of privacy through an unreasonable search and seizure is found in both the Fourth Amendment and Wyoming Constitution arts. 1, 4. Any search, assuming first that it does invade a subjective and legitimate expectation of privacy sufficient to invoke the constitutional protections, must be unreasonable to be impermissible. Whether a search is reasonable is determined from the facts and circumstances of the case in light of the "fundamental criteria" that are found in the Fourth Amendment. The question of reasonableness does not arise unless there has been an intrusion on a legitimate expectation of privacy. The primary, and often ultimate, test for determining whether evidence must be suppressed, at least in the federal arena, has evolved into the determination of whether "the individual's expectation, viewed objectively, is 'justifiable' under the circumstances." Here, the court determined that the Division of Criminal Investigation's (DCI) procurement of Saldana's telephone records, including those linking his name to his unlisted telephone number, did not constitute a "search" invading a "legitimate expectation of privacy" sufficient to demonstrate an invasion of Saldana's constitutional rights. Any person using a telephone, whether on legitimate business or otherwise, assumes a risk that the telephone can and will reveal the numbers that he dials. The subjective expectation of privacy that one would find in connection with an unlisted number is not more "legitimate" than a listed number with respect to criminal investigations because the purpose and the privacy protections of an unlisted number go only to veiling it from the public by not including it in telephone books and directory assistance services. Moreover, since there was no "search" that invaded a legitimate expectation of price, no warrant was required. The DCI did not infringe on Saldana's Fourth Amendment rights by acquiring information through the use of the federal DEA investigative subpoena. Furthermore, the court noted that the DCI's acquisition of Saldana's telephone toll records did not breach the increased expectation of privacy that the Wyoming statutes afford. The records were not "intercepted" and were not acquired, disclosed, or used contrary to the provisions of Wyoming Statute § 7-3-602(a). Moreover, the acquisition of telephone number information is not "aural acquisition of the contents of any oral or wire communication by use of an electronic, mechanical or other device," as required for a violation of Section 7-3-601(a)(v) of the statute.

[Saldana v. Wyoming, 846 F2d 604 (Wyo. 1993)]

¶ 16.05 ELECTRONIC MAIL SYSTEMS

Access authority for purpose of maintaining computer system authorizes access to close down use of computer software. American Computer Trust Leasing, a computer lessor, brought action to collect payments allegedly due for leased computer hardware. The defendants brought a counterclaim alleging that American wrongly deactivated their software. Since one defendant's software was not deactivated, the court granted American summary judgment on that claim. The other defendant, Farrell, sought damages pursuant to Minnesota state law for trespass and statutory nuisance. *Held:* American's right of access to maintain the computer system allowed it access for the purpose of closing down the computer software. Here, the court found that Minnesota's trespass statute was not applicable because the alleged deactivation was not the type of property governed by the statute. Additionally, the court found that Minnesota's nuisance statute was not applicable because there was no injury stemming from an interest in land. Thus, the court granted American's motion for summary judgment on this issue.

[American Computer v. Jack Farrell Implement, 763 F. Supp. 1473 (D. Minn. 1991)]

Defendant is convicted for unauthorized computer use for purchasing a stolen telephone calling card; telephone system used was a computer under state law. Johnson was charged with offering an illegally possessed AT&T credit card number, for a fee, to travelers at the Port Authority Terminal in Manhattan. Among other things, Johnson was charged with unauthorized use of a computer. Johnson contended that this case did not involve the use of a computer, but rather use of a telephone. *Held:* Under New York law, the telephone system is a computer for purposes of the statute. The court noted that the instrumentality at issue in this case is not merely a telephone, but a telephone inextricably linked to a sophisticated computerized communications system. Thus, the court held that a computer was implicated in this case.

[People v. Johnson, 560 NYS2d 238 (NY City Crim. Ct. 1990)]

Computer crime statute applies to pattern of unauthorized access and use of voice mailbox system maintained by hospital. Gerulis was convicted in the Court of Common Pleas, Allegheny County, Pennsylvania, with, among other things, the unlawful use of a computer under Pennsylvania statutory law. Gerulis had gained access to and used the voice mail messaging systems of a hospital and a cellular phone company. The unauthorized users of the voice mail systems used the message space to leave lists of illegally obtained credit and calling card numbers. *Held:* The Superior Court of Pennsylvania sustained the lower court's conviction for unauthorized use of a computer. Under Pennsylvania law, a person unlawfully uses a computer if he "(1) accesses . . . any computer . . . with the intent to interrupt the normal functioning of an organization or to devise or execute any scheme or artifice to defraud or deceive or control property or services by means of false or fraudulent pretenses, representations or promises." Here, the court found that Gerulis "accessed" the computer via her alteration of passwords in the computer systems. Furthermore, the court noted that the voice mailbox systems were "computers" since they are a system that inextricably links a telephone with a sophisticated computer system.

[Commonwealth v. Gerulis, 616 A2d 686 (Pa. Super. Ct. 1992)]

PART B.   GOVERNMENT DATA

¶ 16.06 DATA COLLECTION

Federal constitutional right of privacy is judicially recognized by U.S. Supreme Court in case involving birth control counseling. Defendants-appellants were convicted of violating Connecticut's birth control law. Appellant Griswold was executive director of the Planned Parenthood League of Connecticut. Appellant Buxton was a licensed physician and a professor at the Yale Medical School. The appellants gave medical advice to married persons as to the means of preventing contraception. Under Connecticut law, birth control and the aiding of another to use birth control are illegal. The appellants were each found guilty as accessories. They argued that the accessory statute violated the Fourteenth Amendment. *Held:* Connecticut's law forbidding the use of contraceptives unconstitutionally intruded on the right of marital privacy. The Court found a right to privacy based on emanations or penumbras of various separate federal constitutional guaranties.

[Griswold v. Connecticut, 381 US 479 (1965)]

U.S. Supreme Court invalidates requirement that the NAACP disclose membership rosters on free association and other grounds. Alabama had a statute requiring foreign corporations, except as exempted, to qualify by filing their corporate charters before doing business with the secretary of state and designating a place of business and an agent to receive service of process. The NAACP is a nonprofit membership corporation organized under the laws of New York. The NAACP never complied with the qualification statute. The attorney general of Alabama brought an equity suit to enjoin the NAACP from conducting further activities within, and to oust it from, Alabama. The NAACP contended that its activities did not subject it to the qualification requirements of the statute and that, in any event, what the state sought would violate its members' rights to freedom of speech and assembly guaranteed under the Fourteenth Amendment to the U.S. Constitution. *Held:* The NAACP was not required to produce records including the names and addresses of all its members and agents. The Court found that such a requirement was a denial of due process because it would involve a substantial restraint on the NAACP members' exercise of their right to freedom of association.

[NAACP v. Alabama, 357 US 449 (1958)]

State constitution expressly defines personal privacy as a protected and fundamental right.   California Vehicle Code Section 12800 requires each applicant for a driver's license to submit a fingerprint to the Department of Motor Vehicles (DMV). In August 1982, Perkey applied for a renewal of her driver's license and refused to be fingerprinted. The DMV denied her application for renewal based solely on her refusal to be fingerprinted. Perkey alleged that the collection and retention of fingerprints for unrestricted use in a statewide identification system violates the right of personal privacy guaranteed by the California Constitution (Cal. Const. art. I, § 1). *Held:* Fingerprinting, per se, does not infringe an individual's right to privacy. In light of the unobtrusive nature of the fingerprinting process, California courts have permitted the use of fingerprinting in many noncriminal contexts. However, the DMV's dissemination of fingerprint data to third parties for purposes unrelated to motor vehicle safety was unlawful under several provisions of the Civil and Vehicle Codes; thus, the court did not need to determine the appellant's privacy claim. It should be noted that California's state constitution was amended in 1972 to provide explicit language protecting the personal right of privacy. Article I, Section 1 now reads: "All people are by nature free and independent and have inalienable rights. Among these are enjoying and defending life and liberty, acquiring, possessing, and protecting property, and pursuing and obtaining safety, happiness, and privacy."

[Perkey v. Department of Motor Vehicles, 721 P2d 50 (Cal. 1986)]

New Hampshire Supreme Court imposes due process notice and hearing standards permitting individuals the right to question and contest data in determining that reports of child neglect were "founded, [but the] problem [was] resolved."
Lana and Leon Bagley were married and had five children. In October 1984, the chil-

dren ranged in age from 2 to 11. Additionally, Lana Bagley cared for several other children. On October 14, 1984, there was a domestic dispute that involved the discharge of firearms. The New Hampshire Division for Children and Youth Services (the Division) investigated this incident and Mrs. Bagley's unlicensed day care activities. On November 21, 1984, the Division allegedly called the Bagleys regarding the Division's findings. Petitioners were allegedly told that "(1) the children were in hazardous living conditions, and (2) Mr. Bagley was a danger to others, in conflict with the community and had used defective judgment." The Bagleys, through their attorney, requested a hearing. Subsequently, the Bagleys petitioned the courts of New Hampshire to intervene. *Held:* The Division's notification procedures did not satisfy due process requirements of New Hampshire's constitution. Under New Hampshire law, a determination of whether challenged procedures satisfy due process involve a two-part process: first, determination of whether the challenged procedures concern legally protected interests, and second, determination of whether procedures afforded requisite safeguards. The first part of this test was met since a person's liberty may be impaired when governmental action seriously damages a person's standing and associations in the community. Here, the stigma that attached to child neglect deprived the Bagleys of their liberty. Next, the Division's lack of adequate notice did not afford the Bagleys adequate legal safeguards, thereby violating their due process. Due process requires notice reasonably calculated, under all the circumstances, to apprise interested parties of the pendency of the action and afford them an opportunity to present their objections. Furthermore, to be considered adequate, the notice must give a reasonably complete statement of the information on which the proposed action is based and the full reasons for that action. In this case, the Division failed to adequately notify the Bagleys of the action it took or the reasons for those actions.

[Petition of Bagley, 513 A2d 331 (NH 1986)]

Collection of information regarding patients in state-subsidized mental health care facilities is tailored to meet federal requirements and is therefore justified by need to monitor use of federal monies. In 1982, the Washington state legislature enacted the Community Mental Health Services Act (CMHSA, RCW 71.24). This act established a comprehensive mental health care program that provided patients access to state-subsidized mental health facilities. This statute specifically provided for disclosure of patient information for "management, monitoring and reporting" purposes. In part, this requirement was important to ensure the continuance of funds from federal agencies. Under certain limited circumstances, the Department of Social and Health Services (DSHS) was to have received the names and files of mental health patients as an auditing measure. Additionally, the CMHSA provided for additional disclosure for certain "priority" patients, essentially tracking the patients' cases. Respondents brought this action to enjoin the DSHS from carrying out these tracking systems—known overall as the Community Mental Health Tracking System (CMHTS). Among other things, the respondents claimed that CMHTS would violate the patients' right to privacy. *Held:* The statute was permissible as enacted. The court noted that intimate information can be disclosed if it is carefully tailored to meet a valid governmental interest; furthermore, the disclosure cannot be greater than reasonably necessary. Here, the federal government had specifically required adequate accounting systems to ensure that federal funds were being properly spent. The state of Washington had a similar interest in maintaining adequate mental health care facilities and care for individual patients. Finally, the records were to be kept strictly confidential and included no more that the patient's name and diagnostic code. As such, the statute was not overbroad; indeed, the statute was carefully tailored to meet the state's legitimate interests.

[Peninsula Counseling Ctr. v. Rahm, 719 P2d 926 (Wash. 1986)]

¶ 16.07 DATA MATCHING

Data-matching program relating to welfare eligibility is upheld.   Massachusetts recipients of welfare brought action for declaratory and injunctive relief from an allegedly unlawful welfare fraud investigation commenced by the defendants on the basis of a computer match. The computer analysis compared welfare recipients with unreported employment. *Held:* Computer match information demonstrated a substantial likelihood of unreported employment, a relevant change in the welfare recipients' current status warranting a welfare eligibility redetermination. Here, the court focused on whether the resulting data was sufficiently probative to warrant further action by the agency.

[15,844 Welfare Recipients v. King, 474 F. Supp. 1374 (D. Mass. 1979)]

Data collected for Social Security purposes is validly used to cross-check veterans' records, resulting in reduction of one veteran's disability pension, and does not contravene any right of privacy.   Jaffess was a World War II Navy veteran who had received a Veterans Administration (VA) disability benefits pension since 1943. Those benefits were awarded pursuant to 38 USC § 521 and were based on the payments formula contained therein. That formula determined the amount of benefits payable depending on the veteran's income from other sources, including Social Security benefits. The applicable regulation declared that anyone receiving a VA pension must notify the VA of material or expected changes in income. Jaffess had been receiving disability benefits under the Social Security Act, but failed to report that income to the VA. On January 6, 1975, Jaffess received notice from the VA that his VA benefits would be reduced because of his expected Social Security benefits. This adjustment apparently resulted from a computer comparison of persons receiving both VA and Social Security benefits. Jaffess brought action seeking damages for violation of, among other things, his right to privacy. *Held:* The defendant's motion for summary judgment was granted. The court noted that the thrust of the case law in the area of privacy did not include within its scope the right of an individual to prevent disclosure by one governmental agency to another of matters obtained in the course of the transmitting agency's regular functions.

[Jaffess v. Secretary, Dep't of Health, Educ. & Welfare, 393 F. Supp. 626 (SDNY 1975)]

PART C.   GOVERNMENT DATA DISCLOSURE

¶ 16.08 RIGHTS OF ACCESS AND DUTIES TO DISCLOSE

No privacy interest is infringed by dissemination of list of active shoplifters. In late 1972, two chiefs of police in Kentucky distributed a "flyer" of "active shoplifters" to approximately 800 merchants in the Louisville area. The respondent's name and likeness appeared in the flyer; he had earlier been arrested for shoplifting, but no disposition of those charges had been reached at the time of distribution of the flyer. Shortly after the circulation of the flyer, the charge against the respondent was dismissed. The flyer came to the attention of respondent's employer. The respondent brought suit under 42 USC § 1983, alleging that the petitioners' action under color of law deprived him of his constitutional rights. *Held:* The Supreme Court reversed the court of appeals and dismissed the respondent's complaint. The Court, among other things, held that no privacy interest was infringed. Here, the Court noted that there is no "right of privacy" found within any specific guaranty of the Constitution. However, the Court has recognized "zones of privacy" that may be created by more specific constitutional guaranties that impose limits on government power. The Court found that the respondent's case did not come within any of those zones of privacy. Additionally, the Court noted that there is a justifiable policy interest in deterring shoplifting and that arrest records are public information.

[Paul v. Davis, 96 S. Ct. 1155 (1976)]

Newspaper has First Amendment right of access to forms filed in criminal proceedings. The appellants and their co-defendants were indicted in August 1985 for crimes relating to an armed robbery of a Wells Fargo depot in West Hartford, Connecticut in September 1983. Shortly after the trial commenced, the Hartford Courant Company moved to intervene in the case and for access to the court's files. Among other things, the Courant sought documents relating to payments made on behalf of the defendants, who were indigent, pursuant to the Criminal Justice Act (CJA). The

CJA forms include information regarding, among other things, judicial officers' approval of payments to attorneys and others providing expert services. The district court held that the CJA forms must be made available for the Courant's review. Six appellants moved to have the district court reconsider its ruling. At issue on appeal were forms that list the amounts sought and approved for payment, without detailed material backup. *Held:* The Courant had First Amendment right of access to the forms. The court noted that there is a presumption of public access to criminal trials and pretrial proceedings in criminal cases. This presumption also applies to documents filed in connection with criminal proceedings. Additionally, the court noted that the public has a strong interest in how its funds are being spent in the administration of criminal justice and what amounts of public funds are being paid to particular private attorneys or firms. The court noted that this right to access is a qualified one; it is not absolute. Thus, this right must be weighed against the appellants' rights to effective assistance of counsel, the attorney-client privilege, and work-product protection.

[United States v. Suarez, 880 F2d 626 (2d Cir. 1989)]

Right of access to information regarding government operations is based on constitutional concepts of free speech. Legi-Tech sought to enjoin officials of New York state from denying it access to a state-owned computerized data base containing legislative information. That information was available to the general public only through a governmental subscription service. Legi-Tech argued that Chapter 257 of the New York laws, which was the state's basis for denying Legi-Tech a subscription, was unconstitutional on its face and as applied because it denied the appellant freedom of speech and of the press. *Held:* Legi-Tech's appeal was remanded for further findings. The court of appeals examined the appellant's two-pronged challenge to New York's statute. First, the court looked at Legi-Tech's claim that Chapter 257 unconstitutionally discriminated between a state-owned member of the press and other press entities by providing the former preferential access to pending legislation. Second, the court examined the appellant's argument that Chapter 257 unconstitutionally denied it access to the state's reporting service. The court remanded both of these prongs for further factual inquiry.

[Legi-Tech, Inc. v. Keiper, 766 F2d 728 (2d Cir. 1985)]

Disclosure of abortion reimbursement records is not violation of privacy rights of doctors or patients where there is no showing that such disclosure will alter professional actions. The Kansas Public Records Inspection Act provides that all official public records, which are by law required to be kept and maintained, shall be open for public inspection. The district court, in a declaratory judgment action, decided that the state Act did not require the disclosure of the names of physicians and amounts of public funds paid to each of those physicians for abortions during a certain period. The state appealed. *Held:* Disclosure of this information would not infringe physicians' or patients' constitutional right of privacy. The court noted that there was no reason to believe that the state would not adequately or effectively delete the confidential information contained in the records. Thus, the court held that no patient's right to privacy would be violated. As far as the physicians' right to privacy was concerned, the court found that the public's right to know how and for what purposes public funds were spent outweighed any personal privacy right.

[State ex rel. Stephan v. Harder, 641 P2d 366 (Kan. 1982)]

¶ 16.09 ACCESSIBILITY OF DATA

Federal agencies' record-keeping practice of retaining only amputated paper printouts of electronic records does not comport with Federal Records Act requirements. On appeal, the Executive Office of the President (EOP), Office of Administration, the National Security Council (NSC), White House Communications Agency, and Trudy Peterson, Acting Archivist of the United States, challenged the conclusion of the district court that EOP and NSC guidelines for managing electronic documents did not comport with FRA requirements. More specifically, these government agencies and officials contended that, contrary to the court's ruling, they have in the past reasonably discharged their Federal Records Act (FRA) obligations by instructing employees to print out a paper version of any electronic communication that falls within the statutory definition of a "record" and by managing the "hard-copy" documents so produced in accordance with the FRA. These hard copies, however, often omitted fundamental pieces of information that were an integral part of the original electronic records, such as the identity of the sender and/or recipient and the time of receipt. *Held:* The district court was correct in concluding that the agencies' record-keeping guidance was not in conformance with the FRA. The FRA was promulgated to ensure accurate and complete documentation of the policies and business transactions of the federal government, to control the quantity and quality of records produced by the federal government, and to promote the judicious preservation and disposal of records. If a document qualifies as a record, the FRA prohibits an agency from discarding it by fiat. Many of the electronic communications at issue contained preservable records, as they were made or received by an agency of the U.S. government in connection with the transaction of public business and were appropriate for preservation by that agency as evidence of the organizations's functions, policies, decisions, and activities. The agencies did not have the discretion to convert only part of the electronic records to paper and then manage only the partial paper records in accordance with the FRA. The practice of retaining only the amputated paper printouts was found to be inconsistent with Congress's evident concern with preserving a complete record of government activity for historical and other uses. Consequently, the electronic versions of the electronic mail communications are the official records that must be managed and preserved in accordance with the FRA.

[Armstrong v. Executive Office of the President, 1 F3d 1274 (DC Cir. 1993)]

U.S. Department of State is not obligated to undertake extraordinary reconstruction or analysis of its data to respond to request pursuant to FOIA. Miller was an amateur historian who requested information relating to the Israeli attack on the U.S.S. Liberty. After receiving only a handful of documents approximately one year later, he filed this suit under the FOIA. The Department of State then released various documents to Miller. The State Department moved for summary judgment. The district court granted the State Department's motion and denied Miller recovery of attorney fees. Miller appealed the district court's grant of summary judgment. One of Miller's grounds for appeal was that the district court erred in finding that Miller had failed to raise a substantial issue of fact as to the inadequacy of the State Department's search and as to the good faith of the search. *Held:* The court of appeals affirmed the district court's decision on its merits. The court of appeals noted that the adequacy of an agency's search for requested documents is judged by a standard of reasonableness. The search need only be reasonable; it need not be exhaustive. Here, the agency showed by convincing evidence that its search was reasonable; i.e., it was especially geared to recover the documents requested.

[Miller v. Department of State, 779 F2d 1378 (8th Cir. 1983)]

Federal Privacy Act does not require retrieval or correction of agency reports that are not retrievable under requestor's name or under any other personal records held by government. Plaintiff-appellant, Dr. Baker, was a civilian employee of the Navy serving as a psychologist in San Diego. One of his subordinates, Dr. Rocklyn, filed a grievance against her based on her treatment of him. A naval officer, Lieutenant Commander Davis, was assigned to investigate the charges levied by Dr. Rocklyn. Davis prepared a memorandum relating to his findings and filed it in the employee grievance file under Dr. Rocklyn's name without indexing or cross-referencing that report to Dr. Baker's name or file. Dr. Baker later submitted a request, under the FOIA and Privacy Act, to receive a copy of Davis's report. Dr. Baker later sought to expunge that report from Dr. Rocklyn's file. Subsequently, Dr. Baker filed this suit seeking to force the Navy to expunge that report based on the civil remedies provision of the Privacy Act. The Navy filed a motion for summary judgment, which was granted by the district court. That court found that Davis's report did not qualify as a record within a "system of records" under the Privacy Act because it was not retrievable under Dr. Baker's name or other personal identifier. Dr. Baker appealed. *Held:* The court of appeals affirmed the district court's decision. The court of appeals noted that the legislative history of the Privacy Act indicates that Congress was primarily concerned about the potential misuse of personally identifiable information stored in computers. As a result, the definition of "system of records" makes coverage under the Act dependent on the method of retrieval of a record rather than its substantive content.

[Baker v. Department of Navy, 814 F2d 1381 (9th Cir. 1987)]

State FOIA is held to require that statistical data regarding complaints about judges be disclosed to newspaper reporter. The state Judicial Review Council of Connecticut (JRC) filed an administrative appeal from a decision of the Freedom of Information Committee (FOIC). FOIC ordered the JRC to release information relating to complaints against judges to a newspaper reporter. The issue before the court was whether the public had access to JRC statistical data prior to its compilation and distribution to the public. *Held:* The public had a right of access to this information prior to its compilation. The court reasoned that the keeping and maintaining of statistical data constituted an "administrative function" and thus the sought data was a public record pursuant to Connecticut's FOIA. The JRC sought to distinguish compiled statistical data—which was admittedly within the public domain—and uncompiled statistical data. The court noted that this contention appeared to be a distinction without a difference. The compilation of data was not held to change the nature of the data from inaccessible to accessible. While the JRC had legitimate concerns in reviewing and checking the data before its release, the court found that these concerns had to yield to the public's right to access.

[Judicial Review Council v. Freedom of Info. Comm., 605 A2d 891 (Conn. Super. 1992)]

¶ 16.10 FORM OF DISCLOSURE

Agency has no obligation under FOIA to accommodate requester's preference regarding format of requested information. Dismukes brought action to obtain a copy of a computer tape listing by name and address the participants in six 1982 Bureau of Land Management Simultaneous Oil and Gas Leasing bimonthly lotteries. The Department of the Interior had advised Dismukes that such information is routinely made available to the public on microfiche cards and could be provided to him in that form. Dismukes requested the information in the form of computer tapes. Thus, the single issue presented here was whether an FOIA requester can specify the format of data he seeks from an agency. *Held:* The Department of the Interior did not have to provide the information in the format requested by Dismukes. The court decided that the agency need only provide the information in a reasonably accessible form, and microfiche cards met that standard.

[Dismukes v. Department of Interior, 603 F. Supp. 760 (DDC 1984)]

State statute that mandates that agency disclose "public records" results in agency having to disclose computer tapes. The circuit court determined that Cook County and George Dunne, as president of the county board, had to furnish the American Federation of State, County and Municipal Employees, AFL-CIO (AFSCME) with certain information requested pursuant to Illinois's FOIA in the form of a computer tape. Here, the AFSCME wanted the information requested in the form of a computer tape rather than a printout, which Cook County/Dunne furnished. Cook County/Dunne appealed this decision. The appellate court reversed this ruling, holding that the defendants needed only to provide the requested information in a reasonably accessible format and that the computer printout satisfied this standard. The AFSCME appealed. *Held:* Cook County/Dunne could not choose the format in which to release information. Under the Illinois FOIA, public bodies must make public records available for inspection and copying unless they can avoid so doing by invoking an exception provided in the statute. Here, the court noted that public records include computer tapes.

[AFSCME v. County of Cook, 555 NE2d 361 (Ill. 1990)]

Doctoral student is entitled to obtain computerized, disclosable portions of police data base. On a complaint for a writ of mandamus filed pursuant to the Public Records Act of Ohio, a doctoral student requested the court to direct the respondents to provide her with copies of certain magnetic computer tapes of the Cleveland police department. The respondent police department compiled the records in question by storing some of the information in a computerized data base. The student stated that she needed the computerized records to complete her research into the effectiveness of the deployment and utilization of the city's police force. She sought the computer tapes themselves because, allegedly, her analysis could only be performed via computer because of the large amounts of data involved. *Held:* Writ granted. The court held that the computerized records, as opposed to paper printouts, added value to the information contained in those records. When such value is added, a new set of enhanced public records is created that must be disclosed to the public. Thus, the police department had to allow the doctoral student to copy the portions of the computer tapes to which the public is entitled under Ohio law when that person has presented a legitimate reason as to why paper copies of the information would be insufficient or impracticable.

[State v. City of Cleveland, 584 NE2d 665 (Ohio 1992)]

¶ 16.11 COMMERCIAL DISCLOSURES

Under Federal Election Campaign Act, dissemination of contributors' names without addresses and telephone numbers does not violate statutory prohibi-

tion against using the material for "commercial purpose." A private company was in the business of disseminating Federal Election Commission (FEC) information for a profit to interested third parties. The information conveyed contributors' names and contribution amounts, but no other identifying information. The purpose of relaying the information was to encourage research and reporting on patterns of political contributions. The National Republican Congressional Committee filed an administrative complaint with the FEC alleging that the company's sale and use of the information was in violation of provisions in the Federal Election Campaign Act (FECA) that prohibited use of the information for "commercial purposes." Failing to reach a resolution, the FEC then filed a civil enforcement suit. The district court ruled for the FEC on the commercial purposes prohibition. The appellate court reversed. *Held:* Dissemination of information by the private company did not constitute "commercial use" within the meaning of the statute because it discouraged all kinds of unwanted solicitation and harassment of the contributors. The court concluded that the absence of addresses and telephone numbers discouraged use of the information for solicitation purposes. Each report sold by the company contained on each page a prohibition from using the information "for the purpose of soliciting contributions or for any commercial purpose." Moreover, the "salting" provision of the statute that allowed political committees to insert pseudonyms on each report would help ensure that third parties that attempted to use the lists for any sort of solicitation would be caught.

[Federal Election Comm'n v. Political Contributions Data, Inc., 943 F2d 190 (2d Cir. 1991)]

Commercial motivation in request for state data base information relating to real estate tax records is deemed irrelevant. ATS requested that the Virginia treasurer produce computerized records containing, among other things, certain real estate tax information pursuant to Virginia's FOIA. ATS was in the business of helping its mortgage-lending clients in the payment of their real estate taxes. Essentially, ATS compiled lists for mortgage lenders of that lender's customers, and determined the individual amounts of real estate taxes owed by each customer and the total amount of real estate tax owed by all of the lender's customers in the aggregate. ATS then provided this information, for a fee, to the mortgage lender so that the lender could pay local real estate taxes for its borrowers in one check. In its request, ATS explicitly stated that it would use the requested information to "create tax lists to be used for payment of property accounts that will be paid by lenders we service under contract." The treasurer of Virginia denied ATS's request. ATS filed a petition for a writ of mandamus to compel the release of the records. The trial court ruled in the treasurer's favor, holding disposing of the case on public policy grounds, and dismissed the case with prejudice. *Held:* The Supreme Court of Virginia found that the purpose or motivation behind a request is irrelevant to a citizen's entitlement to that information. The court noted that the proper questions here concerned the status of the requestor as a citizen of the commonwealth, the status of the requested documents as official records, whether any exceptions applied, and whether the requestor would pay the cost of production.

[Associated Tax Serv., Inc. v. Fitzpatrick, 372 SE2d 625 (Va. 1988)]

¶ 16.12 COMPUTER PROGRAMS AND MODELS

IRS is not required to release information that will seriously impair assessment, collection, or enforcement of taxes under internal revenue laws.   Consolidated actions before the court of appeals arose from suits brought under the FOIA. There were three issues brought up for review: (1) whether the IRS had fulfilled its responsibilities under the FOIA in failing to disclose check sheets in connection with the Tax Compliance Measurement Program (TCMP); (2) whether ZIP code information was exempt from disclosure under the FOIA; and (3) whether the records containing data used to create the TCMP were exempt from FOIA disclosure. The court of appeals affirmed in part and reversed in part. *Held:* The IRS, in failing to provide check sheets along with three computer tapes with data, had failed to fulfill its responsibilities under the FOIA, reversing the district court's determination. Since revealing even the first three digits of a taxpayer's ZIP code could result in taxpayer identification, the district court was correct in withholding this information, and thus the appellate court affirmed this holding. Data used to create the TCMP was exempt from disclosure on the ground that in so doing, the disclosure would impair the functioning of the tax laws, affirming the lower court's decision. The court concluded that the latter determination was a factual one. All the disclosure plans for partial disclosure of TCMP records would involve extensive editing in order to create records that would not violate the FOIA. Since this would require the IRS to create new records, this was counter to the FOIA, which does not obligate agencies to create records, only to provide access to those that have already been created if doing so is not in violation of the FOIA.

[Long v. IRS, 825 F2d 225 (9th Cir. 1987)]

Federal Highway Administration must disclose documents pursuant to FOIA describing computer algorithm used in weighing various factors employed in determining a carrier's safety rating.   The Federal Highway Administration (FHWA) promulgated procedures for determining the safety fitness of motor carriers subject to its jurisdiction. In carrying out such safety determinations, FHWA agents inspecting a carrier filled out a form containing 75 questions relating to specific aspects of safety compliance. Based on that information, the FHWA assigned one of three safety ratings: satisfactory, conditional, or unsatisfactory. These ratings determined how closely a carrier was to be monitored and, potentially, were the basis for sanctions. The algorithm used in determining the safety rating generated from the questionnaire was sought herein by the plaintiff under the FOIA. Secretary of Transportation Skinner withheld documents that would have revealed the contents of the algorithm on the grounds that they were "related solely to the internal personnel rules and practices of an agency" and that they "would disclose techniques and procedures for law enforcement investigations or prosecutions, or would disclose guidelines for law enforcement investigations or prosecutions . . . [that] could reasonably be expected to risk circumvention of the law." *Held:* The FHWA was required to disclose the documents. Here, the court rejected the FHWA's assertion that the algorithm was a mere tool to focus the administration's investigatory powers on lax carriers. Instead, the court noted that the algorithm had the effect of immediate action by other agencies. Thus, the algorithm was not solely an internal rule or practice. Next, the court held that disclosure of the algorithm would not facilitate circumvention of the law. Rather, knowing the agency's priorities would allow carriers to concentrate their efforts on correcting what the agency considered to be the most serious safety breaches.

[Don Ray Drive-A-Way Co. v. Skinner, 785 F. Supp. 198 (DDC 1992)]

Commerce Department is not forced to disclose computer programs that were used to determine if a foreign company had violated antidumping laws. A law firm filed an action under the FOIA seeking disclosure of a computer program used by the U.S. Department of Commerce (DOC) to perform calculations used in determining if a foreign steel producer had violated U.S. "antidumping" laws by selling steel in the U.S. market at less than fair market value. The DOC asserted that the program at issue was exempt from disclosure. *Held:* The program was protected from disclosure pursuant to FOIA exemptions for internal personnel rules and practices of the agency and for investigatory records. Here, the court noted that the program was used for "predominantly internal purposes" and disclosure would "significantly risk circumvention of federal statutes or regulations." Thus, the computer program was exempt from disclosure under Exemption 2 of the FOIA, which exempts from disclosure matters that are "related solely to the internal personnel rules and practices of an agency." Additionally, the court found that the program was protected by Exemption 7, which exempts from disclosure "investigatory records compiled for law enforcement purposes, but only to the extent that production of such records would . . . disclose investigative techniques and procedures."

[Windels, Marx, Davies & Ives v. Department of Commerce, 576 F. Supp. 405 (DDC 1983)]

¶ 16.13 PERSONAL PRIVACY RESTRICTIONS

Disclosure of information under FOIA balances public interest against personal privacy interest. A nonprofit cooperative of painting and drywall contractors and labor unions brought an action under the FOIA to require the Department of Housing and Urban Development (HUD) to disclose names and addresses of construction workers that had been redacted from payroll records pursuant to the FOIA. The cooperative requested records relating to three HUD-assisted projects. In providing the records, HUD invoked the FOIA to withhold names, Social Security numbers, and home addresses that would have enabled the cooperative to determine the earnings and work hours of individual employees. The district court, on cross-motions for summary judgment, entered judgment for the cooperative. HUD appealed. On appeal, HUD argued that releasing the requested information would constitute an unwarranted invasion of the workers' privacy and thus the information was properly withheld under Exemption 6 of the FOIA. *Held:* Summary judgment for the cooperative was reversed on the ground that the diminution of privacy rights of the workers outweighed the public interest of disclosure of the information (monitoring enforcement by HUD in compliance with Davis-Bacon and the Copeland Anti-Kickback Act) counter to the intent of the FOIA. In providing such information to the cooperative, disclosure would also have to be provided to others—creditors, salesmen, and union organizers. This disclosure, the court reasoned, would result in a "clearly unwarranted invasion of personal privacy."

[Painting & Drywall Work Preservation Fund, Inc. v. Department of Housing & Urban Dev., 936 F2d 1300 (DC Cir. 1991)]

Government's interest in disclosure must outweigh individual's personal privacy interests for government to prevail on cause of action brought against it by private citizens. A civil rights action was brought by the wife and children of a male citizen with AIDS against an officer and a borough for violation of their privacy rights. Upon arrest of the citizen with AIDS, his wife and a friend, an afflicted citizen, requested police to proceed with caution when conducting a search of his body because he had tested HIV-positive. In a subsequent encounter with neighbors of the afflicted citizen and his wife, a police officer told them that the husband had AIDS. This resulted in the family suffering humiliation and being shunned by their community. The wife and children brought a civil rights action against the police officer and the borough for civil rights violation under 42 USCA 1983. *Held:* Violation of privacy rights was granted on the motion for summary judgment against both defendants on the ground that the constitutional right of privacy of the plaintiffs had been violated by disclosing the citizen's physical condition to those who had no physical contact with him. The government had not shown a compelling state interest in breaching privacy. The court noted that the stigma of AIDS extends to all family members, regardless of whether they have the disease.

[Doe v. Borough of Barrington, 729 F. Supp. 373 (DNJ 1990)]

Police accident report tapes are private where tapes include the names of parties and officers. Mullin filed a written request for a copy of the Detroit Police Department's traffic accident computer tape pursuant to the Michigan FOIA. The Detroit Police Department denied this request based on an exemption to this statute pertaining to "[i]nformation of a personal nature where the public disclosure of the information would constitute a clearly unwarranted invasion of an individual's privacy." At trial, the court found for the police department. On appeal, the police department relied solely on the "invasion of privacy" exemption. *Held:* The trial court's decision was affirmed. The exemption for invasion of privacy applied to this request for the police department's traffic accident computer tape where it contained, among other things, names, addresses, and other information of persons involved in accidents in the city in 1980, reports of any arrests made pursuant to the accidents, allegations of criminal conduct, and investigative techniques and procedures of law enforcement personnel. That information was held to intrude into the private affairs of individuals and potentially contain embarrassing private facts; thus, disclosure would have been an invasion of those individuals' right to privacy.

[Mullin v. Detroit Police Dep't, 348 NW2d 708 (Mich. Ct. App. 1984)]

Itemized telephone bills for long-distance and car phone calls made by community board members are not records required by law to be made, maintained, or kept on file. North New Jersey Newspapers Company requested copies of itemized telephone bills for the Passaic County Board of Chosen Freeholders' office and car phone lines. That request was made pursuant to New Jersey's Right-To-Know law and North New Jersey's common-law right of access to such records. The Board refused to release the telephone bills arguing that the Board's confidentiality interests outweighed the Newspaper's need to review the bills. Under New Jersey's Right-To-Know law, any citizen—without any showing of personal or particular interest—has an unqualified right to inspect public documents if they are, in fact, statutorily defined documents. *Held:* These records were not records that were "required by law to be made, maintained or kept on file"; thus, they were not subject to the Right-To-Know law. Here, the court noted that it doubted that the legislature of New Jersey intended that all detailed information a modern computer system can generate constitutes records subject to this law. As such, these records were not required to be disclosed.

[New Jersey Newspapers v. Passaic County, 601 A2d 693 (NJ 1992)]

¶ 16.14 TRADE SECRETS AND PROPRIETARY RIGHTS

Trade secrets are property that are potentially cognizable as protected value under due process standards. The FIFRA authorizes the EPA to use data submitted by an applicant for registration of a covered product (i.e., a pesticide) in evaluating the application of a subsequent applicant, and to disclose publicly some of the submitted data. The appellee was an inventor, producer, and seller of pesticides in Missouri. The appellee brought this suit in federal district court for injunctive and declaratory relief alleging, inter alia, that the data collection of the FIFRA effected a "taking" of property without just compensation in violation of the Fifth Amendment. The district court held that the challenged provisions were unconstitutional, and permanently enjoined the EPA from implementing or enforcing those provisions. *Held:* To the extent that the appellee had an interest in its health, safety, and environmental data cognizable as a trade secret property right under Missouri law, that property was protected by the Fifth Amendment's taking clause. The court noted that, despite their intangible nature, trade secrets have many of the attributes of more traditional property.

[Ruckelshaus v. Monsanto Co., 467 US 986 (1984)]

Financial or commercial information provided voluntarily is confidential under FOIA disclosure exemptions if it will not customarily be released to the public by the person from whom it was obtained.   The Institute for Nuclear Power Operations (INPO) prepared safety reports that it voluntarily submitted to the Nuclear Regulatory Commission (NRC). INPO was a nonprofit corporation whose membership included all the operators of nuclear power plants in the United States. A condition of INPO's submission of the reports at issue was that the NRC not release the information to other parties without INPO's consent. In 1984, the Critical Mass Energy Project (CMEP) asked the NRC to provide it with copies of the INPO reports pursuant to the FOIA. The NRC denied this request, and CMEP brought suit. *Held:* The NRC was not required to release the reports. These reports were deemed to be "confidential" within the meaning of the FOIA disclosure exemption for confidential trade secrets and commercial or financial information. Here, the information in the reports was considered commercial in nature and the reports were voluntarily provided to the NRC. For reports voluntarily submitted to the government, the critical test is whether the information is such that it would not be customarily released to the public. INPO's custom was not to release such information to the public. The court reasoned that when an FOIA request is made for voluntarily submitted information, the government has an interest in encouraging cooperation by persons having information useful to officials.

[Critical Mass Energy Project v. NRC, 975 F2d 871 (DC Cir. 1992)]

Commercial or financial information that must be submitted under FOIA is subject to two-part test to determine whether information in government's possession is "confidential" under Exemption 4 of FOIA.   The National Parks and Conservation Association brought action to enjoin federal officials from refusing to permit it to inspect and copy records relating to concession operations of the National

Park Service. Section 552(b)(4) of the FOIA exempts "trade secrets and commercial or financial information obtained from a person and privileged or confidential" from FOIA disclosure. To bring a matter (other than a trade secret) within the purview of this exception, a party must show that the information is (1) commercial or financial, (2) obtained from a person, and (3) privileged or confidential. The issue raised on appeal was whether this information was "confidential" within the meaning of the exemption. *Held:* The court applied a two-part test to determine the confidentiality of this information. Such information is confidential if disclosure of the information would be likely either "(1) to impair the Government's ability to obtain necessary information in the future; or (2) to cause substantial harm to the competitive position of the person from whom the information was obtained." The concessionaires were given the opportunity to further develop the record to show that they would be prejudiced by the disclosure of such information. Reversed and remanded accordingly.

[National Parks & Conservation Ass'n v. Morton, 498 F2d 765 (DDC 1974)]

PART D. PRIVATE DATA

¶ 16.15 PRIVATE DATA SYSTEMS

Successful claim brought pursuant to Federal Tort Claims Act is not preempted by Section 7217 of IRC, which provides remedies for violations of 26 USC § 6103. After the IRS issued press releases concerning Johnson's conviction and plea bargain, Johnson sued IRS officials involved in the press release, claiming that the release of tax information violated 26 USC § 6103, the federal statute prohibiting disclosure of tax returns and return information. Johnson subsequently amended his complaint to include an FTCA claim against the United States, based on the state law torts of negligence and invasion of privacy. *Held:* The IRS agents tortiously invaded Johnson's privacy, in violation of Texas law, when they authorized release of confidential taxpayer information to newspapers of general circulation. Moreover, the agents' violation of Section 6103 established their negligence per se under Texas law. Accordingly, Johnson established his FTCA claim. In addition, Section 7217 of the IRC, the federal statute providing remedies for violations of Section 6103, did not preempt Johnson's right to sue under the FTCA. The FTCA constitutes a general but not unlimited waiver of the federal government's immunity from tort claims. Under the FTCA, suits against the United States are authorized "for injury or loss of property . . . caused by negligent or wrongful act or omission of any employee of the Government while acting within the scope of his office of employment, under circumstances where the United States, if a private person, would be liable to the claimant in accordance with the law of the place where the act . . . occurred." To recover under the FTCA, Johnson had to succeed against the government in a state law tort cause of action. Here, Johnson had established the factors of an invasion of privacy cause of action for public disclosure of private facts. In addition, Section 6103 establishes a standard of care applicable to the duty that existed on the part of the IRS agents to refrain from publicly damaging or embarrassing private facts about another person. Under Section 6103, "no officer or employee of the United States . . . shall disclose any return or return information obtained by him in any manner in connection with his service as such an officer or employee. . . ." Actions by the IRS agents, including the releasing of Johnson's middle name, his home address, and his official job title in press releases constituted a violation of the standard of care established in Section 6103 and amounted to negligence under Texas tort law. Such information was contained in Johnson's tax returns but not in any court record. Section 7217 of the IRC merely provides remedies for violations of Section 6103. The statute is not exclusive and therefore does not preempt the FTCA.

[Johnson v. Sawyer, 4 F3d 369 (5th Cir. 1993)]

Award of damages for false light invasion of privacy does not constitute forbidden intrusion on field of free expression.   Globe published archive photographs of Mitchell to illustrate an unflattering and false story in one of Globe's tabloids. Mitchell sued Globe for defamation, invasion of privacy, and intentional infliction of emotional distress. The jury found for Globe on the defamation count, but returned a verdict for Mitchell on the remaining claims, awarding $650,000 in compensatory and $850,000 in punitive damages. Globe appealed, arguing that the evidence was insufficient to support the verdict as a matter of law. *Held:* Evidence supported the verdict awarding Mitchell damages for false light invasion of privacy; the verdict did not constitute a forbidden intrusion on the field of free expression. The district court abused its discretion in not granting remittitur on the compensatory damage award, as it was shocking and exaggerated; however, the district court did not abuse its discretion in declining to remit the punitive damages award. To prevail on a "false light" invasion of privacy claim, a plaintiff must show, by clear and convincing evidence that (1) the false light in which he or she was placed by the publicity would be highly offensive to a reasonable person, and (2) the defendant acted with actual malice in publishing the statements at issue. "Actual malice" in this instance was defined as the intentional or reckless failure to anticipate that readers would construe the publicized matter as conveying actual facts or events concerning Mitchell. A finding of actual malice required a showing of more than mere negligence. Here, besides the assertion of the pregnancy of a centenarian, every other aspect of the charged story was subject to reasonable belief. The tabloid's format and style suggested that it was a factual newspaper; therefore, the Globe's argument that actual malice, as a matter of law, could not exist in a work that was intended to be an obvious fiction was without merit. The First Amendment can tolerate, without significant impairment of its function, sanctions against such calculated falsehoods as found in this tabloid, which mingled factual, fictional, and hybrid stories without overtly identifying one from the other.

[Peoples Bank & Trust Co. v. Globe Int'l Publishing, 978 F2d 1065 (8th Cir. 1992)]

Tort of intrusion into the private affairs of individual may apply to collection of private information for no legitimate purpose.   During 1973 and 1974, Tureen maintained a health insurance policy with the All-American Insurance Company. Tureen suffered a heart attack in 1973 and made a claim for health insurance benefits later that year. Tureen made a claim after a second heart attack in 1974. All-American hired Equifax, Inc., to investigate each of Tureen's claims. Equifax conducted its investigation of Tureen's second claim and issued a report to All-American; that report gave rise to this action. Tureen's suit alleged, among other things, that the investigative report invaded his privacy. At trial, the jury found for Tureen. Equifax appealed. *Held:* The court reversed the trial court's decision and remanded with directions. Here, the court noted that because in certain circumstances there may be a legitimate purpose for the collection—and even the disclosure—of an individual's past insurance history, it had to conclude that Equifax did not invade Tureen's privacy merely by collecting and retaining his past insurance history.

[Tureen v. Equifax, Inc., 571 F2d 411 (8th Cir. 1978)]

¶ 16.16 FAIR CREDIT REPORTING

Computer data collection procedure constitutes negligent failure to fulfill statutory duty under FCRA to establish a reasonable updating procedure.   SARMA provided a computerized credit service to local business subscribers. SARMA depends in large part on information provided to it by its subscribers. SARMA's computerized credit service conducted searches of its data base based on information presented to it by subscribers. When presented with such data, SARMA's system displayed the credit history file that most nearly matched the customer being searched. The decision whether to accept a search as complete and correct was left up to the subscriber itself. Moreover, when a subscriber accepted a given file as pertaining to a particular consumer, the computer automatically captured into its file any information input from the subscriber's terminal that the central file did not have. The flaw with such an automatic capturing feature is that it may accept erroneous data. In this case, SARMA's system captured an erroneous Social Security number that caused the system to report the bad credit history of "William Daniel Thompson, Jr." to subscribers inquiring about "William Douglas Thompson, III." Gulf Oil Corporation and Montgomery Ward denied credit to William Douglas Thompson, III, on the basis of erroneous information furnished by SARMA because of the mixup. William Thompson, III made various attempts to correct this error with SARMA; however, his file remained intertwined with William Daniel Thompson, Jr.'s file. William Thompson, III brought this suit in October 1979. The district court awarded him $10,000 damages pursuant to the FCRA. *Held:* The court of appeals affirmed the district court's decision. Section 1681e(b) of the FCRA provides that, "When a consumer reporting agency prepares a consumer report, it shall follow reasonable procedures to assure maximum possible accuracy of information concerning the individual about whom the report relates." Here, the court noted that SARMA was negligent in failing to exercise reasonable care in programming its computer to capture information into a file without requiring any minimum number of "points of correspondence" between the consumer and the file or having an adequate auditing procedure to foster accuracy. Additionally, SARMA failed to employ reasonable procedures designed to discover conflicting information that would have led to the discovery of the mistake.

[Thompson v. San Antonio Retail Merchants Ass'n, 682 F2d 509 (5th Cir. 1982)]

Credit Bureau does not violate the FCRA when it furnished negative credit information on wrong individual to member of its reporting service. Kenneth V. and Ira Dobson alleged that the Credit Bureau of Middle Georgia either willfully or negligently failed to comply with the FCRA, 15 USC §§ 1681 et seq., and that because of the Credit Bureau's impermissible use of their credit report, they incurred damages. June Dobson had entered into discussions with Hamby Chevrolet regarding the purchase of an automobile. Hamby, a member of the consumer reporting services of the Credit Bureau, used the Credit Bureau's reporting services to evaluate the creditworthiness of June Dobson and her husband, Kenneth D. Dobson. Hamby's finance manager fed the names, current and former addresses, and Social Security numbers of June and Kenneth D. Dobson into the computer. In addition to printing out two files on Kenneth D. Dobson, the computer also printed out the credit report of Kenneth V. Dobson, Kenneth D. Dobson's father. This report contained negative credit information. *Held:* The Credit Bureau maintained and followed reasonable procedures to limit the furnishing of consumer reports to the purposes listed under Section 1681(b)(3); accordingly, the Credit Bureau did not willfully violate the FCRA, and no liability could be imposed against it. Reasonable procedures include requiring "prospective users of the information to identify themselves, certify the purposes for which the information is sought, and certify that the information will be used for no other purposes." Here, the information furnished to Hamby concerning the Dobsons was in response to a legitimate request for a consumer credit report. Moreover, the fact that Kenneth V. Dobson's file, which contained a different Social Security number, was produced was not unreasonable. Valuable credit histories on individual consumers that have been reported under different Social Security numbers or whose Social Security numbers are transposed or erroneous would not be reported if searches were limited to a specific Social Security number.

[Dobson v. Holloway, 828 F. Supp. 975 (MD Ga. 1993)]

Table of Cases

[References are to paragraphs (¶).]

[References are to paragraphs (¶).]

[References are to paragraphs (¶).]

[References are to paragraphs (¶).]

[References are to paragraphs (¶).]

[References are to paragraphs (¶).]

[References are to paragraphs (¶).]

[References are to paragraphs (¶).]

[References are to paragraphs (¶).]

Index

[References are to paragraphs (¶).]

— **S** —

[References are to paragraphs (¶).]